Quicken® 2017

THE OFFICIAL GUIDE

Bobbi SANDBERG

New York   Chicago   San Francisco
Athens   London   Madrid   Mexico City
Milan   New Delhi   Singapore   Sydney   Toronto

Cataloging-in-Publication Data is on file with the Library of Congress

McGraw-Hill Education books are available at special quantity discounts to use as premiums and sales promotions, or for use in corporate training programs. To contact a representative, please visit the Contact Us pages at www.mhprofessional.com.

Quicken® 2017 The Official Guide

1 2 3 4 5 6 7 8 9 0   QFR   22 21 20 19 18 17

ISBN   978-1-25-986201-4
MHID   1-25-986201-1

Sponsoring Editor	**Proofreader**
Wendy Rinaldi	Claire Splan
Editorial Supervisor	**Indexer**
Janet Walden	Jack Lewis
Project Editor	**Production Supervisor**
Patty Mon	James Kussow
Acquisitions Coordinator	**Composition**
Claire Yee	TypeWriting
Technical Editor	**Art Director, Cover**
Mary Higgins	Jeff Weeks
Copy Editor	
Lisa McCoy	

This book is dedicated to my clients, all of my wonderful students, past and present, and the great team at McGraw-Hill Education. And, as always, to Sandy.

About the Author

Bobbi Sandberg has long been involved with computers, accounting, and writing. She is a retired accountant currently filling her time as a trainer, technical writer, and small-business consultant. As a Quicken user since the program launched in the 1980s and a Quicken teacher since its inception, she knows the questions users ask and gives easy-to-understand explanations of each step within the program. She teaches at several venues, offering step-by-step instruction in a variety of computer applications. Her extensive background, coupled with her ability to explain complex concepts in plain language, has made her a popular instructor, consultant, writer, and speaker. She has authored and co-authored more than a dozen computer books, including *Quicken 2012 The Official Guide*, *Quicken 2013 The Official Guide*, *Quicken 2014 The Official Guide*, *Quicken 2015 The Official Guide*, *Quicken 2016 The Official Guide*, *Genealogy QuickSteps*, *Microsoft Office 2013 QuickSteps*, and *QuickBooks 2016: The Guide for Small Business Success*.

About the Technical Editor

Mary Higgins is a long-time Quicken user, having used each version since 1999. She enjoys pushing the limits of what the software is intended to do—clicking every button, navigating every menu path, reading the help files, etc. She reads and posts on the Quicken forums and finds it interesting to see how others are using Quicken and the different approaches to resolving issues.

Contents

Part Two   Organizing Quicken for You

Part Four   Assessing Your "Money's Worth"

Part Five   Looking Toward Tomorrow

Acknowledgments

This book, like most others, is the end product of a lot of hard work by many people. Among them are

- Wendy Rinaldi, sponsoring editor at McGraw-Hill Education, for her ability to hear both spoken and unspoken words, her professionalism, her wonderful can-do attitude, and ALWAYS positive outlook! She creates an atmosphere that makes working a joy.
- The Quicken team, especially Sangeetha Saradha. Sangeetha is knowledgeable, willing to help, patient, and a delight with which to work. Her experience and wonderful attitude, along with her great team, make this project so pleasant. We are honored to work with each team member!
- The support team at McGraw-Hill Education—Claire Yee, Janet Walden, and too many other names to mention—is appreciated much more than words can express. The end result is because of their hard work and dedication.
- Patty Mon, the project editor, is, without a doubt, one of the gems of this project. Always on point; consistently watching all phases of the project; and always caring, fun, and professional. We each benefit from her expertise and constant understanding of what is required.
- The other Patty in our group, Patty Wallenburg of TypeWriting, a composition genius, always gives us her skillful and clever best. She is unfailingly proficient and an artist with graphic presentation, not to mention habitually, awesomely, great! To have BOTH of the Pattys on the project assures you, the reader, that each word is presented in such a way as to make your understanding as clear as possible.
- The technical editor, Mary Higgins, is the brightest star in the galaxy. Her technical expertise, quick understanding, and ability to hone in with the most important ideas in the manuscript, makes each chapter more readable. She is an amazing ally and a wonderful editor. Thank you, Mary, for all that you do.
- Lisa McCoy, the most adroit copy editor, is wonderful. She can see through typos, understands strangely phrased sentences, and always finds the right way to say anything. She is the best of the best, and her talent is amazing.
- Claire Splan, proofreader, who always makes any publication better with her knowledge and talents!
- Jack Lewis, indexer, is the reason you can find quick answers to any questions. His clear eye for detail and understanding of the overall project makes each volume he indexes a minor work of art.

Introduction

Choosing Quicken Personal Finance Software to organize your finances was a great decision. Quicken has all the tools you need to manage your personal finances. Its well-designed, intuitive interface makes it easy to use. And its online and automation features make entering transactions and paying bills a snap. But if that isn't enough, Quicken also offers features that can help you learn more about financial opportunities that can save you time and money—two things that often seem in short supply.

This introduction tells you a little about the book so you know what to expect in the chapters to come.

About This Book

This book tells you how to get the most out of Quicken. It starts by explaining the basics—the common, everyday tasks that you need to know just to use the program. It then goes beyond the basics to show you how to use Quicken to save time, save money, and make smart financial decisions. Along the way, it shows you most of Quicken's features, including many that you probably didn't even know existed. You'll find yourself using Quicken far more than you ever dreamed you would.

Assumptions

This book makes a few assumptions about your knowledge of your computer, Windows, Quicken, and financial management. These assumptions give you a starting point, making it possible to skip over the things that you are assumed to already know.

What You Should Know About Your Computer and Windows   To use this book (or Quicken 2017, for that matter), you should have a general understanding of how to use your computer and Windows. You don't need to be an expert. As you'll see, Quicken uses many standard and intuitive interface elements, making it easy to use—even if you're a complete computer novice.

At a bare minimum, you should know how to turn your computer on and off and how to use your mouse. You should also know how to perform basic Windows tasks, such as starting and exiting programs, using menus and dialog boxes (called just *dialogs* in this book), and entering and editing text.

If you're not sure how to do these things or would like to brush up on them, get any of the Windows books from McGraw-Hill Education. Those resources will provide all the information you need to get started.

What You Should Know About Quicken and Financial Management   You don't need to know much about either Quicken or financial management to get the most out of this book; it assumes that both are new to you.

This doesn't mean that this book is just for raw beginners. It provides plenty of useful information for seasoned Quicken users—especially those of you who have used previous versions of Quicken—and for people who have been managing their finances with other tools, such as Microsoft Money (welcome to Quicken!) or pencil and paper (welcome!).

Because the book assumes that all this is new to you, it makes a special effort to explain Quicken procedures as well as the financial concepts and terms on which they depend. New concepts and terms first appear in italic type. By understanding these things, not only can you better understand how to use Quicken, but you also can communicate more effectively with finance professionals, such as bankers, stockbrokers, and financial advisors.

Quicken Updates   One of the terrific things about computing in 2017 is our Internet connectivity and capability. Quicken's team, like all program developers, is working to improve the software throughout the year, not just when a new version is released. That means Quicken can send small changes to their program each time you update the program. Because of this, you may see illustrations in this book that differ from the ones you see on the screen. The procedures haven't changed; only small changes have been made to make the program more user friendly.

And mentioning illustrations, there may be illustrations in your program that appear a bit strange. For some reason, a couple of the windows in the program have *truncated* text—that is, words that appear to be cut off. We are told that each of these items is being fixed throughout the year as the great Quicken team finds the issues.

Organization

This book is logically organized into six parts, each with at least two chapters. Each part covers either general Quicken setup information or one of Quicken's financial centers. Within each part, the chapters start with the most basic concepts and procedures, most of which involve specific Quicken tasks, and then work their way up to more advanced topics, many of which are based on finance-related concepts that Quicken makes easy to master.

It is not necessary to read this book from beginning to end. Skip around as desired. Although the book is organized for cover-to-cover reading, not all of its information may apply to you. For example, if you're not the least bit interested in investing, skip the chapters in the Investing part. It's as simple as that. When you're ready for the information that you skipped, it'll be waiting for you.

Here's a brief summary of the book's organization and contents.

Part One: Learning Quicken Basics   This part of the book introduces Quicken Personal Finance Software's interface and features. It begins by explaining how to install Quicken and showing you the elements of its user interface, including some of Quicken's online features. It explains Quicken's mobile app and how you can access your financial information from your smart phone or other mobile device.

Part Two: Organizing Quicken for You   This part of the book explains how to set up Quicken Personal Finance Software for everyday use. It starts by explaining the basics of creating accounts and how to categorize your transactions (and why!). You will understand how Quicken account registers work and how to manually record bank and credit card transactions. Then, you will learn how you can take advantage of online transaction entry and payment processing features, such as Transaction Download and Online Bill Pay. It provides details about how you can tap into the power of Quicken to automate many entry tasks, thus saving you time.

Part Three: Tracking Your Money   This part of the book describes how Quicken Personal Financial software helps you track your money. It starts by explaining how to create reminders for your bills and how to organize your spending. You'll learn how to reconcile both bank and credit card statements and why both procedures are important. It then explains the basics of tracking investments in Quicken and then goes on to describe how you can use Quicken's online investment tracking features to download investment information from your brokerage firm and exchange information with Quicken.com. Along the way, it provides a wealth of information you can use to invest wisely and maximize your investment return.

Part Four: Assessing Your "Money's Worth"   This part of the book explains how you can use Quicken Personal Finance Software's features to keep track of your property and loans. It starts by showing you how you can use the Property & Debt tab and other Quicken features to monitor expenses related to your assets and debts. It then continues to explain how to use the Investing tab and some useful Quicken tools.

Part Five: Looking Toward Tomorrow   This part of the book tells you about Quicken Personal Finance Software's planning and reporting features, which you can use to plan for your retirement, major purchases, and other life events. It covers Quicken's built-in financial calculators, as well as features that can help you save money to make your dreams come true. You are introduced to the many tax tools that are available in Quicken to help you prepare for tax time and, finally, you'll learn how to use Quicken's powerful reporting capabilities.

Part Six: Appendixes   This part of the book provides some additional information you may find helpful when using Quicken Personal Finance Software. These appendixes explain how to work with Quicken data files and how to customize Quicken.

Conventions

All how-to books—especially computer books—have certain conventions for communicating information. Here's a brief summary of the conventions used throughout this book.

Menu Commands   Quicken, like most other Windows programs, makes commands accessible on the menu bar at the top of the application window. Throughout this book, you are told which menu commands to choose to open a window or dialog, or to complete a task. The following format is used to indicate menu commands: Menu | Submenu (if applicable) | Command.

Keystrokes   Keystrokes are the keys you must press to complete a task. There are two kinds of keystrokes:

- **Keyboard shortcuts** are combinations of keys you press to complete a task more quickly. For example, the shortcut for "clicking" a Cancel button may be to press the ESC key. When instructing you to press a key, the name of the key is in small caps, like this: ESC. If you must press two or more keys simultaneously, they are separated with a hyphen, like this: CTRL-P. Many of Quicken's keyboard shortcuts are explained in Chapter 1.
- **Literal text** is text that you must type in exactly as it appears in the book. Although this book doesn't contain many instances of literal text, there are a few. Literal text to be typed is in boldface type, like this: **Checking Acct**. If literal text includes a variable—text you must substitute when you type—the variable is included in bold-italic type, like this: ***Payee Name***.

Icons

Icons are used to flag specific types of information.

Sidebars   This book includes "Experienced Users Recommend" sidebars. These sidebars are meant to put a specific Quicken feature into perspective by either telling you how it is used or offering suggestions on how you can use it. You'll learn a lot from these sidebars, but like all sidebars, they're not required reading.

Learning
Quicken Basics

This part of the book introduces Quicken Personal Finance Software's interface and features. It begins by explaining how to install Quicken and showing you the elements of its user interface, including some of Quicken's online features. It explains Quicken's mobile app and how you can access your financial information from your smart phone or other mobile device. The chapters are

Meeting and Installing Quicken 2017

Chapter 1

In This Chapter:

- *Exploring Quicken's uses*

- *Installing Quicken*

- *Starting Quicken*

- *Creating your first account*

- *Exploring the Quicken window*

- *Understanding online financial services*

- *Setting up One Step Update*

- *Meeting the Intuit Password*

- *Understanding the Password Vault*

- *Exiting Quicken*

If you're brand new to Quicken Personal Finance Software, get your relationship with Quicken off to a good start by properly installing it and learning a little more about how you can interact with it. Although the information provided in this section is especially useful to new Quicken users, some of it also applies to users who are upgrading. You'll learn about data files, accounts, and some of the many other features included in this software.

What Is Quicken?

On its face, Quicken is a computerized checkbook. It enables you to balance your accounts and organize, manage, and generate reports for your finances. However, as you explore Quicken, you'll learn that it's much more. It's a complete personal finance software package—a tool for taking control of your finances. Quicken makes it easy to know what you have, how you are doing financially, and what you could do to strengthen your financial situation.

Exploring Quicken's Uses

Although many use Quicken only to manage their bank and credit card accounts, Quicken can help you manage investment accounts and help you organize other data, such as the purchase price of your possessions and the outstanding balances on your loans. It can even store a copy of the warranty that came with your purchases. With Quicken's online features, much of your data entry can be automated. Online banking enables you to keep track of bank account transactions and balances and to pay bills without writing checks or sticking on stamps.

With all financial information stored in Quicken's data file, you can generate net worth reports to see where you stand today. You can also use a variety of financial planners to make financial decisions for the future. Quicken's tax features, including export into TurboTax and the Deduction Finder, can make tax time easier on you and your bank accounts.

Quicken Editions

Quicken offers several editions of Quicken 2017 for Windows for managing personal finances: Starter, Deluxe, and Premier. The features in each edition are shown in Table 1-1.

What You Can Do	Quicken Starter	Quicken Deluxe	Quicken Premier
Track bank accounts and credit cards	x	x	x
Use online services	x	x	x
Categorize transactions	x	x	x
Financial alerts		x	x
Create a budget		x	x
Manage investments		x	x
Tax planning		x	x

Table 1-1 · Quicken Edition Features

This book covers Quicken Deluxe and Premier editions for Windows. Although much of its information also applies to Quicken Starter, this book covers many features that are not included in the Starter edition and a handful not included in the Deluxe edition. If you're a Quicken Starter or Deluxe user, consider upgrading to Quicken Premier so you can take advantage of the powerful features it has to offer. One more thing—Quicken offers two additional Quicken editions. If you're a small-business owner, Quicken Home & Business can handle your personal and rudimentary business financial needs, including the business expenses you need to track for your tax return's Schedule C. If you manage one or more rental properties, Quicken Rental Property Manager can handle transactions and other information for tenants, rental income, and related expenses that you need to track for your tax return's Schedule E. As you can see, Quicken has you covered with a Quicken product for all facets of your financial life.

System Requirements

Quicken 2017 is designed to work with Windows Vista SP2, 7, 8, 8.1, and 10 and both 32- and 64-bit machines with at least a 1GHz processor. You'll need a minimum of 1 gigabyte (GB) of random access memory (RAM) and a minimum of 450 megabytes (MB) of free space on your hard drive. Your monitor should have a minimum resolution of 1024×768. If you are installing from an optical disk, you'll need a CD/DVD drive. You need Internet access for working online and receiving program updates. You also need a printer for printing reports and graphs.

If you choose to use the mobile app, as explained in Chapter 3, Quicken 2017 works with iPhones, iPod touch, and iPads that have iOS 8 or higher installed. Should you want to use the Quicken 2017 app with your Android mobile or tablet, you will need OS 4.0 or newer.

Getting Started

Ready to get started? This section explains how to install, register, and begin using Quicken 2017.

Installing Quicken

Quicken uses a standard Windows setup program that should be familiar to you if you've installed other Windows programs. Insert the Quicken 2017 disk into your optical drive or, if you have downloaded the program, double-click the downloaded .exe file. A dialog should appear, asking if you want to install the program to your hard drive. If so, click Yes to start the Quicken installer. If you have downloaded your program, simply locate the downloaded installation file and double-click to open it. Whether you have downloaded or are installing from a disk, you may see a message asking if you want to allow the following program to make changes to this computer. Click Yes to start the process.

The Install Wizard appears as seen next. The installer displays a series of steps Quicken will take to install your new program. Click Let's Go to get started.

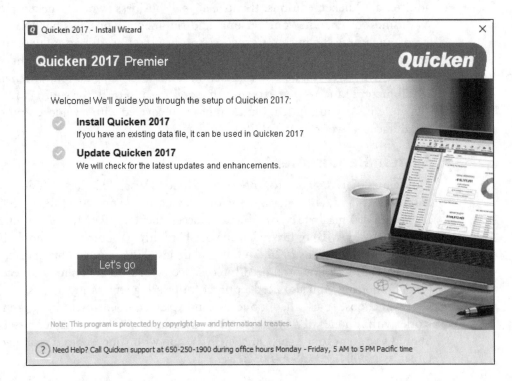

The license agreement appears, as seen in Figure 1-1. Select the I Agree To The Terms Of The License Agreement And Acknowledge Receipt Of The Quicken Privacy Statement option, and click Next to continue. (Unless you select this option, you will neither be able to click Next nor install the software.)

Take the time to click the Quicken Privacy Statement link to open and read this important document in a web browser window. Close the browser window when you're finished to return to the installer. In the Ready To Install The Program screen, the installer displays a summary of what it will do. If this is a first-time Quicken installation, it will install Quicken 2017 along with any updates to the program. However, if you're upgrading from a previous version, the installer will begin by uninstalling whatever version is currently installed. (Only one version of Quicken can be installed on your computer at a time.)

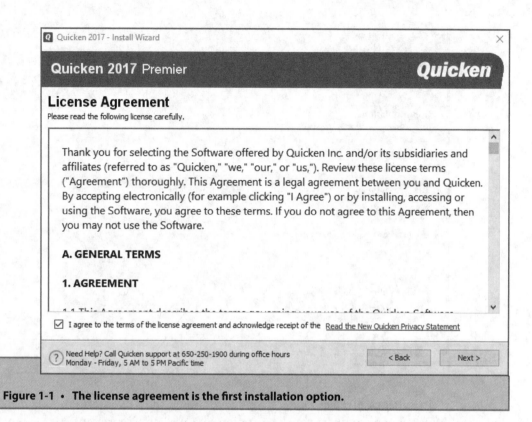

Figure 1-1 • **The license agreement is the first installation option.**

Only the Quicken program files will be deleted; your data files will remain intact so you can use them with Quicken 2017.

If you want Quicken to be installed in other than the default location (C:\Program Files(x86)\Quicken), click the optional Select Your Installation Location link located at the lower left of the dialog. To keep the recommended default location, just click Install. Wait while the installer uninstalls the previous version of Quicken (if necessary), installs the Quicken 2017 program files, and downloads any updates to your hard disk.

For upgraders, the data file you most recently used in a previous version is converted to the Quicken 2017 format with a copy of the previous version's data file placed in a folder called Q*xx*Files, where *xx* shows the version year.

When Quicken is installed, you see a congratulatory message that the installation is complete, as shown next. To start Quicken immediately, select the Launch Quicken And Complete Registration check box. To use Quicken at another time, clear that check box.

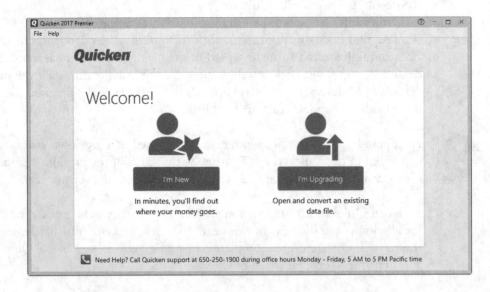

In either case, select Done. If you have chosen the default option to launch Quicken and complete your registration, the Welcome screen appears as seen next. Click either the I'm New or the I'm Upgrading button to continue.

Installing Quicken as a New User

When you select the I'm New button, the Quicken 2017 Sign In screen appears as seen in Figure 1-2. If you have not used Quicken before, use the Create Account button to establish your Intuit ID, which allows you to download information from your financial institution, access your Quicken data on your mobile devices, pay your bills online from within Quicken, and receive e-mail and text alerts from Quicken. To learn more, see "Understanding the Intuit ID," later in this chapter.

After you have completed creating your Intuit ID, click Next to continue. If you are installing Quicken for the first time, you are required to register with your name and other information. Complete the registration and click Next.

If you have used Quicken before on this computer, you are prompted to enter your Intuit ID and password. Click Next to continue.

The next setup screen appears, from which you can enter a decision about using Quicken's mobile features. Should you choose not to use mobile access at this time (our choice here), you can access this feature later, as explained in Chapter 3. After you have made your choice, click Next to continue.

You are told your registration is successful, as shown in Figure 1-3. Information about all the new features in both Quicken 2017 desktop and mobile apps is

Figure 1-2 • Your first task is creating or entering your Intuit ID.

EXPERIENCED USERS RECOMMEND

If you downloaded Quicken 2017, most users strongly recommend saving a copy of your downloaded program onto an external device, such as a flash drive, CD, DVD, or external hard drive, just in case your internal hard drive has any problems in the future.

Keep a copy of your e-mail verification of purchase in the same location. It's much easier for the Quicken staff to verify your information in case of any issues when you can provide purchase information and verification. Use Quicken's Attachment feature to keep all of your purchase information right in Quicken. See Chapter 5 to learn how to attach data to your Quicken transactions.

If you purchased Quicken directly from Quicken.com and need to download it again, you will need your Intuit ID and password.

1. Sign in to Quicken.com with your ID and password.
2. Select Downloads & Unlocks at the left side of the screen.
3. Select the appropriate program to start the download.
4. Save a duplicate copy of the downloaded program on an external drive, flash drive, CD, or DVD.

Figure 1-3 • Once you have completed your Intuit registration, you begin by creating your accounts.

provided. Click Add Account to continue to add your first account as seen in Figure 1-4.

If you try to close the registration screen before you have completed all of the fields, you will receive an error message. Click the Cancel button at the bottom right of the Add Account dialog to start again.

If you click Cancel, Quicken opens to the Main View screen of the Home tab in your newly created data file. This file is in your Documents folder in a Quicken subfolder. The opening screen includes information and buttons that help you finish setting up your Quicken data file, as seen in Figure 1-5. Chapter 2 offers detailed information on working with the Home tab.

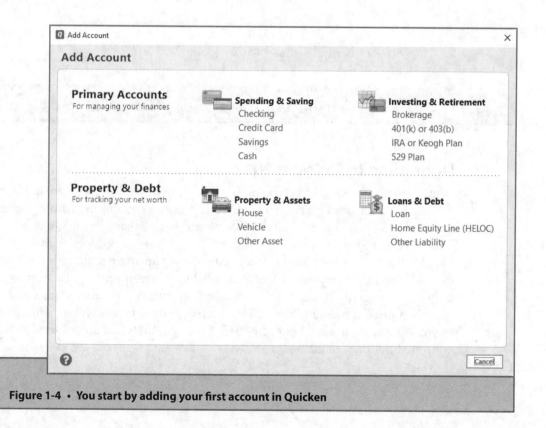

Figure 1-4 • You start by adding your first account in Quicken

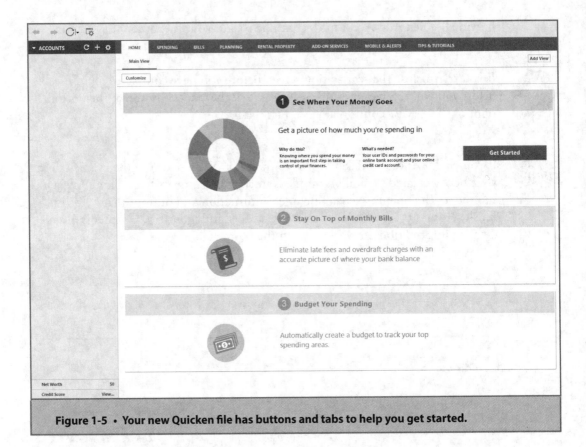

Figure 1-5 • Your new Quicken file has buttons and tabs to help you get started.

Upgrading to Quicken 2017

When you update Quicken on a computer with any Quicken 2015 versions or earlier, the installation process converts your previous data for use with Quicken 2017. This process converts the data file named in the dialog to the Quicken 2017 format and saves the original file in C:\Users*yourname*\Documents\ Quicken\Q*xx*Files. The path for the saved copy of the original file varies depending on the previous version from which you are upgrading. Remember, only one version of Quicken can be installed on your computer at a time, and only the Quicken program files will be deleted. Your data files will remain intact so you can use them with Quicken 2017. Quicken 2016 files do not need to be converted to Quicken 2017.

Existing User Startup on a New Computer

If you have installed Quicken 2017 on a computer without earlier versions of Quicken and choose the I'm Upgrading option, Quicken asks for the location of your data so that you can import it to the new computer. Your earlier file can be restored from another computer on a home (or business) network, an external hard drive, a flash drive, DVD, CD, or Quicken's online backup. This process converts the data file named in the dialog to the Quicken 2017 format and saves the original file in C:\Users\ *yourname*\Documents\Quicken\Q*xx*Files. The path for the saved copy of the original file may vary depending on the previous version from which you are upgrading.

Starting Quicken

You can start Quicken in several different ways. Here are some of the most common methods:

- **Opening Quicken with the Desktop Shortcut or Windows Tile**   The Quicken installer places a Quicken 2017 shortcut icon on Windows 7 desktop. Double-click this shortcut to open Quicken. In Windows 8, 8.1, and 10, a tile appears with the other installed apps. Click the tile to open Quicken.
- **Open Quicken from the Task Bar**   In Windows 7 use the Start button on the Windows task bar to start Quicken and other Quicken components. Choose Start | All Programs | Quicken 2017 | Quicken 2017 to start Quicken. In Windows 10, select Start | All Apps | Quicken 2017. Right-click Quicken 2017 and select either Pin To Start or Pin To Taskbar.

Creating Your First Account

To begin using Quicken, you must tell the program what bank accounts and credit cards you wish to track. During this process, Quicken will go online to download an up-to-date list of participating financial institutions.

The Add Account dialog box, shown earlier, will help you add your first account, which in most cases will be a checking account, as seen next. Choose the name of your bank from the displayed list, or type its name in the Enter The Name Of Your Financial Institution field. If your bank's name does not appear on this first group of names, when you type the first four letters of your bank's name, a new list appears with a list of those institutions that begin with the letters you typed.

Add your Primary Checking Account   ×

Add your Primary Checking Account

Enter the name of your financial institution

Type here to search all supported institutions

Or choose from these popular financial institutions

AllyBank	Citibank
American Express	Discover Card Account Center
American Express Bank FSB	Fifth Third Bank - NEW
Bank of America	HSBC Bank USA
BB&T - Online Banking	PNC Bank - Web Connect
Capital One 360	SunTrust Bank
Capital One Bank	TD Bank Online Banking - New
Capital One Card Services	U.S. Bank Internet Banking
Chase	Wells Fargo Bank
Citi Cards	

Financial Institution not on the list? Prefer not to download? Interested in advanced connection
Use Advanced Setup to create your account.

Cancel   Next

See the Advanced Setup link at the bottom of the window? Use this if your bank name does not appear on any list, if you do not want to download your information, or if your bank offers more than one type of downloading service.

Click Next to continue. In the dialog that appears, Quicken prompts you to enter your user name and password as provided by your bank. (Should you want to save this password in the Quicken Password Vault, click Save This Password. See "Setting Up the Password Vault for Upgraders" later in this chapter for more information.) Some banks require additional information. If so, enter the appropriate information and click Next. If you are not sure of your typing, select the Show Characters check box to see what you have keyed in. Click Connect to continue.

As you enter your user ID and password, Quicken will warn you if your CAPS LOCK key is on.

The Quicken Update Status message appears as Quicken connects to your financial institution. (If there are additional passwords or security phrases required by your bank, you are prompted to enter them. Do so and click OK or Next, depending on the prompt.) You may be prompted to enter your Intuit ID.

If you have more than one account that uses the user ID and password you entered, all of the accounts may be downloaded. If you have not yet set up any accounts in Quicken, each account will be called by the account name shown on your bank's records. Each financial institution uses its own naming method. For example, Bank of America uses the account type plus the full account number as the account name.

You may change the name to something more descriptive if you choose. If you have already entered some accounts, Quicken prompts you to add, link, or ignore each of the downloaded accounts. After changing the account name(s) and selecting Add/Link/Ignore, click Next.

If you have not set up any accounts before, Quicken may not offer to Add/Link/Ignore the account(s) you are creating, nor will you be able to change the account names during the creation process. You go directly to the Accounts Added List. You can still change the account names once the account creation process has completed.

If you have enabled online services with your financial institution and want to sync your accounts for mobile access, select the Sync To Quicken Cloud For Mobile & Alerts check box(es) in the Accounts Added List. See more about mobile access in Chapter 3.

After the download is complete, your account (or accounts if you have more than one at that bank) shows on an Accounts Added List. Click Finish to return to the Home tab's Main View. Each downloaded account appears in the Account Bar with the nickname you entered. You may change the account names if you choose. See Chapter 4 for more information about changing account names.

Your downloaded transactions appear in the account register. You will notice a small blue dot by each transaction in the first column of the register. Positioning your mouse over the word "New" shows an explanation of that transaction as recorded by your financial institution. You may choose to mark that you have reviewed each transaction separately or mark all transactions as having been reviewed.

You can tell Quicken not to download your transactions automatically. Learn how in Chapter 6.

Setting Up Other Banking Accounts

After you have created your primary checking account, you can add more accounts right away by selecting the Add Another Account button. You can create additional new accounts with the Add An Account button that appears at the bottom of your Account Bar. No matter what type of account you create, Quicken steps you through the creation process, prompting you to enter information about the account, such as its name and balance. See Chapter 4 to learn how to use the Add Account dialog to set up more accounts.

The Quicken Interface

Quicken 2017 has been updated to a clean, modern interface. This is designed to be intuitive and easy to use. If you are starting Quicken from scratch, after you have installed and created your Intuit ID, Quicken opens to the Quicken Home page shown earlier in Figure 1-5. This interface puts the information and tools you need to manage your finances right within mouse pointer reach. You never have to dig through multiple dialogs and menus to get to the commands you need most. You'll see more about using this Home page in Chapter 2.

▼ ACCOUNTS	C + ⚙
All Transactions	
◿ Banking	$20,811
● House Checking	1,194
● Main Checking	14,675
● Small Savings	5,094
● House Credit Card	-151
Net Worth	$20,811
Credit Score	View...

Exploring the Quicken Window

This section tells you about the components of the Quicken interface and explains how each feature can help you manage your financial life. The main Quicken window gives you access to most of Quicken's features and your financial information. We'll look at each section separately.

Account Bar

The Account Bar lists each of your Quicken accounts on the left side of the main Quicken window, as shown here. At the top of the Account Bar is a link to the All Transactions register, which shows the transactions for all of your accounts (with the exception of your Investing accounts) in one register. It even shows transactions from linked investment cash accounts.

If you can't see all of your accounts in the Account Bar, use the scroll bar on the right side of the Account Bar to scroll through its contents. You can also click the downward or right-pointing arrow next to a section heading on the Account Bar to hide or display, respectively, the list of accounts beneath it.

By default, account balances, rounded to the nearest dollar, appear in the Account Bar; however, you can right-click anywhere in the Account Bar to open a context menu. Choose Show Amounts to display the amounts, and clear the check mark to hide amounts from view. (Hiding amounts makes the Account Bar narrower so more information appears in the window to the right.) This contextual menu offers additional options for the display of the Account Bar, such as displaying cents in the amounts. You can also change the width of the Account Bar by dragging its right border.

The Show Amounts box is a toggle. If the check box is on, clicking will turn the check box off. If the check box is off, clicking will turn it on. It also toggles the display of the amounts in the Account Bar on and off.

The account names in the Account Bar are links to that account's register. You can customize the Account Bar as discussed in Chapter 2.

Tabs

Tabs, as shown in the following illustration, help you navigate through Quicken. Some tabs, such as the Spending and Bills tabs, provide information about your financial status, as well as links and buttons for accessing Quicken features. Other tabs have views, such as the Main View of the Home tab, that enable you to view and customize Quicken settings for your financial situation. Use the Show Tabs option from View in the Quicken menu to display your tabs. Some tabs are available only in the Home & Business or Rental Property Manager editions of Quicken. Learn about the tabs in Chapter 2.

| ▼ ACCOUNTS | ⟳ + ⚙ | HOME | SPENDING | BILLS | PLANNING | INVESTING | PROPERTY | ADD-ON SERVICES | MOBILE & ALERTS | TIPS & TUTORIALS |

Understanding Online Financial Services

If you're interested in keeping track of your finances with the least amount of data entry, you should be considering Quicken's online features such as Transaction Download and Online Payment. However, you can't use them until you've set up an account with a participating financial institution and applied for the online account services you want to use. Learn more about online financial services in Chapter 6.

Accounts

To track your finances with Quicken, you must create at least one account. Although many of your expenditures may come from your checking account, you probably have more than one account that Quicken can track for you. By setting up all of your accounts in Quicken, you can keep track of balances and activity to get a complete picture of your financial situation. You don't have to add all of your accounts at once. You can start by tracking just the one or two accounts that you use most frequently and add accounts later. As you've learned earlier in this chapter, you get started by entering your primary bank account.

In Quicken, a data file holds all of the information about all of your Quicken accounts. Quicken accounts can be checking, savings, credit card, investing, property, and debt accounts. When would you want more than one data file? For example, you may need two data files if you use Quicken to organize both your own finances and the finances of a community group for which you are serving as treasurer. Each of these data files would have its own separate set of bank, credit, and asset accounts.

Using One Step Update and the Password Vault

Many of Quicken's online features use One Step Update to update information and download transactions from your financial institutions. However, that's not all One Step Update can do. This feature makes it possible to handle many of your connection chores at once. When used in conjunction with the Password Vault feature, you can click a few buttons, enter a single password, and take a break while Quicken updates portfolio and account information for you. You can even schedule updates to occur automatically when Quicken isn't running.

The idea behind One Step Update is to use one command to handle multiple online activities. This eliminates the need to use update commands in a variety of locations throughout Quicken. One command does it all.

Setting Up One Step Update

Choose Tools | One Step Update or click the Update button—the white right-curling arrow at the top of the Account Bar. A dialog appears asking for your Intuit ID and password. After you enter your Intuit ID and password, click Update Now to start the process. The One Step Update Settings dialog appears as seen in the next illustration.

One Step Update Settings   ✕

↻ **One Step Update Settings**

Download transactions and balances (Manage Passwords)

☑ U.S. Bank Internet Banking   Password ▢

Online services (all | none)

☑ Download quotes and investment information (select quotes)

View your investing portfolios online at **Investing.Quicken.com** (Learn more...)

? Schedule Updates...   ↻ Update Now   Cancel

- **Download Transactions and Balances**   Listed in this area are the financial institutions with accounts for which you have enabled online access. These accounts can be both banking and investment accounts.
- **Online Services**   You see this section if you have set up any online services. In it, you tell Quicken which items you want to update.

Click the Update Now button. You will see a One Step Update Progress dialog and, when the update is finished, the One Step Update Summary dialog appears.

If you use your Outlook calendar to "remind" you, make sure to run a One Step Update each time you make changes in the Bill And Reminders dialog. Otherwise, the changes you made in Quicken are not updated in Outlook. Conversely, if you make changes in Outlook, remember to make the same change in Quicken. One Step Update works from Quicken to Outlook, not from Outlook to Quicken.

Small green circles appear to the left of each successfully updated financial institution. You can click the link showing the number of accounts updated to get a pop-up showing the accounts. You can then click the account shown in the pop-up to open that account's register, or click the Close button at the bottom of the window to dismiss the One Step Update Summary.

The One Step Update Summary dialog does not appear if you have previously told Quicken to display the summary only when there is an error.

Scheduling Updates

You can schedule updates to occur when you're not using Quicken. Then, when you start Quicken, your data file is already updated with information from your financial institutions. To set up a schedule, choose Tools | Schedule Updates. The Schedule Updates dialog appears, as shown next. You can set options in each area of the dialog. When you have finished, click OK.

When scheduling an update, you may see a message about the Password Vault (see "Understanding the Password Vault" later in this chapter), which is created automatically when creating a new file. The Password Vault can be unlocked or reset by entering your Intuit ID. The default for the Password Vault is to use the Intuit ID, but you can change it to your own custom password.

These are each of the options:

- **Update These Financial Institutions**   The update area lists all of the items in the One Step Update dialog discussed earlier in this chapter. Click to toggle check marks beside each item you want to include in the schedule.
- **Schedule**   The Schedule area determines when the updates will occur. Select the check boxes for each day of the week you want the updates to occur, and then choose a time from the At drop-down list. Because your computer must be running for the updates to take place, set options for when you know your computer will be turned on. Updates will not occur, however, if Quicken is running; this ensures that the automated feature does not interrupt your work with Quicken.
- **Passwords**   Security options enable you to indicate when your computer should prompt you for the Password Vault password. (The Password Vault feature must be set up and used in conjunction with scheduled updates.) You have two options:
  - **At Windows Startup**   Choosing this option displays the Password Vault Password dialog when you start Windows.
  - **Before Each Scheduled Update**   This option displays the Password Vault Password dialog just before each update.
- **Update Online Services**   Choose the items you want to update.

Using the Schedule

Using the schedule is easy.

1. Exit Quicken, because a scheduled update will not occur when Quicken is running.
2. When you are prompted for the Password Vault password (which happens just before the update), enter the password. (If you have told Quicken to prompt you for the Password Vault password at Windows startup, your Password Vault password will already have been entered.)
3. Click Update. Quicken does the rest.

Changing the Schedule

To change the schedule, choose Tools | Schedule Updates to display the Schedule Updates dialog. Make changes in the dialog as desired to modify settings. To cancel scheduled updates, clear the check boxes beside each day of the week. When you're finished making changes, click OK.

Do take the time to read the link about Quicken's security features that is available in the Schedule Updates dialog.

Understanding the Intuit ID

You can associate the Intuit ID Password with your Password Vault and when synchronizing accounts using your mobile device.

This feature is in response to the concerns of Quicken users who have requested a simplified password recovery system. Because Quicken passwords become part of the encrypted data file in which the passwords were created, the passwords cannot be recovered; they must be removed. There is now an automated password recovery feature, where you answer questions about your data, like account balances or when a payment was made. If you answer enough of the questions correctly, your password is removed. Help refers to this feature as Remove Password. You can find the feature in the Enter Password dialog; the link is titled "Forgot password?"

Intuit Password for New Users

For new Quicken users, the Intuit ID is set as the password for the Password Vault (see "Understanding the Password Vault" next in this chapter), which is created automatically when creating a new file. The Password Vault can be unlocked or reset by entering your Intuit ID. Although the Password Vault password will initially be set to your Intuit ID password, you can choose your own Password Vault password.

Intuit Password for Upgrading Users

For those users who are upgrading from previous editions of Quicken, a Password Vault is created with the Intuit ID password as the password for those users whose previous edition did not include a Password Vault.

Understanding the Password Vault

Because some Quicken users find it a nuisance to have to type in each password each time they use the One Step Update feature, especially if they connect to more than one or two financial institutions, Quicken's Password Vault feature enables you to store all your financial institution passwords in one central location. The passwords are initially protected with a single password in Quicken 2017: your Intuit ID password.

Setting Up the Password Vault for Upgraders

When you have upgraded to Quicken 2017, you can make changes by choosing Tools | Password Vault | Add Or Edit Passwords. The Edit Password Vault dialog, shown next, appears. Enter your Intuit ID password to continue.

1. Select Manage Vault Password to open the Manage Vault Password dialog, seen next.

2. Select Use My Intuit ID Password or Use My Custom Password to continue.

3. Enter your Intuit ID password in the Existing Password field.
4. Enter your custom password in the Create New Password field.
5. Confirm your password by typing it again in the Confirm Password field.
6. Click Save to close the dialog and return to the Edit Password Vault dialog.

The accounts you have activated for online access are displayed. If you have stored a password, Yes appears in the Password Stored column. If you have not yet stored a password, the column will show No. To add a password:

1. Click the password line of the account for which you want to add a password.
2. Click Add Password.
3. Enter the appropriate password in the Password field.
4. Enter the password again in the Reenter Password field.
5. Click Add to close the dialog and return to the Edit Password Vault dialog.

You'll enter each password twice because the characters you type do not appear on screen; this is a secure way of making sure you enter the same thing both times.

Enter as many passwords as you choose, and when all have been entered, click Done. When asked whether you want to enter additional passwords, click Yes to add more passwords or No to close the dialog. The Password Vault dialog closes.

Secure passwords traditionally have at least eight characters, combining both uppercase and lowercase letters, numbers, and symbols.

If you choose to print your passwords, do not leave the printed list in plain sight or affix it to your monitor.

The View Guidance Button

The View Guidance button at the top right of the screens in many (but not all) tabs opens a series of tips and suggestions called Quicken Qcards. Shown next is the introduction to these helpful hints found in the Main View of the Home tab. Click Next to see another hint in that tab's snapshot. As you cycle through the tips, each tip opens in another part of the current tab's view with an explanation of that section. Click the X at the upper right to close the Qcard.

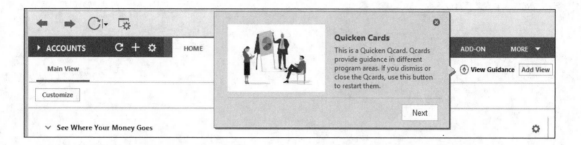

Exiting Quicken

There are several ways by which you can exit your Quicken program. However, consider doing a backup before you close your program. When you choose File | Exit, you are asked if you want to back up the data file. Learn more about Quicken Backups in Appendix A.

- You can close Quicken by selecting File from the Quicken menu and clicking Exit.
- You can close Quicken by clicking the small X in the upper-right corner of the Quicken window.

Starting with Quicken Basics

Chapter 2

In This Chapter:

- *Bookkeeping with Quicken*

- *Reviewing account types*

- *Exploring the Quicken window*

- *Understanding other Quicken features*

- *Finding help in Quicken*

- *Understanding data files and accounts*

- *Creating more accounts*

Quicken is a complete personal finance software package and a useful tool for taking control of your finances. Quicken makes it easy to know what you have, how you are doing financially, and what you could do to strengthen your financial situation. If you have forgotten your high school bookkeeping class (or never took one), the following section describes some of the terminology you will encounter and how Quicken handles your financial transactions.

How Financial Transactions Are Tracked

Quicken is based on the principles of double-entry bookkeeping. If this sounds a bit confusing at first, don't worry. Once you enter (or download) the transaction into one of your accounts and indicate the categories, Quicken takes care of all the other details.

For example, if you transfer money from your checking account into your savings account, there are actually two entries: one entry that takes the funds out of your checking account, which decreases the total balance in that account, and the second that puts the funds into your savings account, which will *increase* the total in that savings account. To save you time, Quicken does this automatically by its use of categories. (Categories are discussed in detail in Chapter 4.)

Bookkeeping with Quicken

Each time you spend, charge, or receive money and enter the transaction into Quicken, it is recorded into one of the accounts you establish. This money transaction can be an Asset, a Liability, Income, or an Expense. These four "ledger" types are the backbone of any bookkeeping system. Each transaction has to fall into at least one of the ledger types.

If you spend money—for example, when you go to the grocery store and write a check or use your checking account's debit card—this "Expense" will show in Quicken as a payment (or reduction of your checking account) and an increase in your Grocery expense category. A deposit, such as the birthday money from Aunt Carissa, is shown by Quicken as "Income" when it increases the amount in your checking account and increases the Gift income category, as shown next.

You can have a transaction that uses more than one category in an account. For example, your telephone bill may include both telephone charges and Internet connection charges, as seen in the illustration. That transaction is an expense, with the check you write reducing the amount of money in your checking account and increasing both your Home Phone Expense and your Internet Expense categories as shown here. These are called "split" transactions, and you'll learn more about them in Chapter 5.

Although the split transaction's category shows as "Split," you can see the individual categories by hovering your mouse pointer over the word "Split."

Reviewing Account Types

As you think about the four ledger types, each account you create in Quicken fits into one of the four. An account is a record of what you either own or owe. Quicken offers various kinds of accounts for different purposes. A link for each account you set up in Quicken appears in one of the sections of the Account Bar as discussed later in this chapter. You can choose to hide accounts from the Account Bar. Table 2-1 summarizes the accounts and how they are organized within Quicken.

- **What You Own**   In bookkeeping jargon, what you own are assets. In Quicken, an asset is one type of account; several other types exist as well:
  - **Spending**   These accounts display in the Banking section of the Account Bar and are used primarily for expenditures. This section displays checking and cash accounts as well as your credit cards.

Account Type	Account Bar Section	Asset or Liability
Checking	Banking	Asset
Savings	Banking	Asset
Credit Card	Banking	Liability
Cash	Banking	Asset
Standard Brokerage	Investing	Asset
401(k) or 403(b)	Investing	Asset
IRA or Keogh Plan	Investing	Asset
529 Plan	Investing	Asset
House	Property & Debt	Asset
Vehicle	Property & Debt	Asset
Other Asset	Property & Debt	Asset
Debt	Property & Debt	Liability

Table 2-1 • Overview of Quicken Account Types

- **Savings** These also show in the Banking section of the Account Bar and are used to record the transactions in savings accounts.
- **Investment** Your investment accounts display in the Account Bar's Investing section and are for tracking the stocks, bonds, and mutual funds in your portfolio that are not in retirement accounts.
- **Retirement** While also included in the Investing section, these accounts track investments in retirement accounts. Quicken distinguishes between different types of retirement accounts. One type includes individual retirement accounts (IRAs) or Keogh Plans, another covers 401(k) or 403(b) accounts, and most 529 Plans are included in this section.
- **Asset** Your asset accounts display in the Property & Debt section of the Account Bar. You use this type of account for tracking items that you own. Quicken distinguishes among three different types of asset accounts: House, Vehicle, and Other Asset.
- **What You Owe** The bookkeeping term for what you owe (your debts) is liabilities. Quicken offers two kinds of accounts for amounts you owe:
  - **Credit Card** Credit cards will normally appear in the Banking section, and this is the best location for them. However, those cards that you have designated as Liability accounts display in the Property & Debt section. See Chapter 5 to learn how to show credit cards in the Property & Debt section of the Account Bar.
  - **Debt** Debt (liability) accounts appear in the Property & Debt section. This section is for tracking loans, mortgages, and other liabilities. While

it is possible to include credit cards in this section, most users opt to show their credit card accounts in the Banking section of the Account Bar.

If you are using either the Home & Business or Rental Property Manager edition of Quicken, you can also enter special business accounts such as Accounts Payable and Accounts Receivable.

Exploring the Quicken Window

The main Quicken window gives you access to most of Quicken's features and your financial information. We'll look at each section separately.

Account Bar

The Account Bar lists each of your Quicken accounts on the left side of the main Quicken window, as seen here. Click on the name of each account to see all the transactions for that account. At the top of the Account Bar is a link to the All Transactions register, which shows the transactions for all of your accounts in one register. The All Transactions register does not show your Investing accounts; however, it does show transactions from linked investment cash accounts.

There can be up to five sections to the Account Bar, depending on how you structure Quicken. The main three are Banking, Investing, and Property & Debt. If the Account Bar is not displayed, click the small right-pointing arrow at the left of the word "Accounts."

If you can't see all of the accounts in the Account Bar, use the scroll bar on the right side of the Account Bar to scroll through its contents. You can also click the downward or right-pointing arrow next to a section heading on the Account Bar to hide or display, respectively, the list of accounts beneath it.

By default, account balances, rounded to the nearest dollar, appear in the Account Bar; however, you can right-click anywhere in the Account Bar to open a context menu, shown next. Choose Show Amounts to display the amounts, and clear the check mark to hide amounts from view. (Hiding amounts makes the Account Bar narrower so more

ACCOUNTS	C + ⚙
All Transactions	
⊿ Banking	$54,628.56
Main Checking	13,144.88
House Checking	2,959.02
Kids Savings	25.56
MMA Account	23,463.47
Old Checking	15,336.25
Main Credit Card	-238.48
Credit Card in Wallet	-70.21
More Accounts	8.07
⊿ Separate ⓘ	$599,205.89
Banking	
Small Savings	3,004.26
Money Market Acct	5,089.82
Major Savings	116,346.05
Investing	
OLD IRA	100,977.65
401(k)	23,854.57
Brokerage 1	7,358.79
Current IRA	43,485.47
Ending Balance	**$54,628.56**
Credit Score	View...

information appears in the window to the right.) This contextual menu offers additional options for the display of the Account Bar, such as displaying cents in the amounts. You can also change the width of the Account Bar by dragging its right border. All of these options are explained in the section "Account Bar Context Menu," later in this chapter.

The account names in the Account Bar are links to that account's register. Click on the link to open the register for that account. You can change the location of an account in the Account Bar from one section to another or to hide an account's name from the Account Bar. For example, if you choose to designate a specific account as a savings or investment account:

1. Right-click on the account name and select Edit/Delete account.
2. In the Account Details dialog that appears, select Display Options.
3. In the Account Intent drop-down menu, select the account in which you want this account to appear, as shown next.
4. After you have made your selection, click OK to save your choice, and the account appears in your chosen section of the Account Bar.

In general, you can designate the section in which you want your account to appear, or you can choose to show all accounts in each section.

- The small downward arrow to the left of the word "Accounts" allows you to minimize the Account Bar to save room when working with other Quicken processes. When you click this arrow to minimize the Account Bar, it turns into a right-pointing arrow. Click that right-pointing arrow to open the Account Bar once again. In the same way, you can collapse and expand the Account Bar sections.
- The white curly arrow to the right of the word "Accounts" is a shortcut for updating your online accounts. See more about online accounts in Chapter 6.
- The plus sign opens the Add Account dialog.
- The small gear icon at the far right of the word "Accounts" opens the same context menu as shown earlier.
- Ending Balance is the total of all of the amounts currently displayed in the Account Bar. The total at the bottom of the Account Bar will be labeled "Ending Balance" if you have selected Show Ending Balance In Account Bar. If you have instead chosen Show Current Balance In Account Bar, the label will be Net Worth.

 If you have chosen to not display amounts in the Account Bar from the Account Bar context menu, you will not see Ending Balance displayed in the Account Bar.

Account Bar Context Menu

As with many context menus in Quicken, the Account Bar context menu allows you to tailor this section to meet your needs.

- If you right-click a specific account, the context menu includes **Edit/Delete Account**. This link opens the Account Details dialog for the account you selected.
- If you right-click in a blank area of the Account Bar, the first item on the list is **Account List**, as seen next. This option opens a list of all of your accounts. You may also open this list with the shortcut keys CTRL-A.

- **Expand All Accounts** tells Quicken to display all of the individual accounts in each separate section of the Account Bar.
- **Standard View** and its companion **Compact View** allow you to choose the way your accounts appear in the Account Bar. Compact View can save some room on your screen. The option for selecting the vertical spacing in the Account Bar is new for Quicken 2017.
- **Show Credit Score** tells Quicken to display the Credit Score button in the Account Bar.
- **Show Amounts** tells Quicken to display the balance of each account. If you choose not to display the balance amount, you do not see the Ending Balance total in the Account Bar.
- **Show Cents In Amounts** tells Quicken to include the cents rather than just the dollar amount of each account's balance.
- **Show Current/Ending Balance In Account Bar** tells Quicken whether to display the balance as of today or include transactions you've entered for future dates in the balance.
- **Show Savings Goals Transactions In Register And Reports** appears only if you have established savings goals. Learn more about the Savings Goals feature in Chapter 13.

Click View | Account Bar to open a menu from which you can choose where the Account Bar physically appears in your Quicken window.

Tabs

Tabs, as seen in Figure 2-1, help you navigate through Quicken. Some tabs, such as the Spending and Investing tabs, provide information about your financial status, as well as links and buttons for accessing Quicken features. Other tabs

Figure 2-1 • Use Quicken's tabs to navigate through the program.

have views, such as the Main View of the Home tab, that enable you to view and customize Quicken settings for your financial situation.

A tab exists for each major area of Quicken:

- **Home** displays customizable views of your Quicken data. See Chapter 7 and Appendix B to learn more about how to work with and customize the Home tab views.
- **Spending** provides information about your income and expenditures for all accounts, only a single account of your choosing, for all dates, or for a custom date that you choose. You can use the drop-down lists to customize the information in both graphical and list formats, as explained in Chapter 7.

EXPERIENCED USERS RECOMMEND

Many Quicken users choose to display all of the tabs until they find which features they use the most. For example, the Budgeting feature of Quicken is included in the Planning tab. Consider exploring the features available in each of the Quicken tabs before you decide to turn off its display. Use the Tabs To Show option from View in the Quicken menu to specify which tabs to display or hide from view. In the Deluxe, Premier, or higher versions of Quicken, you have Investing and Property & Debt tabs that are not available in the lower versions. In the Home & Business edition, you will see a Business tab, and in the Rental Property version, one more: a Rental Property tab.

You can choose to display spending for all accounts or a single account of your choosing, or with Custom, you can choose a selection of your accounts to display.

- **Bills** provides information about your upcoming bills and offers tools for working with bills and reminders, as discussed in Chapters 6 and 7.
- **Planning** gives you access to Quicken's financial planners, as well as the assumptions you need to set up to use the planners effectively, as discussed in Chapter 12.

- **Investing** provides information about your investment and retirement accounts and any stocks or mutual funds you've asked Quicken to watch for you. See Chapters 9 and 11 for investing information.
- **Property & Debt** provides information about asset and debt accounts, including your home, car, related loans, and auto expenses, as discussed in Chapters 10, 11, and 12.
- **Add-on Services** offers links to additional Quicken services, such as Quicken Bill Pay and Quicken Online Backup.

If you have more tabs selected for display than the width of your Quicken window can show, several tab names are shortened. For example, Planning appears as "Plan" and Investing as "Invest," as seen here.

- **Mobile & Alerts** helps you set up your Quicken ID to work with the Quicken Mobile app. See Chapter 3 for more details.
- **Tips & Tutorials** contains how-to guides and other helpful links.

The buttons in each tab indicate the current view or other options within each tab section. If there's more than one button or a menu in either of these areas, you can click a button or choose a menu command to switch to another view or account.

Understanding Other Quicken Features

Quicken uses other windows to display information, depending on what you want to see or what task you are trying to perform:

- **List Windows**   A list window shows a list of information about related things, such as accounts, categories, tags, or scheduled transactions. You can use a list window to perform tasks with items in the list.
- **Report Windows**   Quicken's report windows enable you to create reports about your financial matters. You have the option to change date ranges, create comparisons, and customize reports. You can also use options and

buttons at the top of the window to work with, customize, and save reports. You learn about all of these in Chapter 15.

Quicken offers a number of ways to access its features and commands, including standard Microsoft Windows elements, such as menus and dialogs, and Quicken elements, such as the Toolbar, the Action gear icons, and links and buttons within Quicken windows.

- **Menus**   Quicken has two ways to display menus. The recommended Standard display shows six items on the menu bar. If you choose Classic Menus, you may have an additional nine from which to choose, as shown here. You can choose commands from the menus as follows:

Quicken 2017 Premier - Our Quicken Data - [House Checking]		Search a payment or deposit	∧ – □ ×
File Edit View Tools Home Bills Spending Investing Property & Debt Planning Mobile & Alerts Tips & Tutorials Add-on Services Reports Help			

The Property & Debt menu appears only when you have entered a new account in either the Property & Assets or Loans & Debt sections.

- Click the menu name to display the menu. If necessary, click the name of the submenu you want, and then click the name of the command you want.
- Press the shortcut key combination for the menu command that you want. A command's shortcut key, if it has one, shows to the right of the command name on the menu. See an extensive list of Quicken's shortcut keys in Appendix A. If your Windows program is set up to have keyboard access keys underlined, you can press ALT to activate the menu bar and press the keyboard key for the underlined letter in the menu that you want to open. If necessary, press the key for the underlined letter in the submenu that you want to open, and then press the key for the underlined letter in the command that you want.
- **Context Menus**   Context menus (which are sometimes referred to as shortcut or context-sensitive menus) can be displayed throughout Quicken. Point to the item for which you want to display a shortcut menu and click the right mouse button. The menu, which includes only those commands applicable to the item, appears at the mouse pointer.

EXPERIENCED USERS RECOMMEND

If you are using Windows 7, Windows 8, or Windows 10, you can see more than just the keyboard shortcut sequences. From your Windows 7 Start button, click Control Panel | Ease Of Access Center | Make The Keyboard Easier To Use | Make It Easier To Use Keyboard Shortcuts, and click the Underline Keyboard Shortcuts And Access Keys check box. Then you see the shortcut and access keys you would normally see only if you first press the ALT key on the keyboard. Whether or not you have the keyboard access keys underlined, you can still use the ALT key to view the information. Turning on the underlining just makes it easier to see the sequences.

In Windows 8 and Windows 10, the same options are found by selecting the Search charm and entering **Control Panel**, or if you display your apps by category, select Control Panel in the Windows Systems section. Then select Ease Of Access Center | Make The Keyboard Easier To Use | Make It Easier To Use Keyboard Shortcuts, and click the Underline Keyboard Shortcuts And Access Keys check box.

- **Dialogs**   Like other Windows applications, Quicken uses dialogs to communicate with you. Some dialogs display a simple message, while others include text boxes, option buttons, check boxes, and drop-down lists you can use to enter information.
- **Toolbar**   The Quicken Toolbar is a row of buttons along the top of the Quicken window, just beneath the standard menu bar, that gives you access to other navigation techniques and features. The Quicken Toolbar appears by

EXPERIENCED USERS RECOMMEND

Other menu items affect how you see information in Quicken:

- Use Large Fonts makes the font much larger. This option enlarges the standard Quicken fonts in every tab, as well as in registers and on-screen reports. The downside of this option is that although the font is larger, you will see less information on each screen and some of the windows may be cut off. Also, the menu bar fonts stay the normal size.
- The Use Pop-Up Registers option displays a selected register (or registers) as a pop-up on top of the regular Quicken window. The downside to using pop-up registers is that you cannot set your Quicken Preferences to open to a specific account's register if you use pop-up registers.
- The Account Bar and To Do bars can be docked at the left or right of your Quicken screen. To change the position, select Account Bar and/or Dock To Do Bar.

default, but can be turned off and customized. Learn how to customize it in Appendix B.

- **Back** (an arrow pointing left) displays the previously opened window.
- **Forward** (an arrow pointing right) displays the window you were looking at before you clicked the Back button. This button is only available if you clicked the Back button to view a previously viewed window; otherwise, it is grayed out.
- **One Step Update** (the curling arrow pointing to the right) opens the One Step Update menu, so with your Internet connection you can update all of your online information at once.
- **Customize Toolbar**, which appears when you right-click in a blank area of the toolbar, allows you to make changes and additions to the Quicken Toolbar. Learn more about customizing the Toolbar in Appendix B.

- **Filters**   Filters appear as a row of textual buttons and menus just above the contents of many Quicken windows. Most filter items, which vary from window to window, are drop-down lists. Click the downward-pointing arrows to access the list.

Quicken Title Bar

At the very top of your Quicken screen is the title bar, as seen earlier with the Classic menu displayed. The title bar displays the Quicken version with which you are working, the file that is currently open, and the tab that is currently selected. Toward the right side of this bar is a question mark, which opens Quicken Help as well as a Search box.

Search is a global search feature you can use to search for transactions entered into Quicken. Just enter the search criteria in the field, and press ENTER.

Finding Help in Quicken

In addition to the question mark icon in the title bar and in many Quicken windows and the Help button in some dialogs, Quicken includes an extensive Onscreen Help system to provide more information about using Quicken while you work. You can access most Help options from the Help menu.

Quicken's Onscreen Help uses a familiar Windows Help interface. You can use it to browse or search Help topics or display Help information about a specific window. These days, any decent software program offers on-screen help. So what's the big deal about Quicken's? Quicken's Onscreen Help is especially, well, helpful. It covers every program feature and provides step-by-step instructions for performing many tasks. Clickable links make it easy to jump right to a topic you want to learn more about. And as you'll discover while using Quicken, Help is available throughout the program—not just in the Quicken Help windows. Each additional link on the Help menu is explained here:

- **View Guidance**   This option opens one of the Quicken Qcards. See Chapter 1 for more information about View Guidance.
- **Quicken Live Community**   The Quicken Live Community command uses your Internet connection to take you to Quicken's online user-to-user forum, where you can ask questions, get answers, and share information with other Quicken users. Click links or use the search feature to get the information you need to make the most of Quicken.
- **Quicken Support**   Clicking Quicken Support on the Help menu takes you to the Quicken, Inc., website. Select Support from the list at the top of the page or the Customer Support Team link.
- **Sanitize Data File Copy**   This item is used to strip out or obfuscate personal and financial info from your data file in case you need to send your data file to Quicken, Inc., for troubleshooting.
- **Screen Share**   This option, new in Quicken 2017, opens a screen, seen next, by which you can agree to let Quicken support personnel see your screen to help you when you contact Quicken, Inc.

Quicken Screen Share

By clicking "I Agree," you agree to allow a Quicken representative to view your screen for support purposes. All information displayed on your screen will be visible. Please close all programs that display private information, and do not show any passwords.

Your session may be recorded for quality control and diagnostic purposes.

[I Agree]   [No]

- **Check For Updates**   This option uses your Internet connection to verify that you are using the latest version of Quicken.
- **Privacy Policy**   This option takes you to the Quicken Privacy statement. Quicken, Inc., takes the job of protecting your information very seriously. The policies and procedures the company uses to protect all of your information are displayed in this message. The statement explains what information is collected by Quicken, how that information is used, and how you can find out more about Quicken's specific methods to ensure your information is safe at all times.
- **Log Files**   This link contains other links to several files created in the "background" by Quicken. Should you ever need to contact Quicken Support, the helpful Quicken support person may ask you to refer to these files for

troubleshooting. There
are several types of log
files, and should you
ever need to send them,
Quicken Support will
designate which one is
required.

- **About Quicken**   This
tells you which version
of Quicken you are
using. Also in the About
Quicken message are copyright information and credits to the many people
who have made the program possible. Additional technical information
about your Quicken file and system resources can be displayed by holding
down CTRL and clicking Help | About Quicken. You may be asked for this
information when troubleshooting with Quicken Support.
- **Upgrading Quicken**   If your current Quicken version does not meet your
needs, you can upgrade through Quicken Help. Click Help | Add *nnnn*,
where *nnnn* is the name of the version you prefer. Using your Internet
connection, these commands display a window that provides a bit more
information about other features in Quicken. From this website, you can
purchase either of these Quicken versions.

As You Begin

To use Quicken Personal Finance Software, you must set up your Quicken
data file for your financial situation. This means creating accounts and entering
starting balance information. When you first set up your Quicken Personal
Finance Software data file, it includes a number of default categories. Don't think
you're stuck with just those categories. You can add and remove categories at any
time. The same goes for accounts—you can add them as you see fit. Modifying
the accounts and categories in your Quicken data file is a great way to customize
Quicken to meet your needs.

As discussed in Chapter 1, Quicken opens to the Home tab's Main View,
which appears once you have entered your primary bank account. As you start
using Quicken, it's a good idea to understand how Quicken's data files and
accounts work. You'll also learn what documents to gather to help you set up your
accounts properly.

Understanding Data Files and Accounts

All of the transactions you record with Quicken are stored in a data file on your hard disk. This file includes all the information that makes up your Quicken accounting system.

Data Files

Many new Quicken users confuse data files and their Quicken accounts. A data file holds all of the information about all of your Quicken accounts. Quicken accounts can be checking, savings, credit card, investing, property, and debt accounts. These accounts contain the transactions you enter, either manually or by downloading from your financial institution. You can have any number of accounts within a data file. Think of your data file as a large strongbox in which you store all of your financial transactions.

Although it's possible to have more than one Quicken data file, it isn't usually necessary. One file can hold all of your transactions. In fact, it's difficult (if not downright impossible) to use more than one Quicken file to track a single account, such as a checking or credit card account. Splitting your financial records among multiple data files makes it impossible to generate reports that consolidate all of the information.

When would you want more than one data file? For example, you may need two data files if you use Quicken to organize both your own finances and the finances of a community group for which you are serving as treasurer. Each of these data files would have its own separate set of bank, credit, and asset accounts.

EXPERIENCED USERS RECOMMEND

You'll notice throughout each chapter of this book that you are encouraged to create a backup copy of your files. *How* to do it is covered in Appendix A. *Why* to do it is even more important. If you have ever experienced a hard drive crash, you know the importance of backing up your data on a regular basis. Imagine losing several years of financial information in the blink of an eye. So, as you are reading through the techniques and how-tos in each chapter, remember that the information you are saving on your hard disk using Quicken should be copied or saved to another location as well. Any mechanism that is built can break, and usually at the most inopportune time. Back up, back up, back up your files! You can *never* have enough backup copies.

Also, you may want to have a series of backups in case you need to revert back to an earlier version of your data. Consider keeping annual backups for previous years, monthly backups for the current year, and weekly backups for the current month.

Appendix A covers a number of data file management tasks, including creating additional data files and backing up your data files.

Accounts

An *account* is a record of what you either own or owe. For example, your checking account is a record of cash on deposit in the bank that is available for writing checks. A credit card account is a record of money you owe to the credit card company or bank for the purchases on your credit card. All transactions either increase or decrease the balance in one or more accounts. You create accounts within a Quicken data file so you can track the activity and balances in your bank, credit card, investment, and other accounts.

What You Need

To set up accounts manually, you should have balance information for the accounts that you want to monitor with Quicken. You can get this information from your most recent bank, investment, and credit card statements. It's a good idea to gather these documents before you start the setup process so they're on hand when you need them. To use the online banking services from your financial institutions, make sure you have your passwords and personal identification numbers (PINs).

If you plan to use Quicken to replace an existing accounting system—whether it's paper based or prepared with a different computer program, you may find it helpful to have a list of account names you've used (called the "chart of accounts" by your accountant) or recent financial statements. This way, after you set up your Quicken accounts, you can replace the Quicken default name with your preferred names.

Accounts

To track your finances with Quicken, you first create at least one account. While many of your expenditures may come from your checking account, you probably have more than one account that Quicken can track for you. By setting up all of your accounts in Quicken, you can keep track of balances and activity to get a complete picture of your financial situation. You don't have to add all of your accounts at once. You can start by tracking just the one or two accounts that you use most frequently and add accounts later.

Creating More Accounts

To begin using Quicken, you must tell the program what bank and credit cards you wish to track. Click the plus sign in the Accounts Bar to open the Add Account dialog as described in Chapter 1.

The Add Account dialog box appears, as seen in Figure 2-2. As described in Chapter 1, choose what type of account you want to add, choose the name of your bank from the displayed list, or type its name in the Enter The Name Of Your Financial Institution field. If your bank's name does not appear on this first group of names, when you type the first letters of your bank's name, a new list appears of those institutions that begin with the letters you typed.

Click Next to continue. Depending on your financial institution, you may see a dialog displaying connection services available for that financial institution. If so, make your choice and click Next. In the dialog that appears, as seen in Figure 2-3, Quicken prompts you to enter your user name and password as provided by your bank. Notice that you can display the password items by selecting the word

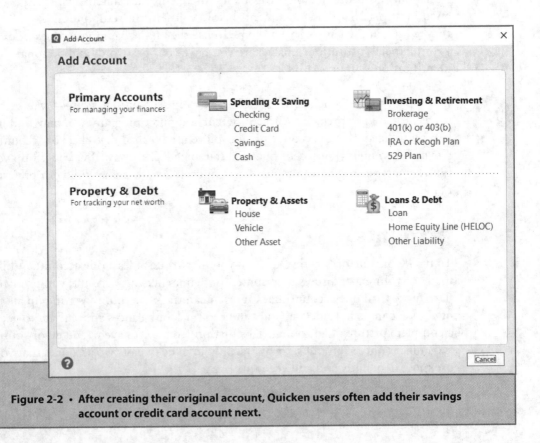

Figure 2-2 • After creating their original account, Quicken users often add their savings account or credit card account next.

Figure 2-3 • **Use the ID and password provided by your financial institution when adding a new account.**

"Show." (Should you want to save this password in the Quicken Password Vault, click Save This Password.) Click Connect to continue.

NOTE As you enter your user ID and password, Quicken warns you if your CAPS LOCK key is on.

The Quicken Update Status message appears as Quicken connects to your financial institution. If there are additional passwords or security phrases required by your bank, you are prompted to enter them. Do so and click OK or Next, depending on the prompt. You may be prompted to enter your Quicken ID here.

If you have more than one account that uses the user ID and password you entered, all of the accounts may be downloaded. If you have not yet set up any accounts in Quicken, each account will be called by the account name shown on your bank's records. You may change the name to something more descriptive if you choose. If you have already entered some accounts, Quicken prompts you to add, link, or ignore each of the downloaded accounts. After changing the account name(s) and selecting Add | Link | Ignore, click Next.

Use the Advanced Setup link at the bottom of the window if you do not want to download your information or if your bank offers more than one type of downloading service. See Chapter 6 for more information.

After the download is complete, your account (or accounts if you have more than one at that bank) shows in your Account Bar. Click Finish to return to the Home tab's Main View. Each downloaded account appears in the Account Bar with the nickname you entered. You may change the account names if you choose.

Consider Quicken Mobile

Chapter 3

In This Chapter:

- *Appreciating mobile*

- *About your mobile companion*

- *Understanding your Intuit ID*

- *Getting started from your desktop*

- *Setting alerts*

- *Showing your budget*

- *Getting started on your mobile device*

- *Working with the Quicken Mobile Overview page*

In today's hectic world, you are not always at your desktop computer when you need financial information. With the Quicken Mobile app you can check your credit card balance using your iPad on the way to work or glance at your smart phone to see if a check has cleared while you're at the gym. This chapter explains how to get started with the Quicken Mobile app and discusses its features.

Understand Mobile Applications

A mobile application (or app) is a small program especially designed to run on smart phones, tablet computers, or other mobile devices. If you have ever downloaded a game onto your cell phone, your favorite tune to your MP3 player, an e-book from the library to your e-book reader, or a map to your tablet computer the last time you took a trip, you have used a mobile app. Many apps, like the Quicken Mobile app, are free, and others are available for a small price. Of the price for the apps sold to the user, a percentage of the cost goes to the distributor (such as iTunes) and the rest goes to the person or company that created the app.

Appreciating Mobile

We hear the words "cloud" and "mobile app" everywhere in our world today: in advertisements, news programs, even schools. Just what is the cloud and how is it used? The term, whose original use is obscure, refers to storing programs and data at a location other than the owners' (or users') physical location and allowing users to access that information via the Internet.

If you have ever viewed a YouTube video, have a Gmail account, or used a website to share family photos, you've accessed the "cloud." The reality is that much of what we do each day on the Internet is done in the cloud. There is even an e-book version of this book downloadable from the cloud!

Meet Quicken's Mobile App

Quicken 2017's Mobile app is designed for Quicken users who want the ability to access their information from anywhere with an Internet connection. Are you required to use the Quicken Mobile app? No. Many Quicken users find the desktop program has all the features they need. However, by installing and using the free Quicken Mobile app on your Android or Apple device, you can keep up with any of your spending accounts—checking, savings, and credit cards—no matter where you may be.

New in Quicken 2017, the mobile app can be used to view the latest synced data and enter transactions, even without an Internet connection. You can also track both your investments and your Watch List.

About Your Mobile Companion

Quicken's Mobile app is available only for those who have purchased Quicken 2017 and installed the program on their laptop or desktop computer. It is used as an add-on to your Quicken program, not as a stand-alone product. Only after you have created your Intuit ID and set up your accounts as discussed in Chapter 1 can you start using Quicken's Mobile app.

Some Quicken users never use this tool. Others find it invaluable. It is up to you to decide. So what are the requirements for using Quicken's Mobile app?

- You must have either an Apple (iOS) or Android mobile device such as a tablet, smart phone, or e-reader that has the ability to connect to the Internet.
- You must have set up your accounts (and budget if you want to use that feature) on your desktop or laptop computer.
- You must have the Intuit ID you created when you first installed Quicken.

The illustrations throughout this chapter are from an Android smart phone and an Apple iPad. On your device, the screens may look a bit different.

Beginning with Quicken's Mobile App

If you are excited about the ability to see your financial information from any location with an Internet connection, it's time to get started. When you first installed Quicken on your computer, you created your Intuit ID. At the time, you may have chosen to use mobile, as using the mobile application is strictly optional. You saw the screens shown in Figures 3-1 and 3-2. However, to access your information from the Quicken Mobile app, this section explains both the advantages of using the app and how to set it up from your desktop.

Understanding Your Intuit ID

Quicken uses your Intuit ID to enable you to access your financial information from anywhere using either your smart phone or a tablet. Having that capability can make your financial life easier and eliminate the "oh my gosh" feeling that you have forgotten to send an important payment. This ID is used by Quicken to send both e-mail and text alerts regarding the accounts you choose to access on your mobile device. It is very useful to know that your salary check was, indeed, deposited yesterday or that a new charge was placed on your credit card.

The ability to monitor your credit card accounts may be one of the most useful features of the Quicken Mobile app. The moment you see a charge that you have not made, you can call your financial institution to report the error.

Figure 3-1 • When your registration is complete, you learn about the new features in Quicken 2017.

Figure 3-2 • You can start using Quicken Mobile as soon as you have installed and registered your Quicken 2017 program.

Getting Started from Your Desktop

If you chose to sync with Quicken Mobile after adding your first accounts, you saw a message that Quicken was syncing your accounts with Quicken Cloud, as seen next. If you did not choose to use the Mobile app when you first installed Quicken 2017, you can do so at any time. From your desktop, select the Mobile & Alerts tab to open the Quicken Mobile Get Started screen as seen in Figure 3-3.

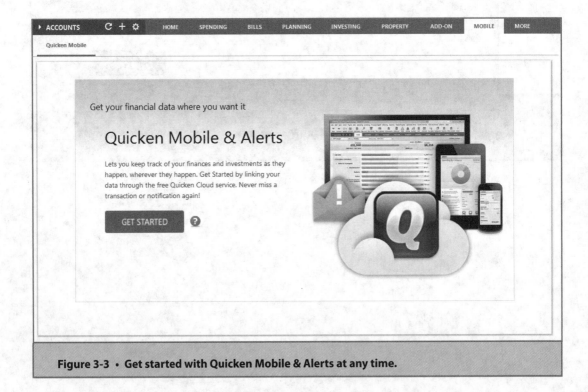

Figure 3-3 • Get started with Quicken Mobile & Alerts at any time.

1. Click the Get Started button. You are asked to sign in with your Intuit ID password. Enter it and click Sign In. The window that appears will depend on how you entered your first account (or accounts) when you installed Quicken 2017. If you don't see the Get Started button, you can change the accounts you have selected to sync; see the section "Edit Account Settings" later in this chapter.

2. You see the Select The Accounts You Want To Access From Mobile Devices dialog as shown in Figure 3-4. Select the accounts you want to see from your mobile devices from the list of available accounts.

3. By default, all the accounts are selected for mobile access. If you do not wish to synchronize all of them, clear the check box for each account you do not want to synchronize with your mobile device. You can choose both banking and investment accounts. However, at this time, only your investment account balances are synced, not the investment transactions.

4. Enter the online banking password for the accounts you do want to synchronize. Although it says to enter your account password, you are actually entering the password for your financial institution's site, where you may have multiple accounts.

5. Click Done to complete the process.

Figure 3-4 • **You can choose which accounts to sync, even though Quicken selects all accounts automatically.**

You may also see a message in your e-mail from Quicken saying you have activated alerts.

You see a message that your accounts are syncing with Quicken Cloud. When the information has been synchronized, a message appears that your sync is complete. (This message appears only if you are setting up mobile access separately from adding accounts.) You are prompted to download the free Quicken app from Apple, Google, or Amazon for your device. Click Done to close the message.

Work with the Quicken Cloud Overview Screen

The Quicken Cloud Overview screen, seen in Figure 3-5, appears. Note that it shows only the accounts that you have chosen to access from your mobile device. There are other useful links in this screen, as discussed next.

Edit Your Profile   When you click Edit Profile at the upper left of the Overview screen, the Quicken Preferences dialog appears at the Intuit ID, Mobile & Alerts section. Your current Intuit ID Profile appears at the top of the dialog. With the options in the Settings section, you can change the accounts you want to sync as well as your Alert settings. See "Setting Alerts" later in this chapter for more information about alerts.

ACCOUNTS ENABLED FOR MOBILE AND ALERTS	[edit account setting]	EMAIL ALERTS	[edit alerts setting]

ⓘ 401(k)-Main

ⓘ 401(k)-Spouse

Local Bank

    Bill Paying Checking

    House Credit Card

ⓘ Money Market Acct

    Wallet Checking

Credit Union

    Credit Card 1

    Emergency Credit Card

    Other

16 accounts synced | 8 eligible accounts not synced

↻ Sync now to check for new alerts

⚠ **Unusual Spending**
In the past 30 days, you spent $592.00 on Home. Usually you spend $197.33.

Figure 3-5 • The Quicken Cloud Overview screen shows your mobile settings.

Clicking either OK or Cancel closes the Preferences dialog and returns you to the Mobile & Alerts tab. Click Cancel to close the Preferences dialog without saving changes. To save changes, click OK instead.

Sync Now   Use the Sync Now link at the upper right of the Overview screen, as seen next, to sync your accounts with Quicken. The message that appears shows that your accounts are being synced with the Quicken Cloud.

When the operation has completed, the following message appears. Click OK to dismiss the dialog and return to the Mobile & Alerts tab. Note you can select the Don't Show This Again check box if you do not want to see the Cloud Sync Complete message each time your data is synced.

Edit Account Settings   Click Edit Account Settings, shown next, in the Accounts Enabled For Mobile And Alerts section to add or delete accounts you want to access via your mobile device. The Edit Account Settings dialog appears, as seen in Figure 3-6. After you are done making changes, click the Update Accounts button to let Quicken know of the changes. Otherwise, click the Cancel button to close.

ACCOUNTS ENABLED FOR MOBILE AND ALERTS	[edit account setting]

Figure 3-6 • You can edit the items to include with your Mobile app at any time.

Edit Alerts Settings   Use this link to open the Edit Alerts Settings dialog, as discussed in the "Setting Alerts" section next in this chapter. Only the Summary Emails drop-down list appears if you have not yet enabled text alerts; the Summary Texts drop-down list does not appear.

Setting Alerts

One of the great reasons to use Quicken's Mobile app is its ability to tell you about various financial happenings, even when you are not at home in front of your desktop computer. To let Quicken know the information you would like to see, from anywhere in Quicken, click the Mobile & Alerts tab. At the Overview screen that appears, select the Edit Alerts Settings link, which opens the Edit Alerts Settings dialog, as seen in Figure 3-7.

Each of the sections, Account Summary Notifications and Email & Text Alerts, allows you to set different types of alerts.

How Often Do You Want Alerts?

The first section of the Edit Alerts Settings dialog lets you tell Quicken how often you want summary e-mail information sent to you. The drop-down list gives you the option of receiving e-mails Monthly, Weekly, or Never, with Weekly being the

Q Edit Alerts Settings   ×

Edit Alerts Settings

Account summary notifications

How often you'd like to receive account activity summaries?

Summary emails [Weekly   ▼]

Email & Text alerts

📨 Email alerts will be sent to

☐ Secondary email for alerts [_____]

Email	Alert Type	
☐	**Bank fees** if my bank charges me fees above:	$ 1000
☑	**Unusual spending** if my spending in any category is above average by:	$ 500
☐	**Large deposits** when a deposit clears my account of atleast:	$ 1000
☐	**Large purchases** if any of my purchases cost more than:	$ 1000
☑	**Low balance** if the balance of any of my accounts drops below:	$ 500
☑	**Overbudget** If I exceed this budget	
☑	**Interest rate** If my interest rate changes	
☑	**Total credit available** if my credit usage is high enough to affect my credit score	

❓   [OK]   [Cancel]

Figure 3-7 • You tell Quicken what alerts you want to receive in the Edit Alerts Settings dialog.

default. You also can specify the frequency for summary texts, if you have enabled notifications via text.

Email and Text Alerts

In this section you can add a secondary e-mail address for Quicken to use for alerts. Your Intuit ID e-mail address is the primary e-mail by default.

What Type of Alerts Do You Want to Receive?

The bottom half of the Edit Alerts Settings dialog is how you tell Quicken both the information you want to see and how you want it delivered. You can choose to have each item delivered via a text message or by e-mail or both. Click the check box to the left of each alert type for the method of delivery and choose from these alert types:

You will not be able to choose the text alert type until you have enabled text alerts.

- **Bank Fees**   If any of the banks you have enabled for mobile access charges a fee above the amount you specify, choosing this option will alert you to that fact. The drop-down list offers five choices: $0, $1, $5, $10, and $50.
- **Unusual Spending**   This alert warns you of above-average spending in any category. The drop-down list lets you choose how much over the average amount requires you to be notified. The options are $200, $500, $1,000, and $2,000.
- **Large Deposits**   Expecting those lottery winnings any day? This option lets you know when a deposit over the amount you designate is posted to your account. You can choose from $200, $500, $1,000, $2,000, or $5,000.
- **Large Purchases**   By choosing this option you are advised of any purchases that are over your designated amount that appear on any of your accounts. You can choose to be told about purchases that are over by $200, $500, $1,000, $2,000, or $5,000.
- **Low Balance**   This selection alerts you to low balances in any of your synced accounts. You can choose to be warned of any balances below $0, $50, $100, $200, $500, $1,000, or $2,000.
- **Overbudget**   Selecting this check box tells Quicken to warn you of any category in which the amount has gone over what you budgeted. This will only warn you if you have entered your budget into Quicken and have selected to display that budget on your mobile device.

- **Interest Rate**   This selection lets you know about any interest rate changes made on any of your spending accounts.
- **Total Credit Available**   Selecting this option sends a warning if you have used so much credit that your credit score might be affected.

   After you have made all of your choices, click OK to continue. You will see that your alert settings are being updated. When that message disappears, you are back at the Mobile & Alerts tab screen.

Showing Your Budget

When you first set up your accounts for mobile access, you may not yet have entered a budget. If not, you can create one by following the directions in Chapter 13. If you have created more than one budget, click the Change link in your Mobile & Alerts Overview screen to choose the budget to use, as seen next.

- If you have more than one budget, choose the drop-down arrow to show the available budgets and select the one you want to use.
- If you do not want to see your budget information on your mobile device, click Don't Sync Budget Data.
- When you have made your selection, click OK to close the dialog. You see the Edit Budget Settings synchronizing to be available on your mobile device, if you have selected to show your budget on your mobile device.
- You may also see any budget alerts on your desktop as shown next.

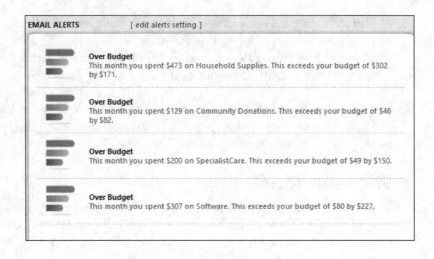

Using Your Mobile Device

After you have completed your settings on your desktop, you are ready to begin using the information on your mobile device. The first step is to obtain the free Quicken Mobile app and install it on your mobile device. You can obtain the app from the sources shown next or visit the Quicken.com website for more details. If your device is an iPhone, you must have iOS 7 to install the app.

- The Amazon App Store
- The Apple App Store
- Google Play

Getting Started on Your Mobile Device

Once your app is installed, go to your apps and you'll see the Quicken icon on your device. Tap the app to begin working with your Quicken Mobile app. On the iPad and Android phone, the icon is a big white Q on a red background with a Quicken label, as seen here.

You may find the Quicken Mobile app in one of the app stores and install it on your mobile device. After you have installed the app and opened it, you may be prompted to purchase Quicken, as you cannot use the app without Quicken 2017 for Windows installed on a desktop.

To ensure your accounts are available on your mobile device, set up your mobile accounts using your desktop Quicken program. Once you've selected the Quicken app on your device, you'll see the Let's Get Started screen. On the iPhone, the screen is not labeled Let's Get Started. It has Quicken at the top and two buttons: Get Started and Sign In.

Because mobile operating systems differ, you may find that some of the illustrations shown in this chapter are different or not available on your mobile device.

The Get Started Message

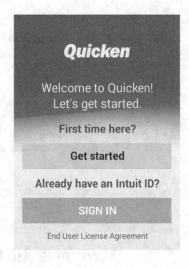

When you tap the Quicken Mobile app icon, you see the following screen, offering two choices. If you choose the Get Started option, you are prompted to buy and install the Quicken program, register, and set up through the Mobile & Alerts tab before using the program. Then, you can sign in with your Intuit ID.

When you tap Sign In to enter your Intuit ID, the sign-in dialog appears. Enter your Intuit ID to continue.

If you see a message that your sign-in failed and you are sure you entered the correct e-mail address, try re-entering your password. Depending on your mobile device, it is very easy to type incorrectly.

Working with the Quicken Mobile Overview Page

After you have correctly entered your Intuit ID, the home or Overview page of the Quicken Mobile app appears, as seen in Figure 3-8. Each section enables you to see more information as discussed next.

Figure 3-8 • As seen on an Android smart phone, the Overview screen in your Mobile app shows information about your accounts.

Since each device and operating system differ, what you see on your device may look different. For example, on an iPhone, you may be prompted with an offer to set a passcode before you see an Updates screen.

Recognize the Quicken Mobile App Tools

Because each mobile device varies, so will your display. If you are using a tablet, small icons appear. The location of the icons depends on your device.

If you use the Mobile app on a smart phone, you may have to swipe through screens or tap an action button. On some devices you see small icons, as shown in Figure 3-9 on an iPad screen.

- **Home**   On some screens you will see a small "house" icon that will take you to the Home page.
- **Search**   The small magnifying glass opens the Search tool dialog. At the bottom of this screen is a keyboard (not shown). With this dialog you can

Figure 3-9 • On an iPad, there are tools represented by icons at the left of the screen.

type the name of a payee, a category, or, if you use them, a tag name. Learn more about tags in Chapter 4.

- Depending on your device, you may only see the Search field once you have opened an account.
- **Transaction**   The Transaction tool opens the Add Transaction dialog, shown here. To work with this dialog, see "Work with the Transaction Tool" next in this chapter.
- **Update**   This tool updates your accounts.

Work with the Transaction Tool

- By default, the transaction is classified as an expense. If this is incorrect, tap that field to change the transaction type, payment type, and account. From this dialog you can select

- Whether this transaction is an income or an expense item.
- Whether the transaction is cash, credit card, or a check.
- The account for this transaction. If the appropriate account for this transaction does not show, tap the right-facing arrow to open the Choose Account list.

- Enter the amount of this transaction. Quicken automatically places a two-place decimal point.
- If the account from which this transaction occurs differs from what appears and you have not changed it earlier, select that field and choose the appropriate account.
- Tap the Choose A Payee field to open the Choose Payee dialog. You may
  - Choose a payee from the list if it is available. On some devices you may not see any payees until you start typing the first letter of a payee name.

  –Or–

  - Tap the Enter Payee Name field to open a keyboard with which you can type a new payee name. After you have typed the name, you will see Create "*nnnn*" (with *nnnn* being the payee name you just typed). Tap Create "*nnnn*" to save the payee name. Depending on your device, you may not see the "Enter Payee Name" text, just the empty field.
- Enter the date of this transaction. Today's date will appear but you can change it.
- Tap the Category field to select the appropriate category for this transaction.
- Tap the appropriate account, and you are returned to the Transaction Type dialog. Enter a check number if necessary and tap Done. Tap Back to return to the Add Transaction dialog. Depending on your device, you may not see a Done button.

You have additional items that look like three vertical or horizontal dots or even a small gear icon in the lower-right corner of the screen, as seen in the next two illustrations. The first illustration is from an Android phone with three vertical dots and the second from an iPad, showing the links (dots) horizontally. Each dot is a link to additional items. The equivalent on the iPhone is the button bar on the bottom of the overview screen; the buttons are Updates, Overview, and Settings.

Depending on your device, selecting these links may open a menu such as the one seen here. Remember, every device shows items in a slightly different manner.

Each device varies with the options discussed next:

- **Accounts**   This dialog displays the accounts with which you have selected to work. Each account shows the name of the financial institution, the account type and name, and the balance that was current as of your last download. You may also see the last update date and time.
- **Security**   If you share your device with someone else, you can protect your financial information by using the Quicken Passcode feature. Tap the link to bring up the Passcode dialog. Use the keyboard to enter a four-digit passcode. Re-enter the code, and after you have done so, you are returned to the Settings dialog.
- **Logout**   Tap here to log out of your Quicken Mobile app. Get into the habit of signing out each time you use Quicken Mobile, to ensure your financial information is no longer "live" on that device. Depending on your device, the message may be Sign Out or Log Out.
- **About Quicken**   This section tells you what version of the Quicken Mobile app you are using and other information about the program.
- **Help**   This option opens the Help dialog. Its label may vary, depending on your device. In the iPhone, there is no About Quicken and no Help listed; instead, there is a Help And Legal entry, which contains similar info.

EXPERIENCED USERS RECOMMEND

Why would someone use a passcode? By creating a passcode, your financial data will only be available when that passcode is entered. In particular, if your device is lost or stolen, you want to prevent anyone else from accessing your data. From your desktop Quicken, you can choose to delete your cloud account. Select Edit | Preferences | Intuit ID, Mobile & Alerts | Delete Your Cloud Data.

You can remove or reset the passcode from the Settings dialog by opening the Passcode dialog and entering your passcode. From the dialog that appears, tap Turn Passcode Off to delete the passcode. After you tap that option you are returned to the Settings dialog.

To change your passcode, choose Change Passcode. After you have made that choice, the Enter A Passcode dialog appears. Enter a new passcode and then enter it again. On an iPad, you are then returned to the Settings dialog. If you have another device, you may be returned to the Passcode Lock screen and be required to tap Settings to get back to the Settings screen.

To return to the Overview, tap the small Quicken icon at the upper left of your screen or the three horizontal bars at the upper left of your smart phone screen. On the iPhone, to return to Overview from Settings, click the Overview icon at the bottom center of the screen.

The Spending By Category Snapshot

In most devices, the top of your Overview page shows a colorful chart with the categorized and uncategorized expenses for the current month, as shown earlier in Figure 3-8. At the upper part of the screen is the total amount you have spent for the current month. On other devices, such as a smart phone, you may see a bar chart.

The iPhone shows a colorful donut chart displaying spending for the month on the Overview. For the first few days of each month, the Spending By Category chart will show the previous month's spending. This is because it takes a few days to accumulate enough transactions to trend the new month's spending.

On some smart phones or other devices, you might tap in the Earned And Spent section to see this detail. When you tap that option, you can review further detail by tapping Category or Payee and then tapping the category or payee you wish to review.

Tap any of the category sections in the Category donut to open a larger screen from which you can look at the totals for that category and any others.

On the iPhone, tapping any segment of the donut opens the Spending screen, displaying the top spending category by amount. Then tapping on any segment in the donut displays the amount of spending for that segment. You can then see the transaction detail by tapping the *nn* transactions link below the donut.

From this screen you can

- See the total spent in that category in the current month. To see the amounts spent in a previous month, tap the name of the month at the bottom of the window. Use the calendar icon at the bottom right of your screen to open the View Time Range dialog from which you can view the amounts you spent in this category for This Month, Last Month, or This Year. Your device may not have this capability.
- Tap on any other category in the donut to see the detail for that category.
- Tap the Transactions link to see what transactions are included in this total.
- Tap the See Details link to see additional information about the expenditures.
- Tap the Overview icon to return to the Overview page.

More Spending Reports

If you slide the Spending By Category snapshot seen on tablets, you will see two more snapshots.

Spending Over Time   This snapshot displays your total spending for the last six months as a columnar graph. Tap any column to enlarge the graph. When you select a month, the total spending for the month (or month to date if you are working with the current month) displays at the bottom of the graph. The graph may vary, depending on how much data you have entered into Quicken.

Not all mobile devices contain the Spending Over Time graph.

Tap Transactions to see each transaction for the month. Tap See Details to open a Spending By Category snapshot. Your mobile device may not have these capabilities.

Net Income Over Time   When using your tablet, slide once again to see the Net Income Over Time snapshot. The information again shows in columnar graph form. Select any month to see both the income and expenses for that month.

Your smart phone may not have a Net Income Over Time snapshot.

There are three small circles at the bottom right of the Spending By Category snapshot. Tap each circle to cycle through the main Spending By Category, Spending Over Time, and Net Income Over Time snapshots. You can also swipe to see the other snapshots.

Your Budget in Quicken Mobile

If you have chosen to include budget information, that data displays on your Overview page. Tap the section to open the Budget window. The budget categories you have chosen to include show how much you have spent in addition to how much you have left for each category, as well as the total for each month. On some smart phones, you may see a small gray circle with a pencil at the right end of each budget bar.

If you have set a budget alert, as described in "Setting Alerts" earlier in this chapter, you will receive either an e-mail or a text warning if you are going over budget for the selected categories. This alert appears on both your Mobile app Overview page and the Mobile & Alerts Overview page on your desktop computer. You may also receive an e-mail warning you that you have gone over budget, depending on the settings you created in the Edit Alerts Settings dialog on your desktop Quicken program.

Account Totals

Below your budget information is the balance for each of the accounts you have selected to be part of the Quicken Mobile app. Tap any account name to see the recent transactions for that account. Depending on your device, it may take two taps to accomplish this task. The first tap takes you from the Overview Accounts section to Accounts. Tapping any account on the list takes you to a list of the transactions for that account. Tap any transaction to open the Transaction Detail window.

The position of the Accounts listing depends on the device. It looks like Accounts is listed below Budget on an Android in the Overview and above Budget on an iPad in the Overview. On the iPhone, the Accounts listing is at the top of the Overview screen, which shows Alerts, Accounts, Budget, Cash Flow, and Spending. You are not returned to the Overview screen unless you tap back from the Budget screen.

Transaction Detail Window

When you choose a specific transaction, the Transaction Detail window allows you to make changes, view information, and split the categories for the transaction. Depending on your device, there are several ways to access a specific transaction. One way is to click Accounts and select the account in which the transaction is posted.

Split a Downloaded Transaction   Tap on a transaction. In the Transaction Detail window, tap the Split button to open the Split dialog. (On an iPhone, the Split button is at the top right of the transaction details screen.)

- To add a new category, tap Add or the white cross within the green circle. A new category line appears along with a calculator. Tap the right-facing arrow in the category field to choose from the list of categories.
- Tap the amount field for that category and enter the numbers from the calculator. You do not need to enter the decimal point, as Quicken enters it automatically. For example, tapping 3465 will show as 34.65.
- Repeat the process for each new category. As you enter new amounts, the original amount adjusts to reflect your entries. If you enter a number that would make the total less than zero, you will see a warning that the amount you are entering is too large.
- Tap the white minus sign inside the red circle by any category, and a small Delete message appears in the amount field. Press the message to delete that category.
- Tap Save when you have completed your changes, or Cancel if you decide you don't want to split the transaction. Your transaction appears. After you have reviewed your transaction, tap the Back button at the upper left of the screen to return to the previous screen. Repeat the process until you are back at the Overview page.

 In some mobile devices, you may have to tap the *<Your Account Name>* button to return to the transaction listing for the account.

Organizing
Quicken for You

This part of the book explains how to set up Quicken Personal Finance Software for everyday use. It starts by explaining the basics of creating accounts and how to categorize your transactions (and why!). You will understand how Quicken account registers work and how to manually record bank and credit card transactions. Then, you will learn how you can take advantage of online transaction entry and payment processing features such as Transaction Download and Online Bill Pay. It provides details about how you can tap into the power of Quicken to automate many entry tasks, thus saving you time. This part has three chapters:

Utilizing Accounts and Categories

In This Chapter:

- *Reviewing account and transaction types*
- *Working with bank accounts*
- *Adding new accounts*
- *Working with the Account List window*
- *Establishing categories and subcategories*
- *Working with the Category List window*
- *Organizing categories into groups*
- *Using tags*

Now that you have added your first account in Quicken, you have an idea of its power and capabilities. This chapter discusses setting up other accounts and some ideas on using your accounts to make your financial life easier.

Setting Up Other Banking Accounts

After you have created your primary checking account, you can create additional new accounts with the plus button that appears at the top of your Account Bar, as seen here. No matter what type of account you create, Quicken steps you through the creation process, prompting you to enter information about the account, such as its name and balance. In this section, you'll learn how to use the Add Account dialog to set up new accounts.

Reviewing Account and Transaction Types

Many of the transactions you track with Quicken will involve one or more of its bank, credit card, and cash accounts. Here's a closer look at each account type, along with some transaction examples. As you read about these accounts, imagine how they might apply to your financial situation.

Bank Accounts

Quicken offers two types of accounts that you can use to track the money you have in a bank:

- Checking accounts, which are usually the first type of account you create in Quicken.
- Savings accounts are for your savings. These accounts normally don't have as much activity as checking accounts. You can use a Quicken savings account to track the balance in a certificate of deposit (CD), vacation savings plan, or similar savings account.

 Some financial institutions consider CDs to be investment accounts, so you may not be able to download interest as you would with a regular savings account.

Both of these account types have the following types of transactions:

- **Payments**   Funds going out of your account.
- **Deposits**   Funds put into your account.
- **Transfers**   Movement of funds from one account to another.

Credit Card Accounts

Credit card accounts track money you owe, not money you own. Some credit cards, such as MasterCard, Visa, American Express, and Discover, can be used in many locations. Other credit cards, such as Macy's or Shell, can be used only in certain stores. They all have one thing in common: if there's a balance, it's usually because you owe the credit card company money.

Credit card account transactions can also be broken down into four categories:

- **Charge**   Charges result when you use your credit card to buy something or the credit card company charges a fee for services.

- **Credit**   The opposite of a charge is a credit. Think of it as a negative charge; don't confuse it with a payment. An example is when you return an item to a store where you bought it and receive credit on your Visa card.
- **Payments**   Amounts you send to a credit card company to reduce your balance, such as paying the balance on your American Express card or $150 of the $227 balance on your Visa card, as the rest of the balance is not yet due.
- **Transfers**   An example of a transfer can be points or cash from your credit card rewards account to your credit card when you redeem your rewards.

Cash Accounts

From within Quicken, you can also use a cash account to track your cash expenditures. For example, you might create an account called My Wallet or Spending Money and use it to keep track of the cash you have on hand. Cash accounts are like bank accounts, but there's no bank. The money is in your wallet, your pocket, or the Mason jar on your dresser.

Cash accounts have three types of transactions:

- **Receive**   When you receive cash, you increase the amount of cash you have on hand, such as receiving a $20 bill in a birthday card.
- **Spend**   When you spend cash, you reduce your cash balance.
- **Transfer**   When you withdraw cash for spending money from a bank or credit card account using an ATM.

Working with Bank Accounts

In earlier chapters, you learned how to add new accounts. Here are a few additional things to keep in mind when creating Quicken accounts:

- Ensure that each account has a name that clearly identifies it. For example, if you have two checking accounts, don't name them "Checking 1" and "Checking 2." Instead, include the bank name (such as "USA Bank Checking") or account purpose (such as "Joint Checking") in the account name. Using familiar names can keep you from accidentally entering a transaction in the wrong account register. Remember, the name of the currently selected account register displays on the title bar of the Quicken window, is highlighted in the Account Bar, and displays at the top of each register, as seen in Figure 4-1. In addition, at any time you can change an account's name in the General tab of the Account Details dialog.
- If you create an account for which you both download and manually enter transactions, be careful not to enter transactions that have already cleared the bank.

Quicken 2017 Premier - Our Quicken Data - [House Checking]   Search a payment or deposit

File   Edit   View   Tools   Home   Bills   Spending   Investing   Property & Debt   Planning   Mobile & Alerts   Tips & Tutorials   Add-on Services   Reports   Help

Back   Forward   Update

▾ ACCOUNTS   HOME   SPEND   BILLS   PLAN   INVEST   PROPERTY   ADD-ON   MORE ▾

All Transactions   **House Checking**
△ Banking $15,649   Last download October 19, 2016 - 4:38 pm
   Main Checking   14,675
   House Checking   1,125 | All Dates ▾ | Any Type ▾ | All Transactions ▾ | Reset | Search |
   House Credit Card   -151
△ Investing $5,094 | Date ▲ | Chec... | Payee | | Payment | . | Deposit | Balance |
   Small Savings   5,094 | | | Category | Memo | | | | |
                                   | ▶ ⬭ | | | | | | | |
                                   | 10/14/2016 | DEP | | | | R | 75.00 | 1,401 80 |
                                   | | | Gifts & Donations | birthday from Aunt Carissa | | | | |
                                   | 10/15/2016 | 65 | Jim's Hardware Store | | 188 67 | c | | 1,213 13 |
                                   | | | --Split-- | Download from usbank.con | | | | |
                                   | 10/17/2016 | 64 | Safeway | | 87 96 | c | | 1,125 17 |
                                   | | | Food & Dining:Groceries | Download from usbank.con | | | | |
                                   | 11/14/2016 | Check # | Payee | | Payment | | Deposit | |
                                   | ▶ ⬭ | | Category | Memo | | | | Save ⚙ ◂ |

   Net Worth $20,743   **Online Balance:**   1,193.68   **Ending Balance:**   1,125.17
   Credit Score   View...

Figure 4-1 • Your Quicken window displays the name of your currently selected account in several ways.

Some Quicken users choose to manually enter transactions as reminders. See Chapter 7 for more information.

• Entering your credit limit for a credit card account enables Quicken to alert you when you get close to (or exceed) your limit. If a credit card account doesn't have a credit limit—for example, a store charge card— you may want to enter your own personal spending limit. This makes it possible to take advantage of Quicken's alerts feature to prevent overspending in that account. You can enter either the preset credit limit or your personal spending limit in the General tab | Set Up Alerts section of the Account Details dialog, as seen here. In checking and

Account Details

Account Details

| General | Online Services | Display Options |

Account name   House Checking
Description
Account type: Checking
Tax deferred   ○ Yes   ⊙ No
Interest rate   %

┌ Set up alerts ─────────────────────
   Max. Balance   8,000.00
   Min. Balance   1,500.00
└────────────────────────────────────

❓   Delete Account   Tax Schedule

savings accounts, you can enter either (or both) a minimum or maximum balance for Quicken to track in the same area.

- Using a cash account to track every penny you spend, from the cup of coffee you buy at work in the morning to the half-gallon of milk you pick up on your way home that evening, isn't for everyone. You may prefer to track only items that might be income tax related, such as donations or large purchases, and record the rest as miscellaneous expenses.

Adding Other Account Information

As you work with your accounts, there may be other information you want to include, such as interest rate changes on a money market account. To enter the new information:

- From the Account Bar, right-click the name of the account you want to edit. From the context menu, shown here, select Edit/Delete Account to open the Account Details dialog.
- Enter or change the account information on the left side of the General tab. The dialog has different fields depending on the type of account. All account types allow you to change their account name and description.

In addition, checking and savings accounts let you change the following:
- Whether the account is tax deferred (before indicating an account is tax deferred, check with your tax professional)
- Interest rate
- Maximum and minimum balances for which you can be alerted

In credit card accounts, you can change the following:
- Interest rate
- Credit limit

Investing accounts let you change the following:
- Whether the account is tax deferred
- An option to show the cash in some types of investment accounts in a checking account

Chapter 9 has more information about investing accounts.

For all account types, the information on the right side of the dialog is similar, depending on the account type. You can modify the information only if the account is not set up for online services. Once the account is set up for online services, you may not change the financial institution name, account and routing numbers, or customer ID. (However, if you deactivate an account you have enabled for online access, you can edit the fields.) You see the following, as shown in the illustration.

Account Details	✕

Account Details

| General | Online Services | Display Options |

Account name: House Checking   Financial institution
Description: _____   Account Number: _____
Account type: Checking   Routing Number: _____
Tax deferred: ○ Yes ⊙ No   Customer ID: _____
Interest rate: ___ %

Set up alerts
Max. Balance: 8,000.00   Contact name: _____
Min. Balance: 1,500.00   Phone: _____
                                  Home page: Bank Web page   Go
                                  Activity page: Activity Web page Go
                                  Other page: Other Web page   Go
                                  Comments _____

? | Delete Account | Tax Schedule | OK | Cancel

- The financial institution
- The account and bank routing numbers
- Your customer ID, if applicable to this type of account

You can always change

- A contact name or the phone number at the financial institution

- The financial institution's web page, including the banking activity pages
- Any other comments you have about the account

Before you set up an account for online services, there are two tabs in the Account Details dialog. After that, there are three. From all three, you can access the Delete Account dialog and change the Tax Schedule information. Use the appropriate tab to make these changes:

- Use the **General** tab to make changes to the account name and other fields in that tab.
- Use the **Online Services** tab to activate or deactivate online services, including online payment services, if they are available through your financial institution.
- Use the **Display Options** tab to tell Quicken how to display this account, as shown in Table 4-1, later in this chapter.

When you have made all of your changes, click OK to close the Account Details dialog.

Adding New Accounts

Quicken calls its default method of adding accounts "Simple Setup." This process begins by opening the Add Account dialog. You can open this dialog in several ways, as listed here:

1. Click the plus icon at the top of the Account Bar.
2. Choose Tools | Add Account.
3. Press CTRL-A to open the Account List. Click the Add Account button at the bottom-right corner of the window.

You can also open the Account List by choosing Tools | Account List.

The Add Account dialog begins by asking what type of account you want to create. From there its options change, depending on the account type and whether you want to set it up for available online account services.

Creating a Spending and Saving Account

This section covers how to enter spending and saving accounts, such as Checking, Credit Card, Savings, and Cash accounts. You learn how to work with Investing and Retirement accounts in Chapter 9 and Property & Assets as well as Loans & Debt accounts in Chapter 10.

Using one of the methods discussed earlier, open the Add Account dialog. Then select the type of account you want to create. If you choose Checking, Credit Card, or Savings, the Add <type of account> Account dialog screen opens, as seen next. You'll notice that the dialog is similar to the screen you saw when you entered your primary account. The only difference is that instead of Add Primary Checking Account, it says Add <type of account>.

If your bank is not included on this list, typing the first few letters will open a list of banks that either start with those letters or include those letters as part of the bank's name, as shown next.

Q Add Savings Account   ✕

Add Savings Account

Enter the name of your financial institution

her|

All results

Heritage Bank & Trust
Heritage Bank - KS
Heritage Bank - Olympia, WA

1st Heritage Bank N.A.
American Heritage Bank
American Heritage Bank NM
American Heritage FCU
American Heritage National Bank
Bayer Heritage FCU
Century Heritage FCU PA

Financial Institution not on the list? Prefer not to download? Interested in advanced connection
Use Advanced Setup to create your account.

? Cancel   Back   Next

Choose a bank from the list or enter the first few letters of your bank or credit union's name. A second list appears. For many of us, our bank's name will be on the list. Click the name of your bank and click Next. If your bank's name is not on the list, you can still create an account and enter your transactions manually. Click Advanced Setup at the bottom of the window. (See "Using Advanced Setup to Create a Manual-Entry Account" later in this chapter.) When you click Next, you may see a message "Getting information about <your bank name>."

Enter the user ID and password provided by your bank in the appropriate fields and click Connect. A spinning circle appears along with "Looking for your accounts at <bank>" and then "Adding your accounts at <bank>." These messages indicate Quicken is receiving information from your financial institution. If this is the first time you have logged on today, you may be prompted for your Intuit ID.

 Depending on your financial institution, you may be prompted for additional information as you connect to the website. To ensure you type the correct information, you can select the Show Characters check box.

After the information is downloaded, the Account Added window appears with the name of your account. Click Add Another Account or click Finish to close the window. There is also a check box to enable you to select this new account to synchronize with the Quicken Mobile app.

 Depending on your financial institution, you may see how many days of transactions are available to download and how many were downloaded in this session.

Using Downloaded Accounts

If your user name and password connect to more than one account at a specific financial institution, all of the accounts may be downloaded when you connect. If you have already created accounts in Quicken, you will see a dialog from which you can perform an action for each of the downloaded accounts:

- **Add**   Use Add to create a new Quicken account with this information. You may rename the account to something more useful to you.
- **Link**   The Link option is used to identify a current Quicken account and combine the information in the download with that account. Make sure you have chosen the correct account.

 If you find after the fact that you have linked accounts incorrectly, you can still correct it later. See how to deactivate and reactivate online accounts in Chapter 6.

- **Ignore**   If you choose to ignore this downloadable account, the information will not be downloaded into Quicken.

EXPERIENCED USERS RECOMMEND

You can also use a combination of manual-entry and downloaded transaction methods. This enables you to have more control over the data entered and to compare your transactions with the bank's records without having to wait for a monthly statement. You can set up the account for downloading transactions, but enter your transactions manually. Then when you download transactions, they will match your manually entered transactions.

Review each choice before you continue to ensure you have connected the correct Quicken account with each downloaded account. After you have made your choices, click Next. You'll see the Account Added screen listing only the accounts you set as Add or Link. Click Finish to close the Account Added dialog.

You may have noticed one of Quicken's features. As you opened the Add Account dialog, the Quicken window from which you started dims. This feature ensures you will never be confused about which dialog or window you're working with. You can adjust or even turn off the dimming. Click Edit | Preferences | Startup | Quicken Colors | Dim Disabled Windows.

Using Advanced Setup to Create a Manual-Entry Account

As mentioned earlier, if you prefer to enter transactions manually, you can use the Advanced Setup option. This option also allows you to select the downloading method. To access Advanced Setup, from the Add <type of account> dialog, click Advanced Setup at the bottom of the dialog. Select I Want To Enter My Transactions Manually, and click Next.

Enter both a nickname for this account and how you will use this account and press Next again. Enter the statement date of your last statement and the balance shown on that statement and press Next. The Account Added screen appears with the name you selected. Note that you can choose to sync this account to the Quicken Mobile app. Also, from this screen you can select either Add Another Account or Finish, as seen in the following illustration.

![Account Added dialog showing "Savings 2..." with a "Sync to Quicken Cloud for Mobile & Alerts" checkbox, explanatory text about the number of days of transactions, and "Add Another Account" and "Finish" buttons]

Working with the Account List Window

You can view a list of all of your accounts at any time. Choose Tools | Account List or press CTRL-A. The Account List window appears (see Figure 4-2). This window displays a list of all accounts organized by type. If you want to see just one set of accounts—for example, your Banking accounts—click the name in the column to the left of the list. However, if you have entered only one type of account, such as banking accounts, there will be no other column at the left side of the Account List window.

Viewing Account Information

By default, Quicken displays each account in the Account List window (refer to Figure 4-2) by the account name (grouped by account type), along with columns for transaction download settings and the current balance. If you have told Quicken to hide any of your accounts in either the Account Bar or the Account List, you can opt to display them in the list by clicking the Show Hidden Accounts check box at the bottom-left corner of the list. This option does not appear unless you have opted to hide any of your accounts.

Add informational columns to the Account List by choosing commands from the Options button at the bottom-left corner of the Account List window. Just

Figure 4-2 • The Account List displays information about all of your accounts.

select a command on the menu to toggle the display of information on or off. This makes it possible for you to customize the appearance of the list and the information shown. See "Working with Accounts" later in this chapter for more information.

Select an account on the Account List, and click Edit to open the Account Details dialog, as seen earlier in this chapter. Here you can change the name of an account, enter additional account information, tell Quicken how to display the account, and modify the account's online services. Move between the tabs by clicking the tab with which you want to work:

- **General Tab**   The General tab displays basic information about the account that you can view or edit. From this dialog, you can enter information such as the interest rate you receive on this account and the account number, and you can create a link to the bank's home page. There are a number of options, of which only the account name is required. Not all of the options mentioned here will be available for all types of accounts:
- **Account Name**   By default, this is the name you (or the bank) entered when creating the account. You can change it here if you choose.
- **Description**   Add any information to further identify this account in this field.
- **Account Type**   This field cannot be changed. It is the type of account you established when you first created the account.
- **Tax Deferred**   Click Yes to tell Quicken this is a tax-deferred account; click No if it is not.
- **Interest Rate**   Enter the rate of interest, if any, for this account.
- **Set Up Alerts**   Use this section to ask Quicken to alert you if this account reaches a maximum or minimum balance. See Chapter 7 for more information about setting alerts.
- **Financial Institution**   If you have activated online services for this account, the name in this field cannot be changed. If you have set this account to enter transactions manually, you may enter or change the name of your financial institution in this field. In accounts set up for online services, you may see the Account and Routing Number fields filled in as well.
- **Customer ID/Contact Name/Phone**   While the Customer ID field appears only for accounts that have been activated for download, the Contact Name and Phone fields always appear.
- **Home/Activity/Other Page**   Use these fields to enter the website(s) for your bank. Use the Go button to connect to these websites using your Internet connection.
- **Comments**   Use this field for any additional information about this account.

On the bottom of the Account Details dialog are several other option buttons. From here you may access Quicken Help by clicking the question mark, delete this account, or assign income tax information for this account. However, the Tax Schedule button does not appear if you have turned off the Planning tab in View | Tabs To Show.

When you first create an account, you tell Quicken what "type" it is—that is, Checking, Savings, Cash, and so on. For downloaded accounts, Quicken decides the account type based on the information from your bank. Once this type of account is set, you cannot change it. For example, if you create a money market account as a "checking" type account, you cannot change it to a "savings" account.

The Delete Account button opens the Delete Account dialog. If you really want to delete an account, you must confirm the removal through this dialog. Quicken purposely does not make this process easy. You must type **yes** into the dialog and click OK to delete the account. If you have scheduled bills or deposits for this account, they must be removed before you can delete it. See Chapter 7 for more information about scheduling transactions. Remember that when you delete an account, you permanently remove all of its transactions from your Quicken data file. To get the account out of sight without actually deleting it and its data, consider hiding it instead, as shown in Table 4-1. The display options in Quicken 2017 are quite different from those in Quicken 2012 or earlier versions, so if you are upgrading, review them carefully. If you are upgrading from Quicken 2013, 2014, 2015, or 2016, you will not see a difference.

Keep Account Separate	Hide in Transaction Entry Lists	Hide in Account Name and Account Bar	Account Shows
			Directly in Banking, Investing, or Property & Debt Account Bar section
	X		Does not appear when entering any type of transaction
		X	In More under Banking, Investing, or Property & Debt Account Bar section
X			Directly in Separate at the bottom of the Account Bar
X		X	In More under Separate at the bottom of the Account Bar

Table 4-1 • Account Display Options

- **Tax Schedule Information** If the account has income tax implications and you have turned on the Planning tab, click the Tax Schedule button to use the optional Tax Schedule Information dialog. As always, if you have any questions about the tax status of an account, check with your tax professional.
- **Online Services Tab** The Online Services tab, seen in Figure 4-3, allows you to modify the settings in each account for your institution's online services. You can change the connection method, and if your financial institution offers the ability to use Quicken's One Step Update or Online Bill Pay, you can set those options here. You can also set up Quicken Bill Pay through this dialog. And, as seen here, click the Automatic Entry link to tell Quicken how to handle transactions for this account. (See Chapter 6 for more information about the online services offered by many financial institutions.)

Figure 4-3 • Use the Online Services tab in the Account Details dialog box to tell Quicken how to communicate with your financial institution.

- **Display Options Tab**   Use this tab to tell Quicken how you want to display this account, as seen next. You may keep the account separate, hide it in the transaction entry list, or hide the account name in both the Account Bar and in the Account List, as seen in Table 4-1. You may also tell Quicken to close the account entirely, which sets the balance of the account to zero and stops any downloads you've set up.
  - **Keep This Account Separate**   When this check box is selected, Quicken prevents the account from being displayed in lists, menus, and reports. This choice removes the account from view in its regular location on the Account Bar. The account is available in the Separate account section of the Account Bar, which includes the balances of all accounts you have marked with this display choice. Its balance is included in this Separate accounts section, as well as the Net Worth total at the bottom of the Account Bar. If you have also chosen to hide the account in the Account Bar, its balance will show in the Separate section of the Account Bar, grouped with More Accounts. Some Quicken users choose to separate accounts that are not used every day for the sake of convenience.

Many Quicken users do not mark any of their accounts as Separate, choosing instead to include all of their accounts in the appropriate section. One use for this designation might be a Savings Goal. See Chapter 13 for more information on Savings Goals.

  - **Hide In Transaction Entry Lists**   The selection makes the account unavailable when you are entering transactions in any part of Quicken. This is most often done for convenience sake when users have several accounts and the hidden account is one they seldom use.
  - **Hide Account Name In Account Bar And Account List**   Although the account remains visible in other lists and menus where it would normally appear, it no longer appears in its normal location (i.e., Banking, Investment, Property & Debt) in the Account Bar. Instead, it is grouped in that section as a part of "More Accounts." Its balance is still included in the Net Worth total in the Account Bar.
  - **Close Account**   This option closes the account entirely. Its balance is set to zero, and you will not be able to download transactions into a closed account. This is a permanent action. If you have set it up for online services, you must contact the bank to close the account on their end as well.

In Figure 4-3, you may notice a link stating "Automatic Entry is Off." When you select this link, the following dialog appears. From this dialog, you can tell Quicken to automatically enter all downloaded transactions into this account's register, or instruct the program to never add your transactions automatically, as you want to review each individual transaction.

> **Q** Automatic Transaction Entry   ✕
>
> ### Automatic Transaction Entry
>
> For House Checking
> **Automatically add downloaded transactions to your**
>
> ⦿ Use the general account preference that applies to all Banking acco
> ○ Yes - Always automatically add transactions for this account.
> ○ No - Never automatically add transactions for this account.
>   (I will review and accept transactions individually.)
>
> ❓ | OK | | Cancel |

Your other option in this dialog is to use the general setting you set in Quicken Preferences. As discussed in detail in Appendix B, you can set Quicken Preferences from the menu bar. Select Edit | Preferences and, in this case, Register | Downloaded Transactions | After Downloading Transactions.

Many Quicken users choose to review each downloaded transaction to ensure the transaction is categorized and entered in the way they intended. Learn more about Categories later in this chapter.

Account Intent

The Account Intent section seen in the Display Options tab lets you tell Quicken how you plan on using this account. For example, you might have a savings account that you actually are using as an additional retirement account. (However, you might want to check with your financial advisor to see if this is a wise use of your money.) To let Quicken know how you intend this account to be used, choose a value from the drop-down lists. These choices determine the section in which the account will display in both the Account Bar and other lists and reports. Once you have made all of your modifications for this account, click OK to close the Account Details dialog and return to the Account List.

Working with Accounts

You can use options in the Account List window to reorganize accounts so they appear where you want them in the Account Bar:

- **Changing the Order of Accounts**   By default, accounts are shown in alphabetical order in your Account List until you first move an account. As you first add accounts, they automatically sort themselves alphabetically. If you later decide to change the order and then add more accounts, the newly added accounts are inserted at the bottom of the section. To change the order in which accounts appear in the Account List window and Account Bar, select an account by clicking the line in which the name appears. Note that you must click somewhere on the account's line other than the name of the account or the Edit button. When you click the account name, the account's register opens. Clicking the Edit button opens the Account Details dialog. To move the account within its group, click the up or down Order button arrow to change the account's position. You can move an account to any position within its group. If you have only one account per account type, you do not see the Order button.

The order in which your accounts are shown in the Account List is how the accounts display in the Account Bar as well.

- **Viewing Your Accounts**   Each time you open the Account List, you can reset it to display only the group you choose on the left side of the Account List window.
- **Show Hidden Accounts**   Click the Show Hidden Accounts check box at the lower-left corner of your Account List window to display accounts you have marked as hidden. To hide them from the Account List, clear the check box. The Show Hidden Accounts option is also available in many areas throughout Quicken, and the settings you've set in the Display Options tab of the Account Details dialog determine how each account is "hidden."
- **Help Icon**   Clicking the small question mark at the lower-left corner of the Account List opens Quicken Help to the section on managing your accounts.
- **Printing the Account List**   Click the Printer icon at the bottom of the Account List window to print your list. The Print dialog appears. Click Preview to see how your list will appear. Click Close to close the preview window. Click Print to print the list. See "Using the Account List Options" next to learn more about printing details in your list.

EXPERIENCED USERS RECOMMEND

To set options or make changes to the display status of your accounts, click Tools | Manage Hidden Accounts. A useful dialog, as seen next, is displayed. From here you can select how each account is to be displayed within Quicken. If you have many accounts, consider using this dialog rather than using the Account Details dialog in each account.

Manage Hidden Accounts

Hiding Options ⑦

Account Name	Hide in Account Bar and Account List	Hide in Transaction Entry Lists	Keep this Account Separate	Close Account*
401(k)	☐	☐	☑	Close Account...
Car 2	☐	☐	☐	Close Account...
Cash Account	☐	☐	☐	Close Account...
Checking Account	☐	☐	☐	Close Account...
Credit Card	☐	☐	☐	Close Account...
Gabe's Car	☐	☐	☐	Close Account...
Home Inventory	☐	☐	☑	Close Account...
House	☐	☐	☐	Close Account...
House Loan	☐	☐	☐	Close Account...
IRA	☐	☐	☐	Close Account...
Lake Land	☐	☐	☑	Close Account...
Land at the Lake	☐	☐	☑	Close Account...
Letti's Truck	☐	☐	☐	Close Account...
Loan from Aunt Mabel	☐	☐	☑	Close Account...
Loan From John	☐	☐	☐	Close Account...

* A closed account cannot be re-opened. Learn more about when to close an account.

⑦   Done

Using the Account List Options

The Options menu offers you several ways to display the accounts in your Account List:

- **Include Additional Info When Printing**   When you choose this option, each time you print the Account List, it will include all of the options you've chosen in the Options menu. Unfortunately, you need to reset this option each time you open the Account List, as the selection disappears once you close the Account List.

- **Show Net Worth In Account Bar**   The Net Worth number that displays in the Account Bar is the sum of the current balances of all of your entered transactions on each of your nonhidden accounts. This option tells Quicken to display that sum labeled as Net Worth in the Account Bar.

- **Show Ending Balance In Account Bar** As mentioned earlier, the Net Worth balance on the Account Bar is the sum of today's balance of each of your nonhidden accounts. The Ending Balance takes into account the bills or deposits you have entered for future dates.
- **Show Payments To Send/Checks To Print/Number Of Transactions/ Description/Financial Institution** These options create new columns in the Account List that display the selected information. If you have chosen to include the additional information when printing, these columns will appear on your printed Account List report.
- **Show Current/Ending Balance** This is similar to Show Net Worth/Ending Balance In Account Bar, but it refers to the Account List. You may display both the Current and Ending Balances in the Account List.
- **Show Transaction Download Status/Show Online Bill Pay Status** These options appear if you have activated any of your accounts for online services.
- **Show Last Reconcile Date** Choosing to display this column in the Account List shows the last time an account was reconciled with the bank's records. Bank and credit card reconciliation procedures are discussed in Chapter 8.
- **Show Last Download Time** Choosing to display this column in the Account List shows the date and time from the last time the transactions were downloaded into an account.

You may only choose one option at a time in the Options menu. Each time you make a selection, the menu closes and you must reopen it to make another selection.

- **Add Account** On the bottom-right corner of the Account List is the Add Account button. Choose this button to open the Add Account dialog.
- **Done** When you have made all of your adjustments and are through with the Account List, click Done to close the dialog.

Categories

When you first create a data file, Quicken automatically creates dozens of commonly used categories. Although these categories might completely meet your needs, at times you may want to add, remove, or modify a category to fine-tune Quicken for your use.

Establishing Categories and Subcategories

Quicken starts with two category types. Income includes, but is not limited to, receipts such as your salary, commissions, interest income, dividend income, child support, gifts received, and tips. The other type is Expense, some examples of which are insurance, groceries, rent, interest expense, bank fees, finance charges, charitable donations, and clothing.

A subcategory is a subset or part of a category. It must be the same type of category as its parent category. For example, you may use the Auto category to track expenses to operate your car. Within that category, however, you might use one of the subcategories to record specific expenses, such as auto insurance, fuel, and repairs. Subcategories make it easy to keep income and expenses organized into manageable categories, while providing the transaction detail you might want or need.

Working with the Category List Window

You can view a list of all of your categories at any time. Choose Tools | Category List, or press CTRL-SHIFT-C. The Category List window appears as seen in Figure 4-4. Depending on which edition of Quicken you are using, the category groups may be different.

Figure 4-4 • The Category List shows the categories in your Quicken data file with which you can classify your transactions.

EXPERIENCED USERS RECOMMEND

Categories? Subcategories? Sounds confusing and like a lot of work? It is truly not much work, and using categories is well worth the time you spend doing it.

To use this wonderful feature, when you enter a transaction in Quicken, Quicken will enter one of its many predefined categories. The next time you enter a transaction for the same payee, Quicken automatically assumes the transaction will use the same category, so Quicken enters it for you.

When you do define a new category, often you don't have to type the entire category and subcategory—usually just the first few letters. For example, type "Au" and the Auto category displays. Type a colon (:) and an "S" and your category and subcategory are entered as Auto:Service.

So don't leave the category field blank when entering your transactions. That extra step results in more complete reports and a clearer understanding of your finances.

In this section, you'll learn how to use the Category List window to display, add, modify, delete, and perform other tasks with categories.

 If you have added an Investment account, you may notice a group of categories with an underscore before their name. These are special categories used by Quicken for such transactions as computing realized gains on investing accounts. They do not exist until you create your first investment account and are then hidden.

You can also choose commands to determine what information appears with the category names in the Category List window. Click the gear icon seen at the right of the Action column to open a list from which you can choose what columns to display.

Creating a New Category

To create a new category, click the New Category button at the upper right of the Category List window to open the New Category dialog. Enter information about the category, as seen in this example, and click OK. You won't be able to switch to the Tax Reporting tab in the New Category dialog until you have entered a category name in the Details tab. The following is a quick summary of the kind of information you should provide for each category:

- **Category Information**   Basic category information, entered in the Details tab, includes the category name, which is required, and the description and the main category if this is a subcategory. You have the option of entering additional information in the Description field.

If you are familiar with charts of accounts as used by many accounting folks, you can even use numbers in your Category name—for example, 61000–Auto Expense.

- **Tax Reporting**   You can use the Tax Reporting options to specify whether a category is tax related and, if so, what tax form and even the tax line item on which it appears. This can be a real time-saver at tax time by enabling you to organize your income and expenditures as they appear on tax forms. You learn more about using Quicken at tax time in Chapter 14. You are not required to enter anything in this area.

When you have set a tax line item and tax form for your categories, Quicken displays a small red circle with a check by each transaction. The tax information symbol shows only for tax-related transactions, not for all transactions.

Click Save to close the New Category dialog and return to the Category List.

Adding Multiple Categories at Once

Quicken makes it easy to add multiple related categories at the same time. Click the Options button at the bottom of the Category List window and choose Manage Categories to open the Manage Categories dialog, shown here.

Select an option from the Available Categories drop-down list at the top of the dialog. In the Category list on the left, click to add a green check mark beside each category you want to add. When you click Add, the selected categories appear in the Categories To Add list. Click OK to add the categories and close the dialog.

Organizing Categories into Groups

Budgets in Quicken (see Chapter 13 to learn more about creating budgets) are based on transactions recorded for categories and subcategories. (That's why it's important to categorize all your transactions—and not to the Miscellaneous category!) Quicken also enables you to organize categories by customizable category groups.

Some Quicken users see category groups as an annoyance when working with budgets, as each group displays in the Everything Else total, which clutters the Budget display.

Choose Tools | Category List to display the window or press SHIFT-CTRL-C. If the Group column does not appear in your list, choose the Category Action gear icon at the far right of your Category List, click the Group check box, and then click Done.

By default, Quicken assigns nearly every category to either the Personal Income or Personal Expense group. Your bank and investment accounts have no groups assigned. See "Assigning a Group to a Category," later in this chapter, to learn how to assign a group.

The Default Groups

By default, Quicken includes three category groups that it assigns to the categories it creates when you first set up your Quicken data file:

- **Personal Income** is for earned income, such as your salary, and miscellaneous income items, such as interest, dividends, and gifts received.
- **Personal Expenses** are all of your personal expenses, items you pay for and record in your account registers.

- **Transfers** are for transfers between existing accounts. You may not see this available until you have added several accounts to your Quicken file.

Creating a New Custom Category Group

Earlier versions of Quicken offered the use of custom groups. While today Quicken, Inc., recommends using tags, as discussed later in this chapter, custom category groups are still available.

To create a new custom category group, open the Category List by clicking Tools | Category List and at the bottom of the dialog, select Options | Assign Category Groups to open a dialog. If this is the first group you are creating, the Assign Category Groups dialog displays a message that you have not created any custom groups.

Click the New Custom Groups button (or if you have already added a custom group, click the Add/Rename Custom Groups button) to open the Custom Category Groups dialog. When it appears, click New to open the New Custom Group dialog. Type the name of your custom group and click Save. Click Done to close the New Custom Groups dialog and return to the Assign Category Groups dialog.

To add categories to your new group, select a category from the list on the left side of the dialog and click Add. The categories will appear on the right side of the dialog in the Assign It To A Custom Category Group column. Continue through the list of categories until you have finished selecting the categories you want to include in this group.

On some device screens, the font for the currently assigned category groups in the pane on the left makes the currently assigned category groups difficult to see.

You can add more than one item at a time by choosing the first item in a group of categories in the left column, holding down your SHIFT key, and choosing several categories in a row. You can select categories from several locations in the list on the left side as well. To do this, hold down your CTRL key and while continuing to hold it down, click the items you want. If you have to scroll, keep holding down the CTRL key until you have selected (clicked) all the categories you want to include. Then, release the CTRL key and click the Add button. All of your selected items will appear in the right column.

Should you want to include categories you have hidden, click the Show Hidden Categories check box.

If you want to remove a category, select it from the list in the right column and click Remove. It will once again appear in the left column.

After you have completed your choices for this custom group, click Done to close the Assign Category Groups dialog and return to the Category List.

Assigning a Group to a Category

You can assign a new or existing category to a standard or a custom category group. To assign a custom group to a new category, in the Category List window, click New Category to create a new category. The New Category dialog appears. Enter the category name and whether it is an income, an expense item, or a subcategory of an existing category. Click the arrow next to the Group box to display the drop-down list and choose a group from the list. Click OK to save your new category and its category group assignment.

You can also assign a standard group to a category.

1. Right-click the category you want to assign. Select Edit. The New Category dialog appears.
2. Select one of the three radio buttons: Income, Expense, or Subcategory.
3. Clear any information in the Group field by putting your cursor in the field and pressing DELETE on your keyboard.
4. Click Save to close the dialog and return to the Category List.
5. Click Done to close the Category List.

If you have not yet created any custom category groups, you will not see the Group field in the New Category dialog. Return to the Category List, click Options | Assign Category Groups, and create at least one custom category group.

To add a group to an existing category, right-click the category, and click Edit to open the New Category dialog. Click the arrow next to the Group box to display the Group drop-down list. If the category is one of the default Quicken categories, the Personal Expenses group may appear in the Group box, although it is not an option in the group list. Simply click the group to which you want this category assigned, and click OK. The custom group is now assigned to this existing category.

Modifying the Custom Category Group List

You can modify or delete custom category group names. From the Category List, click Options | Assign Category Groups, and click Add/Rename Custom Groups. The Custom Category Groups dialog appears. Select a group name, and click Rename to rename an existing group. To delete a custom category group, select the group name and click Delete.

After you have made your changes, click Done to return to the Assign Category Groups dialog. Click Done one more time to close the Assign Category Groups dialog and return to the Category List. Click Done once more to close the Category List.

Editing, Deleting, and Merging Categories

You use the Category List window to edit, delete, or merge categories. Select the name of the category with which you want to work. The Action options arrow displays in the Action column on the right side of the window. You will not be able to make changes to the items on the Category List enclosed in square brackets ([ ]). These items are transfer "categories" used when you transfer money to and from the indicated account.

Before making any changes, back up your Quicken data file. That way, if you don't like the changes you've made, you can quickly go back to the file's state before you made the changes. See Appendix A for information on backing up Quicken data files.

- **Edit**   Click a category to display the Action arrow. Click the arrow to see several options. Edit displays the New Category dialog (shown earlier) for the selected category. You can use this to make just about any change to a category. You can even "promote" a subcategory to a category by clearing the Subcategory Of: field.
- **Merge With Another Category**   This button allows you to merge transactions using the currently selected category with transactions using another category. This, in effect, recategorizes all of the transactions for the selected category. Clicking Merge With Another Category displays the Merge Category dialog. Choose the category to which you want to merge from the drop-down list. If you want to delete the category you selected, turn on the check box—this makes the dialog work the same way as the Delete Category dialog. Click OK to perform the merge. One thing to keep in mind: if the category you selected is not used in any transactions, you do not see an option to merge the category. You can simply edit or delete it.
- **Hide**   Clicking this option hides the category. It performs the same function as clicking the Hide check box.
- **New Subcategory**   Click this option to open the New Category dialog to create a subcategory.
- **Category Report**   Category Report is very handy for getting a quick report showing a summary listing payees and the number of times each payee/

category combination has been used in your transactions. You can then choose to get a full report showing all transactions for the selected category.

- **Delete**   When you choose to eliminate a category, first ensure you have a current backup. Then, select the category to display the Action arrow in the Action column. (You may have to make your window wider to see the Action column.) Choosing Delete displays different dialogs, depending on the category that is selected. Quicken begins by warning you that the category and any subcategories beneath it will be deleted. Then:
  - If you selected a category without transactions, when you click OK, the category is deleted.
  - If you selected a category or subcategory with transactions, a warning message appears that this category has been used in transactions or has subcategories. If you choose to delete the category, the Delete Category dialog appears. You can use this dialog to replace the category with another category throughout your data file. Choose another category from the drop-down list, and click OK. If you click OK without choosing a replacement category, any transactions that referenced the category you deleted will be marked as uncategorized. If the category you deleted has subcategories, this dialog appears for each subcategory that has transactions, and you cannot cancel the action. If you have made an error deleting a category, you must create the old category again and recategorize all of the uncategorized transactions. If the category happens to be only used in future-dated transactions, the deletion will act like the category is unused and just delete the category.

NOTE Categories used only in future dated transactions are still treated like an unused category and can be deleted without the user being informed that they are deleting a category that is actually used. Although this does not happen often, users can be left with uncategorized transactions.

Tags

A tag is an optional identifier used to specify what a transaction applies to. For example, if you want to keep track of all the money you spent for your last vacation, no matter the category, you can create a tag named Vacation. Then each expense you incur, whether categorized as Clothing, Auto Maintenance, Dining Out, or whatever, can be "tagged" as part of that Vacation tag. Because Quicken can produce reports based on categories, tags, or both, tags offer an additional dimension for tracking and reporting information.

Using Tags

Using tags is completely optional. It's your decision. Quicken maintains a list of all the tags you create. You can display the Tag List window by choosing Tools | Tag List, or by pressing CTRL-L. An example of a Tag List with a couple of tags is shown here.

Tag	Hide	Description	Action
Kids Car	☐	2008 Subaru	Edit Delete
Main Car	☐	2010 Ford	

Creating a New Tag

Click the New button in the Tag List window. The New Tag dialog appears. Use it to enter information about the tag.

Only one piece of information is necessary: the tag name. You may want to make it short so it's easy to remember and enter. The description can be used to provide additional information on the tag's use. The copy number enables you to associate tags with different but similar activities. For example, if you have two separate businesses for which you report activity on two Schedule Cs, you can assign Copy 1 to one business's tags and Copy 2 to the other business's tags.

When you click Save, the tag is added to the list. You can create as many tags as you like.

Working with the Tag List Window

You can use buttons that appear beside a selected tag in the Tag List window, as shown earlier, to work with the tag list or a selected tag:

- **Report**   Click in the space to the left of each tag in the list to generate a report showing all transactions tagged with the selected tag.
- **Edit**   The Edit button enables you to modify the currently selected tag name or other information.
- **Delete**   This button enables you to delete the currently selected tag. When you delete a tag, the tag name is removed from all transactions in which it appeared, but the transaction remains properly categorized.

You can easily toggle the Tag display off and on in your register.

1. Open the account register. Click the small gear icon found at the top of the scroll bar below the Action gear icon. You can also click the Action gear icon | Register Columns to open the same list.
2. From the drop-down list, check or clear the Tag check box.

When you are finished working with Quicken, close the program by clicking the red X on the title bar or choosing File | Exit.

Remember always to back up your Quicken data file. See how to do it in Appendix A.

Delving into Your Bank and Credit Transactions

Chapter 5

In This Chapter:

- *Using account registers*

- *Understanding splits*

- *Tracking credit cards with Quicken*

- *Writing and printing checks with Quicken*

- *Printing Quicken checks*

- *Transferring money*

- *Searching for transactions*

- *Adding notes, flags, and alerts*

- *Attaching checks, receipts, or other images*

- *Watching your credit score*

The heart of Quicken is its ability to manage your bank accounts, and this is probably Quicken's most used feature. You enter or download the transactions, and Quicken Personal Finance Software keeps track of the source of your money, where you spent it, and your account balances. Quicken will even print your checks.

In much the same way, Quicken helps you track your credit card accounts. You may choose to enter transactions as you make them, download your transactions daily, or enter an entire month's charges and payments when you receive your credit card statement. Quicken keeps track of balances and offers you an easy way to monitor what you used your credit card to buy. Equally important, by using Quicken and monitoring costs and fees, you will have a record of how much your credit cards cost you in terms of finance charges and other fees.

Getting Started

As you learned in earlier chapters, Quicken groups its account types into four general categories. This chapter focuses on what Quicken calls the "Spending & Savings" accounts, such as those you have at banks, credit unions, or similar financial institutions. Before you can use Quicken to track bank and credit card transactions, you prepare by creating the necessary accounts and learning how recording transactions works. This section provides an overview of the spending account types, along with examples of transactions you might make.

Quicken's Registers

To make the most of Quicken, you must enter transactions for the accounts you want to track. You can do this manually, as discussed in this chapter, or, if the account is enabled for Online Account Services, you can track your account activity automatically via download, as discussed in Chapter 6. Even if you intend to only download transactions, understanding the basics of manual transaction entry will help should anything go awry with the transaction downloads. Either way, you'll need to know how to work with register transactions for your accounts.

You can enter transactions in several ways, based on the type of transaction:

- Use registers to record virtually any type of transaction, including manual checks, bank account payments and deposits, credit card charges and payments, and cash receipts and spending.
- Use the Write Checks window to record and print checks in Quicken.
- Enter transfers to transfer money from one account to another.
- You can also enter transactions via a transaction reminder or scheduled transaction.
- You can also link your bills to a specific vendor using the Quicken Bill Linker. See Chapter 7 for a full explanation of this useful feature.

Using Account Registers

Quicken's account registers offer a standard way to enter all kinds of transactions. As the name suggests, these electronic account registers are similar to the paper checking account registers that come with your checks. To open an account's register, from the Account Bar, click the name of the account you want to open. The register opens to the right of the Account Bar, as seen in Figure 5-1.

Overview of the Account Register

Before we discuss entry techniques, let's take a closer look at the account register window seen in Figure 5-1.

Range Selection Options   At the top of most account registers are options to customize the information displayed in your register. Drop-down lists enable you to filter the transactions that appear in the current register, as described on the following page.

Figure 5-1 • Use the account register to work with your bank accounts.

- The All Dates drop-down list lets you filter the register to include all dates or specific time periods, or create a customized date range to display.
- The next drop-down list in bank account registers gives you the ability to filter for Any Type (meaning the type of transaction), Payment, or Deposit. In credit card account registers, your choices are Any Type, Charge, or Payment. A cash account shows Any Type, Spend, or Receive.
- The third drop-down list allows you to filter the register by several criteria: All Transactions (the default), Uncategorized, Unreconciled, Cleared, Uncleared, and Flagged.
- Reset sets the transactions register back to the default settings of All Dates, Any Type, and All Transactions.
- The Search field allows you to search for transactions within this register.
- The Reminders menu lets you set reminders to appear in your register. See "Reminders Menu" later in this chapter. If you don't see the clock icon that represents the Reminders menu, see the "Actions Menu" section later in this chapter to learn how to add the Reminders menu.
- The Action gear icon, seen here, gives a variety of options for your accounts, as described in the "Actions Menu" section.

Transactions	
Set up online	
Edit account details	Ctrl+Shift+E
Write checks	Ctrl+W
Reconcile	Ctrl+R
Transfer money	Ctrl+Shift+T
Reporting	
Account attachments	Ctrl+Shift+A
Account overview	Ctrl+Shift+O
More reports	▸
Print transactions	Ctrl+P
Export to Excel compatible file	
Register views and preferences	
Reminders to show in register	▸
Two-line display	Ctrl+2
Sorting options	▸
Register columns...	
Global Preferences(All registers)	
Register Row Height Spacing	▸
Register preferences	
Customize action bar	

Downloaded Transactions   Although Quicken prefers you use the more updated setting that automatically adds your downloaded transactions to your register, as more fully explained in Chapter 6, you do have an option to manually add transactions that have been downloaded. To verify your settings, from the menu bar, click Edit | Preferences | Register | Downloaded Transactions | Downloaded Transactions Preferences | After Downloading Transactions, as seen next.

Preferences   ✕

Select preference type: Select preferences:

Startup   Downloaded transactions preferences
  Navigation
Setup   After downloading transactions   ⓘ ──────
  Calendar and currency
  Backup   ☑ Automatically add to banking registers
  Web Connect   ☐ Automatically add to investment transaction lists
Alerts
Investment transactions   Compare account portfolio after   ⓘ [Edit Settings...]
  Investing.Quicken.com port...   download
Register   During transaction download ──────────────
  Data entry and QuickFill
  Notify   ☑ Automatically categorize transactions
  Write checks   ☑ Automatically apply Quicken's suggested name to payee
  Downloaded transactions   ☑ Capitalize first letter only in downloaded payee names
  Transfer detection
Reports and Graphs   Your renaming rules ──────────────────
  Reports only
Intuit ID, Mobile & Alerts   ☑ Use my existing renaming rule   [Renaming Rules...]
                                              ☑ Automatically create rules when I rename payees
                                                 ☑ Let me review/confirm the automatically created rules

  ⊘   [OK]   [Cancel]

Even if you clear the file preference, you may still have an individual preference set for the particular account register. Check the Online Services tab of the Account Details dialog to verify your settings.

1. If you do not want your investment accounts transactions added automatically to your investment account register, clear the Automatically Add To Investment Transaction Lists check box. See Chapters 6 and 9 for more information about downloaded investment transactions.
2. Click OK to save your settings and close the Preferences dialog.

Downloaded Transactions displays either a link to set up downloading for each account or a list of transactions that have already been downloaded but not yet accepted into the account, respectively. Learn how to set up and work with the Transaction Download and Online Payment features in Chapter 6.

Bill and Income Reminders   The Bill And Income Reminders tab at the lower part of the register displays a list of upcoming, due, and overdue scheduled transactions. See Chapter 7 for more information about scheduled transactions, the Bill Linker feature, and other reminders.

Reminders Menu

Appearing at the left of the Action gear icon is the Reminders menu, as seen here. You have a choice of how far ahead the reminders should appear or to not show them at all. Use the choices on this menu to tell Quicken when (or if) to display Bill & Income Reminders that you have set. The icons and status text for these scheduled reminders display in the register in the first (Status) column. If you widen the column, you will also see status text.

 To display the Status column, select the Register Columns gear icon at the top of your register. (This gear icon is in the same line as Date, Check #, Payee, and so on.) From the list that appears, select Status.

Actions Menu

This register window's Action gear icon, seen earlier, includes a number of options you can use while in the register. There are four sections: Transactions, Reporting, Register Views And Preferences, and Global Preferences (All Registers). Note that many of the sections include keyboard shortcut commands. Learn more about keyboard shortcuts in Quicken Help and Appendix A.

Transactions Section   From the Action gear icon, use the Transactions section to:

- Click Set Up Online to activate Online Account Services for the current account. If you have included the financial institution's home page or an activity or other page in the Account Details dialog, you will note additional options that are links to those websites.

 If the account is set up for Web Connect, when you click Update Now, your Internet connection will open your browser at the login page for that financial institution's website.

- Click Edit Account Details to open the Account Details dialog.
- Click Write Checks to open the Write Checks dialog. See "Writing and Printing Checks in Quicken" later in this chapter. If this is a cash or credit card account, that option is not available.

- Click Reconcile to open the Reconcile Details dialog. See Chapter 8 for complete instructions on reconciling your accounts so that the bank and your Quicken files are in agreement. Depending on the account type and online status of the account, you may see an Update Balance dialog, or you may be prompted to download transactions before reconciling. If the account is a checking or credit card account not enabled for online access, you will go directly to the Reconcile Details screen.
- Use the Transfer Money option to move money from one of your Quicken accounts to another. See "Transferring Money" later in this chapter for more information.

Reporting Section   The Reporting section allows you to:

- Click Account Attachments to open the Account Attachments dialog. See more information in the section "Working with Attachments" later in this chapter.
- Click Account Overview to display a graphical recap of the selected account as well as the account's current status.
- Click More Reports to see the information about this account in various report formats. Read more about creating reports in Chapter 15.
- Click Print Transactions to open the Print Register dialog where you can print the register for this account. See Chapter 15 for more information about printing reports and graphs.
- Click Export To Excel Compatible File to export the transactions in the account register to a tab-delimited text format. See more information about exporting files in Chapter 15.

Register Views and Preferences   The Register Views And Preferences section lets you set how this register displays:

- Click Reminders To Show In Register to open the Reminders menu as discussed earlier in this chapter.
- Click Two-line Display to show your register information on two lines. This option displays the Category and Memo on a second line in the register. One-line display is the default for Quicken 2017.
- Click Sorting Options to tell Quicken how to organize your transactions in this register. See "Sorting Transactions" later in this chapter for more information.
- Click Register Columns to open the Register Columns list. You can also click the small gear icon at the top of the register's vertical scroll bar to see this

list. Learn more about this topic later in this chapter in the "Using Register Columns" section.

- In the Global Preferences section, select Register Row Height Spacing to set the spacing of your register, as seen next. New in Quicken 2017, you have three options from which to choose. As you can see in the illustration, there are three options: Comfortable, Standard, and Compact. Test each of them on your device to see which setting is best for you.

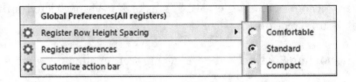

- Click Register Preferences to open the Preferences dialog at the Register section. See Appendix B for more information on Quicken Preferences.
- Click Customize Action Bar to open the Customize Action Bar dialog, as seen next. From here you can add toolbar buttons that will show to the left of your Action gear icon at the top of your account register. As seen in our Customize Action Bar illustration, the Reconcile shortcut and the Write

Checks icon will appear between the Reminder icon and the Action gear icon on our action bar. Click Done when you've completed your choices. This feature is a great way to display action bar items that you often use and may save you several mouse clicks.

Basic Entry Techniques

To enter a transaction into a register, open the register by clicking the account in the Account Bar. Begin by clicking in the first empty line at the end of the account register window. If you have chosen to sort your date column in descending date format, the blank line will be at the top of your register. This activates a new, blank transaction. (You will see highlighted indications of what is to be entered in each field.) Enter transaction information into each highlighted field using your TAB key to move from field to field if necessary. Press SAVE to complete the transaction.

Although the entry process is straightforward, here are a few things to keep in mind when entering transactions.

Many users feel more comfortable using the ENTER key to move between fields. To set this option, go to Edit | Preferences | Register | Data Entry And QuickFill | Data Entry. Click the Use Enter Key To Move Between Fields check box.

Using Icons/Buttons   In many locations throughout Quicken, including Register preferences and Quicken Help, these icons are referred to as buttons. Since they appear as icons, the terms are used interchangeably throughout this chapter. Icons appear when certain fields are active:

- When you are using the Date field, a calendar icon appears. You can click it to display a calendar, and then click calendar buttons to view and enter a date.
- When either the Payment or Deposit Amount field is active, a calculator icon appears. You can click it to use a calculator and enter calculated results.
- When the Payee or Category field is active, a small Report button appears. Click the Report button to display a pop-up report of transactions in that category or for that payee as seen here. Click the X to close the report.

Food & Dining:Groceries		✕
Last 60 days ▼ (All accounts)		
Payee		Amount
Payless Foods		-84.03
Safeway		-87.96
	Total:	-171.99
	Average:	-85.99
	Monthly Average (6 mo):	-28.66
	Show Report	

If you do not see the calendar, calculator, or report icons, you can turn them on by going to Edit | Preferences | Register | Data Entry And QuickFill and ensuring that the Show Buttons On QuickFill Fields check box is selected.

Menu buttons, which look like triangles pointing down to a horizontal line, display drop-down lists of items applicable to the active field. You can enter an item by choosing it from the list's options or by simply typing the information.

Using the Number Field   The Check # (or Reference # in nonbanking accounts) field is where you enter a transaction number or type. You can enter any number you like, or use the drop-down list to display a list of standard entries; click an option to enter it for the transaction. You can also press the + or – key on the keyboard to increase or decrease the check number, respectively, while the field is active.

Savings and Credit Card accounts have a default one-line display with no reference field. Turn on the Reference # field by clicking the Register Columns gear icon at the top of your register (above the vertical scroll bar). Click the Reference # check box and then click Done to close the list.

- **Check #** automatically increments the most recently entered check number and enters the resulting number in the Check Number field.
- **ATM** is for ATM transactions. You may also want to use it for debit or check card transactions.
- **Deposit** is for deposits.
- **Print Check** is for transactions for which you want Quicken to print a check. Quicken automatically enters the check number when the check is printed.
- **Send Online Payment** is for accounts for which you have enabled Online Bill Pay.
- **Online Transfer** is for accounts you have activated to transfer funds from one online account to another online account.
- **Transfer** is for a transfer of funds from one account to another.
- **EFT**, which stands for electronic funds transfer, is for direct deposits and similar transactions.
- **Edit List** opens a dialog with which you can create your own item names. For example, if you have periodic items, such as insurance payments, withdrawn from your account, you might create an item named INS.

The Payee Drop-Down List and QuickFill   When you begin to enter information in the Payee field, a drop-down list of existing payees or payers appears. As you type, Quicken narrows down the list to display only those names that match what you have typed. You can enter an existing name from the list by selecting it. Quicken will fill in details from the most recent transaction for that name for you. This is Quicken's QuickFill feature, which you will learn more about in Chapter 7.

Automatic Categorization   When you use manual entry, you must assign categories. When you use downloaded transactions, after entering a payee for the first time, Quicken may fill in the category for you. This is Quicken's automatic categorization feature, which enters categories based on thousands of payee names programmed into it. You'll find that in most cases, Quicken assigns an appropriate category. But you can change the category if you like and, from that point on, Quicken's QuickFill feature uses your newly assigned category for future transactions to that payee.

Using the Category Drop-Down List   The Category drop-down list organizes category and transfer accounts in the Category list window, as discussed in Chapter 4. This drop-down list may appear automatically when you begin to enter a category in the Category field of the transaction. If it does not, click the menu button on the right side of the field to display the Category list, as seen next. You can narrow down the display of categories by clicking any of the headings that appear on the left side of the drop-down list. Then click the category name to enter it into the field.

EXPERIENCED USERS RECOMMEND

There is an issue that affects users with smaller monitor screens. The Category list drop-down (or in this case, pop-up) may be too tall to display the full dialog. The top or the bottom of the dialog will be cut off. We see many complaints on the Quicken Community of this problem. There are a few tricks you can use to work around the issue—they are all basically variants of making more room for the dialog to display. Using one-line display instead of two-line display and pressing F11 to toggle to Full Screen mode are two of the work-arounds. You can also go old school and use the category entry shorthand to enter categories and subcategories, like typing **au:f** for category Auto and subcategory Fuel. To work around not seeing the Split button at the bottom of the dialog due to the screen cutoff, you can press CTRL-S on the keyboard to open the Split dialog.

Entering New Categories   If you type in a category that does not exist in the Category List and press ENTER, Quicken displays a message asking if you want to create a new category with that name. (You may also see the prompt if you use the TAB key to move between fields.) Click Yes to open the New Category dialog to create a new category, or click No to return to the register and enter a different category. See more about categories in Chapter 4.

Entering Subcategories   In earlier versions of Quicken, when you chose a subcategory from the Category field's drop-down list, Quicken automatically entered the subcategory's parent category name, followed by a colon (:) and the subcategory name. To type a subcategory, use the first letter or two of the category, the colon, and then the first letter or two of the subcategory. QuickFill matches the category:subcategory.

In Quicken 2017, you need only enter the first few letters of the subcategory—the entire parent category and subcategory name will appear as you type. Folks who have used earlier Quicken versions and are upgrading will likely be more comfortable with the category letters, colon, subcategory letters approach. New users might be more comfortable with the subcategory letters method.

Entering Multiple Categories   To enter more than one category for a transaction, click the Split icon, the small two-headed arrow. See how to enter transactions with splits a little later in this chapter, in the section "Understanding Splits."

Using Register Columns   Use the small gear icon at the top of the vertical scroll bar to tell Quicken which columns to display in your register and which ones to hide. (You can either click the Register Columns gear icon at the top of the vertical scroll bar or choose Register Columns from the Action gear icon menu to open the list, as shown here.) Each item toggles the selected column in your register off and on. While many of the items seem self-explanatory, there are several that might cause some confusion, so we explain the options here. You may see a slightly different list, depending on your register, its online services activation, and its configuration.

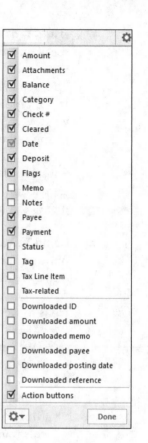

- **Amount**   Selecting this option adds an amount column before the balance column. It displays deposits in black and payments in red. However, deposits and payments may have different labels in other types of accounts.
- **Attachments, Flags, Status, Tax Line Item, and Tax-Related**   If any of these items are selected, the appropriate button (Sort By Attachments and/or Sort By Tax-Related) appears at the top of the Date column. The small flag and attachment icons also appear before or underneath the date when entering a new transaction. See "Sorting Transactions" later in this chapter for more information.
- **Balance**   This column shows the balance in the account after each transaction.
- **Action Buttons**   When this is selected, the Save, More Actions, and Split Transaction Into Multiple Categories buttons display in the selected transaction. See "Using Transaction Buttons" later in this chapter for more information.
- **Date**   This column cannot be omitted.
- **Downloaded *xxxxx***   These items are covered in Chapter 6.

After you have made your selections, click Done to close the Register Columns list.

If you don't like the way your register columns appear, open the Register Columns list and click the small gear icon at the bottom-left corner. From there, you can choose to make all of your registers display the same one-line or two-line registers as your current register, or reset the columns to their default settings.

Using Tags   As discussed in Chapter 4, a tag is an optional identifier for specifying what a transaction applies to. Quicken displays a Tag field in the register. To include a tag in a transaction, simply enter the tag in that field. Quicken may display a drop-down list of valid tags from which you can choose. If you type a tag name that is not on the Tag List, Quicken displays the New Tag window so you can create the tag on the fly. Review how to create tags in Chapter 4. You can use the Register Columns menu to turn off the Tag field display.

Entering Memos   You can enter a brief memo (up to 64 characters) about the transaction in the Memo field to the right of the Category (or Tag) field. This memo can help you recall why you made the transaction.

Using Transaction Buttons   If you have set the option to display the action buttons, three icons appear in the second line of a two-line display register, as shown here, and in line with the active transaction in a one-line display register. You can use these icons to work with the transaction, as follows:

- **Save** enters the transaction into the account register. If Quicken's sound option is turned on, you should hear a cash register cha-ching sound when you click it. (You can turn Quicken sounds on or off in the Preferences dialog, as covered in Appendix B.)
- **More Actions**, a small black gear icon, displays a menu you can use to edit this transaction. See some of the More Action menu commands later in this chapter, in the section "Changing Transactions."
- **Split Transaction Into Multiple Categories**, a small arrow pointing left, opens the Split Transaction window. The next section explains how to enter a transaction with splits.

Understanding Splits

A split is a transaction with more than one category. For example, suppose you pay one utility bill for two categories of utilities—electricity and water. If you want to track each of these two expenses separately, you can use a split to record each category's portion of the payment you make. This enables you to keep good records without writing multiple checks to the same payee.

To record a transaction with a split, click the Split icon in the account register or the Split button in the Write Checks window when entering the transaction. The Split Transaction window, shown here, appears. Click in the first blank line and select a category. If desired, enter a memo for the category in the Memo field. Then enter the amount for that category in the Amount field. Repeat this process for each category you want to include in the transaction. The illustration shows what the Split Transaction window might look like with four categories entered.

	Category	Memo	Amount	
1.	Shopping:Sporting Goods	volleyball set	39	88
2.	Home:Lawn & Garden	grass seed	29	12
3.	Pets:Pet Food & Supplies	pet carrier	71	22
4.	Auto & Transport:Service & Parts	engine repair	48	45
5.				
6.				
7.				
8.				
9.				
10.				
11.				
12.				
13.				
14.				
15.				
16.				

Split Transaction

Enter multiple categories to itemize this transaction; use the Memo field to record more details.

Add Lines   Clear All   Allocate

Adjust

Split Total: 188.67
Remainder: 0.00
Transaction Total: 188.67

OK   Cancel

If you entered a transaction amount before clicking the Split button, you can monitor the Remainder and Transaction Total values in the Split Transaction window to make sure you've accounted for the entire transaction amount. If you entered an incorrect amount, click the Adjust button to adjust the transaction amount to match the split total. If you want to allocate what is remaining, clear the unallocated amount in the split window and click OK. You can then allocate how the split distributes a remainder amount.

If you need more lines to record all of the split amounts, click Add Lines. To clear all of your entries and start over, click Clear All.

The Quicken default for a split transaction is 30 lines. If you need that number of lines or more, it is likely you are using the split transaction to record your credit card account transactions when paying the account. It's better to create the credit card account in Quicken so you can track the credit card transactions in the credit card account register instead of a split transaction.

When you're finished entering transaction categories, click OK. If you left the transaction amount empty before clicking the Split button, a dialog appears, asking if you want to record the transaction as a payment or deposit. Select the appropriate option and click OK to close the Split Transactions dialog.

 If the split is in a credit card account, the dialog will be "Charge Or Payment."

The word "Split" appears in the Category field for the transaction in the account register window.

Three buttons appear beside the Category field when you activate a transaction with a split:

- The green check mark displays the Split Transaction window so you can review and edit the transaction.
- The red X opens a message that allows you to clear all lines from the split. Use this option with care—it removes all category information from the transaction. You can then add new category information or redo the previous category information. If you clear the split using the red X and decide you didn't really want to clear the split info, just press the ESC button on your keyboard. Pressing ESC restores the transaction to its original state. However, this only works if you have not yet saved the transaction.
- Clicking the Report icon opens a mini-report pop-up showing a report about the categories in this transaction for a time period you can set.

EXPERIENCED USERS RECOMMEND

As you are entering categories in a split transaction, you may notice that the Allocate button at the bottom of the Split Transaction dialog is activated. If you have entered several amounts and have just one remaining amount, you have two options for that remainder.

1. Click Allocate to open the Allocate Empty Split Line dialog.
2. Choose Distribute Proportionally Between All Other Split Lines to apportion the remaining amount in the same ratio as the other lines.
3. Choose Distribute Evenly: $nn.nn To All Other Split Lines.

Tracking Credit Cards with Quicken

Tracking bank account transactions and balances is just one part of using Quicken. It's also a great tool for tracking credit cards. Knowing how much you owe on your credit cards helps you maintain a clear picture of your financial situation.

How you use Quicken to track your credit cards depends on how accurate you want your financial records to be and how much effort you're willing to spend to keep Quicken up to date.

Credit Card Tracking Techniques

You can use either of two techniques for paying credit card bills and monitoring credit card balances with Quicken:

- Use your checking account register or the Write Checks window to record amounts paid to each credit card company for your credit card bill. Although this does track the amounts you pay, it doesn't track how much you owe at any one time.
- Use a credit card account register to record credit card expenditures and payments. This takes a bit more effort on your part, but it tracks how much you owe and categorizes what you bought. And, if you utilize Quicken's Transaction Download feature for your credit card accounts, as discussed in Chapter 6, it won't take much time or effort to get the job done.

Many Quicken users feel it is well worth the effort to track their credit card expenditures and balances in individual credit card accounts.

Recording Strategies

You can also use two strategies for recording transactions in credit card accounts. Choosing the strategy that's right for you makes the job easier to handle.

Enter as You Spend   One strategy is to enter transactions as you spend. To do this, you must collect your credit card receipts—which might be something you already do. Don't forget to jot down the totals for any online or telephone shopping you do. Then, every day or every few days, sit down with Quicken and enter the transactions.

While this strategy requires you to stay on top of things, it offers two main benefits:

- Your Quicken credit card registers always indicate what you owe to credit card companies. This prevents unpleasant surprises at month-end or at the checkout counter when you're told you've reached your card's limit. It also enables you to use the alerts feature to track credit card balances. Learn more about those features in Chapter 7.

- At month-end, you won't have to spend a lot of time entering big batches of transactions. All (or at least most) of them should already be entered.

Many just don't like holding on to all those pieces of paper. Once you have signed up for Transaction Download, all of the information can be downloaded from your card company and entered automatically. This method has an added bonus, as it allows you to spot any fraudulent charges earlier than waiting for a paper statement.

Enter When You Pay   The other strategy is to enter transactions when you get your monthly statement. With this strategy, when you open your credit card statement, you'll spend some time sitting in front of your computer with Quicken to enter each transaction. If there aren't many, this isn't a big deal. However, it can take some time if you have a large number of transactions to enter.

Of course, the main benefit of this strategy is that you don't have to collect credit card receipts and spend time throughout the month entering your transactions. However, you still have to enter them either manually or via download! And it may be harder to spot fraudulent charges.

Entering Credit Card Transactions

Entering credit card transactions isn't very different from entering checking account or savings account transactions, as seen in Figure 5-2.

Entering Individual Charges   Open the account register for the credit card account. Then enter the charge transaction, using the name of the merchant that accepted the charge as the payee name. Press TAB to move between the fields.

If you want to record a reference number for a credit card transaction, choose the Register Columns icon at the top-right area of the register and click in the Reference # check box at the bottom of the list. This column then appears to the immediate right of the Date column. Don't forget to click Done to save your column display changes.

Entering Credits   Enter the transaction just as if it were a charge, but put the amount of the credit in the Payment box. This subtracts it from your account balance.

Figure 5-2 • **Your credit card register looks much like your checking and savings registers.**

Entering Finance Charges In the credit card account register, enter the name of the credit card company as the payee and the amount of the finance charge as a charge. You can choose Interest Exp or any other category for the transaction. You can also enter any finance charges during the reconcile process for manual credit card accounts. Chapter 8 explains how to use Quicken to reconcile your credit card accounts to the bank's records.

Entering Payments In the account register for your checking account or in the Write Checks window, enter a payment transaction with the credit card company name in the Payee box. Enter the credit card account name in the Category text box; you should find it as a transfer account in the Category drop-down list that appears when you activate the field.

Recording Credit Card Rebates Some credit card companies offer rebates for purchases. How you record a rebate depends on how the rebate is received:

- To record a rebate received as a check, deposit the check as usual and enter the amount of the rebate as a deposit in that account.
- To record a rebate received as a reduction in the credit card account balance, enter the amount of the rebate in the credit card account as a payment. (Just remember that a rebate is not a payment that counts toward your monthly obligation to the credit card company.)

What you use as a category for this transaction is completely up to you. You may want to use the Interest Exp(ense) category, thus recording the rebate as a reduction in your interest expense. Or, perhaps, if the rebate applies to a certain purchase only, use the category you originally used for that purchase. For example, if you have a credit card that gives you a 5 percent rebate on fuel purchases, you might record the rebate using the Fuel category you created to track fuel expenses. If you have many credit cards that offer rebates, you may want to create a rebate income account or rewards account and use that as the category for all rebate transactions. These are just suggestions. There is no right or wrong way to do it.

Entering Cash Transactions

Although Quicken enables you to keep track of cash transactions by creating a "cash" account, not everyone does this. The reason: most people make many small cash transactions every day. Is it worth tracking every penny you spend? That's something you need to decide.

Many people track only expenditures that are large or tax deductible—for example, the $20 you gave to the local Lions Club. You may want to do the same. If so, you still need to set up a cash account, but you don't need to record every transaction.

Cash Receipts   Cash receipts may come from using your ATM card, cashing a check, or getting cash from some other source. If the cash comes from one of your other accounts through an ATM or check transaction, when you record that transaction, use your cash account as the category. That increases your cash balance.

Important Cash Expenditures   In your cash account, record large, tax-deductible, or other important cash expenditures like any other transaction. Be sure to assign the correct category.

Other Cash Expenditures   Throughout the week, you may spend $1 for a newspaper, $3 for a soft drink, and about $12 for lunch at your favorite coffee shop. Recording transactions like these can be tedious, so don't bother if you don't want to. Instead, at the end of the week, compare your cash on hand to the balance in your cash account register. Then, enter a transaction to record the difference as an expenditure. You can use the Misc category and enter anything you like in the Payee field.

Writing and Printing Checks in Quicken

Quicken's Write Checks window uses a basic check-like interface to record checks. You enter the same information that you would write on an actual check. You then tell Quicken to print the check based on the information you entered.

To open the Write Checks window, from your account register, click the Action gear icon | Write Checks or press CTRL-W. You can also access this window by selecting Tools | Write And Print Checks. The Write Checks window, shown in Figure 5-3, appears. The name of the account from which you are writing this check appears in the drop-down list near the top of the window. If you need to choose another account, click the down arrow. Enter the necessary information for a check, and record the transaction.

Figure 5-3 • The Write Checks window makes it easy to print checks from Quicken.

Overview of the Write Checks Window

The top of the Write Checks dialog looks much like the checks you write by hand, including a space for a memo. If you have enabled Online Bill Pay for the selected account, the Use Online Bill Pay check box will appear to the right of the account name. Other options are discussed here:

- **Edit Address** If the address that appears in the Bill Pay Address field is incorrect, click Edit Address to open the Edit Address Book Record dialog. The Address Book is discussed at length in Chapter 7.
- **Message** Use this field to enter any message for the payee.
- **Memo** This field can also be used to send information to the payee. However, if you use window envelopes to mail your checks, consider using the Message field rather than the Memo field for account numbers so that information does not appear through the window.
- **Category** Use the Category field to enter the category for this check. Click the Split icon should you need to use more than one category.
- **Split** Use the Split Transactions icon to split the categories as you do in your check register.
- **Record Check** The Record Check button records your check in the appropriate check register. You do not have to enter it twice! You may see a pop-up telling you the check has been successfully recorded and a Don't Show Again check box. This is one of the default warnings you can reset in Preferences. See Appendix B for more information about Quicken Preferences.
- **Check Data** Quicken uses the space below Category, Split, and Record Check to show a list of the checks that are ready to print. This makes it easy to enter a number of checks and print them all at once.
- **Date** This is the date you entered in the Date field in your check body.
- **Type** Normally, Print will appear in this field because the check is to be printed using Quicken.
- **Payee/Category/Amount** These are all entered directly from the check body above.

You can use the Write Checks window to enter your online payments for accounts that are enabled for it. These show up as Send transactions when entered. See Chapter 7 for more information on paying bills online.

- **New Check** Select the New Check button to add the next check in sequence for this batch of checks. You will be prompted to save the current check before a new blank check form appears.

- **Ending Balance**   The amount that displays in this field is the balance in your selected checking account after all of these checks have been printed.
- **Order Checks**   This link opens a page that displays the QuickBooks logo. Select Checks to see checks that are compatible with Quicken. You may also be able to order compatible checks through your financial institution.
- **Reports**   The Reports button allows you to print a Register Report for the account from which you wrote the checks.
- **Print**   Click this button when you are ready to print your checks. Learn more about that later in this chapter, in the section "Printing Quicken Checks." If the account is enabled for Online Bill Pay and the Use Online Bill Pay check box is selected, you will not see a Print button. Instead, the button will be labeled Send. When you have made all of your choices and entered all the checks for this work session, click Done to close the dialog box.

To delete a check from the list of checks to be printed, select the check and click the small, white circle with a blue, right-facing arrow at the right of the check information. Click this arrow and select Delete. A message appears asking if it is okay to delete the current transaction. Choose OK or Cancel. You can use this same menu to void or memorize a check. You can also use Restore to move the check information from the Check Data area back into the check fields at the top of the Write Checks window.

Entering Transactions in the Write Checks Window

The Write Checks window (refer to Figure 5-3) is like a cross between a paper check and Quicken's account register window. You fill in the check form just as you would fill in the blanks on a paper check. Quicken's QuickFill feature makes data entry quick and easy by recalling entry information from similar transactions to the same payee. You must enter a valid Quicken category in the Category field, just as you would when entering a transaction in the account register. Clicking the Record Check button completes the transaction and adds it to the checks to print list as well as the account register.

You must also fill in the check amount. In earlier versions of Quicken you could leave it blank to be filled in by hand at a later time.

Consult the section "Using Account Registers," which appeared earlier, for details about the information that should be entered into most fields. Here are a few additional things to consider when entering transactions in the Write Checks window.

Addresses on Checks   If you enter an address on the check, you can mail the check using a window envelope. The address is automatically added to the Quicken Address Book. You can click the Edit Address button in the Write Checks window to display the Edit Address Book Record dialog, which you can use to modify an address in the Address Book.

Check Memos   Be careful when using the memo field if you are using window envelopes. Some envelopes display part of the memo field. If you have included account numbers or other personal information in the memo, that information may be visible to others.

EXPERIENCED USERS RECOMMEND

In earlier versions of Quicken, you had to select Edit | Preferences | Write Checks and select the check box Allow Entry Of Extra Message On Check to have the message field display when writing a check. In Quicken 2017, this message field is the default. To turn it off, clear the Allow Entry Of Extra Message On Check check box.

There is another option that may be useful for you. To include text "Rental house" with payee Electric Company, type **Electric Company {Rental house}** in the payee field for the check. The printed check will show "Electric Company" as the payee, but the account register and Write Checks window will show the full "Electric Company {Rental house}" text.

Printing Quicken Checks

Once you have completed the initial setup for check printing as described in Appendix A, you're ready to print checks.

Open the account register for which you want to print checks. Then insert the check stock in your printer and choose File | Print Checks, or click the Print button in the Write Checks window. The Select Checks To Print dialog appears. Enter the number of the first check to be printed in the First Check Number box. Then set other options as desired. If you select the Selected Checks option, you can click the Choose button to display a list of checks and mark off the ones you want to print. Click Done in that window to return to the Select Checks To Print dialog.

When you click Print First Check or OK, Quicken sends the print job to your printer. It then displays a dialog asking if the checks printed correctly. You have the following two options:

- If all checks printed fine, just click OK.
- If a problem occurred while printing the checks, enter the number of the first check that was misprinted, and then click OK. You can then go back to the

Select Checks To Print dialog and try again. Click OK or Cancel to close the Select Checks To Print dialog.

Transferring Money

You can easily record the transfer of funds from one account to another. You might find this feature especially useful for recording online or ATM transfers.

Recording a Transfer in the Account Register Window

You can record a transfer in the account register window of either the source or destination account. When you choose Transfer (TXFR) from the Check # drop-down list, the Category drop-down list displays only transfer accounts. Choose the other transfer account from the list and complete the transaction. (If you don't see a Check # column in your account register, you can display it by clicking the Register Columns gear icon at the upper-right corner of your account register and marking the Check# check box in the list. Click Done to close the Register Columns list.) This process does NOT contact the bank; it simply records the information. See Chapter 6 for information about transferring money with an online account.

You can also click the Action gear Transfer Money icon to open the Transfer Money Within Quicken dialog, or simply enter the transfers directly into an account register.

Working with Existing Transactions

So far, this chapter has concentrated on entering transactions. What do you do when you need to modify a transaction you already recorded? That's what this section is all about.

Searching for Transactions

All account registers, except for Investing accounts, have a specific Search field with which you can search the register for specific payees, categories, and even amounts. Simply type the item into the Search field, and all transactions that match what you typed will appear in the register, as seen in Figure 5-4. When you have finished reviewing the information, click the X in the Search field to return to the register with its normal display.

As you type into the Search field, it filters the register to show transactions that match the text you type in the field. You can use this to make a quick register report or find a set of transactions quickly, which is a great feature.

	►	Date ▼	Chec...	Payee	Category	Tag	M...	N...	🔗	Payment	.	Deposit		Amount		Balance	⚙

Main Checking   🕐▾ ⚙▾

All Dates ▾ | Any Type ▾ | All Transactions ▾ | Reset | Payless ✕

	11/3/2016	58552	Payless	Groceries					67 00			-67 00	17,706 76
	9/4/2016	58525	Payless	Groceries					76 00			-76 00	17,630 76
	7/21/2016	58446	Payless	Groceries					62 37 R			-62 37	17,568 39
	7/8/2016	58484	Payless	Groceries					184 50 R			-184 50	17,383 89
	6/21/2016	58492	Payless	Groceries					63 44 R			-63 44	17,320 45
	6/16/2016	58489	Payless	Groceries					33 45 R			-33 45	17,287 00
	2/27/2016	58430	Payless	Groceries					48 00 R			-48 00	17,239 00
	1/11/2016	58392	Payless	Groceries	Tag	Me...	Notes		29 62 R Deposit			-29 62	17,209 38

483 Transactions | Online Balance: | 26,290.43 | Current Balance: | 14,470.88 | Ending Balance: | 17,691.31

› Downloaded Transactions (0)   Bill and Income Reminders (0 Due)

Figure 5-4 • Using Search to display all items in which the Payee name is Payless.

The search is register specific, meaning that it is only for the register in which you are working. Should you want more detailed information, use the Quicken Find command as discussed next. You can also use Search in the All Transactions register to search all registers except Investment accounts. All Transactions can be found at the top of the Account Bar.

NOTE The Search field is available in asset registers as well as spending registers. Investment Transaction Lists use the Find command. The Search field is also available in Debt and Loan (except online-enabled loans) registers. Find is available in all registers via the keyboard shortcut CTRL-F.

Using the Find Command

The Quicken Find dialog includes several drop-down lists to help you locate and work with transactions. To use the Find command, first place your cursor in the field with which you want to search. Then, from the Quicken menu, click Edit | Find or press CTRL-F. (In an Investment Transaction List, use the Find icon, which is a small magnifying glass, found at the right side of the list.)

The Quicken Find dialog appears. Start by choosing an option from the Find drop-down list, which includes all register fields for a transaction. Then choose the matching option from the next field to indicate how the search criteria should be matched (this field is not labeled, but the first choice on the list is "Contains"). Enter the search criteria in the next field. To search backward (relative to the currently selected transaction), turn on the Search Backwards check box.

After setting up the search, if you click the Find All button, Quicken displays the window, which lists all the matches it found. You can double-click a match to view it in the account register window.

The window will be titled Search Results if you start with Find and then click Find All. The window will be titled Find And Replace if you start with Edit | Find/Replace.

Using the Edit Transaction Command

To edit transactions, you must first find them. Then, in the Found window, select the transaction(s) by clicking the check box(es) in the Select column. Then click the Edit Transaction(s) button at the bottom right of the Search Results window.

You can also access the Find And Replace dialog by pressing CTRL-H or choosing Edit | Find/Replace.

The items you selected in the Find And Replace dialog appear in the Found section of the dialog. You can turn on the Show Matches Within Splits check box at the bottom of the dialog if you want Quicken to find all matches, including those that appear in splits. Once you set up the search and click the Find button, a list of matches appears in the Found section of the dialog. Click beside each found item you want to change to place a check mark there. Then set options in the Replace and With fields. Click Replace All to replace all selected items with the replacement option you specified. The Replace All button changes to Replace Selected if you have only selected some and not all transactions. Click Done to close the Find And Replace dialog. As always, remember to create a backup before you make any mass changes to your data.

Sorting Transactions

You can click a register's column heading or use the sort options to change how your transactions are displayed. Click the Action gear icon | Sorting Options in an account's register to open the Sorting Options menu. For example, sorting by check number groups the transactions by the Check field, making it easy to find a specific check. You can quickly move up and down your register to a specific date or transaction number by dragging the scroll box on the scroll bar. However, except for the last two sort options pertaining to Order Entered, it is easier to sort by clicking the account register's column headings.

You can even sort by the flags. See "Adding Notes, Flags, and Alerts" later in this chapter.

Changing Transactions

Quicken enables you to change a transaction at any time—even after it has been cleared. This is especially useful when you find that a check has been categorized as groceries when it should have been categorized as a charitable donation.

Making Simple Changes

If all you want to do is change one of the fields in the transaction—such as the category, date, or number—simply find the transaction in the appropriate account register, make changes as desired, and click the Save button to record them.

Using the More Actions Menu   When you need to make additional changes, use the More Actions menu. The More Actions menu appears when you click the small gear icon between the Save and Split icons. These icons are available when you have selected a specific transaction (or multiple transactions) in your register.

The More Actions menu, as shown here, offers a number of options for working with your transactions. Each is explained here:

Many of these actions can also be accessed by right-clicking and choosing from the resulting context menu.

Save	
Restore transaction	Esc
Split...	Ctrl+S
Notes and flags...	
Attachments...	
Tax line item assignments	
Copy transaction(s)	
Cut transaction(s)	
Paste transaction(s)	
Edit transaction(s)	
New	Ctrl+N
Delete	Ctrl+D
Undo delete	
Insert transaction	Ctrl+I
Move transaction(s)	
Undo accept all transactions	
Memorize payee...	Ctrl+M
Add reminder	
Void transaction(s)	
Reconcile	▸
Review downloaded payee	▸
Find...	Ctrl+F
Find next	Ctrl+Shift+F
Go To matching transfer	
Go to specific date...	Ctrl+G
Use Calculator	

- **Save** enters the transaction in the register. Choosing this command is the same as clicking the Save button or pressing ENTER.
- **Restore Transaction** enables you to change a transaction back to the way it was before you started changing it. This

option is available only if you have made changes to the selected transaction.

- **Split** opens the Split window for the transaction. Choosing this command is the same as clicking the Split button. You learned how to use the Split feature earlier in this chapter, in the section "Understanding Splits."

You can also press CTRL-S on your keyboard to open the Split window.

- **Notes And Flags** displays the Transaction Notes And Flags dialog (which is shown later in this chapter, in the section "Adding Notes, Flags, and Alerts") so you can add transaction notes, flag the transaction in a specific color, or create an alert for follow-up.
- **Attachments** displays the Transaction Attachments dialog (shown later in this chapter, in the section "Attaching Checks, Receipts, or Other Images") so you can attach scanned copies of both paper and electronic information to the transaction.
- **Tax Line Item Assignments** displays the dialog with which you can assign a tax line item to the transaction's category as discussed in Chapter 14.
- **Copy Transaction(s)** copies the selected transaction without removing it from the account register.
- **Cut Transaction(s)** selects the selected transaction and removes it from the account register so that it can be put in another register.
- **Paste Transaction(s)** pastes the last-copied transaction into the current account register. This option is available only after a transaction has been cut or copied. You might want to cut a transaction to paste it into another register if you realize that you entered it in the wrong register.

The copy, cut, and paste commands can all be used with multiple transactions. You just need to select the transactions first before selecting the command.

EXPERIENCED USERS RECOMMEND

Cutting, copying, and pasting are basic computer processes that many programs use. Often, it is quicker to copy a transaction and simply paste it into the new register. While that does require you to return to the first register to delete the transaction from its original location, using copy protects against loss of the transaction. If you have children, pets, or power issues that might affect your computer during a cut-and-paste process, you might want to consider using copy instead of cut when moving information. Or, you can use the Move Transaction option to move the transaction back to its original register.

- **Edit Transaction(s)** displays the Find And Replace dialog (shown earlier in this chapter, in the section "Searching for Transactions") so you can use the Replace feature to modify the selected transaction(s).
- **New** enables you to create a new transaction for the account. This does not affect the currently selected transaction.
- **Delete** deletes the selected transaction. Remember that deleting a transaction removes the transaction from the Quicken data file, thus changing the account balance and category activity.
- **Undo Delete** restores the transaction you just deleted. You must use this command immediately after deleting a transaction to restore it.
- **Insert Transaction** enables you to insert a transaction before the selected transaction in the account register. This does not affect the currently selected transaction. However, depending on your sort order, the inserted transaction may sort to another position in the account register after you have entered it.
- **Move Transaction(s)** displays the Move Transactions(s) dialog, which you can use to move a transaction from the current account register to a different account register. Simply choose an account name from the drop-down list and click OK to complete the move. This is sometimes a better option than the cut-and-paste option.
- **Undo Accept All Transactions** restores accepted transactions to unaccepted status when you have accepted all transactions. This command is available only if the last thing you did was accept the transactions. Learn more about accepting transactions in Chapter 6.
- **Memorize Payee** tells Quicken to add the selected transaction to its list of memorized payees.
- **Add Reminder** enables you to schedule the transaction for a future date or to set up the transaction as a recurring transaction. Learn more about scheduling transactions in Chapter 7.
- **Void Transaction(s)** marks the selected transaction as void. This reverses the effect of the transaction on the account balance and category activity without actually deleting the transaction. You can void a single or multiple transactions.
- **Reconcile** enables you to indicate whether the transaction should be marked as Not Reconciled, Cleared, or Reconciled. Learn how to reconcile accounts in Chapter 8.
- **Review Downloaded Payee** allows you to review the payee name downloaded from your financial institution's server. This option only appears if the transaction has been downloaded and its payee name has changed.
- **Find** displays the Find dialog, which is discussed earlier in this chapter, in the section "Searching for Transactions."

- **Find Next** searches for transactions matching the previously entered Find criteria.
- **Go To Matching Transfer** displays the selected transaction in the account register for the other part of a transfer. For example, if the selected transaction involves the checking and savings accounts and you are viewing it in the checking account register, choosing the Go To Transfer command displays the same transaction in the savings account register. This command is available only if the selected transaction includes a transfer.
- **Go To Specific Date** enables you to move to a different date within the register. This does not affect the currently selected transaction.
- **Use Calculator** (not shown) opens the Quicken Calculator. The Use Calculator selection is available only when the cursor is in an amount field (Payment or Deposit).
- **Cancel Payment** (not shown) sends a cancel payment instruction to your bank to stop an online payment. This option is available only for online payments that have not yet been made.
- **Payment Inquiry** (not shown) shows the status of an online payment and offers a link to create an e-mail to your financial institution.
- **Properties** (not shown) displays the date this transaction was posted by your financial institution.
- **View As A Check** (not shown) displays the selected transaction as a check in the Write Checks dialog if the transaction is marked to print. You can then easily print the transaction or make any other changes.

The following items appear if your cursor is in the Category field when you select More Actions:

- **Amount Spent On** *<category>* will display a Category Report for this category if your cursor is in the category field in the selected transaction.
- *<category>* **Budget** displays budget information about the selected category if your cursor is in the category field. This action works only with a single category you have included in a Quicken budget.
- **Launch Mini-Report** displays a small report window of the current category's transactions. The option that appears depends on the field that is selected when you display the menu.

The following items appear if your cursor is in the Payee field when you select More Actions:

- **Payments Made To** *<payee>* will display a Payee Report for this payee if your cursor is in the Payee field in the selected transaction.

- **Launch Mini-Report For Payee** *<payee>* displays a small report window of the current payee's transactions.

Selecting More Than One Transaction   You may need to work with more than one transaction at a time. To do this, you need to select multiple transactions. Here's how:

- To select several individual transactions in an account register, hold down CTRL and click each transaction you want to include. The transactions change color to indicate they are selected.
- To select a range of transactions, click to select the first transaction in the range. Then hold down SHIFT and click the last transaction in the range. All transactions between the first and the last transaction change color to indicate they have been selected.

It may be helpful to sort the register first to get the transactions you wish to select grouped together. You can also filter using the drop-down boxes at the upper left of the register, or use the Search field to enter a payee, category, or name on which to filter.

Quicken's Other Account Features

If you have ever spent several hours (or even days) looking for an invoice that contained a guarantee, Quicken's attachment feature is for you. You can add notes, flags, reminders, and image files to any transaction in your account. This makes it possible to store all kinds of digital information in your Quicken data file, including canceled checks, receipts, or photographs.

If there's such a thing as a "Paperwork Reduction Act," then why do we seem to keep accumulating more and more paper? Bank statements, canceled checks, receipts . . . it seems endless. Then, somehow, the moment we throw away an important property tax–related document, the next day we get a letter from the county, asking to see it.

This is when Quicken's electronic image attachment feature can help. If you have a scanner, you can digitize important papers and attach their image files to the transactions or accounts they relate to. Then, when you need to consult the document, you can quickly and easily find it in Quicken and view it on screen. You can even print a copy with the click of a button! Sure beats dealing with file boxes.

As with all Quicken and other computer data files, ensure your backup procedures are being followed on a regular basis so that when disaster strikes, your files are recoverable.

Adding Notes, Flags, and Alerts

You can add a note, color-coded flag, or follow-up alert—or all three—to any Quicken transaction. First, select the transaction to which you want to add the item. Click the More Actions button, and from the menu, click Notes And Flags to open the Transaction Notes And Flags dialog seen next. You can also use the small flag or paper clip icons beneath or to the left of the date on a register line.

- To add a note, type the text into the Notes box. This adds a small piece of paper icon to the transaction beneath the date. Pointing to the icon displays the note in a screen tip box.
- To flag the transaction, click the Flag This Transaction check box. Then choose a color from the drop-down list. This colors the flag icon that you set.
- To create a follow-up alert, turn on the Alert For Follow-Up On check box and enter a date in the box beside it. (You can add a follow-up alert only if the transaction is already flagged.) This adds an alert to the Alerts Center window, which is discussed in Chapter 7.

Click OK to save your settings.

Attaching Checks, Receipts, or Other Images

With Quicken you can attach image files to transactions or accounts. These files can be on your hard drive, a flash drive, a CD or DVD, or your computer's clipboard. You can also use your scanner to create a digital image to attach to your transaction. Use this feature to connect digital copies of important documents with the transactions or accounts to which they relate.

Attaching Images to Transactions

You attach an image to a transaction in the account register window. Begin by selecting the transaction to which you want the item attached. Then click the More Actions button and select Attachments.

The Transaction Attachments dialog appears as shown here. Click the Add downward arrow to open the drop-down list. Choose the location of the attachment you want to add:

- **Add File** displays the Select Attachment File dialog, with which you can locate, select, and open a file on either your hard drive or another device. The file must be in a format readable by your browser, such as JPG, GIF, TXT, DOCX, HTML, PDF, or PNG. When you select the file, it appears in the Transaction Attachments dialog.
- **Add From Scanner** displays the Select Source dialog, which you can use to select your scanner. It then displays your scanner's standard scanning interface, which you can use to scan an image. When the scan is complete, the image appears in the Transaction Attachments dialog.
- **Add From Clipboard** pastes the contents of the clipboard into the Transaction Attachments dialog.

To add other attachments, just repeat the process. Quicken allows you to add as many attachments as you like to a transaction. When you're finished, click Done to close the Transaction Attachments dialog. An Attachment icon appears beneath the transaction date to indicate that items are attached.

Working with Attachments

Once a file is attached to a transaction, you can view, export, delete, or print it at any time. To work with a transaction attachment, click the More Actions icon for the transaction and select Attachments, or select the small paper clip icon in the Status column of the transaction. The paper clip icon appears in the Date column for account registers using the two-line format, and in its own column in one-line format registers.

The Transaction Attachments dialog opens. Click the ellipsis (three dots) to the right side of the transaction date to open a small menu. Once you have clicked the ellipses button, several buttons become available in the Transaction Attachments dialog:

- **View/Open** opens the attachment using the application that created it.
- **Export** saves the attachment as a file on a disk.
- **Delete** removes the attachment.

The menu items you see will depend on the type of attachment you have created.

Click Done to close the Transaction Attachments dialog.

Watching Your Credit Score

With news every day about identity theft and hacking intrusions on financial records, guarding your credit history has become nearly a necessity. Quicken, in combination with Experian, has created an option from within the program for you to easily review your current score to ensure that all is well.

By default, the Account Bar shows Credit Score at the bottom of the list. If this icon does not appear, right-click anywhere in the Account Bar and choose Show Credit Score. The option will appear at the bottom of your Account Bar list.

> ### EXPERIENCED USERS RECOMMEND
>
> The Attachment feature in Quicken is a favorite. Users scan paid bills, packing slips, insurance policies, and many other documents. Then, instead of buying another filing cabinet, they shred the documents, secure in the knowledge that Quicken has kept them on the hard drive. When you perform your daily backup, these attachments are included with all of the rest of the Quicken data.

Click on Credit Score to open the application. Fill in all of the boxes, including your Social Security number. Agree to the Quicken Terms of Use and click Continue.

Follow the instructions. Once you have completed and submitted all of the information, you will see your actual score at the bottom of the Account Bar instead of the words "Credit Score."

 This is not a required task in Quicken. Many users do not use this service, nor do they want to connect their Social Security number with online services. It is your choice as to how to handle this option.

Connecting Online

Chapter 6

In This Chapter:

- *Understanding Transaction Download*

- *Introducing Online Payment and Quicken Bill Pay*

- *Setting up Online Account Services*

- *Checking Online Account Services status*

- *Using the Online Center window*

- *Downloading transactions*

- *Making online payments*

Life can be hectic sometimes, too hectic to keep track of your bank accounts, pay bills before they're overdue, and buy stamps to mail those bills. Quicken Personal Finance Software's Online Account Services enable you to do most (if not all) of your banking from the comfort of your own home so banking can be a lot less of a chore. You can use these features separately or together:

- **Transaction Download** enables you to download bank and credit card account activity and transfer money online between accounts.
- **Online Payment** enables you to pay bills online without manually writing or mailing a check. (Quicken Bill Pay offers the features of Online Payment, even if your bank does not support it.)

Just a reminder: Quicken does not handle the characters &, <, or > as part of a password. In addition, each financial institution designates both the password length and its allowable (and disallowable) characters.

Online Account Services

Here's a closer look at Quicken's Online Account Services, including what the services are, how they work, and how you can expect to benefit from them.

Understanding Transaction Download

Quicken's Transaction Download feature can perform several tasks, depending on your financial institution. Generally speaking, financial institutions support Transaction Download three ways. You can quickly determine which method is used for a specific account. Press CTRL-A to open your Account List. (You can do this from any screen within Quicken.) The type of connection for each account shows in the Transaction Download column of the list. If you do not see the Transaction Download column in your Account List, click the Options button at the bottom left of the Account List and choose Show Transaction Download Status. See Table 6-1 for the download features that are available for each method.

If you have more than one account that uses Web Connect, consider downloading one account at a time the first time you download, if your financial institution allows it. This way you won't inadvertently import the wrong account's information into your register.

One important feature of Web Connect is you may be able to download a greater range of transactions by date than you can with Direct Connect and Express Web Connect. This is especially useful when you first set up your accounts so you can get the longest transaction history possible. You can switch download methods if needed. For example, you might start out using Web Connect to get a more complete set of historical transactions, then switch to Direct Connect for its easier transaction downloading.

Introducing Online Payment and Quicken Bill Pay

Online Payment enables you to send a check to anyone without physically writing, printing, or mailing a check. You enter and store information about the payee within Quicken. You then create a transaction for the payee that includes the payment date and amount. You can enter the transaction weeks or months in advance if desired—the financial institution sends payment on the date you specify.

Item	Connection Type		
	Direct Connect	**Express Web Connect**	**Web Connect**
Bill Pay	Available from within Quicken if your financial institution offers it.	Not available from within Quicken. Consider Quicken Bill Pay services.	Not available from within Quicken. Consider Quicken Bill Pay services.
Data	Two-way connection with your financial institution. Data is stored on the financial institution's server. All passwords are stored on the financial institution's server. And, if you choose to sync a Direct Connect account to a mobile device, the password is stored on Quicken, Inc., servers as well.	One-way connection for download and updating account balances. Data and passwords are stored on Quicken, Inc.'s aggregation servers.	One-way connection for downloading and updating account balances. All imported information is encrypted and stored on your computer.
Features	Download transactions; update account balances; pay bills; transfer money between accounts. You can transfer funds between accounts and send e-mail to your financial institution.	Download transactions and update account balances in Quicken.	Download transactions and update account balances in Quicken.
Fees	Check with your bank, as many institutions charge a fee for this type of connection. Your financial institution pays a fee to Quicken, Inc., for this support.	Normally, there are no fees charged by your financial institution. Your financial institution pays a fee to Quicken, Inc., for this support. Your financial institution may charge you an excessive usage fee as the aggregation service will log into your bank site every day to retrieve transaction data.	Normally, there are no fees charged by your financial institution. Your financial institution pays a fee to Quicken, Inc., for this support.
Setup	Contact your financial institution.	Use the financial institution's website login when you create the account in Quicken.	Create a login on the financial institution's website to be used each time you want to download your data.
Use	No need to leave Quicken to use all of the banking features.	Just update your account and all transactions and balances are downloaded into Quicken.	Log on to your financial institution's website, using their login information. Locate a link called "Download" or "History" and follow the directions on that website.

Table 6-1 • Connection Options for Downloaded Transactions

As explained in Chapter 7, you can also link some of your bills directly with a payee.

Explaining the Process

Suppose you use Quicken to send online payment instructions to pay your monthly bill at Jim's Hardware Store. You've already set up Jim's Hardware as a payee by entering the name, address, and phone number of his store, as well as your account number there. Quicken sends your payment instructions to your bank, which stores it in its computer with a bunch of other online payment instructions. When the payment date nears, the bank's computer looks through its big database of payees that it can pay by wire transfer. It sees phone companies, credit card companies, and other banks. However, because Jim's store is small, it's probably not one of the wire transfer payees. In that case, the bank's computer prepares a check using all the information you provided. It mails the check along with dozens of others due to be paid that day.

The date the money is actually withdrawn from your account to cover the payment varies depending on your bank. There are four possibilities: one to four days before the payment is processed for delivery, the day the payment is processed for delivery, the day the payment is delivered, or the day the paper check or electronic funds transfer clears your bank.

Check with your bank to find out when they withdraw the funds from your account for online payments. You can also search the Quicken Community to see the experiences other Quicken users have had with that financial institution. To access the Quicken Community, from the Quicken Toolbar, click Help | Quicken Live Community. (While the name is now the Quicken Community, the link still says "Quicken Live Community," although the forum is not "live" and is not a "live chat" service.)

Online Service Costs

The cost of Quicken's Online Account Services varies from bank to bank. However, usually Express Web Connect and Web Connect services are offered at no charge. Check with your bank to determine the exact fees. Also, ask about how to get the fees waived. Often, a sufficient balance or a combination of balance and auto-deposits will qualify you to have the online services fee waived.

Setting Up Online Account Services

To use the Online Account Services supported by Quicken, you must configure the appropriate Quicken accounts. If you did not set up your accounts for online services when you created the accounts, you will need to do so before you can download any transactions. You must first contact your financial institution and tell them you want online services.

To apply for online account services, normally all it takes is a phone call, although some banks and credit card companies allow you to apply online. The financial institution will usually supply you with some or all of the following:

- **Password PIN (Personal Identification Number)**   You'll enter this code into Quicken when you access your account online. This is a security feature, so don't write down your PIN on a sticky note and attach it to your computer monitor. Many financial institutions send this information separately for additional security.
- **User Name (Customer ID Number)**   Each bank uses a different numbering system.
- **Bank Routing Number**   Although your bank might send routing number information, Quicken won't need it. It knows what financial institution you're using based on the information you provide when you create the account. That's why it's so important to choose the correct financial institution when you create each account. You may see the routing information received by Quicken in the Routing Number field in the General tab of the Account Details dialog.
- **Account Number for Each Online Access–Enabled Account**   This tells your financial institution which account you want to work with. Quicken may not need this information. Depending on your financial institution, the account number may appear in the Account Number field of the General tab of the Account Details dialog.

Getting Started with Online Account Services

With customer ID and PIN in hand, you're ready to set up your account (or accounts) for Online Account Services. You can verify this by following the instructions in the "Checking Online Account Services Status" section, later in this chapter.

Some companies, such as department stores, that offer online access on their web pages, may not have the capability of downloading your transactions into Quicken. Check with the company to determine if they have transaction download capability.

Setting Up for Direct Connect, Express Web Connect, and Quicken Bill Pay

If you entered some of your accounts manually when you first used Quicken, from the Account Bar, click the account you want to set up to open its register. Click the Action gear icon. From the menu, select Set Up Online as shown here. (If the account is already set up for online access, the Actions menu shows Update Now instead of Set Up Online.)

Transactions	
⚡ Set up online	
🗐 Edit account details	Ctrl+Shift+E

 The Action gear icon is at the top right of your account registers. If you have customized an account to show Account Toolbar icons, there may be additional icons showing. The Action icon is farthest to the right. You can always use the keyboard shortcut CTRL-SHIFT-N to open the Actions menu.

 When logging in to your financial institution, you may have to physically place the mouse cursor in the proper field each time. Quicken does not always place the cursor in the appropriate field.

Checking Online Account Services Status

You can confirm that an account has been set up for Online Account Services and determine what kind of connection it uses. Right-click the account from the Account Bar and choose Edit/Delete Account. Then, click the Online Services tab to display the type of connection, as shown next. (If your bank offers another connection method, you may see a message with a link describing this.)

- **Deactivate** Use this button if you want to stop Direct Connect services for the account. However, you must still contact the bank to deactivate the connection on their side. To deactivate (or disable) an account from online services:
    - Click Deactivate. (If you currently have unaccepted transactions, you must either accept the transactions or delete them before you can deactivate online services.) A message appears asking if you would like to deactivate the service. Click Yes to complete the deactivation.

Account Details

General   **Online Services**   Display Options

Online setup

Main Checking
is set up for transaction download.   Automatic entry is: Off   Deactivate

Financial Institution: U.S. Bank Internet Banking
Connection Method: Express Web Connect   Reset Account

No account data will be deleted.

Online bill payment

Pay your bills online without
leaving Quicken.   Set up Now...

☐ Reconcile using online balance

Delete Account   Tax Schedule   OK   Cancel

- A connection message box briefly appears while the service is deactivated. Depending on the type of connection your financial institution offers, you may see a Remove Connection button. If so, click it.

If your financial institution has changed or if you have problems deactivating an old (or closed) account, try disconnecting your Internet connection before you deactivate.

- **Reset Account** can be used when a download problem has occurred. None of your data is deleted from Quicken; the account is reset to hopefully solve the issue. Click this button, enter your bank password, and the account's online access is reset. You are prompted to choose the account with which downloaded transactions are connected. Make your choice and click OK.

  During the Reset Account process, the Reset Account button is grayed out and inactive. Once the Reset Account process has completed, the Reset Account button will no longer be grayed out and a small green check mark will appear to the left of the button. If there are new transactions to be downloaded, they will be downloaded during the Account Reset process.

- **Automatic Entry Is: On/Off**   This link opens the Automatic Transaction Entry dialog, shown next. From this dialog, you tell Quicken how to handle downloaded transactions for this specific account.

- **Connection Method**   This link shows the current method by which you connect to your financial institution.
- Click OK to close the Account Details window and complete the process.

Be aware that some banks use different passwords for Direct Connect services than for Web Connect or Express Web Connect.

EXPERIENCED USERS RECOMMEND

Many Quicken users avoid automatically adding downloaded transactions to the account register. In Quicken Preferences, you can select to enter all downloaded transactions into your register. While this may seem to save time, if the matching does not work correctly, it's sometimes difficult to determine what went wrong. You may want to start out with reviewing and accepting each downloaded transaction into your account register, then, once the matching is working well, switch to automatically adding the downloaded transactions to the register.

However, if you do want all downloaded transactions to be loaded into your register automatically, click Edit | Preferences | Downloaded Transactions | Downloaded Transaction Preferences | After Downloading Transactions, and ensure that the Automatically Add To Banking Registers check box is selected.

The Online Center

While you can access online services from several of the various tabs, you can also use the Online Center to work with Quicken's online features. This window gives you access to all the lists and commands you need to download transactions and, if you have Direct Connect, to create payments, transfer money, and exchange e-mail with your financial institution.

Using the Online Center Window

To open the Online Center window, choose Tools | Online Center. You will see the available tabs, such as Transactions, Payments, Transfer, and E-Mail, with one financial institution selected.

 Depending on each account's type, you may not see all the tabs for every account.

A number of buttons and menus enable you to work with the window's contents:

- **Delete** removes a selected item. This button is not available in all tabs of the Online Center window.
- **Payees** (if you have set up online payments) displays the Online Payee List window, which is discussed later in this chapter in the section "Entering Online Payee Information."
- **Repeating** (if you have set up online payments) displays the Repeating Online tab of the Bill And Income Reminders list window. Learn more about using this feature later in this chapter, in the section "Making Online Payments."
- **Contact Info** displays the Contact Information dialog for the currently selected financial institution, if it is offered. You can use the information in the dialog to contact the bank or credit card company by phone, website, or e-mail. Not all financial institutions have these options.
- **Print** prints the transactions that appear in the Payments tab window. It will also print any e-mails you have in the E-mail tab. You may be able to print downloaded transactions that have not yet been accepted.
- **Options** displays a menu of commands for working with the current account or window.

Downloading Transactions

One of the main features of Online Account Services is the ability to download transactions from your financial institution into Quicken. There are several ways to start downloading your transactions after you have set up your online accounts:

- Use the Update/Send button of the Online Center window.
- Click the white right-curling arrow at the top of the Account Bar.
- Click the One Step Update button (a right-curling arrow) on the Quicken Toolbar.
- From an account's register, click the Action gear icon at the top right of the register and choose Update Now from the menu that appears.
- From the Quicken menu, choose Tools | One Step Update.

Connecting to the Financial Institution with Direct Connect or Express Web Connect

If your financial institution supports Direct Connect or Express Web Connect, you can download all transactions from within Quicken.

Using the Online Center window, choose the name of your bank or credit card company from the Financial Institution drop-down list. Click the Update/Send button. The One Step Update Settings dialog for that institution appears. Enter your password, and click Update Now.

Wait while Quicken connects to your bank. A status dialog may appear while Quicken collects your data. When Quicken has finished exchanging information, the status dialog disappears and the One Step Update Summary window takes its place. Continue following the instructions later in the chapter, in the section "Comparing Downloaded Transactions to Register Transactions." Depending on your preference settings, you may only see the One Step Update Summary window if there is an error in the online session.

Downloading a Web Connect File

If your financial institution supports Web Connect but not Express Web Connect, you'll log in to your financial institution's website and manually download the statement information, just as you did when you first set up the account for Online Account Services. Even if your financial institution supports Express Web Connect, you can download using Web Connect if you wish. The availability of Express Web Connect does not preclude use of Web Connect.

However, if you have chosen Express Web Connect or Direct Connect as your download method for an account, to download via Web Connect, you will need to start from the financial institution's website rather than from within Quicken.

EXPERIENCED USERS RECOMMEND

Many Quicken users set up accounts in Quicken and decide later to activate online services for these accounts. The first time you download transactions into a Quicken file for which accounts have been set up, you are prompted to either add the downloaded transactions into a new account or link to an existing account.

If your link is to an incorrect account, the transactions download into that incorrect account. If you have not accepted the transactions, simply delete the downloaded transactions. Then, download the information into the correct account. If you have accepted the transactions and they are in the register of the wrong account, you can move them into the correct account. However, if you have linked the accounts, you have to deactivate the accounts to break the connection to the incorrect account.

 It's not so easy to delete transactions from the Downloaded Transactions tab. You must delete the downloaded transactions one at a time. If you have many transactions in the Downloaded Transactions tab, it may be easier to accept them all, sort your account by date/order entered, and then select all the downloaded transactions and either delete or move them to the correct account. Another alternative is to restore a recent backup from before you performed the transaction download.

If you have several months' (or years') worth of downloaded transactions, one way to solve this issue is by deactivating online services for both accounts, moving any transactions that are in the wrong account into the correct account, and then reactivating the online service for both accounts. See "Moving Transactions" later in this chapter. However, as always, before making any changes, back up your Quicken data, "just in case."

In the Online Center window, choose the name of your bank or credit card company from the Financial Institution drop-down list. If necessary, click the Update/Send button to see the dialog shown next. Quicken connects to the Internet and displays your financial institution's login page. Log in, navigate to the page where you can download statements, and download the statement or transactions you want. For a Web Connect account, choosing Update/Send from the Online Center will open your browser and display the financial institution's login page, not shown in the illustration.

If necessary, switch back to Quicken. It should automatically import the transactions you downloaded into the correct account. If you have chosen to accept your downloaded transactions automatically, you will see a small blue ball icon at the left of each of the downloaded transactions in your account register. Transactions that have been matched to scheduled transactions have a calendar icon in the same location.

If Express Web Connect or Direct Connect is available for an account, you may see a dialog offering to upgrade your connection. You may see a prompt to handle your Web Connect transactions now or save the transactions for later processing. To set this, go to Edit | Preferences | Downloaded Transactions and make your selection.

Click the Close button in the One Step Update Summary window to dismiss it. Then, click that account's name in the Account Bar to open the register for that account.

Unless you have chosen to turn on the Automatically Add To Banking Registers preference, your downloaded transactions will appear in the Downloaded Transactions tab at the bottom of the register window. From there, you can use the directions in the next section "Comparing Downloaded Transactions to Register Transactions."

Keep in mind that the first time you connect via Direct Connect, the bank normally sends all transactions from the past 90 or more days. (Some banks send a full year of transactions!) After that, only new transactions (items that have not been downloaded) will be downloaded. For Web Connect downloads, you can often specify the transaction period when you set up the download.

Comparing Downloaded Transactions to Register Transactions

If you have opted to accept downloaded transactions manually, you will compare the downloaded transactions to the transactions already entered in your account register. This process enables you to review or identify transactions that may have been entered incorrectly by either you or the bank.

If you do not see the Downloaded Transactions tab at the bottom of your register, you may have minimized the window or you may have told Quicken to automatically add downloaded transactions to the banking registers. To allow the tab to display, click Edit | Preferences | Downloaded Transactions | Downloaded Transaction Preferences | After Downloading Transactions, and clear the Automatically Add To Banking Registers check box.

EXPERIENCED USERS RECOMMEND

If you have trouble downloading your transactions from a specific financial institution using One Step Update, use the Update Now command from the Action gear icon menu in your account's register. If that doesn't solve the problem, try going online to your bank's site and downloading the transactions manually. Some users experience issues when there were no transactions to download, and downloading manually solved the problem.

If the account is set up for Direct Connect or Express Web Connect, being able to successfully download from the financial institution's website does not necessarily eliminate that institution as the cause of the issue. Often Direct Connect and Express Web Connect use entirely different servers. Because the servers are different, it may be that the problem is with one of the server computers.

Consider using the Quicken Community forums using the name of your financial institution as the search term. If the financial institution is having problems, it's very possible another Quicken user has already posted a question. To access the Quicken Community, from the Quicken Toolbar, click Help | Quicken Live Community.

The bottom half of the account register window is the Downloaded Transactions tab (refer to Figure 6-1). It shows three ways to identify downloaded transactions:

- **Match** identifies transactions that match those in the register. This will happen if the transaction has already been entered in the Quicken register and matches the information in the downloaded transaction.

Status	Date	Num	Payee	Payment	Deposit
Match	10/24/2016	66	Check / Download from usbank.com.	60.07	
Accepted	9/2/2016	61	Check / Download from usbank.com.	34.10	
New	9/23/2016	58	Check / Download from usbank.com.	60.81	
Accepted	10/3/2016	59	Check / Download from usbank.com.	41.48	
New	10/11/2016		Account Maintenance Fee / Download from usbank.com.		6.95
New	10/11/2016		Account Maintenance Fee / Download from usbank.com.	6.95	

Figure 6-1 • Many Quicken users choose to review transactions before accepting them into the register.

Especially the first time you are downloading transactions for an account, you will want to closely check the Match transactions to ensure the downloaded transaction is matched to the correct register transaction. Incorrect matches can make downloaded transactions seem to disappear and can cause your reconciliation to fail to balance. To check the match, click the Match transaction in the Downloaded Transactions tab. The corresponding transaction in the account register will be highlighted.

- **New** identifies transactions that are not in the register or that are in the register but are different from the downloaded transactions. Maybe you transposed a number or the date is different. You need to manually match these transactions so you do not get duplicates.

  Be sure to check each New transaction carefully to ensure that you were the one who actually initiated the transaction and that the transaction is to the payee and in the amount you created. If you suspect any type of fraud, call your bank immediately.

- **Accepted** identifies matched transactions that you have accepted. When a downloaded transaction has been accepted, a small "c" appears in the Clr column of the account register to indicate that the item has cleared the bank but has not yet been reconciled.

  When you select an item in the Accept Cleared Transactions list, the transactions below it shift down to make room for a blank line with an Accept button and an Edit menu. You can use these to work with the selected transaction.

- **Accepting a Matched Transaction**   If a transaction matches one in the register, you can accept it by selecting it in the list at the bottom of the window and clicking the Accept button. If Quicken sees what appears to be a transaction that matches one in your register, a small, uncleared icon appears in the Status column at the left of your register, as seen here. The icon is a pencil and the icon label is "Uncleared." Click the icon to match the register entry to a downloaded transaction. Even if there is not an apparent match, any time you see the uncleared icon, you can click it to get the Match To A Downloaded Transaction context menu item and, by clicking that menu item, get to the Manual Match window.

●	▶	Date	Chec...	Payee	Category	⬚	Payment	.	Deposit	Amount	Balance	⚙
✏ Uncleared		10/13/2016	56	Jims Hardware	Home:Home Supplies		75 76			-75 76	565 74	
✏ Uncleared	⬚	10/22/2016	66	Safeway	Food & Dining:Grocerie ⬚		60 07		*Deposit*	-60 07	505 6T	Save ⚙ ◁

All Dates   ▼   Any Type   ▼   All Transactions   ▼   Reset   Search   🔍

- **Entering and Accepting a New Transaction**   To enter and accept a new transaction, select the transaction in the bottom half of the window. If the information on the transaction is complete and correct, click Accept. If you have entered the part of the transaction in the register (the top half of the window), fill in any missing details, including the payee, category, and memo. Then click Save in the top half of the window or Accept in the bottom half. Quicken marks it as Accepted and a small "c" appears in the Clr column of the register.

- **Unmatching a Matched Transaction**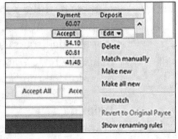
  If a matched transaction really shouldn't be matched, select it in the bottom half of the window and choose Unmatch from the Edit pop-up menu as seen here.
  - **Unmatch** tells Quicken that it got the match wrong, but this command lets Quicken attempt to match it to another transaction. As a result, it may come up with another match. It's your job to determine whether the new match is correct. If it can't find a match, the status changes to New.
  - **Make New** tells Quicken that the transaction shouldn't match any existing transaction. The status changes to New, and Quicken can then treat it as a new transaction.
  - **Make All New** tells Quicken to make all of the downloaded but not yet accepted transactions new so you can manually match them or enter them as a new transaction.

- **Manually Matching a Transaction**   If a downloaded transaction identified as New should match one in the register, or if a single transaction corresponds to multiple transactions in your account register, you can manually match them up. In the bottom half of the window, select the transaction that you want to match manually, and click the Edit button. Click Match Manually to open the Manually Match Transactions dialog. Turn on the check box(es) for the transaction(s) you want to include in the match. When you click Accept, Quicken marks the transaction in the Clr column with a small "c."

If the transaction included multiple register transactions, the entry Quicken creates includes each of the register transactions on a separate split line. You can click the Split button for the transaction to edit it as desired. See Chapter 5 to review working with split transactions.

If you see a transaction that displays as "New" but you're sure you've entered it, check for small discrepancies, perhaps in the amount. You can either force a manual match or simply correct the item you've entered into your register and the item status will change to Match.

If you choose to have Quicken automatically add your downloaded transactions into your banking register, you can still manually match a transaction. Register transactions that have not been matched with a downloaded transaction have a small pencil icon near them. If you use a one-line register, this icon appears to the left of the date. Click the icon and choose Match To A Downloaded Transaction. You can use this matching method whether you auto-enter your downloaded transactions or manually review/accept your downloaded transactions.

Deleting a New Transaction

To delete any transaction, select it in the bottom half of the account register window, click Edit, and choose Delete from the Edit pop-up menu. A confirmation dialog appears; click Yes to remove the transaction from the list.

> **EXPERIENCED USERS RECOMMEND**
>
> New users sometimes reconcile accounts using a paper statement and do an online reconciliation at a later time. If they don't download before doing the reconciliation, they may encounter a transaction that indicates it has been reconciled in the register but appears as a "New" transaction when downloaded. Use the Match Manually procedure to connect the two and prevent future downloaded transactions from incorrectly matching to the transaction.

Sometimes matching issues can be resolved, especially when reconciling an account, by choosing to display the Downloaded Posting Date column in your register. Display this column (field) in your register by choosing the Action gear icon | Register Columns | Downloaded Posting Date. Since reconciliations are date-driven, the posting date may be after the cutoff date of the reconciliation. Click Done to close the Register Columns list and return to the register.

Moving Transactions   If you have several accounts at the same bank and inadvertently accept transactions into the incorrect account, you can move either a single or multiple transactions. You can use this procedure to move transactions between accounts at different banks or to move transactions between accounts that are not online accounts.

To move a single transaction:

1. Right-click the transaction in the account register. Choose Move Transaction(s) from the context menu.

2. The Move Transaction(s) dialog box appears. Choose the account into which you want to move the transaction from the drop-down list, shown here.

> **Q** Move Transaction(s)   ×
>
> Move to account: | Main Credit Card   ▼ |
>   House Checking
>   MMA Account
> **?**   Money Market Acct
>   Old Checking

3. Click OK and Quicken returns you to the original register.

To move multiple transactions as a group in your register:

1. Click the first transaction in the register to highlight it.
2. Hold down your SHIFT key and, while still holding it, click the last transaction in the group. All of the transactions will be selected. Release the SHIFT key.
3. Right-click in the highlighted area, and from the context menu that appears, choose Move Transaction(s).
4. The Move Transaction(s) dialog box appears. Choose the account from the drop-down list into which you want to move the transactions.
5. Click OK to return to your original register.

To select multiple transactions that are scattered throughout your register:

1. Click the first transaction in the register to highlight it.
2. Hold down your CTRL key and, while still holding it, click each transaction you want to move. All of the selected transactions will be highlighted. Release the CTRL key.
3. Right-click in the highlighted area, and from the context menu, choose Move Transaction(s).
4. The Move Transaction(s) dialog box appears. Choose the account from the drop-down list into which you want to move the transactions.
5. Click OK. You are returned to the original account register.

You may be able to get all the transactions together in a contiguous group by sorting or filtering the account register.

In each case, the transactions are moved to the account you designate.

If you are moving reconciled transactions, you will see a prompt for each transaction you are moving, asking you if you are sure you want to move a reconciled transaction. This can be tedious if you are moving many transactions. You may want to use Copy Transaction(s) and Paste Transaction(s) instead, as this method will not show the prompt asking if you are sure about changing the reconciled transactions.

Accepting All Downloaded Transactions   The Accept All button accepts all transactions into your account register. If you select this without reviewing them one by one, some transactions may not be properly categorized. Also, some transactions may be matched to the wrong transaction, making it appear as if the downloaded transaction disappeared. Most Quicken users don't use Accept All without first examining each downloaded transaction to ensure it matched to the proper register transaction.

After you have reviewed all of your transactions and accepted, matched, or deleted the transactions, click Done to close the Downloaded Transactions tab. Choose Finish Later to close the dialog if you cannot complete the task at one sitting.

Renaming Downloaded Payees

One of the potentially annoying things about entering transactions by accepting downloaded activity information is the way your bank identifies payees. For example, one bank identifies the payee as "Shell Oil 12384658" instead of plain old "Shell Oil." Fortunately, Quicken's Renaming Rules feature can automatically rename bank-assigned payee names with names you prefer. You can also create and apply your own renaming rules. You do this with the Renaming Rules dialog, which allows you to control how Quicken deals with the differences between the payee names in your records and those of the bank's.

To open this dialog, click the Renaming Rules button at the bottom of the Downloaded Transactions tab of the register window, or choose Tools | Renaming Rules. You can also select a payee in your register. Click the small downward arrow at the right of the Payee field, and select the Renaming Rules button. This process is available only if your account is enabled for transaction download.

The Renaming Rules dialog lists all the renaming rules you have already created, as well as the rules Quicken has created automatically. Click the Add A Rule link, or the white cross within the green circle icon next to the Add A Rule link, to add a new rule. Click the Do-Not-Rename Rules tab to add a payee to the Do Not Rename list. (You can add a rule from that tab as well; just click the Add A Rule link.)

If you want to delete a rule, simply select the rule, and click the icon with the small white line within the red circle. A confirmation message appears. Click OK in the confirmation dialog to remove the rule.

To modify a rule, select the payee to display three icons: a pencil, a green circle with a white plus sign, and a red circle with a white line, as shown here. Click the pencil icon to open the Edit Payee Name dialog. Use this dialog to change the selected payee name. Click OK to save your renaming rule edits and return to the Renaming Rules dialog.

	Renaming Rules	✕
	Renaming Rules	

Rename Rules	Do-Not-Rename Rules

Rename the downloaded payee to:

▸ **Linds**

▸ **Paypal**

▸ **Pickles Deli**   ✎ ⊕ ⊖

▸ **Radioshack**

▸ **Regence**

▸ **Shell Oil**

▸ **TigerDirect**

▸ **US Bank**

▸ **Wal-Mart**

▸ **Walgreens**

⊕ Add a rule

? | Preferences | Having trouble | Done

After you have made all of your changes, click Done to return to the register.

Be careful when renaming generally named downloaded transactions. For example, if we write a check to Car Repair By Royce in the amount of $202.26, our US Bank account downloads transactions as "CHECK Download from usbank.com." If we use the Add A Renaming Rule dialog, all downloaded checks will be renamed as Car Repair By Royce! The best workaround for this is to enter checks in your register manually and then match those checks to the downloaded transactions.

When you are in the Renaming Rules dialog and select the Add A Rule link; it opens the Add A Renaming Rule dialog. Enter the name you want to see as the payee name in the Change Payee To box. Then, from the drop-down list, choose If Quicken Name Is or If Payee Contains and then enter the word (or words) that most likely will appear in the downloaded transaction. When you click OK in the dialog, you are returned to the Renaming Rules dialog and will see the new renaming rule added to the list.

EXPERIENCED USERS RECOMMEND

One of the reasons to download your transactions is to eliminate the need to enter all of your checks into your register. However, some banks do not include check numbers or payees in their downloaded transactions. For these accounts, you might consider entering your checks so that you only need to match them to the downloaded item. Otherwise, if you have many transactions, it can take a bit of time to enter the information for each downloaded item. You can cut down on your data entry time by using scheduled reminders and memorized payees.

Making Online Payments

Paying your bills from within Quicken can save you both time and effort. If your bank supports Online Bill Pay, this may be the best choice for you. This section explains how to set up online payees, enter payment information for one-time and repeating payments, and work with payment instructions.

Entering Online Payee Information

To send payments from your account, your bank must know who each payee is and where they are located. To ensure that your account with the payee is credited properly, you must also provide account information. You do this by setting up online payees in the Online Center.

- From the Tools menu, click Online Center to open the Online Center dialog. Select Payees to open the Online Payee List. You can also choose Online Payee List from the Tools menu to open the list.
- The Financial Institution drop-down list shows the institutions for which you have enabled Online Bill Pay. If there is more than one, choose the institution that has the account from which you will be paying this payee. The payees you have added for the displayed institution will be listed, showing the payee name, the lead time for this payee, and the account number. Some financial institutions do not provide the lead time for online bill payments. There are several buttons at the bottom of the list, as discussed later.

If you have not yet set up Online Bill Pay, the Payees menu item will not be listed in the Online Center and the Online Payee List entry in the Tools menu will be disabled.

- **New** opens the Set Up Online Payee dialog.
    - Enter the name of the online payee in the Name field and any description that might be needed in the optional Description field. Verify (or enter, if this is a new payee) the mailing address, account number, and phone number. If you skip over one of these required fields, Quicken will prompt you for the information.
    - Click OK when you have completed entering the information. The Confirm Online Payee Information message appears displaying the information you just entered. Check the information in this box carefully. When you're satisfied that the information is correct, click Accept. The new payee is added to the Online Payee List. If the information is not correct, click Cancel and you are returned to the Set Up Online Payee dialog.

The following items appear on the Online Payee List:

- **Help** (the small question mark) opens the paying bills online section of Quicken Help.
- **Print** (the printer icon) prints a list of online payees.
- **Edit** enables you to modify the information for the selected online payee. However, note that you cannot change the account number without deleting the payee and setting up a new payee.
- **Use** switches you back to the Payments tab of the Online Center window and inserts the selected payee into the payment form.
- **Report** displays a report of all payments made to the selected online payee.
- **Delete** removes the selected online payee. Deleting a payee simply deletes the payee's information from the Online Payee List window. It does not change any transactions for a payee. You cannot delete a payee for which unsent payment instructions exist.
- **Done** closes the Online Payee List.

Entering Payment Instructions

To enter additional online payment instructions, click Tools | Online Center | Payments. Ensure you are using the correct financial institution if you have more than one set up for online payments. Fill in the fields in the middle of the window with the payment information on the following page.

- **Processing Date** is the date the bank should begin processing the payment. For some banks, this date is fixed based on the Delivery Date field and can't be changed. When the Processing Date is fixed based on the Delivery Date, the Processing Date's value will be grayed out.
- **Delivery Date** is the date you want the payee to receive payment. This should be before the date the bank creates and mails the check. The check may be received before the delivery date, depending on the mail (if the check is mailed). The date you enter, however, must be at least the same number of business days in advance as the lead time for the payee—often four business days. For some banks, the delivery date cannot be changed; instead, specify a processing date that allows enough time for the payment to be made on a timely basis.
- **Payee** is the online payee to receive payment. Quicken's QuickFill feature fills in the payee's name as you type it. If desired, you can choose it from the drop-down list of online payees. If you enter a payee that is not in the Online Payee List window, Quicken displays the Set Up Online Payee dialog so you can add the new payee's information. This enables you to create online payees as you enter payment instructions.
- **$** is the amount of the payment.

If you have set your Quicken Preferences to use the ENTER key when moving between fields, this process ignores your Preference setting and uses ENTER to enter the online payment.

- **Category** is the category for the transaction. You can enter a category, choose one from the drop-down list, or click the Split button to enter multiple categories.
- **Memo**, which is optional, is for entering a note about the transaction.

When you've finished entering information for the transaction, press ENTER. Depending on your financial institution, a message box may appear reminding you that you need to allow enough time for the payment to be processed by your financial institution. Click OK to continue or Cancel to return to the payment. Click the Don't Show This Message Again check box to keep the message from appearing for future transactions.

The transaction appears in the list in the bottom half of the window with the words "Payment request ready to send" in the Status column beside it. You can repeat this process for as many payments as you want to make.

You can also enter an online payment instruction directly into the appropriate account register and choose Send Online Payment in the Check # column.

Sending Payment Instructions

Once your payment instructions have been completed, you must connect to your bank to send the instructions. In the Online Center window, click the Update/Send button. Quicken displays the One Step Update Settings dialog, which lists all of the payment instructions, including any repeating payment instructions. If you are prompted, enter your password and click the Update Now button.

Quicken connects to your bank's server and sends your payment (or payment cancellation) instructions. When the process is complete, you see the One Step Update Summary window. Click Close. In the Payments tab of the Online Center window, the words "Scheduled for delivery on" followed by the payment date appear in the Status column beside the payment instructions that have been sent to your bank.

Canceling a Payment

Occasionally, you may change your mind about making a payment. Perhaps you find your spouse already sent a check or that you set up the payment for the wrong amount. For whatever reason, you can cancel an online payment that you have sent to your bank, as long as there's enough time to cancel it before the payment is to be paid.

When you send a payment instruction to your bank, it waits in the bank's computer. When the processing date (determined by the number of days in the payee's lead time and the payment date) arrives, the bank makes the payment. Before the processing date, however, the payment instructions can be canceled. If you send a cancel payment instruction to the bank before the processing date, the bank removes the instruction from its computer without sending payment to the payee. Quicken won't let you cancel a payment if the processing date has already passed. If you wait too long, the only way to cancel the payment is to call the bank directly and stop the check.

Keep in mind that canceling a payment instruction is not the same as stopping payment on a check. If you send the cancel payment instruction in time, the bank should not charge a fee for stopping the payment. In the Online Center window, click the Payments tab, select the payment that you want to cancel, and click the Cancel Payment button. Click Yes in the confirmation dialog that appears. Use the Update/Send button to send the cancel payment instruction. The Cancel Payment button changes to Don't Cancel Pmt if you have a payment with the cancel payment instruction ready to send selected.

Transferring Money Between Accounts

Quicken makes it easy to record your transfers between accounts. If you have more than one account enabled for Online Bill Pay via Direct Connect at the same financial institution, you can even transfer money from one account to the other directly from within Quicken.

To record a transfer of funds that you make with a phone call or on the financial institution's website:

1. From the Account Bar, select the account from which you want to transfer the funds.
2. Click the Action gear icon | Transfer Money or press CTRL-SHIFT-T to open the Transfer Money Within Quicken dialog as seen here.

3. Enter the transfer information—From Account (source account), To Account (destination account), and amount—in the fields in the middle of the window.
4. Click OK. The transaction will appear in both check registers.
5. If you do not have Direct Connect, be sure to call the bank or go to the website to actually *send* the instructions to transfer funds.

To create an online transfer, both accounts must be activated with Direct Connect and be at the same bank under the same customer identification number. Some financial institutions allow you to pay a credit card that is associated with the same identification number in this manner as well.

To create the online transfer:

1. In a new transaction line, click the Date field and enter today's date. While you can schedule an online transfer for a future date, the transfer will show on the date you actually sent the transfer. Financial institutions process transfer instructions on the same day the request is received.

2. In the Check # field, click the downward arrow, and select Online Transfer from the list. It will appear in your Check # field as OXfr.
3. Enter a description, if you choose, in what is normally the Payee field.
4. In the Payment column, enter the amount of the transfer. Press TAB to move to the Category field. Choose the account to which you want to transfer the money from the drop-down list that appears.
5. Click Save to enter the transaction.

Use the One Step Update dialog to send the instructions to your financial institution. You may also use the Online Center to send an online transfer.

1. Click Tools | Online Center.
2. Select the appropriate financial institution from the drop-down list.
3. Click the Transfers tab.
4. In the Transfer Money From field, choose the account from which you want to transfer the funds from the drop-down list.
5. In the To field, choose the account where the money is going from the drop-down list. Enter the amount in the Amount field.
6. Press ENTER. The transfer is added to the list at the bottom of the Online Center window.
7. Click Update/Send to send the instructions to the bank.

Whether you use the Online Center method or the account register method, you must send the transfer instructions to the bank in order for the transaction to take place.

Unlike Online Bill Pay, there is no way to delete the unsent transfer instruction in the Online Center Transfers tab. However, you can delete the unsent transfer from the account register.

Transfer Detection

A Quicken feature scans your transactions as they are being downloaded to detect transfers between your accounts. When Quicken finds what looks like a matched pair of transfer transactions, it automatically creates the transfer in Quicken for you. The default in Quicken 2017 is this setting. To change this feature, from the Quicken menu bar, click Edit | Preferences | Register | Transfer Detection and clear the Automatically Create Transfers When Detected option. Even if you choose to keep this option, be cautious with this preference—it may detect matches that are not truly transfers. Consider including the option for Quicken to ask for confirmation first. To set this option, from the Quicken menu bar, click

Edit | Preferences | Register | Transfer Detection and click the Confirm Possible
Transfers Before Entering In Register option.

Exchanging E-mail with Your Financial Institution

You can use the E-mail tab of the Online Center window to exchange e-mail
messages with financial institutions for which you have enabled Online Account
Services via Direct Connect. Keep in mind that not all financial institutions
support this feature. Also, remember that this communication is between you
and your financial institution, not Quicken, Inc. (the makers of Quicken). It is
intended primarily for exchanging information about your account, not technical
support for using Quicken.

- **Creating an E-mail Message**   In the E-mail tab of the Online Center
  window, click Create. When a Create dialog appears, use it to set general
  options for your e-mail message. If your message is about an online payment,
  choose the account from the Account drop-down list, and select the payment
  from the Payments list. Even if there is only one payment in the list, you
  must select it or the OK button remains disabled. When you click OK, a
  Message window appears. Use it to compose your e-mail message. Click OK
  again to save the message. The message appears in the bottom half of the
  E-mail tab of the Online Center window, ready to be sent to your financial
  institution.

  If you currently have no online payments scheduled, the option E-mail About
  An Online Payment will be grayed out. If you elected to e-mail your financial
  institution regarding a payment, the window is titled Payment E-mail.
- **Exchanging E-mail Messages**   In the Online Center window, click the
  Update/Send button. Quicken displays the Online Update window, which
  includes any e-mail messages you may have created that need to be sent.
  Enter your password and click the Update Now button. Then wait while
  Quicken establishes an Internet connection with your bank and exchanges
  e-mail.
- **Reading an E-mail Message**   When your bank sends you an e-mail
  message, it appears in the E-mail tab of the Online Center window. To read
  the message, select it and click Read. The message appears in a message
  window. If desired, you can click the Print button to print the message for
  future reference. You can also click Delete to delete the e-mail once you no
  longer need it.
- Click **Close** to close the Online Center window.

Tracking Your Money

This part of the book describes how Quicken Personal Financial Software helps you track your money. It starts by explaining how to create reminders for your bills and how to organize your spending. You'll learn how to reconcile both bank and credit card statements and why both procedures are important. It then explains the basics of tracking investments in Quicken and then goes on to describe how you can use Quicken's online investment tracking features to download investment information from your brokerage firm and exchange information with Quicken.com. Along the way, it provides a wealth of information you can use to invest wisely and maximize your investment return. This part has three chapters:

Part Three

Monitoring Your
Bills and Paychecks

In This Chapter:

- *Being reminded*

- *Creating reminders from downloaded transactions*

- *Using the Bill Linker*

- *Managing reminders*

- *Using QuickFill and memorized payees*

- *Using the financial Calendar*

- *Minding your bills*

- *Using the Paycheck Setup Wizard*

- *Exploring the Spending graph*

- *Using the Spending register*

- *Creating the Address Book*

- *Viewing available alerts groups*

Chapter 7

L ife can be hectic sometimes, too hectic to pay bills before they're overdue, monitor your spending, and all of the other day-to-day chores involved in managing your money. Quicken Personal Financial Software provides tools to help you keep track of your bills and your spending, set reminders and alerts for any financial occurrences, and, at the same time, keep watch on your earnings.

Bill and Income Reminders

A favorite Quicken feature is the ability to tell Quicken about the bills, deposits, and other transactions that need to be made in the future, especially the ones that happen on a regular basis. This feature, when fully utilized, doesn't just prevent you from forgetting to pay bills; it can completely automate the transaction entry process. Starting from the time you first create your Quicken file, you can create reminders to help you stay on top of your monthly bills. This part of the chapter discusses bill and income reminders, including how to set up and use them.

Being Reminded

Reminders aren't only for payments. You could create a reminder for incoming funds, such as an expected bonus or a quarterly annuity check you receive. You can even schedule your paycheck—but it's better to use Quicken's Paycheck Setup feature, which is discussed later in this chapter, to do that.

Quicken's Reminders feature is one of the best timesaving features Quicken offers. By taking full advantage of this feature, you can minimize the time you spend entering transactions into Quicken and you can use those same reminders for cash flow forecasting so you can be sure you always have funds available when it's time to pay those bills. Generally speaking, you can be "reminded" about two types of transactions:

- One-time transactions are future transactions that you expect to record only once. For example, suppose you are arranging to purchase some furniture. You have already paid a deposit for the furniture and you know that the balance will be due at month-end, when the furniture is delivered. You can schedule that month-end payment in advance.
- Recurring transactions are transactions that occur periodically on a regular basis. Many of your monthly bills are good examples: rent or mortgage payments, car payments, utility bills—unfortunately, there are too many to list!

Throughout this chapter and this book; bill reminders, scheduled transactions, and scheduled reminders all are used and mean the same process, saving information about a payee or a transaction so that you can pay or enter the information at a future time.

Remember that creating a reminder is not the same as recording a transaction, even if you opt to show the reminder in your account register. You must print a check or send an online payment instruction to record the transaction. Creating the reminder is only part of the job.

Creating Reminders from Downloaded Transactions

You can create a scheduled transaction in Quicken in several ways. When you first install Quicken, in the Home tab's Main View, click the Get Started button in the Stay On Top Of Monthly Bills snapshot. If you have downloaded your bank account transactions, you may already see outgoing transactions that appear to be recurring transactions. The Review Bills dialog lists these transactions, as seen in Figure 7-1. (If you do not see the Get Started button in the Stay On Top Of Monthly Bills snapshot, skip ahead to "Work in the Home Tab's Main View," later in this chapter.)

If you have not downloaded your transactions, or created a bank account, you may see three different Get Started buttons. However, until you create your first bank account, the only available Get Started button will be in the See Where Your Money Goes snapshot.

Q Stay On Top of Monthly Bills   ✕

Stay On Top of Monthly Bills

Review Bills

Let's take a look at the bills we found in your transaction history. Getting these identified correctly makes sure that Quicken can help you keep track of recurring bills, pay them on time, and avoid late fees. You can always add other bills later.

Due ▲	Pay To / Receive From	Linked to Biller	Amount	How Often	Action
1/5/2017	Dish Network	Link it now	-90.81	Monthly	
1/7/2017	AT&T	Link it now	-91.82	Monthly	
Schedule These?					
1/16/2017	Puget Sound Energy		-192.43	Monthly	Edit Remove

Add a bill

Cancel   Next »

Figure 7-1 • You can schedule your monthly bills from your downloaded transactions.

You may remove the transactions or edit them. If you do not want to enter a transaction as a recurring transaction into Quicken, select that transaction and click Remove in the Action column.

Remember, you are editing a transaction reminder, not the transactions already listed in the account register.

To edit a transaction:

1. Select the transaction and click Edit. The Edit Bill Reminder dialog appears, as seen next.

Q Edit Bill Reminder   ×

Edit Bill Reminder

| Pay to | Puget Sound Energy |

Due next on: 1/16/2017   16th of every month (change)

Amount due: **$173.75** (estimated amount) (change)

From account: Main Checking   ±

Details

Category: **Bills & Utilities:Utilities**
Tag: *no tag*
Memo: **Download from usbank.com. PUGET SOUND ENER**

▶ Optional Settings

?   Cancel   Delete   Done

---

2. Click in the Pay To field to change or correct the payee of this transaction.
3. Click in the Due Next On field to change the date if necessary. You may either type the information or use the calendar at the right of the field.
4. Click Change to the right of the Due Next On field to open a dialog in which you tell Quicken how often to pay (or receive) this item. Make any appropriate changes and click OK (or Cancel if you've not made any changes) to return to the Edit Bill Reminder dialog.

See the "Link It Now" in the Review Bills dialog? This feature in Quicken 2017 is discussed later in this chapter in the section "Using the Bill Linker."

EXPERIENCED USERS RECOMMEND

One of the most common questions in the Quicken Community is how to schedule a reminder on a frequency like every 3rd Friday. To do so, open the Add Reminder button and choose Add Bill Reminder.

1. Enter the vendor name in the Pay To field and select Next.
2. Click the Change link next to the calendar in the Due Next On field to open the illustration shown next.

Cleaning Wizards, Inc.

Start date: 1/20/2017

How often: Monthly   Every 1   month on the   3rd   Friday

End date: No end date

OK   Cancel

3. Set the Start date and if this is to be paid on the 3rd Friday of each month, select 3rd from the on the drop-down list and Friday in the last field.
4. Set the end date or leave the field set to No End Date, the default.
5. Click OK to return to the Add Bill Reminder dialog. The pay date will show as the 3rd Friday of every month.

5. Click the Change link to change the amount, if necessary. You may either type the new amount or use the small calculator to the right of the field. If necessary, open the drop-down list in the From Account field to change the account.

6. Click anywhere within the Details section to add a category, tag, or memo. Click OK (or Cancel) to close the dialog and return to the Edit Bill Reminder dialog.

You may also see the split button to the right of the Category field, a small two-headed arrow. Read more about split transactions in Chapter 5.

7. The Optional Settings section is covered in the section "Setting Up Reminders in the Bills Tab" later in this chapter.

8. After you have completed changing or entering the information, click Done/Next. If you have additional recurring items, the Stay On Top Of Monthly Bills | Review Bills dialog asks that you follow the same process for each item on the list.

If you have recurring income items, follow the earlier steps for each income item. When you have completed the income items, click Done. You are returned to the Home tab's Main View in the Stay On Top Of Monthly Bills snapshot. Note that the Bill And Income Reminders section now includes the recurring items. If your paycheck is listed in the recurring income items, click Remove, as you will want to set it up using the Paycheck Setup feature, which is discussed later in this chapter.

Work in the Home Tab's Main View

After you have set up recurring bills from downloaded transactions, you can continue to work in the Stay On Top Of Monthly Bills section in the Home Tab's Main view. Click the Options gear icon to show the menu from which you can do the following:

- Change the displayed date range to display the reminders for the next 7, 14, 30, or 90 days, or 12 months.
- Open the Add Reminder dialog to add a new Bill, Income, or Transfer reminder. Each option opens the appropriate reminder dialog for that specific task.
- Go to the Bills tab, from which you can work with reminders, see what bills and income are due in the near future, and see your projected balances for the next 12 months or even longer, if you choose. See the upcoming section "Setting Up Reminders in the Bills Tab" in this chapter.

Each reminder displayed on the Stay On Top Of Monthly Bills list is a link. Click the small, right-facing arrow to the right of the amount to see a menu, from which you can do the following:

- Enter the reminder into the appropriate register, which opens the Enter Expense Transaction (or Enter Income Transaction) dialog. With this dialog, you can enter the transaction into the register immediately rather than waiting for the date you set earlier. The transaction will reflect the date you specify, showing in the register with that date in the future.

- Skip This One entry. If there is more than one instance of the reminder overdue, the Skip button will be labeled "Skip" and have two options available: Skip This One and Skip All Overdue Reminders For This Payee. Unfortunately, in most of the bills views, the button is not visible, just the ellipsis indicating there is more info available. Right clicking on the reminder with multiple instances overdue shows both skip options. Note that the one view you can see the Skip button in is the Stack view. If you have not selected "Don't show me this again" in the confirmation prompt, you will see a confirmation prompt asking you to confirm skipping the reminder. This is true of all instances where you have the option to Skip This One entry.

- Click Edit to open a submenu from which you can choose from three options in its submenu.
  - Edit This Instance of the reminder, which enables you to edit the amount or date of the next occurrence of the reminder.
  - Edit This And All Future Instances, which opens the Edit Bill Reminder dialog. If the reminder is an income or transfer reminder, the Edit Income Reminder or Edit Transfer Reminder dialog opens.
  - Delete This And All Future Reminders, which opens a message that you are about to delete a scheduled bill or deposit. You must click OK to delete the reminder or click Cancel to close the message without deleting the reminder.

If you double-click the reminder amount, the Edit Transaction dialog appears. This dialog allows you to make changes to the transaction, not the reminder.

See What's Left

The What's Left section at the left of the Stay On Top Of Monthly Bills section shows how much is available for the date range you selected in the Options menu. If any of your accounts will be overdrawn, you will see "Risk of Overdraft" displayed at the left of the What's Left section. Click the link to display the Projected Balances dialog.

If your accounts are all positive (not overdrawn), you will see a See Projected Balances link instead of the Risk Of Overdraft link. Click See Projected Balances to display the balances in each of your spending accounts. This is the same information you see in the Bills tab's Projected Balances view. Click Close to dismiss the Projected Balances dialog.

Credit card accounts are not considered spending accounts in the Projected Balances dialog.

Working with the Bills Tab

When you select the Bills tab, the first option you see in Quicken 2017 is the online Bill Linker feature. This allows you to connect your Quicken program to vendor websites so that Quicken can retrieve bill amounts and due dates and display that information in Quicken.

When you first select this option, you see the dialog shown in Figure 7-2. Learn about this feature in "Using the Bill Linker" next in this chapter.

Using the Bill Linker

As seen in Figure 7-2, Quicken 2017 can help make your life easier by connecting online bills with your payments. If your vendor allows you to see your bill on their website, you can connect a bill reminder to that online bill.

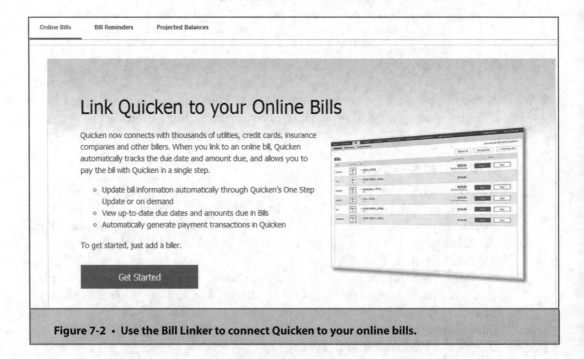

Figure 7-2 • Use the Bill Linker to connect Quicken to your online bills.

Once you select the Online Bills button and click the Get Started link, the Link Bill dialog appears, as seen next. If you do not see the Get Started button, click the Add Reminder button and select Link Reminders To Online Bills from the drop-down list.

Click the drop-down list to select a bill reminder, or select Click Here To Search For Billers That Are Not In The Reminder List Above. When choosing to search for online billers, a list of online billers with which you can link to Quicken appears. Enter the name of the biller as it appears on the biller's website.

Once you have selected a biller, click that biller's name to link your bill. You may be prompted for your Intuit ID. Fill in the user name and password you use with that biller's website. If you have not yet established a user name and password, first connect to that website to set them up. Once your credentials have been verified, your bill is now linked with your vendor, as shown next.

Quicken will automatically retrieve the amount of the bill when it is posted to the website. When you perform a One Step Update or refresh the bill from the Bills tab, the bill is entered into Quicken. While not a true bill "presentment" option where you would get an electronic copy of your bill, Quicken's Bill Linker retrieves the payment due and the due date, and the reminder is updated with that amount and due date. The reminder is not entered until the date you specified in the reminder and the bill is not paid on the biller site, but only through your Quicken program.

To link another bill, select Link Another Bill, or click Close to close the dialog.

Work with Linked Bills

You can edit or remove a linked bill. Select the Bills tab and choose Online Bills. You will see a list of your currently linked bills and three additional options:

- **Update All**   Select this option to update all of your currently linked bills to download the amount and due date for your current bills.
- **Manage Bills**   With this option, you can edit the password on the biller's website or remove a currently linked bill. If you select Remove, Quicken will no longer retrieve bill amounts and due dates; you can still receive and view your bills online at the biller's site.
- **Add New Bill**   Use this option to add another linked bill.

The Bills tab will display the last view you used. If this is the first time you have opened the Bills tab, the view defaults to Online Bills.

Use Bill Reminders

You can view your reminders in your account registers if you have elected to Show Reminders in the account registers, or:

- From the Quicken menu bar when you click Tools | Manage Bill & Income Reminders.
- From the default Main View of the Home tab, in the Stay On Top Of Monthly Bills section, as discussed in the section "Work in the Home Tab's Main View," earlier in this chapter.

Use the Bills tab's Bill Reminders view, shown in Figure 7-3, to view upcoming bills and other scheduled transactions in a number of different ways.

Setting Up Reminders in the Bills Tab

The Bills tab is the place to work with your reminders. The first time you click the Bills tab, it opens to the Online Bills view. Otherwise, when you click the Bills tab, it opens to the last view you used there. If you have not yet set up any reminders or did not download any recurring transactions, you will see a Get Started button in both the Online Bills view and in the Bill Reminders view. If you have already created one or more reminders, select Bill Reminders. You can then click the Add Reminder button and choose from Bill Reminder, Income Reminder, Transfer Reminder, or Link Reminders To Online Bills from the drop-down list.

When you are first working with your Quicken file, you only see the choice to add bill and income reminders. As you add more accounts, you see the Transfer Reminder option.

So, to set up reminders from the Bills tab, click Bill Reminders to see the Stay Ahead Of Your Bills window, as seen in Figure 7-3. Select the Get Started button. The Review Bills dialog displays. If you have not downloaded any transactions that appear to Quicken to be recurring, you will see no bills listed.

1. If you see no bills in the Review Bills dialog, click Add A Bill to open the Add Bill Reminder dialog. (If this is a bill reminder and you have entered payees before, click the drop-down arrow to choose from a list of existing payees. If you are setting up a bill reminder in a new Quicken file, you will probably not yet have any payees on your list.) You may also see the Add Income Reminder link. This opens a similar dialog named Add Income Reminder.

Figure 7-3 • The first snapshot when you choose Bill Reminders in the Bills tab helps you Stay Ahead Of Your Bills.

2. The Add Bill Reminder dialog appears. Enter the payee name in the Pay To field and click Next. From the dialog that appears, enter a date in the Due Next On date field, as seen in the following illustration. You can also choose a date from the calendar to the right of the field.

3. Click Change to set how often you need to be reminded about the bill. The
    Change dialog appears, as shown next. From this dialog, you can change

    Local Power Company
    _____

    Start date: 1/20/2017

    How often: Monthly   Every 1   month on the   20th   Day

    End date: No end date

    OK   Cancel

- The start date.
- How often the item is deducted from your account. Choose an option
  from the drop-down list. Your options are Weekly, Bi-Weekly, Monthly,
  Twice A Month, Quarterly, Yearly, Twice A Year, Only Once, and To Pay
  Estimated Taxes (which follows the IRS estimated tax payment schedule).
  Then set options in the area to the right of the How Often field; the
  options change based on the frequency you select.
- Click the End Date field's drop-down arrow to display the End Date
  options. These specify when the recurring transaction should end.
  - **No End Date**, the default option, keeps the transaction scheduled until
    you delete it or set another option in this dialog.
  - **End On** enables you to set a specific date for the last transaction.
  - **End After** enables you to specify the number of transactions before they
    automatically end or the date on which the payments end. What you
    see will depend on what you enter in the How Often field.

    If all of the information on the Change dialog is correct, click OK to close
    the dialog and return to the Add Bill Reminder dialog.

4. Enter an amount in the Amount Due field, or use the Calculator to the right
    of the Amount Due field. You cannot leave this field blank, but you can
    change the amount when it is time to enter the bill in the register. Enter the
    account from which this bill is to be paid in the From Account field. You
    may also choose from the drop-down list, which will display all of your non-
    hidden accounts.

The drop-down list displays all of your non-hidden accounts, including credit
card, savings, and investing accounts. If you have used an earlier version of
Quicken and hidden some of your accounts, you may need to update how those
accounts are displayed so that you can see them in the Add Reminder dialog.

5. Click anywhere within the Details section to add a category, tag, or memo. (It is best to enter at least the category; that way, each time this reminder is entered into the account register, it will be categorized correctly.) The Category dialog appears:

    •   Type a category or choose one from the drop-down list. You can even split the category—see the split icon to the right of the Category field? (Learn more about splits in Chapter 5.)

    •   Enter a tag if you choose. Review how tags work in Chapter 4.

    •   Enter a memo, such as the account number for this payee.

    •   Click OK to return to the Add Bill Reminder dialog.

6. Click the Optional Settings link to set additional information for this bill. Click the Change link by the Remind Me 3 Days In Advance option to be reminded according to a different time schedule. From this dialog:

    •   Use the up or down arrows to increase or decrease the number of days before the bill is due to be reminded. You can also type in the number of days.

    •   Tell Quicken to enter the bill for you automatically and specify the number of days before the bill is due that you want the bill to be entered.

    •   Tell Quicken to count only business days when calculating the reminder days.

    •   Click OK when you've made your changes to return to the Add Bill Reminder dialog.

7. Click the Add link next to the Related Website option to add the payee's website. Click OK after you have typed the website address to return to the Add Bill Reminder dialog. You can also copy the web address directly from the appropriate website and paste it in the field. This will ensure you don't make a typo when you enter the web address.

8. Click the Change link next to the Estimate Amount For Me option to open the Estimate dialog.

    •   The Fixed Amount option displays a text box you can use to enter a dollar amount that the transaction will always use. You can change the amount when the transaction is entered, if necessary.

    •   Click the drop-down list to choose Previous Payments. This option tells Quicken to create an estimate based on the payments you have made previously. Actually, it's not previous payments, per se; it is previous payments created by entering the bill reminder. If you have not created payments by entering the bill reminder, there will be no data from which to create the estimate.

    •   The other option on the drop-down list is Time Of Year. This is used when you make recurring payments at a specific time of year, such as real estate or other taxes.

If your Quicken file does not have enough data to estimate either Previous Payments or Time Of Year information, you will see a pop-up message telling you this.

9. If you have set any estimates in the Estimate dialog, click OK. Otherwise, click Cancel to close the dialog and return to the Add Reminder dialog.
10. If you use Microsoft Outlook, select the Sync To Outlook check box to synchronize your due date reminder with the Outlook calendar.
11. Select the Print Check With Quicken check box to tell Quicken to print the check for this bill when it is due. Print Check With Quicken records the transaction as a payment using a check to be printed. Entering the transaction, of course, decreases the balance in a banking account. The Check Number field in the account register is set to PRINT, which signals Quicken to include the transaction with other checks to be printed.
12. Click Done to close the Add Bill Reminder dialog and return to the Review Bills dialog, so we can continue creating more reminders or click Next/Done to close the Review Bills dialog and return to the Stack View.

The Stack View of the Bill Reminders view appears as seen in Figure 7-4. This view shows all payments scheduled for the time period you choose in the Due

Figure 7-4 • Use the Stack view in the Bill Reminders view of Quicken's Bills tab to see payments you must make soon.

Within drop-down list. In addition to the options in this view, you have the Add Reminder and Manage Reminders buttons available.

Bills Reminders View

The Bills Reminders button's view, as seen with View As Stack selected in Figure 7-4, shows each upcoming scheduled transaction with a note-like interface. Click one of the reminders, and its details appear in the middle of the window. Use the horizontal scroll bar at the bottom of the window to display upcoming reminders. You can use a transaction's buttons to enter, skip, or edit the transaction. Clicking a Show History button displays a payment history for that payee.

You may change the way the information shows by clicking the View As drop-down list.

- **Stack** displays each item in a "stack" as if they were papers on top of each other. You can use the Due Within Next drop-down list to choose the date range. Your options are 7, 14, and 30 days. You can choose to not include items that have been paid by clearing the Include Paid check box, located to the right of the Due Within Next field.
- **List** displays information about the status, due date, pay to or receive from information, and amount of each reminder. From this view you can enter, edit, or skip the reminder. The Due Within Next and Include Paid options are the same as in the Stack view.
- **Calendar** shows all reminders in a calendar view that includes transactions and their amounts, as well as the ending total banking account balance. You can use the arrows by the current month area to scroll through months.

 You cannot indicate which accounts to include on the Bills tab's Calendar view, even if you have designated those accounts in the full Calendar view. See "Using the Financial Calendar" later in this chapter.

- **Monthly List** shows all scheduled transaction reminders for the current month. You can choose another month by using the arrows to the left and right of the current month.
- The **Account** drop-down list allows you to select the accounts to show in each view, except the Calendar view, which does not have any sort of account selection option available.
- Select the date range for which you want the reminders displayed in the **Due Within Next** drop-down list. You may choose to see what is due for the next 7, next 14, or next 30 days in the Stack view and the next 7, 14, 30, 90 days or 12 months in the List view.

Projected Balances

This option's view, shows projected balances and your upcoming reminders in a list view. While the default is to display all spending accounts, you can select a single account to view from the Select Accounts drop-down list or choose Multiple Accounts to open the Projected Balances selection dialog. This dialog allows you to choose two or more spending or credit card accounts to display. Click the Show (Hidden Accounts) check box to include them in the cash flow view. Click Tools | Manage Hidden Accounts if you don't see the accounts you expect to see here.

NOTE Selecting Multiple Accounts in the Select Accounts drop-down list opens the Customize dialog, where you can select the accounts you wish to include in the Projected Balances graph.

Click Select All to choose all displayed accounts or Clear All to start over with your selection. Click OK to close the dialog.

You may choose a date range to display by clicking the Time Range drop-down list. You may choose the next 7, 14, 30, or 90 days; the next 12 months; or create a customized date range.

The Projected Balances graph snapshot includes all of the accounts you have selected for the date range you select. A legend showing the account or accounts represented in the line graph appears at the bottom of the section. In the Upcoming Bills And Income From *nn/nn/nnnn* to *nn/nn/nnnn* section, you can work with your transaction reminders as follows:

- Click the right-pointing arrow in the circle icon in the Action column to enter, skip, or edit the selected transaction. You will only see the right-pointing arrow in the circle icon for the first instance of the reminder.
- Click the account name in the Account To Use column to be taken to that account's register.
- Click the transaction's amount in the Amount column to open the Edit Reminder dialog.

Working with Reminders

Scheduling a transaction was the hard part. (Not very hard, though, was it?) Entering, editing, and skipping a scheduled transaction is easy. Here's one way that some say is the quickest and easiest to work with reminders.

Click the Bills tab, then click the Bill Reminders button to display the view you prefer, and select a reminder. The options described here may be in the List or Monthly List views, the Calendar date in the Calendar view, or the reminder itself in the Stack view.

While the Calendar view does not feature an Edit button, you can double-click each day's transactions to open a dialog with which you can choose to enter, edit, or skip the transactions.

- **Enter**   If the transaction has not already been entered, the Enter button displays the Enter Transaction dialog. Use this dialog to finalize settings for a transaction. When you click Enter Transaction, the transaction is entered into the account register. The dialog will be labeled Enter *X* Transaction, where *X* is Expense or Income. If a reminder has already been entered, there will be no Enter button displayed. Instead, the button will be Go To Register.
- **Skip**   The Skip button skips the transaction if it has not already been entered into the account register. The transaction moves down in the list, and its due date changes to the next due date. If a reminder has already been entered in the register, there will not be a Skip button.

When you are working with reminders for scheduled transactions, pressing the ENTER button puts the transaction into the proper register as a scheduled payment, while the Skip button tells Quicken to change the reminder to the next date the transaction is scheduled.

- **Edit**   The Edit button displays the Edit Transaction Reminder dialog when the transaction has not yet been entered into the account register. This dialog looks and works very much like the Add Income Reminder dialog shown earlier. Use this dialog to modify settings for the transaction's future entries. If the transaction is an instance of a recurring transaction, the Edit button appears as a menu with the following two options:
  - **Edit This Instance** displays the Edit Reminder dialog that enables you to change the date and amount of the transaction. It also displays a button that will enable you to link the bill with the Bill Linker feature. This is not available in the Calendar view.
  - **Edit This And All Future Instances** displays the Edit Transaction Reminder dialog, as discussed earlier.

The dialog will be titled Edit Bill Reminder, Edit Income Reminder, or Edit Transfer Reminder. You will only see the Edit button without the Edit menu for a reminder that is scheduled to occur only one time. You will not see either the Edit button or the Edit menu if the reminder has already been entered in the account register.

Managing Reminders

In the Bills tab, click Manage Reminders or press CTRL-J to open the Bill And Income Reminders window, as seen in Figure 7-5, which displays both current and future transactions. If you have previously scheduled transactions or repeating online transactions, the Bill And Income Reminders window has four tabs. Until you have created either one or both or if none of your accounts are enabled for Online Bill Pay, there are only two tabs visible.

Bill and Income Reminder Button Options

You can use button options in both the Monthly Bills & Deposits and the All Bills & Deposits tabs to enter, skip, create, edit, or delete scheduled transactions. You must select a transaction to activate all but the Create New option.

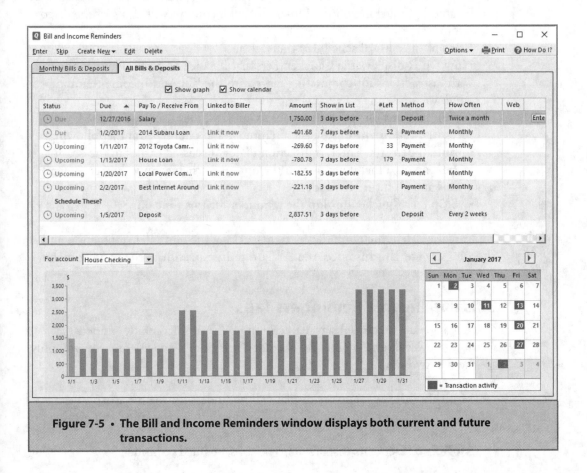

Figure 7-5 • The Bill and Income Reminders window displays both current and future transactions.

- **Enter** opens the Enter [*type of*] Transaction dialog. Enter the appropriate information, and click Enter Transaction. If the reminder is for investment income, you may see a dialog titled Edit Income – Income (Div, Int, etc.).
- **Skip** enables you to skip this payment (or next payment) of that transaction.
- **Create New** enables you to create a new scheduled transaction. See "Setting Up Reminders in the Bills Tab" earlier in this chapter.
- **Edit** opens the Edit Bill (or Income) Reminder dialog in which you can modify each area of the reminder.
- **Delete** removes the scheduled transaction. It does not remove any transactions that have already been entered in a register.
- **Options** offers commands for changing the way the Bill And Income Reminders window is sorted. You can also change the sort order by clicking the Due, Pay To/Receive From, Payments, or Deposits column header. Depending on the tab in which you are working, you may also be able to sort by amount. Clicking on the Linked to Biller column will also sort the listed reminders.
- **Print** prints a list of scheduled transactions.
- **How Do I?** displays the Quicken Personal Finance Software Help window with instructions for completing tasks with the Bill And Income Reminders window.
- **Action buttons** on individual transaction reminders can also be used. To access the action buttons, select a reminder and choose from the following:
  - **Enter** opens the Enter Transaction dialog discussed earlier in the chapter.
  - **Edit** opens a menu giving you the option to change only this reminder or this and all future reminders.
  - **Skip** tells Quicken to skip the reminder for this time only.

 You can also delete the reminder by right-clicking the reminder transaction and choosing Delete This Instance And All Future Instances from the context menu.

Bills and Income Reminders Tabs

There may be up to four tabs available in the Bill And Income Reminders window. However, until you have scheduled some online payments, you will only see the first two tabs.

- **Monthly Bills & Deposits** displays all reminders for the month. You can click the arrows beside the name of the month to view reminders for other months.
- **All Bills & Deposits** displays all types of scheduled reminders.

- **Scheduled** displays the deposits and payments that you have scheduled for this month. Remember, until you have set up an account with Online Payment capabilities, you will not see the Scheduled tab.
- **Repeating Online** lists repeating payments you have scheduled for online payment.

Display Check Boxes   In each tab, two check boxes enable you to display additional information in the window:

- **Show Graph** displays a column chart showing cash flow for selected accounts for the month.
- **Show Calendar** displays one or two calendars (this month and the next month) that indicate scheduled transaction dates.

Schedule These?

You may see a Schedule These? list at the bottom of a Bill And Income Reminders window, as seen in Figure 7-5. When this is present, it displays transactions that Quicken "thinks" you might want to schedule for the future. It builds this list based on categories used in the transactions or transactions you have entered more than once.

- To schedule a transaction in the list, click the Yes button beside it. Quicken displays the Edit Bill (or Income) Reminder dialog so you can turn the transaction into a scheduled transaction.
- To remove a transaction from the list, click the No button beside it.

You will not see the Yes/No buttons until you have selected a suggested reminder in the list.

Scheduling Repeating Online Payments

Some payments are exactly the same every month, such as your rent, a car loan, or your monthly cable television bill. You can set these payments up as repeating online payments.

 The process begins when you schedule the online payment once, indicating the payee, amount, and frequency. Quicken sends the instructions to your bank. Thirty days before the payment is due, your bank creates a new post-dated payment based on your instructions and notifies you that it has created the payment. Quicken automatically enters the payment information in your account register with the appropriate payment date. The payment is delivered on the payment date. This happens regularly, at the interval you specify, until you tell it to stop. Because you don't have to do a thing to continue paying regularly, the more payments you make with this feature, the more time you save.

1. From the Bills tab, choose Add Reminders | Bill Reminder.
2. Enter the name of your payee in the Pay To field. Click Next.
3. In the Add Bill Reminder dialog, set the date, the amount, and the account from which you will be paying this bill. Be sure to choose an account in which you have activated Online Bill Pay.
4. Enter a category, tag, or memo if necessary.
5. Click the Use Online Bill Pay check box. If you don't see the Use Online Bill Pay check box, you have not selected an account that is enabled for online bill pay.
6. Click Optional Settings if necessary to display your options. Click the Make This A Repeating Online Payment check box. If you have made the payment a repeating online payment, you cannot ask Quicken to remind you to enter the payment or estimate the amount of the payment.
7. Click Done.

If this is a new online payee, Quicken prompts you to enter address and account number information so that your payment can be processed by your bank.

There are two very important things to remember when using the Add A Reminder dialog to create a repeating online payment:

- Click the Use Online Bill Pay check box to tell Quicken that the payment will be made online.
- Click the Make This A Repeating Online Payment check box if you choose. This tells Quicken to send one instruction for multiple repeating payments.

When you click Done to save the payment instruction, it appears in the Repeating Online tab of the Bill And Income Reminders dialog. You can use the buttons at the top of the Bill And Income Reminders dialog to work with items listed in the Repeating Online list window. In each instance, if you have not clicked a transaction to select it, the appropriate button option is grayed out even if there is only one online transaction in the Repeating Online list.

- **Enter** records the selected repeating online payment in the register.
- **Skip** skips payment of the selected repeating online payment.
- **Create New** enables you to create a new scheduled transaction or paycheck.

- **Edit** displays the Edit Repeating Online dialog so you can modify the details of the repeating online payment.
- **Delete** removes the repeating online payment from the list, thus canceling future payments. You must click Delete in the confirmation dialog that appears to remove the transaction, as well as run a One Step Update to send the instruction to your bank.
- **Options** offers commands for changing the sort order of payments in the list; however, you may have to click the header of the column by which you want to sort to make it sort properly.
- **Print** prints a list of repeating online payments.
- **How Do I?** displays the Quicken Personal Finance Software Help window with instructions for managing your spending and completing tasks with the Bill And Income Reminders list.

Stopping a Single Repeating Online Payment

In the Online Center window's Payments tab, select the payment you want to stop, and click the Cancel Payment button. Click Yes in the confirmation dialog that appears. Use the Update/Send button to send the cancel payment instruction. Note that the payment may not appear in the Online Center window unless you have reviewed and approved all downloaded payment transactions, as explained in Chapter 6.

Stopping All Future Payments for a Repeating Online Payment

Press CTRL-J to open the Bill And Income Reminders window. In the Repeating Online tab of the Bill And Income Reminders window, select the payment you want to stop, and click Delete. Click Delete in the confirmation dialog that appears. The transaction is removed from the list. Then use the Update/Send button in the Online Center window to send the cancel payment instruction.

Using QuickFill and Memorized Payees

As you enter transactions, Quicken is quietly working in the background, memorizing transaction information for each payee. It creates a database of memorized payees. It then uses the memorized payees for its QuickFill feature. QuickFill works in two ways:

- When you enter the first few characters of a payee name in the Write Checks or account register window, Quicken immediately fills in the rest of the name. When you advance to the next text box or field of the entry form,

Quicken fills in the rest of the transaction information based on the last transaction for that payee. The search looks for the letters you type anywhere in the payee name.

- You can select a memorized payee from the drop-down list in the Payee field of the Write Checks or account register window. Quicken then fills in the rest of the transaction information based on the last transaction for that payee.

QuickFill entries include amounts, categories, and memos. They can also include splits and tags. For example, you might pay the cable or satellite company for television service monthly. The bill is usually the same amount each month. The second time you create an entry with the company's name, Quicken fills in the rest of the transaction automatically. You can make adjustments to the amount or other information as desired and save the transaction. It may have taken a minute or so to enter the transaction the first time, but it'll take only seconds to enter it every time after that.

By default, the QuickFill feature is set up to work as discussed here. If it does not, check the QuickFill options to make sure they are set properly. To check these options:

1. Click Edit | Preferences | Register | Data Entry And QuickFill.
2. Ensure all of the check boxes are selected in the QuickFill and Memorized Payees section.
3. Click OK to close Quicken Preferences.

EXPERIENCED USERS RECOMMEND

If you use memorized transactions and the QuickFill feature is completing more information than you want it to, edit the transaction in the Memorized Payee List. For example, if you pay activity fees for each of your children to the local community center, you may want to use a different memo for each child's dues. After you have memorized the transaction, open the Memorized Payee List and clear out the Memo field or Tag fields. Then, click the Lock check box. Use either the keyboard shortcut CTRL-T or select Tools | Memorized Payee List to access the list.

 You could also memorize the payee with a different memo for each child or create a tag for each one. Learn more about tags in Chapter 4.

To show the Lock column in the Memorized Payee List, click Options and click Show Locked Status Column In List. Each time you enter the transaction, just change or enter the information that is different from the transaction that has been memorized.

Utilizing the Memorized Payee List

If desired, you can view a list of your memorized payees. Just choose Tools | Memorized Payee List or press CTRL-T. The list displays the last transaction you entered for each payee. (Depending on the type or category for a specific memorized payee, you may see more than just the last transaction in the Memorized Payee List.)

If a payee does not appear on the Memorized Payee List and you believe it should, check your Preferences. Click Edit | Preferences | Data Entry And QuickFill.

Select a memorized payee to display the Edit and Delete action buttons. Edit displays the Edit Memorized Payee dialog for the currently selected transaction. You will also see the Report button when you select a memorized payee.

- The **Payee Name** field displays the payee name as it is currently entered. You may change the name or any of the other fields as required.
- The **Type Of Transaction** field is established when you set up the payee.
- The **Category** field allows you to set or change the category for this memorized payee, as well as set up split categories.
- You can change the **Tag**, **Memo**, and **Amount** fields or leave them blank. The **Never Auto-categorize This Payee During QuickFill Or Downloads** option tells Quicken you wish to enter the proper category for this payee.
- Click **Lock** to leave this memorized payee unchanged when transactions for this payee are entered or edited in the account register. It will not ensure the memorized payee stays blank, however, unless you saved the memorized payee with blanks—for example, the Category field in the memorized payee will remain blank if you saved it with no category selected.
- **Show This Payee In The Calendar Memorized Payee List**, which is selected by default, determines how this item is displayed in the Calendar. See "Using the Financial Calendar" later in this chapter.

If the two check boxes do not appear, select the Options button and click Show Locked Status Column In List and Show Calendar Status Column In List.

- When you have selected a payee, **Delete** displays a dialog asking you to confirm that you really do want to delete the selected item. If you delete the transaction, it is removed from the Memorized Payee List only, not from any register in the Quicken data file.
- With a selected payee, click **Edit** to open the Edit Memorized Payee dialog box from which you can make any necessary changes.

- The **Memorized Payee Report** icon is hard to see. It is located to the right of the Delete button in a selected payee. Click this icon, seen here, to open and print a Payee Report about this payee.

You can also use the Memorized Payee List as follows:

1. Open the register from which the item will be paid, and click the next available line. Use the CTRL-T keyboard shortcut to open the Memorized Payee List.
2. Right-click the memorized payee transaction you want to use.
3. From the context menu that appears, click Use to paste the item into your register.
4. Click Save or use the ALT-A keyboard shortcut to save the transaction.

You may want to build a Memorized Payee List from all of your existing cash flow accounts. To do so:

1. From the menu bar, click Tools.
2. Hold down CTRL-SHIFT and click Memorized Payee List.
3. Your new Memorized Payee List displays.

Memorized Payee List Activities

You can use buttons at the bottom of the Memorized Payee window, as seen next, to change what displays in the list and add, merge, rename, or delete memorized payees on the Memorized Payee List:

- **New Payee** displays the Create Memorized Payee dialog, which is similar to the Edit Memorized Payee dialog. You use the Create Memorized Payee dialog to create brand-new transactions without actually entering them into any register of your Quicken data file. Just fill in the fields to enter transaction information, and click OK. The new transaction appears in the Memorized Payee List window.
- **Options** opens a menu that allows you to choose to display the "Lock" and the "Show On Calendar" columns in the Memorized Payee List. Click View Locked Items Only to display locked memorized payees only.

- **Merge/Rename** displays the Merge And Rename Payees dialog, which you can use to enter a new name for the selected payee. When you enter the new name, the Add A Renaming Rule dialog appears. Enter the new payee name, choose either If A Payee Contains or If Quicken Name Is from the drop-down list, and click OK.
- Use the **Delete** button to delete one or more payees from the list. You must first select the memorized payees to be deleted.
- The **Renaming Rules** button opens the Renaming Rules dialog, covered in Chapter 6.
- The question mark icon opens the **Quicken Personal Finances Help** window with additional information for completing tasks with the Memorized Payee List window.
- The printer icon opens the **Print** dialog with which you can print the Memorized Payee List.
- Click Done to close the Memorized Payee List.

Use the CTRL-M keyboard shortcut after you have entered a transaction to memorize the payee and the category.

Using the Financial Calendar

Quicken's Calendar, shown in Figure 7-6, keeps track of all your transactions, past and future, by date. You may open the Calendar by choosing Tools | Calendar or by pressing CTRL-K.

Calendar Buttons

You can use buttons to work with the calendar's contents:

- **Today** (new in Quicken 2017) enables you to select today's date in the calendar.
- **Go To Date** enables you to go to a specific calendar date. Click the Calendar icon to open a tiny calendar, and select the date you want. Or, enter the date in the Go To Date field and click the Go button.

You can also use date field keyboard shortcuts, like M for the first of the month, T for today, and H for the end of the month. Learn more about keyboard shortcuts in Appendix A.

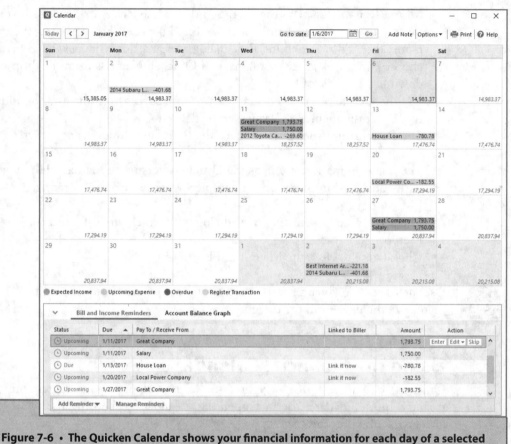

Figure 7-6 • **The Quicken Calendar shows your financial information for each day of a selected month.**

- **Arrow buttons** by the date and month names enable you to move from one month to another.
- **Add Note** enables you to enter a note for a selected date. You can even change the color of your note. The Note icon then appears on the Calendar on the date you select. After you have selected the color of your note, check your monitor settings. Depending on your monitor, the icon may be hard to see!
- **Options** offers commands for viewing and working with the contents of the Calendar window.
- **Print** opens the Print dialog from which you can print the Calendar.
- **Help** displays the Quicken Personal Finance Software Help window with information about using the Calendar.

The Transactions Window

When you double-click a calendar date (or single-click an already selected date), the Transactions window, which lists all the transactions for that date, appears, as seen in the following illustration. You can use the buttons in the Transactions window to work with transactions:

- **Enter** opens the Enter Expense Transaction dialog from which you can enter the selection into the register. If the transaction has already been entered into the account register, this button changes to Go To Register and opens that transaction in the register where it is entered.
- **Edit** enables you to modify the currently selected transaction. If this transaction has not been entered into the register, the Edit <*type*> Reminder dialog displays, where <*type*> is income, bill, or transfer. If it has been entered into the register, the Edit Register Transaction dialog appears.
- **Delete** removes the selected transaction. This option is only available for transactions that have already been entered into the register and does not appear in this illustration.
- **Skip** lets you skip the transaction for this date. This option is only available for transactions that have not been entered.
- **Schedule** enables you to create a new scheduled transaction based on the selected transaction. This option is only available if the currently selected transaction is not a scheduled transaction. Unfortunately, the payee name is not transferred from the selected transaction to the Add Reminder dialog. You must type in or select the payee name from the drop-down list.
- The **Help** icon opens Quicken Help at the section explaining how to work with the Calendar.
- **Add** enables you to enter a new transaction. From this menu you can add an expense or income transaction as well as a new reminder.
- **Close** closes the window.

   The dollar amounts that appear in the bottom of each calendar date box show the total account balances for the accounts displayed in the window after taking all payments into consideration. (You can specify which accounts to include by choosing Select Calendar Accounts from the Options menu in the button bar.) This feature works, in effect, like a simplified forecasting tool.

Useful Quicken Features

In addition to the Bill and Income Reminders, Memorized Payees, and QuickFill, Quicken offers a number of other useful functions to help you with your financial recordkeeping.

Minding Your Bills

Quicken's optional Billminder feature makes it possible for you to monitor upcoming bills and scheduled transactions without starting Quicken. This application displays a window that summarizes upcoming transactions. It also includes a convenient button to run Quicken, should you decide to take action on a listed item.

How you open Billminder depends on your operating system:

- **Windows 7 and earlier**   Choose Start | All Programs | Quicken 2017 | Billminder.
- **Windows 8.1**   Choose the Billminder tile located near your Quicken 2017 app.
- **Windows 10**   Choose Start | All Apps. Scroll to Quicken 2017. Click the downward pointing arrow and choose Billminder.

To make the most of Billminder, you may want to configure it so it automatically starts each time you start your computer. To do this, click the Options button in the Billminder button bar to display Billminder Options as shown here. Select the Enable Billminder On Windows Startup check box. You can set other configuration options as desired to determine when Billminder should appear. Then click OK. Click Exit to close Billminder.

Using the Paycheck Setup Wizard

Quicken's Paycheck Setup Wizard feature offers yet another way to automate transactions. You use it to enter information about your regular payroll check and its deductions. Then, when payday comes along, Quicken automatically enters the payroll deposit information based on the Paycheck Setup transaction.

Quicken allows you to set up your recurring paycheck so that all the deductions can be fed into the appropriate categories. There are three ways to access the Paycheck Setup Wizard.

1. From the Planning tab, select Tax Center and from below the Taxable Income YTD section, click the Add Paycheck button.
2. From the Tools menu, click Manage Bill & Income Reminders | Create New | Income Reminder and choose the Paycheck Setup Wizard at the bottom of the dialog.
3. Some experienced Quicken users prefer to use the Classic menus instead of Standard menus as these menus offer easy access to the Paycheck Setup Wizard. Click View | Classic Menus | and then click Bills | Add Reminder | Paycheck Reminder. Until you have selected Classic Menus, you will not see the Bills menu.

In all cases, the Paycheck Setup Wizard appears as shown in Figure 7-7. As you can see, you can choose to enter either the net amount of your paycheck or the

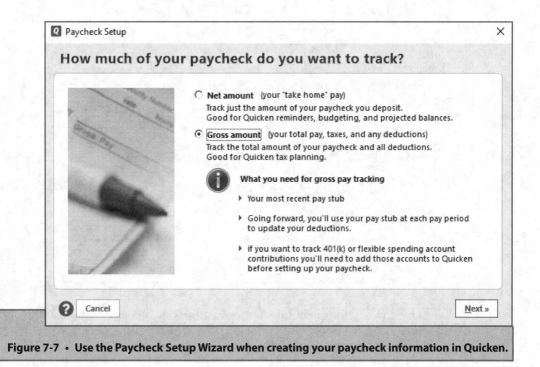

Figure 7-7 • Use the Paycheck Setup Wizard when creating your paycheck information in Quicken.

gross amount, which will help you track tax and other deductions. In the example outlined next, we have chosen to record the gross payroll. Quicken says that you will need your most recent paycheck and that you'll need to add any 401(k) accounts to Quicken before you begin.

1. Once you have all the required information at hand and have entered any 401(k) or other accounts in Quicken, from the Paycheck Setup screen, select Gross Amount and then click Next.

2. Select the paycheck owner (you or your spouse), and type the name of the company from whom you earn the paycheck. Press TAB to move to the Memo field. Type any additional information in this optional field, for example, if you receive two checks, one for base pay and one for commissions. Click Next to open the Track Paycheck dialog, shown here.

3. Click the Account field down arrow, and select the bank account into which this income is deposited. Press TAB, ENTER, or select the payment date, indicate whether you want it automatically entered or just a reminder. You

can also change your mind and choose to track your net pay only by selecting the Track Net Only button.

4. Scroll down and click Edit or Amount opposite Salary to open the Amount field. Enter the gross amount of income you receive. If you do not receive the same amount each time, enter an average.

5. If you have other components of your income, such as a regular bonus or commissions, click Add Earning, select the category of other earnings, enter the amount, and click OK.

6. If you have pre-tax deductions, such as 401(k) contributions, click Add Pre-Tax Deduction, select the category, select the account, enter both the contribution and employer-matching amounts, if applicable, and click OK.

 Depending on your company's insurance plan, some health insurance premiums are deducted after taxes, not before.

By entering deduction information from your regular paycheck, Quicken can create tax reports, help you plan for taxes, and export information to TurboTax for year-end tax reporting.

7. Click in the amount field next to each of the tax items that are on your pay stub and enter the amount as shown next. If you want to make any changes to the name and category, click Edit, make the changes, and click OK. However, it is best to stay with the standard tax categories, as Quicken has already linked those categories with the proper tax-line items.

Name	Category	Amount		
Federal Tax	Tax:Fed	455.00	Edit	Delete
State Tax	Tax:State	45.00	Edit	Delete
Social Security (FICA)	Tax:Soc Sec	155.00	Edit	Delete
Medicare Tax	Tax:Medicare	36.25	Edit	Delete
Disability (SDI)	Tax:SDI	15.00	Edit	Delete
Total		706.25		

Add Tax Item ▼

∨   **After-Tax Deductions**

Done   Cancel

8. Click After-Tax Deductions, which can include health insurance and stock purchases, correct the name if needed, select the category you want to use

to collect this deduction, enter the amount, and click OK. Repeat this for multiple deductions.

9. If you want to split your paycheck deposit over two or more accounts, click Add Deposit Account, select the additional account, type any memo information you want, enter the amount of your paycheck that will go into that account, and click OK.

10. When you have entered all of the paycheck information you want to track, click Done to close the Track Paycheck dialog.

11. Quicken asks if you want to enter year-to-date information. If you choose to enter that data, click OK, click in each of the Year To Date amount fields, type the requested information, and, when you've entered all the data you choose to include, click Enter to close the dialog box. Otherwise, click I Do Not Want To Enter This Information, and click OK. You can view or edit the Year To Date amounts in the Tax Planner. The Tax Planner is covered in Chapter 14.

A Closer Look at the Spending Tab

By now, you may agree that entering financial information into Quicken Personal Finance Software is a great way to organize it. However, sometimes organizing information isn't enough. Sometimes you need to see concise summaries of the information you entered in the form of balances, activity reports, and graphs.

Quicken provides the kind of information you're looking for in the form of snapshots, reports, and graphs. The next sections discuss Quicken's Spending tab by telling you about the snapshots of the information found there and how you can take advantage of its alerts. You can create, modify, and save standard and custom reports and graphs for all Quicken tabs. See Chapter 15 for detailed information about creating Quicken reports.

The Spending tab offers a place for examining the results of your work with your banking accounts. In the following section, you will go on a guided tour of the Spending tab's reporting and graphing features so you can take advantage of all of the elements found in that section of Quicken.

Exploring the Spending Graph

When you click the Spending tab, a graph appears that displays the total amount you have spent from all of your banking accounts for the period you choose. While the default is the last 30 days, we have chosen to show the last 12 months (see Figure 7-8). The top of the window shows the total in all categories. Next is a

| ▸ ACCOUNTS | | C + ✿ | | HOME | SPENDING | BILLS | PLAN | INVEST | PROPERTY | | BUSINESS | RENTAL | ADD-ON | MOBILE | MORE |

Transactions

View Guidance | Reports ▾

| All accounts ▾ | Last 12 Months ▾ | Spending without t ▾ | Reset |

Search 🔍

Last 12 Months

$23,481

in all categories
Percent of total: 100%

Category	Amount	Percent
Education	$3,794.24	16.16%
Bills & Utilities	$3,790.27	16.14%
Home	$3,305.09	14.08%
Shopping	$2,421.58	10.31%
Food & Dining	$2,202.36	9.38%
Maintenance	$1,782.74	7.59%
Repair	$1,386.15	5.90%
Auto & Transport	$942.66	4.01%
Gifts & Donations	$859.28	3.66%
Health & Fitness	$745.00	3.17%
Loan Payment	$610.25	2.60%
[House Loan]	$312.27	1.33%
[2014 Subaru Loan]	$293.66	1.25%
Subscriptions	$270.00	1.15%
Total	**$23,480.71**	

Date	Payee	Category		Amount	✿
1/2/2017	2014 Subaru Loan	--Split--	✓✗	-401.68 Save ✿ ◁ ▸

151 Transactions | | | | Total: | -23,480.71 |

Figure 7-8 • **Use the Spending tab information to generate a number of graphs and reports for a specific time period.**

colorful donut chart with a legend to the right explaining the category associated with each of the "donut slices." The lower part of the window displays the transactions in register format.

If you choose to hide an account from the Transaction Entry List in the Display Options tab and its name in the Account Bar and Account List, the account will not show on the Account Bar, but will show in the Spending tab list of accounts. (Accounts you have designated as Keep Separate will not show in the Spending tab list of accounts, but you can choose them using the Custom entry in the Accounts drop-down list.)

Account Filter

The Accounts drop-down list lets you decide which accounts to display in the Spending graph. You can choose from the following:

- All Accounts includes all of the accounts that appear in the Banking section of the Account Bar.

If you pay from a brokerage account, you must use the Custom account setting from the drop-down list and select the account from that list.

- All Checking/Savings/Cash/Credit Cards includes the accounts you have so named in Quicken.
- At the bottom of the drop-down list, all of your banking accounts are listed so that you can choose to use just one in your Spending graph.
- Choose Custom to open the Customize dialog, which allows you to choose more than one account to display in your graph. You can choose to display all of your accounts, even your hidden ones, by selecting Show (Hidden Accounts) and Select All. The Customize dialog lists all of your accounts, not just your banking accounts.

If you do not have any accounts designated as Keep Separate, you will not see Show Hidden Accounts. If you do have one or more accounts designated as Keep Separate, you will see the Show Hidden check box. Upon checking the Show Hidden check box, you will see those hidden accounts in the list enclosed in parentheses.

If you don't see the accounts you expected, use the Manage Hidden Accounts dialog to change your account settings. From the menu bar, select Tools | Manage Hidden Accounts.

Date Filter

While the default for your Spending graph is the last 30 days, you can use this drop-down list to choose any time period you wish. The pre-set options are as follows:

- **All Dates**, which includes every date for which you have entered a transaction into Quicken.
- **This Month**, which displays just the spending you've done since the first of the current month and includes future-dated transactions that occur in the selected month.
- **Last Month** includes your expenditures in the last calendar month.
- **Last 30/60/90 Days** options are self-explanatory.
- **Last 12 Months** includes all of your expenditures for the last 365 days (or 366 days in leap years).
- **This Quarter** includes the information from the first day of this calendar quarter through the end of the calendar quarter.
- **Last Quarter** presents your spending for the most recent calendar quarter before this quarter.
- **This Year** presents all of your spending through the end of the current year, starting with January 1.

- **Last Year** displays all of last year's spending.
- **Custom** lets you set the date range for your graph.

This Month, This Quarter, and This Year display all of the spending for those respective time periods, even future-dated transactions. For example, if today is 10/05/2017 and you have entered a transaction dated 10/30/2017, the transaction will show in the spending for This Month, This Quarter, and This Year.

Transaction Types Filter

The Income/Spending drop-down list has three options. You can choose to show how much you have spent without taxes (Spending Without Taxes), how much you have spent in total (Spending), or how much has been added to your accounts (Income).

Reset Button

The Reset button, located to the right of the Spending/Income drop-down list, resets your graph to the default of All Accounts, Last 30 Days, and Spending Without Taxes.

Search Field

Enter a category or payee name in the Search field at the far right of the Spending tab view. After you have typed in the name, the register displays the category, payee, or account name that you have entered. The register will show all of the transactions with that name for the time period and accounts you have selected. Click the X to clear the field.

If the matched transactions correspond with the graph settings, the graph updates to show the totals for the matched transactions. For example, if the graph setting is This Year and Spending and your search matches spending from this year, the graph will update to show the matched spending. If you instead searched for income, the spending graph displays "You have no spending in the selected date range or the total may be positive."

Using the Spending Register

The register shown at the bottom of the Spending tab's Transaction view displays all of the transactions from the accounts you have chosen in the Accounts drop-down list at the top of the Spending graph. You may choose to include an Account column, in which Quicken displays the account into which the

transaction was entered. To show this column, click the
Register Columns gear icon and select Account.

By default, this register is sorted by date, with the
earliest date first. If you have chosen more than one
account, the amounts shown in the Total column may
not be useful. However, if you want to know how
much you've spent at a particular store, use the Search
field and set the Account filter to All Accounts. After
you type in the name of that specific store, the total you
have spent for the time period you have set will display
at the bottom of the register in the Total column.

You can tell Quicken which columns to display and
which columns to hide. To access the list of Register
Columns, click the small gear icon at the upper-right
corner of the register. When you click the icon, the
Register Columns list will appear as shown here. Click
the check box for each column you want the register
to display. Clear each check box for columns you don't
want to use. When you have finished your selections,
click Done. If you find you do not like the way your
selections look, click the gear icon once more and, at
the bottom-left corner of the column list, click the
gear icon drop-down arrow and click Reset To Default
Columns. Once again, click Done to close the list.

 Your Register Columns list may not look the same as the one in the illustration.
Listed items and order vary by the type of account and the services you have
activated on each account.

You can adjust the width of each of the register columns by placing your cursor
on the line between two columns and dragging to the left or right. The default
one-line display shows the Date, Payee, Category, and Amount columns. You can
display additional columns by selecting from the Register Columns list. Click the
gear icon at the right of the register to display the list.

The Spending Tab's Register

The register you see in the Spending tab is different from the individual registers
you see for each banking and credit card account. The register you see may

contain information from more than one account, depending on your settings in the Account filter's drop-down list. To print from the Spending tab register, press CTRL-P to open the Print Register dialog. The date range will be the range you set in the Date Filter's drop-down list. To change the date range, adjust the date filter in the Spending tab. You see only the default columns in the printout, not any columns you have elected to show optionally, such as Account.

The Reports Button

The Reports button in the Spending tab makes it easy for you to print a variety of reports. See Chapter 15 for an overview of the reports that Quicken can produce for you.

Creating the Address Book

Quicken's Address Book feature stores the address information you enter when using the Write Checks window. You can also use this feature to modify or delete existing information or add new records. Keeping track of addresses with the Address Book makes it easy to insert addresses when writing checks and to look up contact information when you need to follow up on transactions.

Choose Tools | Address Book to display the Address Book window. This window lists all of the records in the Address Book.

Address Book window showing records.

The window contains:

Address Book : <All Groups>

Payee	Street	City ▲	State	Zip	Country	Attn Line	Email
General Hospital	101 N Main	Anytown	WA	95668			
Orthopedic Sur...	P O Box 770	Anytown	WA	95066			
Chevron/Texaco ...	P O Box 530950	Atlanta	GA	30353...			
Local Power Co...	BOT-01H//PO ...	Bellingview	CA	98009...			
Commerical Indu...	1601 114th Ave...	City	IA	98004			
Bank Of America	P O Box 60069	City of In...	CA	91716			
Local Telephone...	P O Box 329	Langley	VA	36822			

You can use buttons and menus to work with Address Book window contents as shown here.

- The **Group** drop-down list lets you choose between All Groups and any other groups you have established within Quicken.
- The **Column Sets** drop-down list lets you view each of the various Address Book tabs in a columnar display. There are different columns in each column set. Each column set allows you to display different Address Book record data.
- **New** opens the Edit Address Book Record from which you can enter a new entry to the Address Book.
- **Edit** enables you to edit the selected record.
- **Delete** removes the Address Book record. It does not affect transactions that used the deleted Address Book record.
- **Options** opens a menu with which you can work with your Address Book entries:
  - **Switch Names And Organization** swaps the name you have entered as a contact into the Organization field in the Contact tab of the Address Book record.
  - **Switch Payee & Secondary Addresses** changes an address you have entered as the primary address to a secondary address.
  - **Format Address** opens a dialog with which you can format how the payee's address will appear on the checks you print.
  - **Assign To Groups** opens a dialog with which you can assign this payee to a group within Quicken.
  - **Select All/Select None** selects all or none of the payees in the Address Book.
- The **Help icon** displays the Help window with instructions for working with the Address Book.
- **Print** offers commands for printing Address Book record information.

 Depending on your printer, you may be able to print envelopes from this section.

Adding or Modifying Address Book Records

To add a new Address Book record, click the New button in the Address Book window. The Edit Address Book Record dialog, shown next, appears. You also use the Edit Address Book Record dialog to edit an existing record. Simply select the record in the Address Book window, and click the Edit button in the button bar. You can also double-click the entry to open it if you choose.

The Edit Address Book Record dialog has five tabs for recording information. Click a tab to display its options, and then enter the information you want to store. Here's what you can enter in each of the five tabs:

- **Payee** is for the information that would normally appear in a Write Checks window, as well as some additional contact information. From this tab, you can also tell Quicken to include this payee in other lists.
- **Contact** is for the name, title, phone numbers, and website of a specific person.
- **Secondary** is for a secondary mailing address and e-mail address.
- **Personal** is for personal information, such as spouse and children's names, birthday and anniversary, an ID number if you need one, and still more phone numbers.
- **Miscellaneous** is for additional information, such as user-defined fields and notes. Click OK to save your entry.

Printing Entry Information

You can print the information in the list in three formats: list, labels, and envelopes.

Start by selecting a group from the Group drop-down list at the top of the Address Book window. From the group of records that displays, select a payee or several payees whose information you want to print. To change the format of a specific record, choose that record and click Options | Format Address to open the Format Print Check Address dialog. Set the options and click OK.

From the Address Book window, click the Print icon to open a drop-down list of printing options. These options are List, Labels, and Envelopes.

- **List** Choose List to display a Print dialog just like the one that appears when printing Quicken reports. Use it to enter printing options, and then click Print to print the list.
- **Labels** Choose Labels to display the Print Labels dialog. It includes a list of commonly used Avery label products; be sure to select the right one. Then select from the Contact To Print at the bottom of the Print Labels dialog. Click Print to open another Print Labels dialog from which you select the printer you want to use. Make sure you have label stock in the printer and choose the orientation of your labels, either Portrait or Landscape. Select Print Preview to see how your printed labels will look and click Print to print your labels.
- **Envelopes** Choosing Envelopes displays the Print Envelope dialog. Use it to print #10 envelopes for Address Book records. To print your envelopes:

  1. Select the payees for which the envelopes are to be printed.
  2. Click the Print icon and select Envelopes.
  3. From the Print Envelope dialog, you may print either the contacts you have selected or select Print All Contacts to create envelopes for everyone in the group.
  4. Click Print Return Address if you want a return address printed on your envelopes. Select the return address.
  5. Click Print to open the Quicken Print Envelopes dialog. Your default printer appears in the Print To section.
  6. Select either a Horizontal or Vertical feed, depending on your printer's envelope printer. Set the Margin Offsets if necessary.
  7. If you want to use another printer, select Printer Setup and choose another printer.
  8. Click Font if you want to change the size of the printed information.
  9. Ensure you have envelopes in your printer's envelope feeder. When you have made your choices, click OK to print your envelopes.
  10. Click Done to close the Address Book window.

About Alerts

When you're juggling multiple bank, credit card, and investment accounts along with taxes, reminders, and several insurance policy renewal dates, Quicken's Alerts feature can really help you keep your sanity. After all, who can keep track of all those balances and keep them where they should be? Quicken can! Financial superstar!

The Alerts feature can also prevent embarrassment at a checkout counter by warning you when a credit card balance is getting dangerously close to its limit. Likewise, it can remind you to pay your credit card bill so even if your balance is relatively low, you won't forget to make that monthly payment on time.

This section discusses the kinds of alerts Quicken offers and explains how to set them up.

Viewing Available Alerts Groups

Quicken offers four different groups of items for which you can set alerts. To enable them, open the Tools menu, and choose Alerts Center. Click the Setup tab, as seen in Figure 7-9, and then open the group with which you want to work. Here's an explanation of the alerts you can set in each group.

Banking Alerts

- **Account Min. Balances** enables you to set minimum balances for your checking and savings accounts. Quicken alerts you when the account balance falls below the reminder amount you specify.
- **Account Max. Balances** enables you to set maximum balances for your checking and savings accounts. Quicken alerts you when the account balance climbs above the amount you specify.
- **Credit Card Limits** enables you to set limits for your credit card accounts. You can set a limit amount and a reminder amount. Quicken alerts you if the balance exceeds the reminder amount.
- **Check Reorder Notice** tells Quicken to alert you when you reach a certain check number.
- **Monthly Expenses** enables you to specify maximum monthly spending amounts for any Quicken expense category. If you exceed the limit you specified, Quicken alerts you to the fact.
- **Savings Goals** tells Quicken to alert you when you fall behind on a savings goal. This option works directly with Quicken's Savings Goals feature, which you learn about in Chapter 13.

Figure 7-9 • The Alerts Center's Setup tab helps you manage alerts.

- **Online Services Available** tells Quicken to alert you when one of your financial institutions supports Online Account Services.

In addition, Quicken offers three other General group reminder alerts that fall in the banking group:

- **Online Transactions** tells Quicken to remind you to download transactions from your financial institution if you haven't done so for 30 days or more.
- **Scheduled Bills Or Deposits Due Soon** tells Quicken to remind you in advance of any scheduled transactions that are due.
- **Send To Quicken.com** tells Quicken to remind you to export your portfolio to Quicken.com when holdings change.

Investing and Tax Alerts

Chapter 9 discusses setting the Investing group alerts while you can see Chapter 14 for a discussion on the three Taxes group alerts that are available for your use.

General Alerts

In addition to the three alerts discussed earlier in this section in "Banking Alerts," you can set alerts for the following:

- **Insurance Reappraisal**   Use this alert to remind you of insurance policy renewal dates and to ensure that your current coverage amounts are up to date.
- **Mortgage Reappraisal**   This is a particularly useful alert if your mortgage has a variable interest rate, requires a balloon payment, or requires other, periodic attention.

Setting Up Alerts

You set up alerts from the Setup tab of the Alerts Center window. Click the name of one of the alerts to view and set it. To set an alert, select the name of the alert on the left side of the window. If necessary, click the check box to select it. Then click the value you want to change on the right side of the window and enter a new value. Not all alerts have values you can change; for example, the Online Services Available alert is a simple on or off setting made with the check mark.

You can tell Quicken how to notify you with the options in the bottom half of the Setup window.

- **Text In The Alert List** displays the alert as an item in an Alerts snapshot only, which you can see in the Alerts Center Show All tab and when you add alerts to another view.
- **Urgent (Pop Up Dialog Box)** displays the alert in a dialog when you first start Quicken each day.
- **Keep The Alert In The List For** lets you tell Quicken how long the alert should remain in the Alerts snapshot. The default setting is One Month, but you can use the drop-down list to choose One Day, One Week, One Month, One Quarter, or One Year.

When you're completely finished setting alerts, click OK to close the Alerts Center window. The alerts will work quietly in the background, watching your financial dealings. When it's time to go to work, they appear as you specified.

Working with Alerts

Once you've set up alerts, you can view, modify, or delete them as desired. Here's how:

- **Viewing Alerts**   View alerts in the Show All tab of the Alerts Center window. Click Tools | Alerts Center | Show All to display them.
- **Modifying Alerts**   Change the way an alert works at any time. Open the Tools menu, and choose Alerts Center | Setup. Then follow the instructions in the previous section titled "Setting Up Alerts" to change alert settings.
- **Deleting Alerts**   To delete an alert, display the Show All tab of the Alerts Center. Click the Delete button beside each alert you want to delete. A confirmation dialog appears. Click OK to delete the alert.

To prevent a deleted alert from appearing again, use the Setup tab of the Alerts Center window to clear the check box for the alert in the list on the left side of the window.

You can select multiple alerts and click one of the selected Delete buttons to delete all of the selected alerts. To select multiple alerts, click the first alert, then hold down SHIFT and click the last alert you want to delete. Click any of the Delete buttons within the highlighted selection.

Banking and Reconciling

Chapter 8

In This Chapter:

- *Starting a reconciliation*

- *Comparing transactions to a paper statement*

- *Identifying reconciled items*

- *Finishing up*

- *Reconciling credit card accounts*

- *Printing a reconciliation report*

- *Undoing reconciled transactions*

Once you have set up your banking and credit card accounts, it is important that you reconcile your Quicken information to that shown by your financial institution. Often, the task of reconciling or manually balancing your bank account each month is not your favorite chore. However, you may open your bank statement each month and, using the paper form and a calculator, total all the checks and deposits. There's a lot of adding when it comes to totaling the outstanding checks and deposits, and the longer you wait to do the job, the more adding you'll need to do. And for some reason, it hardly ever comes out right the first time you try. Maybe you've even failed so many times that you've given up.

In the first part of this chapter, you will learn why it is important to reconcile your bank statements and how you can do it, quickly and easily, with Quicken Personal Finance Software.

Reconciling Bank Accounts

Reconciling an account refers to the process of comparing transactions in your account register to transactions on the account statement sent to you by your bank. Transactions that match are simply checked off. You'll need to account for transactions that appear only in one place, such as in your account register or the bank's account statement.

In this section, you'll review the basics of reconciling a bank account with Quicken: comparing transactions, making adjustments, and finishing up.

Starting a Reconciliation

You may either reconcile your bank statement with the traditional paper statement sent by your bank or reconcile your account online. We'll begin with the paper statement with which you may already be familiar.

Open the account register for the account you want to reconcile. Click the Action gear icon at the top far right of the register to open the menu seen here. Choose Reconcile. What happens next depends on whether the account is enabled for online access.

You can also open this menu by pressing CTRL-SHIFT-N or start reconciling at once by pressing CTRL-R.

Quicken does not supply a reconciliation form for cash accounts. However, you can update the balance, which marks the cash transactions with an "R" to indicate they have been reconciled.

Accounts Without Online Account Access

If the account is not enabled for online access, the Reconcile Details dialog appears. It gathers basic statement information prior to reconciling the account. Enter information from your bank statement in the appropriate boxes. (Enter service charge and interest earned information only if you have not already entered it in the account register.) Then click OK to continue. For the rest of the process, see "Comparing Transactions to a Paper Statement" later in this chapter.

Reconciling Accounts with Online Account Access

When you choose Reconcile for an account enabled for Online Account Access, Quicken begins by displaying a message that your account may be out of date, as seen here. If your account is not up to date, take the time to go online and update your account. Downloading is the

> ## EXPERIENCED USERS RECOMMEND
>
> While reconciling online may save you time, there are advantages to using your paper statement when reconciling your account:
>
> - Paper statements make it easier to spot errors by your bank.
> - You may have forgotten to enter a debit card purchase or even a check. Using a paper statement will remind you to enter those transactions into your Quicken check register.

only way you can be sure that all transactions recorded by the bank are included in your account register, unless you enter everything by hand. Choose Download Transactions For This Account, and click OK to download this account's latest transactions. You will also see a warning if you have unaccepted transactions.

Downloading Transactions   The One Step Update Settings dialog appears. Enter your password for this account, and click Update Now. If you have gone online with Quicken before and you store your passwords in the Password Vault, you may see the prompt to enter/create your Intuit ID at this step.

If your bank requires additional information, enter that information. You have the option to show the characters of the additional information to ensure you are typing correctly. After your update is complete and you have accepted the downloaded transactions, the One Step Update Summary dialog box displays. Click Close to close it and return to the account's register. If you have downloaded transactions, you will see a dialog stating you have unaccepted transactions. Quicken asks if you want to review them or continue reconciling

EXPERIENCED USERS RECOMMEND

Even when using an account with online access, be sure that the new statement ending date that you enter in the Reconcile Details dialog is the same as the ending date shown on the paper statement. Users may inadvertently enter the date they are doing the reconciliation instead of the bank statement's ending date and may be unable to quickly complete the reconciliation process. Also, ensure the service charge and interest income dates are the dates shown on the bank statement. If your statement is dated the 29th of the month and you inadvertently enter the service charge as of the 30th, you will be off by the amount of the service charge when trying to reconcile as of the 29th.

If you keep track of all bank account activity with Quicken, reconciling your bank accounts is easy. You won't need to use the form on the back of the bank statement. You won't even need a calculator. Just use Quicken's reconciliation feature to enter beginning and ending balances, check off cleared transactions, and enter the transactions you missed. You'll find you're successful a lot more often with Quicken helping you out.

You can use Quicken's reconciliation feature to balance any Quicken banking account—including credit card accounts. You can also reconcile checking accounts linked to investment accounts. This is useful if you write checks or pay bills with the linked account.

without reviewing or accepting the transactions. You may not see the prompt asking if you want to review unaccepted transactions, however, until you manually restart the reconciliation.

Depending on your Preferences settings, you may not see the One Step Update Summary unless there are errors during your download. Also, unless you have told Quicken to automatically enter your downloaded transactions into your banking account register, you will have to accept and match your downloaded transactions. See Appendix B for additional information on setting your Preferences in Quicken.

Reconciling Without Downloading   If you have opted not to update your online account, click Reconcile Without Downloading to continue with the reconciliation, and click OK. Click Cancel if you want to stop the reconciliation process entirely. After you are up to date, or if you have chosen not to update at this time, Quicken displays the Reconcile *<account name>* dialog, shown next. If you have downloaded transactions, you will have to restart the Reconcile dialog.

This dialog offers two options for reconciling the account:

- **Use Paper Statement** helps you reconcile the information in your Quicken account register to your bank statement. It is a traditional account reconciliation, and it works just like the account reconciliation you perform for an account without Online Account Access. If you select this option, enter the bank statement ending date and ending balance in the appropriate boxes, as shown in the illustration. The opening balance is the sum of all of the transactions in the register with "R" in the Clr column.
- **Use Online Balance** enables you to reconcile the account to the balance that was last downloaded for the account. When you select this option, you don't have to enter anything in the boxes. The first option, Always Use Online Banking For This Account. Don't Ask Me Again, sets the account to permanently use the online balance when reconciling. Selecting the Auto Reconcile Downloaded Transactions check box tells Quicken to reconcile the account to your financial institution's online balance automatically each time you download and accept transactions. With this Auto Reconcile feature enabled, you never have to reconcile the account again. However, you must trust the bank to make no mistakes.

After selecting your option in this dialog, click OK to continue.

The fact that the "opening balance" is the sum of all of the register transactions that have been marked with an "R" can cause Quicken users some aggravation. If there are any changed transactions in the register, you may have to re-reconcile in order to obtain the correct beginning balance. Also, when using the Quicken Mobile app, some users report missing or dropped transactions, which can also cause an opening balance error.

EXPERIENCED USERS RECOMMEND

Be careful when working with both online and paper reconciliations. If you have reconciled with a paper statement and marked a transaction as being reconciled (marked with an "R" in the Clr column) and the transaction is later downloaded from the bank via Web Connect, depending on your financial institution, that transaction may show in your Downloaded Transactions list as "New" or Unmatched.

Select the transaction in the Download Transactions tab, and click Edit to match the transaction manually to the transaction in your register. If the transaction does not appear on the displayed list, click Delete from the Edit option menu to delete the downloaded transaction. If you click Accept, both the downloaded transaction and your earlier, reconciled transaction will appear in your check register.

Some users tend to keep the downloaded transaction and delete the previously entered reconciled transaction. If you delete the downloaded transaction, the previously entered transaction won't get the downloaded posting date populated and could be inadvertently matched to an incorrect downloaded transaction in a future download, so use this method with caution.

Comparing Transactions to a Paper Statement

The next step in reconciling the account is to compare transactions that have cleared on the statement with transactions in your account register. For this, Quicken displays the Reconcile window, shown next, which displays the posting date and all payments, checks, and deposits that fall within the statement period for the account you are reconciling.

For accounts with downloaded transactions, the transaction's date for consideration for inclusion in the Reconcile dialog is the downloaded posting date, which is not necessarily the same as the transaction date shown in the account register.

Understanding the Buttons

Quicken 2017 displays all of your button bar choices at the bottom of the Reconcile window, as seen in the previous illustration. While by default the Reconcile window entries sort in ascending order with the most recent date at the bottom, you can sort the entries in either ascending or descending order by clicking the heading in each section. For example, to sort by check number, click Chk #. To reverse the order by which the column sorts, click the heading name a second time. Clicking any column heading re-sorts the columns in both the Deposits and the Payments and Checks sections. Credit card accounts use Charges and Payments as labels and do not have a Chk# column. Use each button as follows:

- Click **New** to switch to the account register window for the account you are reconciling so you can enter a new transaction. To return to your reconciliation, click the Reconcile:<*name of account*> button at the bottom-left corner of the check.
- Select a transaction and click **Edit** to switch to the account register window so you can modify that selected transaction.

Selecting the transaction "toggles" the check mark. A better practice is to right-click the transaction you want to edit and select Edit from the context menu that appears. In that way, your "Clr" status is preserved.

- Click **Delete** to remove a selected transaction. A prompt appears asking if you want to delete the transaction. Click Yes to remove the transaction from the account register.
- The **Balances** button displays the Online Balance in the account or the Reconcile Paper Statement dialog (which is similar to the top half of the Reconcile Online Account dialog shown earlier) so you can check or change entries there.
- The **Mark All** button is a toggle between Clear All and Mark All that either eliminates the green check marks beside a marked item or marks all of the items in the Reconcile window as cleared by the bank.
- Click **Cancel** to leave the reconciliation. Quicken asks if you want to save your work.
- The **Finish Later** button saves your work, closes the Reconcile window, and returns you to the account register. The difference between Cancel and Finish Later is that Finish Later remembers your reconcile settings, such as statement date and reconcile balance, while Cancel does not.

To open the Quicken Help window when reconciling your accounts, click the question mark at the bottom-left corner of the Reconcile window. Click Done to close the Reconcile window and display the Reconciliation Complete dialog box.

Reconciling to a Bank Statement

While you're checking off transactions in Quicken and on your bank statement, look for differences between them. Here are some of the differences you might encounter:

- An item that appears on the bank statement but not in your account register may be an item that you did not enter. You may have omitted the transaction for a number of reasons. Perhaps it was a bank adjustment that you didn't see. Or maybe you simply forgot to enter a check. To enter an omitted transaction, click the New button in the Reconcile dialog to switch to the register

> **EXPERIENCED USERS RECOMMEND**
>
> If you have set up Savings Goals (see Chapter 13), you may see "Contributions To Goals" or "Withdrawals From Goals" as items on your account register. These are only for your information and do not affect your bank account. To hide them while you are reconciling your account, click the Action gear icon, and in the Register Views And Preferences section, clear the Show Savings Goal Transactions In Register And Reports check box.

window. Enter the transaction in the register, click Enter, and click either the Reconcile:<*account name*> button at the bottom-left corner of the register or the Return To Reconcile button at the upper-right corner of your register to continue the reconciliation. Then click to place a check mark in the Clr column beside the item to mark it as cleared.

- An item that has a different date or amount in your register than that shown on the bank statement may be due to an error, either yours or the bank's. If the error is yours, you can edit the transaction by double-clicking it in the Reconcile window. This displays the account register window with the transaction selected. Edit the transaction and click the Save button. Then click the Reconcile:<*account name*> button at the bottom-left corner of the register or the Return To Reconcile button at the upper-right corner of the register to continue the reconciliation.
- If the amount of an error is small, many people simply adjust their register to reflect what is shown by the bank, especially if the check has been written by hand. The check-reading machinery at the bank has sometimes mistaken

---

EXPERIENCED USERS RECOMMEND

A hidden field, Downloaded Posting Date, controls which transactions are presented in the Reconcile window for accounts with downloaded transactions. You can have this field display in your register by selecting the Action gear icon | Register Columns. In the menu that appears, check Downloaded Posting Date, and a new column appears on your register to the right of the Date column, as shown next. This is handy information if transactions you expect to appear in the current reconciliation do not appear—the date the bank posted the transaction may be outside the date range of your reconciliation. Notice on the same menu there are other fields you can show in your register as well, such as Downloaded Payee and Downloaded Memo. While these may not have any effect on your reconciliation, the fields may make categorizing these downloads easier. After you have made your choices, click Done to close the menu.

the number 7 on my handwritten checks for a number 1, for example. If the mistake occurs in the cents section, it may not be a problem. Otherwise, you may want to contact the bank to fix the issue.

• Items that appear in your account register but not on the bank statement are items that have not yet cleared the bank. These are usually transactions prepared just before the bank's closing date, but they can be older. Do not check them off. Chances are you'll check them off the next time you reconcile. If, during a bank reconciliation, you discover any uncleared items that are older than two or three months, you should investigate why they have not cleared the bank. You may discover that a check (or worse yet, a deposit) was lost in transit.

Reconciling to an Online Balance

If you've recently downloaded and accepted transactions for the account, reconciling to an online balance shouldn't take much time. Items you've already reviewed and accepted will be checked off. Some more recent transactions may not be checked off because they haven't yet cleared your bank. Your job is to look for older transactions that appear in your Quicken account register that aren't checked off. These could represent stale payments that may have been lost in transit to the payee or errors (or duplications) you made when manually entering information into your Quicken account register. Follow up on all transactions more than 60 days old to see why they haven't been included with your downloaded transactions.

EXPERIENCED USERS RECOMMEND

Some users have reported that reconciling to online balances does not seem to work after updating their bank accounts. If you have chosen Reconcile Using Online Balances in this account and you find that Quicken is asking you to use a paper statement, follow these steps:

• Right-click the problem account and choose Edit/Delete Account.
• When the Account Details dialog box opens, select Online Services.
• Clear the Reconcile Using Online Balance check box at the bottom right of the dialog box.
• Update this account. When the update is complete, open the register for this account and select the Action gear icon. Choose Reconcile. Recheck the Reconcile Using Online Balances option.

Identifying Reconciled Items

When you download your transactions during the month, Quicken marks the Clr column with a "c" because the transaction has been posted at the bank. This does not mean it has been formally reconciled. Once you have finished the reconciliation, whether reconciling to a paper statement or using the online balance as your accepted balance, Quicken will mark each of the transactions in the Clr column with a capital "R," meaning the transaction has been reconciled.

You can change a "c" to an "R" or clear the Clr column entirely. Click in the column to bring up the menu, as shown in the illustration. Be careful about changing a reconciled item unless you are making corrections. Quicken uses the Clr column in an account register to identify items that either have cleared the bank or have been reconciled.

C	Uncleared
C	Cleared
C	Reconciled
⦿	Reconcile Ctrl+R

If you want to change a transaction's cleared status, choose from the following:

- **Uncleared** indicates that the transaction has not yet been cleared by the bank.
- **Cleared** indicates that the bank has cleared the item, but the item has not yet been reconciled.
- **Reconciled** shows that the item has been reconciled. To make it even more obvious that a transaction has been reconciled, reconciled transactions appear in gray print rather than black if you have set that preference. For more information about Preferences, see Appendix B.
- **Reconcile** (CTRL-R) begins the reconcile process as discussed earlier in this chapter.

You can toggle the gray color of reconciled transactions to black by clicking Edit | Preferences | Register | Register Appearance and unchecking Gray Reconciled Transactions, which is selected by default.

If you change back to using your paper statements after using online reconciliations, Quicken warns you the change may cause a problem. This is because your paper statement may not contain all of the items you have marked as cleared when reconciling online.

Finishing Up

When you reconcile a bank account with Quicken, your goal is to make the difference between the cleared balance and the statement ending balance zero. You can monitor this progress at the bottom of the Reconcile window, as seen earlier.

When the Difference Is Zero

If you correctly checked off all bank statement items and the difference is zero, you've successfully reconciled the account and you can click the Done button.

If You Can't Get the Difference to Zero

Sometimes, try as you might, you just can't get the difference to zero. Here are a few last things to check before you give up:

- Make sure all the amounts you checked off in your account register are the same as the amounts on the bank statement. Keep in mind that if you made a transposition error—for example, 87.91 instead of 87.19—the difference between the two amounts will be evenly divisible by 9. In this case, 87.91 minus 87.19 is .72—a number evenly divisible by 9.
- Make sure you included any bank charges or earned interest, no matter how small the interest.
- Make sure the ending date and balance you entered are the same as those on the bank statement.
- Check to see if any of the deposits were entered as checks or checks as deposits.
- Verify that none of the transactions were entered twice.
- Watch for penny differences. Occasionally, the bank will see an 8 as a 3 or a 4 as a 1.
- Ensure that the opening balance shown in the Reconcile Details dialog matches your statement's opening balance. If there is a difference, you may have deleted or changed a previously reconciled transaction.

If you checked and rechecked all these things and still can't get the difference to zero, click Done. Quicken displays a message indicating the amount of the difference and offers to make an adjustment to your account register for the amount. Click Adjust to accept the adjustment. The amount of the adjustment will be recorded without a category. If you want to continue trying to find the difference, click Cancel to return to the Reconcile window.

EXPERIENCED USERS RECOMMEND

From time to time a deposit shows on the bank statement that does not seem to match anything in your register. It is possible you've deposited two or more checks together at the bank yet entered the deposits separately in your register. If you often have several checks to deposit at the same time, create a split deposit as explained in Chapter 5. This way, the total deposit will match the bank statement.

   If any of the checks in a group is a "form," such as a payroll check, consider using two deposit slips so that each deposit shows separately on the bank statement. Some folks even create an Undeposited Checks account in Quicken where they enter the individual checks, then enter a transfer from the Undeposited Checks account to their checking account in the total amount of the group, because it is that total that will appear on your bank statement.

Be careful of old checks you have written that may suddenly clear. A good example of this is a check you wrote as a donation to a local charity. It may sit in someone's desk for several months before that person notices it and puts it into the bank. Each bank has their own policy on "stale-dated" checks, meaning that only checks within a certain period are honored. However, checks can slip through with dates as old as last year!

Other Reconciliation Tasks and Features

Quicken offers a number of other reconciliation features that you might find useful. Here's a quick look at them.

Reconciling Credit Card Accounts

You can reconcile a credit card account the same way you reconcile a bank account. If you try to enter all credit card transactions as you make them throughout the month, it's a good idea to use the reconciliation feature to compare your entries to the credit card statement, just to make sure you didn't miss any. If you simply enter all credit card transactions when you get your statement, reconciling to the statement really isn't necessary.

   However, if you are going by what is on your credit card statement, you're counting on your financial institution to be correct. If you just enter in the transactions from your credit card statement, you may miss fraudulent charges or mistakes made by your financial institution.

When you access your credit card accounts online, you can quickly download or manually record your credit card transactions into your Quicken credit card account register. You can also use the Quicken Mobile app to enter your credit card charges as you make them!

Many Quicken users go online frequently to view both their bank account and credit card balances to ensure there are no fraudulent or unidentified charges.

Reconcile a Credit Card Without Online Access

Choose the account you want to reconcile from the Account Bar to open that account's register. Press CTRL-R to begin the reconciliation. When you reconcile an account for which you have not enabled Online Account Access, Quicken displays the Reconcile dialog as shown next.

Reconcile: Credit Card   ✕

Reconcile: Credit Card

* Required fields

The prior ending statement date:

Enter the following from your statement.

Charges, Cash (other than finance	*	33.00	
Payments,	*	0.00	
Ending	*	33.00	
New Statement Ending	*	9/30/2016	

Enter and categorize your interest charges, if any.

Finance Charges: [   ]   Date: 9/30/2016

Category: Interest Exp

OK   Cancel

As you can see, Quicken asks for the total charges, including cash advances, you made during the billing period, as well as any payments or credits that have been made on the account. You can find this information on your paper credit card statement. Enter the new statement ending date, any finance charges, and the date they were assessed. Note the red asterisks by the required fields. You must enter a number or date in these fields, even if the number is zero. Click OK to move to the Reconcile window, which looks and works almost exactly like the Reconcile window that was shown earlier.

As shown in the illustration, as you click each cleared transaction, a small green check mark appears. Click Mark All to mark every transaction shown in the Reconcile window as cleared. Click Done when the Difference field shows zero. A dialog appears asking if you want to make a payment on that credit card now, as seen here. If you choose to make a payment now, first select the account from which you want to make the payment from the Bank Account drop-down list.

Select the payment method:

- **Printed Check** opens the Write Checks dialog. Once all the information has been entered, simply click Record to add the print check instruction to the payment account register.
- **Hand Written Check** posts the check (without the check number) in the credit card register and opens the register from which that check was written so you can enter the check number of that handwritten check. Until you enter the check number and save the transaction, the check appears as a payment in the credit card register, but until you actually write and send the check, no payment is made.
- **Online Payment (not shown)** opens a message that online payments are not active for this account. Click OK to continue.

If you do not want to be reminded to make a payment after each reconciliation, click Don't Show Me This Screen Again. Be very sure you don't want to be reminded to make a payment after reconciling your credit card account. Once you've selected the Don't Show Me This Screen Again check box, there is no way to undo this action.

Click Yes if you have chosen one of the payment options, or click No if you will be making the payment later. You are returned to the account register, where you will see each reconciled transaction displays an "R" in the Clr column.

Reconcile a Credit Card with Online Access Enabled

Open the register for the credit card account you want to reconcile. Click the Action gear icon | Reconcile. Quicken prompts you to either download any current transactions or proceed to the reconciliation process without downloading. See "Reconciling Accounts with Online Account Access" earlier in this chapter for more information. For this example, we are choosing to reconcile without downloading.

Click Reconcile Without Downloading, and click OK to proceed. The Reconcile Online Account window for the current account appears. Note this window's similarity to the dialog for checking accounts. You may choose to reconcile to a paper statement, in which case you must enter a value (which can be zero) in each of the fields. If you accept the online balance method, note the "balance as of" date and recognize that the balance displayed is what the bank has cleared as of that date.

The manual account Reconcile dialog notes required fields with a red asterisk. Online-enabled accounts do not note the required fields in the Reconcile dialog.

If you have chosen to reconcile the account to your online balance, click Auto Reconcile Downloaded Transactions to change the "c" in the Clr column of your register to an "R."

After you have completed the reconciliation, if there is a balance on the account, Quicken asks if you want to make a payment. If you choose to make a payment, select the bank account from the drop-down list and tell Quicken if you are going to print a check through Quicken or write the check or pay online. If your choice is to print or write a check, the Write Checks window displays. If you choose Online Payment or Printed Check, the Write Checks dialog also opens with an option to use Online Bill Pay if you have enabled that feature. However, if you select Hand Written Check, the Write Checks dialog does not appear. If you choose not to make a payment at this time, click No.

When your credit card balance is zero, a message box appears stating that there is no payment required, as you have an outstanding balance of zero. You will see a similar message if your credit card balance is a credit. Click OK to close the message box.

Adjusting Your Register

If you can't successfully get the credit card reconciliation to balance, Quicken offers to make adjustments. If you simply cannot balance an account, use the Adjust Balance dialog to make your adjustments. Choose a date for the adjustment, and click Adjust to make the entry, which will show as a balance adjustment in your register as of the date you enter in this dialog.

Be careful about clicking any Don't Show Me This Screen Again check boxes when reconciling credit card statements. You only get one chance to do this, and at some point, you may want to see the dialog. Resetting the Quicken Warnings preference does *not* reset the Don't Show Me This Screen Again check box. To "reset" the warning, you have to create a new credit card account and move/copy all the transactions from the old account to the new account.

Streamline Your Reconciliations

To make the reconciliation process even easier, you can place a reconciliation tool on the Quicken Toolbar. To do so, from the Quicken menu bar, click View | Customize Toolbar. Scroll to Reconcile An Account, and click the Add button. This moves the Reconcile An Account button to the right side of the screen. You may move the Reconcile An Account button to another position with the Move Up or Move Down buttons in the Customize Toolbar dialog. Once you are satisfied with the location of the new button, click OK. The Reconcile An Account button appears on your Quicken Toolbar.

Still quicker is adding a reconcile button to the top of your register. Click the Action gear icon. From the menu, choose Customize Action Bar. In the Available Toolbar Buttons list, choose Reconcile and click Add. A reconcile icon appears pinned to the top of the register between the Reminders icon and the Action gear icon. Click Done to close the dialog. The reconcile icon is a small white check mark inside a green circle, as seen here.

 Although you will see the new icon on the account action bar as soon as you click Add, the new icon is not saved to your account action bar until you click Done.

Printing a Reconciliation Report

After you have completed a bank account reconciliation, Quicken displays a dialog that offers to create a reconciliation report, as seen next. If you click Yes, the Reconciliation Report Setup dialog appears. Give the report a title if you wish, set the date at which the balance is to be shown, and tell Quicken to show either all of the transactions as of the bank balance date or just a summary of all the transactions and each transaction that has not yet cleared the bank. No such prompt appears for a credit card account.

Reconciliation Complete   ×
Your account is balanced. The items you have marked have been reconciled in your register.
Would you like to create a reconciliation report?
☐ Don't show me this screen again.
❓   Yes   No

 You can create a reconciliation report for a credit card account by opening the account register and then using the menu to select Reports | Banking | Reconciliation.

Click OK to open the Print dialog shown next. You may choose to print the report on paper or to a PDF printer, as seen in the illustration. Saving your report as a .pdf file allows you to electronically store the report in a location you choose on your hard drive. You can print your report in either Portrait or Landscape orientation.

If your report is a long one, you can choose to print just one or two pages. In the Print Range section of the Print dialog, click Pages and enter the page number from which you wish to start in the From field and the page number with which you want to end in the To field.

When you have finished making your choices, click Print to print the report.

You can print a current reconciliation report at any time. Open the register for which you want the report, and from the Reports menu, click Banking | Reconciliation to open the Reconciliation Report Setup dialog. It is best to do this soon after reconciling the account to get the current reconciliation and transactions.

Because Quicken does not save copies of your reconciliations from previous months, if your reconciliation required an adjusting entry, it is a good idea to document it by creating a report, either as a digital .pdf or a paper copy. You can then file the paper report with your bank statement and canceled checks, or store the .pdf with an electronic copy of your statement and pictures of your processed checks. To ensure you have a copy, either print a hard copy or save your report as a .pdf through the Quicken PDF Printer.

Undoing Reconciled Transactions

At times, you may have to clear previously reconciled transactions or even undo an entire reconciliation. Be aware, this is not recommended! However, computers are not always consistent, banks occasionally merge and their records get skewed, a user will sometimes make a mistake, and so on. Before you make any changes to any reconciled transaction, do a backup of your data. See Appendix A for instructions on creating a backup.

To unclear a transaction you have inadvertently marked as reconciled:

1. Select the transaction and click in the Clr column.
2. Change the notation to Uncleared if it has not been downloaded or to Cleared if the transaction has cleared the bank.

If you need to clear several transactions in a row:

1. Click the first of the transactions, hold down your SHIFT key, and click the last transaction in the group.
2. Note that each selected transaction is highlighted. Right-click someplace within the highlighted area, and from the context menu that appears, click Reconcile and choose either Not Reconciled or Cleared:
   • Quicken opens a prompt asking if you want to mark the currently selected transactions. Choose Yes to mark the selected transactions or No to cancel the change.
   • Each transaction in the group now shows that it has not been cleared, assuming you chose Not Reconciled.

If the transactions you want to change are not in a row (listed one after the other), follow the procedure shown in step 1, but hold down your CTRL key and click each transaction you want to change. These transactions are selected, and you can continue. You can also choose to sort and/or filter and/or search the register to get the transactions of interest in a contiguous set.

Managing Your Investments

Chapter 9

Many people find that investing in stocks, bonds, mutual funds, or other types of assets are ways to save for future goals or retirement. Although more risky than deposits made to an FDIC-insured bank, certain types of investments have the potential to earn more and make money grow faster. In this chapter, you are introduced to investment transactions management and then you will learn how to use Quicken Personal Finance Software to keep track of the money you invest and learn how to obtain information about other investment opportunities.

Quicken Investment Basics

An *investment* is a security or asset that you expect to increase in value and/or generate income. But what, exactly, are *securities*? In Quicken, a security is a single investment that has value based on share price. Examples of securities include stock shares for a specific company, bonds for a specific company, and mutual funds offered by investment firms. Normally, when you own a security, you own a certain number of shares. To calculate the total value of the security, you multiply the number of shares you own by the most recent per-share price.

This chapter concentrates on the investments you can track with the features in Quicken's Investing tab. Before you learn how to use Quicken to track your investments, here's a review of Quicken's investment accounts and a more detailed explanation of why investment tracking is so important.

Understanding Your Portfolio

The term *portfolio* refers to the total of all of your investments. For example, if you have 50 shares of one company's stock, shares in a mutual fund, and a 401(k) plan account at work, these items make up your portfolio.

Types of Investment Accounts

Your Quicken portfolio can include four types of investment accounts. You can have as many investment accounts as you need to represent the investments that make up your portfolio.

- A Quicken brokerage account is for tracking a wide variety of investments handled through a brokerage firm, including stocks, bonds, mutual funds, and annuities. Like the account at your brokerage firm, it can track income, capital gains, performance, market values, shares, and cash balances for multiple securities.
- A 401(k) or 403(b) account is for tracking 401(k), 403(b), or 457 plans, in which you make regularly scheduled, pretax contributions toward investments for your retirement. This type of account can track performance, market value, and distribution among investment choices. If you (and your spouse) have more than one plan, you should set up a separate account for each.

- An IRA or a Keogh account is for tracking a variety of retirement accounts, including standard IRA, Roth IRA, Coverdell Education Savings Account (formerly known as Education IRA), SEP-IRA, SIMPLE-IRA, and Keogh plans.
- A 529 plan account is for tracking 529 Educational Savings Plans. These plans enable multiple family members to make pretax contributions to invest money for a family member's college education. This type of account enables you to track cash, money market, and securities activity and balances.

 There are two distinct account types in Quicken for 529s. One is a 529 plan you can find under Investing & Retirement in the Add Account dialog. The second is under IRA or Keogh Plan in the same dialog. This second type is the account type referred to as Coverdell ESA in the IRA dialog and as Education IRA in Quicken Help.

The various types of Investing & Retirement accounts help you track your investments in Quicken as follows:

- Quicken uses the brokerage accounts to track stocks you have in your possession, brokerage accounts holding one or more securities, employee stock options, Employee Stock Purchase Plans (ESPPs), Dividend Reinvestment Programs (DRIPs), bonds (including U.S. savings bonds), real estate investment trust (REIT) accounts or partnerships, variable or fixed annuities, and Treasury bills. As you can see, brokerage accounts handle pretty much anything that doesn't fall into one of the other types listed here.
- Single mutual funds with no cash balance are tracked either in a standard brokerage account or as a single mutual fund account.
- 401(k) or 403(b) plans are tracked in an account specifically for them.
- Quicken tracks IRA, Keogh, SEP-IRA, and/or SIMPLE-IRA plans with an account type tailored just for these plans.
- 529 plan accounts are tracked in another special account type for these plans.
- Quicken tracks certificates of deposit (CDs) and money market funds as either a savings account or a standard brokerage account.
- Real estate holdings, including your primary residence, are tracked as asset accounts.

Choosing the Right Type of Account

Keep in mind that you can also track many types of investments in asset accounts. But Quicken's investment accounts enable you to better track and report on the income, capital gains, and performance of your investments. While this chapter concentrates on investment accounts tracked in standard brokerage, IRA or Keogh, 401(k) or 403(b), and 529 plan accounts, it is important that you consider what type of account your financial institution requires for downloading transactions as you decide between a single mutual fund account and a standard brokerage account.

If you want to track the maturity dates of your CDs, you may need to use the brokerage account, as Quicken considers CDs to be investment instruments.

Managing Your Portfolio

You may be wondering why you should bother including investment information in your Quicken data file. After all, you get quarterly (or even monthly) statements from your broker or investment firm. Brokerages only keep records for so long, so if you have had dividend-paying stocks where you have reinvested the dividends for many years, Quicken will handily keep track of every lot even if your brokerage's history does not go back that far. Consider the benefits when you manage your portfolio with Quicken's tools:

- Centralizing your investment records
- Knowing your portfolio's value on any day
- Easily calculating capital gains

Brokerage statements tell you the value of your investments on the statement's ending date, but not what they're worth today—or what they were worth on July 20, 1994. Quicken, however, can tell you what your portfolio is worth on any day for which you have entered, or better yet, downloaded, security prices, and it can estimate values for dates without exact pricing information.

Manually compiling a complete pricing and performance history for an investment is no small task, especially for periods spanning multiple statements. If you consistently enter (or download) investment information into your Quicken data file, however, preparing performance charts and reports is as easy as choosing a menu command or clicking a button.

If you change brokerages or your brokerage is acquired by another brokerage firm, often your cost basis information is not retained by either financial institution. When your investments are in Quicken, you can easily transfer the cost basis information from the old account to the new account.

If any of your securities have gone through an acquisition or merger, the tax treatment and associated changes to your cost basis are not always tracked, or tracked correctly, by your brokerage firm. Use Quicken to accurately track these events.

If you are keeping custodial accounts for a minor, when that minor is old enough to take over handling of the account, you can give them a complete buy/sell/cost basis history.

When you use Quicken to track your investments, the data integrates seamlessly with the Lifetime Planner, as discussed in Chapter 12. This way, you can see the impact of investment value changes on your retirement plan at a glance.

Additional Enhancements in Quicken Premier

Those using Quicken Premier or higher can opt to update stock quotes every 15 minutes, although those quotes may be delayed up to 20 minutes. Other features found in the Premier and higher versions are the ability to create snapshots of your portfolio value versus its cost basis, a "Growth of 10K" chart, and average annual return. And the Portfolio X-Ray feature (found in Quicken Deluxe and higher versions) connects you directly with Morningstar for in-depth information about your portfolio. Learn more about Portfolio X-Ray in Chapter 11.

EXPERIENCED USERS RECOMMEND

Many brokerage and investment firms support the downloading of transactions. If you set up your investing account as a manual account using Advanced Setup, consider changing to online services if your brokerage offers them. Downloading transactions saves time and effort, and ensures that your Quicken records match those of your broker. However, your broker's records, or at least the records your broker might download, may not be accurate or complete, especially in the case of corporate mergers, ESPP buys and sells, and other complex investment transactions. You'll want to ensure what gets downloaded makes sense.

Creating Investing Accounts

Before you can begin tracking your investments with Quicken, you must set up the investment accounts you'll need. As you'll see on the following pages, when you create an investment account, Quicken not only prompts you for basic account information, but also gathers information about your security holdings. When you're finished creating an account, it's all ready to use for entering new transactions and creating reports.

Applying for Transaction Downloads

Before you can download transactions into your investment accounts, you may need to apply for download access. Normally, all it takes is a phone call, although many brokerage and investment firms allow you to apply online through the company website. If you do need to apply for online access to your account, it may take up to a week for the application to be processed. You'll know that you're ready to go online when you have your password and other setup information.

Choosing the Type of Investing Account

Begin by clicking the small plus sign at the top of the Account Bar or selecting Tools | Add Account. In the Add Account dialog that appears, shown next, click the type of account you want to create. It is quite important to choose the right account type as the account type cannot be changed after the account has been created. See "Types of Investment Accounts" elsewhere in this chapter for help in deciding. The option you select will determine certain settings for the account. For example, if you choose an IRA or Keogh plan, Quicken will set tax-deferred options that are not set if you select a brokerage account. After you choose a brokerage (or the name of your 529 plan) from the list that appears, you may see a message that Quicken is updating.

Using Simple Setup to Create an Investment Account

Quicken's extensive online account access features make it possible to automate data entry for accounts held in participating financial institutions, including many brokerage firms. To take advantage of these features, Quicken starts the account creation process for standard brokerage, IRA or Keogh Plan, 401(k) or 403(b), or 529 Plan accounts by prompting you to enter the name of your brokerage firm or choosing one from the provided list.

Whether you choose the default Simple Setup or the Advanced Setup to create your account, you may be prompted for your Intuit ID. If so, enter it and continue entering the information for your investment account. (Chapters 1, 2, and 4 also discuss account setup.) When you have typed or clicked the name of your broker, you are prompted for the user ID and password given to you by your broker. (Quicken may display dialogs that prompt you for additional information about the account. The dialogs that appear and the order in which they appear vary, depending on your financial institution.)

Once you have entered your login information, click Connect to proceed with the account setup. After you have proceeded through any dialogs prompting for additional info, Quicken retrieves the account information and transactions, creates the account, and displays an Account Added screen.

As explained in earlier chapters, it is not uncommon to set up accounts in Quicken and decide later to activate online services for these accounts. The first time you download transactions into a Quicken file with online access, Quicken prompts you to create a new account for these downloaded transactions or to link them to an existing account. If you are linking to an existing account, ensure it is the correct one for these downloaded transactions. (If you do not see an offer to link to an existing account that has already been set up for downloading, you may need to back out of the setup and deactivate downloading from the existing account before Quicken offers to link to your account.)

Using Advanced Setup   If your institution's name is not on the Simple Setup list, has other connection methods, or you just prefer not to download, you can set up your account manually. After you have chosen the type of investing account you want to set up, at the dialog where you are prompted for your institution's name, click Advanced Setup at the bottom of the window. From this dialog, you have two options:

- **I Want To Select The Connection Method Used To Download My Transactions**   Select this option if your institution offers more than one online service or if you have been given specific instructions how to connect to their website.

- **I Want To Enter My Transactions Manually**   Select this option if your account is held by an entity that does not offer online services, or you just prefer to enter your transactions by hand. Also, use this option if the account you are creating is not held at a financial institution—for example, an account to track the value of securities in your safe deposit box.

Account Name and Other Basic Information   Depending on the type of account you are adding, Quicken displays dialogs that prompt you for other basic information, including the account name, statement ending date, and cash and money market balances.

- For IRAs and Keoghs you need to indicate
  - Who owns the IRA
  - The type of IRA, such as traditional, Roth, Keogh, and so on
  - If you have not entered a cash value or more than one mutual fund, you may be asked whether this is a single mutual fund account
- 401(k) or 403(b) accounts require
  - Statement ending date
  - Employer name (either current or previous employer)
  - Who owns the account
  - Whether you have loans (and how many) against the account
  - What securities you have in the account

Although you will be prompted to list the securities in the account during account creation, it is not required to list the securities at that time. You can create the account and then go back and add the securities at a later time.

- Whether you want to set up your paycheck information
- If the account tracks the number of shares, whether the statement lists the number of shares of each security

For 401(k) or 403(b) accounts, Quicken displays a dialog that asks whether you want to track loans against the account. If you have any loans against the account, be sure to indicate how many you have. Quicken will then display one or more dialogs prompting you for information about your loan(s).

Securities Held   For securities held in a brokerage account, a dialog (seen next) prompts you to enter security ticker symbols and names. Enter one security per line, using the TAB key to move from one box to the next. If you don't know the ticker symbol for a security, click the Ticker Symbol Lookup button to look it up online. If you need to enter more than five securities in the dialog, click the Add More button to add more lines. Don't enter bonds in this dialog; you add them later. You may only see this dialog when you are doing a manual account setup. After you have entered the information for the first five securities, just use the scroll bar at the right of the screen to scroll down and fill out the next five securities.

Current Holdings   After you have entered the ticker symbols for your securities, click Next. With your Internet connection, Quicken updates and verifies the symbols and displays a dialog like the one shown next. (This screen is another example of the word Other being cut off at the right-hand side.) Enter the total number of shares for each security. For a 401(k) account, you may see a Total Market Value column. If the type of security—Stock, Mutual Fund, or Other—is incorrect, select the correct option.

Q Quicken Account Setup   ×

Enter your current holdings information.

This information will be used to set up your initial security holdings. For each security, enter the
total number of shares you own and select a security type (if the security is not a stock or mutual
fund, click Other - you can edit the security later).

Ticker	Security Name	Total Shares	Stock	Mutual Fund	C
GM	General Motors	150	●	○	
USG	USG Corporation	25	●	○	
OGS	ONE Gas	50	●	○	
DY	Dycom Industries	25	●	○	
IRT	Independence Realty Trust	25	●	○	

When you are finished, Quicken will give you a chance to enter cost basis information.

Cancel   Back   Next

When you click Next, Quicken displays a summary dialog confirming your
entries and encouraging you to enter the complete transaction history for each
of your holdings. To do so, click Done and then follow the directions on the
window that appears.

You may see a message asking if this is a single mutual fund account if you
have not entered a cash balance and have entered only one mutual fund security.
If you are creating this type of account, click Yes. Otherwise, select No and click
Next again. Quicken displays an Account Added window. Click Finish to close
the window.

Paycheck Setup   When you create a 401(k) or 403(b) account, Quicken
displays a dialog, asking whether you want to set up your paycheck. (If you have
already set up a paycheck in Quicken, you will not see this message.) Quicken's
Paycheck Setup feature is great for automatically entering 401(k) contributions
and loan payments. Learn about setting up your paycheck in Quicken in Chapter
7. Click Yes to set up your paycheck. Click No to continue, and then in the
Account Added dialog, click Finish.

Working with Placeholder Entries

Quicken automatically creates special transactions, called placeholder entries,
in investment accounts when you enter, either manually or via Online Account
Access, currently held securities as part of the account setup process. These

transactions make it possible to get up and running quickly with Quicken's investment tracking features, but they often lack the information Quicken needs to create accurate investment reports.

Here's how it works. When you create an investment account, you tell Quicken what securities are in the account and how many shares of each security you currently own. However, Quicken doesn't know when you bought those shares or what you paid for them. Without this historical cost information, Quicken can't calculate your return on investment or your capital gains (or losses) when you sell the security.

Although you can work with a Quicken investment account as soon as it's created, to get the most out of Quicken's investment tracking features, you should replace the placeholder entries it creates with investment cost information. This section explains how.

The placeholder "locks" the number of shares and cash balance for the given date to the number specified in the placeholder. If you enter transactions before the placeholder date, the cash balance will not be affected. This can be a good thing, as you don't have to account for where the cash came from for securities purchased long before you started tracking in Quicken, but it can also be a bad thing if you don't understand how the placeholder works. Many Quicken users wonder why cash is not subtracted from the account when they enter a "buy" transaction. Thus, many users don't use placeholders to avoid these sorts of complications.

You can find an account's placeholder entries with the rest of the transactions for that account. Choose the account from the Account Bar to open its Transaction List (register). You can also click the Portfolio button after clicking the Investing tab and click the name of the account you want. You will see the placeholder transaction on the Transaction List, as well as in a Placeholder Entries tab at the bottom of the Investment Transaction list, along with the Downloaded Transactions tab and the Bill and Income Reminders tab.

You may see a little calculator icon in the Clr column for each placeholder transaction. You may also notice another calculator icon at the bottom left of the Transaction List just above the Download Transactions tab, as well as a legend explaining what the placeholder transactions are and how to work with them.

If placeholder entries are not visible, you may need to set the preference for viewing hidden investment transactions. Select Edit | Preferences. Click Investment Transactions, and then select the Show Hidden Transactions check box. Click OK to save the preference and close the dialog.

Entering Cost Information for Placeholder Entries

To enter security cost information, begin by selecting the placeholder entry you want to work with. Click the Enter Cost link to display the Enter Missing Transactions dialog, which may take several seconds. See the next illustration for an example.

NOTE Transactions entered in the investment account before the date of the placeholder entry will not affect the cash balance of the investment account. It is often better to delete the placeholder and then enter all the historical transactions. You're going to have to enter the same data whether you enter your investment buys/adds via placeholder or using the Enter Transactions dialog. You might as well do it right and use the Enter Transactions dialog.

Two buttons at the bottom of the dialog offer methods for entering historical cost information for a security: Enter Missing Transaction and Estimate Average Cost.

Enter Missing Transactions

ⓘ This security is missing all or part of its transaction history. When you downloaded or manually entered transactions, the total number of shares in those transactions did not equal the total number of shares you own. Quicken has added a Placeholder Entry to account for missing transactions.

To get complete performance reporting and tax calculations, enter the missing transactions now.

Transactions as of 6/12/2016

Date	Transaction	Description
		Enter Missing Transactions to complete cost basis

Holdings as of 6/12/2016	Shares	Cost
Total Shares You Own:	88.3652	*
Shares from Transactions (Above)	0	0.00
Shares in Placeholder Entry	88.3652	Unknown

[Enter Missing Transaction...]   [Estimate Average Cost...]

❓   [Finish Later]

Enter Missing Transaction   Click the Enter Missing Transaction button to open the appropriate correcting dialog. From here, you can enter the individual transactions that make up the total number of shares you hold. In many cases, these transactions include purchases, stock dividends, and stock splits. This option gives you the most accurate records, but if you have many transactions, entering them all can be time consuming. (If the account is a 401(k) account, you may see an extra button labeled Cash Source.) See how to enter new transactions, such as purchases and stock dividends, later in this chapter, in the section "Entering Common Transactions." It is better to delete the placeholder and enter transactions directly into the Investment Transaction list.

For this dialog, complete the transaction information by moving through the fields with your TAB key. The transaction date should already be filled in. If you get a prompt about it, enter the correct date.

If you need to change a date for a placeholder transaction, it must be before the date you have entered for the placeholder when you set up the account.

- The Account and Security Name fields are prefilled, and you cannot change the information.
- Enter the number of shares you purchased on the date of the placeholder transaction. If this placeholder contains more than one lot, enter the oldest lot first. You will have to enter each lot separately to ensure your investment account is correct.
- Enter the price you paid for each share in the Price Paid field.
- Enter the amount of any commission you paid for this transaction. Quicken calculates your total cost.
- If you have made any errors, click the Clear button. If you want to start over, click the Cancel button. Otherwise, click Enter/Done.

A warning message appears telling you that you are attempting to record a transaction on the same date as a placeholder transaction, that your share balance will not be affected, and are you sure you want to do this, as shown next. Click Yes to close the message and return to the Enter Missing Transactions dialog. If you have entered all the transactions to account for all the shares in the placeholder, you will have the option to click Done to close the Enter Missing Transactions dialog. Otherwise, you will see a button labeled Finish Later.

Q Quicken 2017   ✕

? You are attempting to record a transaction on the same date as a Placeholder Transaction.   Your share balance will not be affected.

Are you sure?

[Yes]   [No]

Estimate Average Cost   This option enables you to enter an average estimated cost for all of the shares you hold. Although this method is less accurate than entering individual transactions, it's a lot quicker and may be sufficient if you don't need detailed records of stock costs. You can always go back later and use the Enter Missing Transaction button to record more accurate acquisition details. If needed, click the Enter Cost link in the placeholder transaction, and then click the Estimate Average Cost button at the bottom of the dialog. This opens the Enter Missing Transactions dialog from which you can enter either the total cost or price per share, as seen next.

When you click the Estimate Average Cost button, you can enter either the total cost of the shares in the Cost box or the average price per share in the Price/Share box. Quicken makes any necessary calculations. Click OK to save the entry and return to the register. The item then shows as a placeholder entry in the Investment Transaction list. If you enter the cost first, then decide to enter price/share, once you have entered your desired price/share you will need to click in the Cost field to see the updated cost value.

Setting Up Transaction Downloads

After you have created your investment accounts and downloaded for the first time, you can download current account information using One Step Update, as detailed in Chapter 1, or from the Online Center, as explained in Chapter 6.

Using the Online Center Window

You can use the Online Center to download account information and compare it to data in your Quicken file. From the menu bar, choose Tools | Online Center. If necessary, choose the name of your brokerage firm from the Financial Institution drop-down list near the top of the window.

Unusual in Quicken, there is no Help button or icon in the Online Center. However, you can always press the F1 key from within Quicken to open Quicken Help.

EXPERIENCED USERS RECOMMEND

As our world becomes smaller, some investors are finding they need to use multiple currencies with their transactions. Quicken supports this need in several ways.

To set up multicurrency usage, click Edit | Preferences | Calendar And Currency, and click the Multicurrency Support check box. The Portfolio view in the Investing tab will now include a field for the currency to be used. While the default is the U.S. dollar, you do have a number of other choices. Click OK to save the Preferences change.

When you have enabled multicurrency usage, your One Step Update downloads will automatically include currency exchange rates. If you do not want to include the exchange rates, clear the Get Currency Exchange Rates check box in the One Step Update Settings dialog.

Downloading Transactions

To download transactions, make sure the brokerage firm is selected in the Online Center window, and then click the Update/Send button. Depending on the type of connection offered by your financial institution, you may see the One Step Update Setting dialog or be connected directly to your financial institution's webpage. You may be prompted for your Intuit ID during the process.

Enter any user names and/or passwords as required. If you are using One Step Update Settings, click Update Now. Wait while Quicken connects to your financial institution. If you want to see what you are typing when entering a password, select the Show Password Characters check box.

When Quicken is finished exchanging information, a One Step Update Summary window appears to summarize the activity that took place while you waited. (Depending on your preference settings, you may not see the One Step Update Summary dialog unless there is an error.) Click Close. If you have downloaded the information from a Web Connect website, sign off, if required, and close the connection to your institution's website.

If you display the Online Center window again, any transactions you downloaded show in the bottom half of the window's Transactions subtab for the selected financial institution.

Reviewing and Accepting Transactions

After you download, the One Step Update Summary appears showing that the account has been updated successfully. A small red flag to the left of your account in the Account Bar indicates that there are transactions to review. Click the account to review the transactions.

Depending on your preference settings, you may not see the One Step Update Summary unless there is an error.

Automatic Transaction Entry

Quicken has the ability to accept and enter your downloaded transactions automatically. To enable this action, click Edit | Preferences | Register | Downloaded Transactions | Downloaded Transaction Preferences | After Downloading Transactions, and click the Automatically Add To Investment Transaction Lists check box as seen next.

Many Quicken users do not enable the automatic transaction entry. Instead, they review the downloaded transactions and accept the individual transactions one by one, or they click Accept All after they have reviewed the download.

You can also tell Quicken which accounts to use for this automatic entry:

- Right-click the account's name in the Account Bar, and choose Edit/Delete Account to open the Account Details dialog for that account.
- Click the Online Services tab.
- Click the Automatic Entry Is: On (or Off) link. The Automatic Transaction Entry dialog appears, as shown next.

Q Automatic Transaction Entry   ✕

Automatic Transaction Entry

Automatically add downloaded transactions to your

◉ Use the general account preference that applies to all Investing accc

○ Yes - Always automatically add transactions for this account.

○ No - Never automatically add transactions for this account.
    (I will review and accept transactions individually.)

❓   [OK]   [Cancel]

Choose one of the three choices:

- **Use The General Account Preference That Applies To All Investing Accounts** if you want to have the option you chose in Preferences apply to this account.
- **Yes – Always Automatically Add Transactions For This Account** if you want Quicken to enter all downloaded transactions without your acceptance.
- **No – Never Automatically Add Transactions For This Account. (I Will Review And Accept Transactions Individually.)** This is your choice if you want to review each transaction before it is entered into the account's Transaction List.

Click OK to close the Automatic Transaction Entry dialog. After clicking OK, you may see a warning dialog explaining more about your selection. Click OK or Cancel to dismiss this warning, and then click OK to close the Account Details dialog.

When you are in the account's Transaction List, click Downloaded Transactions to review and accept the items that have been downloaded. If you have elected to automatically add your investment transactions to the Investment Transaction list, you will no longer see the Downloaded Transactions tab, nor will you see the Bill and Income Reminders tab. You may handle your downloaded transactions in two different ways:

- **Review Each Transaction**   Use this method if your account information is currently up to date. It allows you to look at each of the downloaded transactions before deciding to accept them into your "official" Transaction List. Usually, you'll simply select a new or matched transaction and click the Accept button to put it in your register. Once you have accepted the transaction, it appears in your Transaction List (register) with a small "c" in the Clr column, indicating that the transaction has been processed by your financial institution.
- **Accept All**   This choice may be best the first time you download transactions because it is the fastest, but not necessarily the safest or most accurate. When you click this, all of the transactions are transferred to the Transaction List and the Cash Amt and Cash Bal fields are updated. The Downloaded Transactions pane disappears. You can use a hybrid approach by reviewing each downloaded transaction and changing any transaction that needs special handling. Then, click Accept All to accept the rest.

Remember that unaccepted downloaded transactions are not entered in your Investment Transaction list. Thus, your Transaction List and portfolio balances may be misstated until you accept all downloaded transactions.

 If your account balance as downloaded does not match your Quicken balance, Quicken adds an adjusting transaction.

Renaming Transactions

Renaming rules are not very helpful in investment accounts. The rules only affect payee names, and only cash transactions have payees. However, you may want to rename some transactions in order to make them consistent with your naming conventions, or to avoid cluttering your Transaction List with a variety of names that don't give you the information needed. In this case, you can create rules telling Quicken how to change the names of downloaded transactions. You can "rename" securities in downloaded transactions by matching the downloaded security to a security in your Security List. Once the Matched With Online

> ### EXPERIENCED USERS RECOMMEND
>
> Many Quicken users seldom, if ever, use Accept All for any type of downloaded transactions. If they do, they will often perform a backup first from which they can restore their original data. At a minimum, users have recommended that after doing a backup, you take the time to review all of the downloaded transactions thoroughly before you click that Accept All button.
>
> When you click Accept All, if there are sold or removed transactions in the download, you may need to follow prompts so you can enter additional required information. However, after the first time you download, be sure to back up before you accept all the transactions. If you have been entering transactions manually, the download may be slightly different, causing duplication and incorrect balances.

Security link is established, the security will be renamed to the name from the Security List. For example, TD Ameritrade downloads GE as GENERAL ELECTRIC CO COM, but you may prefer your Security List to use "General Electric," so transactions for GE are renamed to General Electric.

NOTE Quicken generally matches to an online security automatically, but if you find the wrong security is matched, you can edit the security and clear the Matched With Online Security option. Then, at the next download, Quicken should prompt you to match the security. Editing the security and changing the name changes the security name displayed in the Transaction List. This process is useful after your first download to change the security names to the name you want displayed.

To rename transactions, click the Renaming Rules button in the Downloaded Transactions tab, or choose Tools | Renaming Rules. The Renaming Rules dialog displays. It shows the list of existing rules. If you have not yet established any Renaming Rules for downloaded transactions, there will be text in light gray font stating that no rules have been defined. Learn more about renaming rules in Chapter 6.

Adjusting the Cash Balance

If the cash balance in your Quicken account doesn't match the cash balance at your brokerage firm, you can adjust the cash balance with the Update Cash Balance dialog. From the Account Bar, click the account you want to adjust. The account's Transaction List appears. From the account's Transaction List, click the Action gear icon | Update Cash Balance. Enter the correct cash balance and the date, and click Done. Quicken adjusts the account accordingly.

In the same way, use the Update Share Balance option to make any corrections to the number of shares in an account.

Reconciling Your Investment Account

To keep your electronic investing accounts reconciled to your statement, you can perform a periodic reconciliation. If your account does not match your statement, you can adjust it with the Reconcile dialog. Select the account in the Account Bar to open the Transaction List. From the Action gear icon's menu, select Reconcile. The Reconcile dialog appears. Enter the starting and ending cash balance amounts and the statement ending date, and click OK.

If the brokerage account has a linked checking account, you will see a warning message telling you the account can only be reconciled from the linked checking account. Click OK to dismiss the warning. For the accounts with linked checking accounts, you'll need to perform the reconciliation in the linked cash account instead. In this case, Quicken will not display the list of transactions in your brokerage account.

A list of the transactions displays. On the left are those transactions that decrease the cash balance, and on the right those that increase it. As you click each transaction, the difference in the lower-right area of the dialog reflects the increase or decrease. Your account is successfully reconciled when the difference is equal to zero. If you want to start by marking all of the transactions, click Mark All. This is particularly helpful when you have many transactions. When you have marked all and are finished, click Done. If you want to return to this later, click Finish Later.

When you have reconciled your account, a message will be displayed offering you the opportunity to create a reconciliation report. Click Yes or No.

- If you choose Yes, the Reconciliation Report Setup dialog appears. Enter a title name.
- Enter a date in the Show To Bank Balance As Of field.
- Choose to create a report including All Transactions or Summary And Uncleared, which shows only the uncleared transactions and a summary of the cleared items.
- Select Show Savings Goal Transactions if you choose to include them.
- Click OK to open the Print dialog. You may choose to print the report to a paper printer or to the Quicken PDF printer. You can also print to a file using the Export To option.
- If you choose No, you are returned to your account's Transaction List.

EXPERIENCED USERS RECOMMEND

As with banking and credit card statements, Quicken does not keep prior period reconciliation reports. To keep your reports, you must either print them or use the Quicken PDF printer to create a "digitally" printed file that you can view with the free Adobe Reader program. (If your operating system is Windows 10, you also have the option of using the Microsoft Print to PDF utility.)

1. In the Print dialog, click the Printer drop-down list and choose Quicken PDF Printer.
2. Click Print. A Save To PDF File dialog box appears.
3. In the Save In field, enter the name of the folder into which the report should be saved, or choose one using the drop-down arrow.
4. Name your file. Use a name that will mean something, perhaps something like Retirement Acct Reconciliation 3-31-2017.
5. Click Save. Your report is "printed" and saved to your selected folder and you are returned to the account's register or Transaction List.

If you click the Don't Show Me This Screen Again check box in the Reconciliation Complete dialog and want to be prompted to print a reconciliation report when completing future reconciliations, you will have to reset the warning in Preferences. From the Quicken Toolbar, click Edit | Preferences | Alerts | Warnings | Reset Quicken Warnings. Click OK to close the Preferences dialog.

Adjusting Holdings

If the holdings amounts in Quicken don't match what you've downloaded, the Enter Transactions dialog can be used to adjust your holdings. Select the account you want to adjust from the Account Bar to open the account's Transaction List. Click the Enter Transactions button located under the name of the account.

From the Enter Transaction drop-down list, select the type of transaction you want. Fill in the information needed, and when you are finished, click Enter/Done. For additional information see the "Entering Common Transactions" section later in this chapter.

If you enter a transaction that has a date more than one year from today's date, you may see a warning message. If you are sure the information you are entering is correct, click Yes.

Working with Investment Accounts

To view an account's information, select the account name from the Account Bar. This opens the register for this account, which looks similar to a spending account's register. From this Transaction List you can enter transactions and perform other activities.

The most important part of properly tracking investments is recording all investment transactions. This includes purchases, sales, dividends, and other activity affecting your portfolio's cost basis and value. This will make life much easier when you are ready to sell the security.

Before you enter a transaction, you must have all of its details. In most cases, you can find the information you need on the monthly statement, confirmation form, or receipt you receive from your broker or investment firm. The information varies, depending on the transaction, but it generally should include the security name, transaction date, number of shares, price per share, and any commissions or fees.

For income tax purposes, it is better to record total cost rather than price per share, as that is the value you enter on Schedule D of your federal income tax return. Quicken will then calculate the price per share for you.

This section provides some information and advice for understanding the Investment Transaction list and entering the most common transactions into investment accounts.

Understanding the Investment Transaction List

The Investment Transaction list looks very much like the check registers. However, instead of the familiar Date, Check Number, and Payee fields, the Investment Transaction list has fields that pertain to your investing activities. See Figure 9-1 for an example.

The Investment Transaction list includes the following:

- **Attachment Icon** (the small paper clip)   When you attach a receipt or other item to this transaction, this icon appears in this column. See Chapter 5 for more information on attachments.
- **Clr**   When you reconcile your investment account, this column shows the cleared status of transactions.
- **Date**   The date of the transaction. Click the small arrow to sort transactions by date.

Figure 9-1 • The Investment Transaction list in Quicken is similar to a spending account's account register.

- **Action**   What this transaction represents. See "Investment Actions" later in this chapter for more information. Click the column to display the small arrow that allows you to sort by this column. It sorts in alphabetical order by action.
- **Security**   This column shows the name of the security. Since a single investment account can contain a wide variety of securities, each security is named.

The five columns that appear with a bold font in the Investment Transaction list are sort fields. Click in the column name you want to use to sort by that column.

- **Description**   What action is represented. For example, if the Action column says "Bought," the number of shares of the named security and the price paid show in this column.
- **Share Bal**   This is the balance of the cumulative number of shares for all the transactions pertaining to that security in the account. This is not the amount of shares for the individual transaction unless the transaction is the first or only transaction in the account for that security.

- **Inv Amt** Shows the amount of the investment in dollars. For example, if you purchased 50 shares of stock at $10.00 per share with a $35.00 commission/fee, this amount would be $535.00.
- **Cash Amt** This column displays the cash amount for transactions for this account where cash is received or spent; for example, for a dividend, you receive cash, so the amount of the dividend would show in the Cash Amt column.
- **Cash Bal** This column displays any cash balance in the account after the transaction on this line of the register.

 Share Balance is the cumulative total of shares for that security on the date of the transaction. If you have three transactions for a security, each buying 10 shares, the Share Balance will show 10, 20, and 30 for the corresponding three "buy" transactions. You need to select the transaction to see how many shares were involved in that particular transaction. The number of shares involved in a transaction also appears in the Description column.

 If your account has a linked checking account, the Cash Amt and Cash Bal columns do not appear in the Investment Transaction list. In an investment account with a linked checking account, you will see a column for investment amount labeled Inv Amt.

Working with the Buttons

In addition to the register lines, at the top of the Transaction List are the Enter Transactions and Holding buttons, each with several options:

- **Enter Transactions** Clicking the Enter Transactions button opens the investment transaction dialog. See "Using the Investment Transaction Dialog" later in this chapter.
- **Holdings** Click the Holdings button to open an Account Overview window for this account. Similar to the Portfolio view in the Investing tab, you can see the current value, recent and historical performances, and the tax implications of the transactions in this account, as explained in "Exploring the Account Overview Window" later in this chapter.

Account Actions Click the Action gear icon at the right of the Investment Transaction list to open the menu, shown next. This menu gives you access to several investment-related activities. The menu is divided into three sections: Transactions, Reporting, and Global Preferences (All Registers). Each is described next:

- **Update Transactions** opens the One Step Update Settings dialog. Enter your password and click Update Now to update your accounts.
- **Set Up Download** (not shown) appears when you have not yet activated this investing account for online services. If your financial institution offers online services, click Set Up Download to start the process.
- **Update 401(k) Holdings** (not shown) starts the Update 401(k) Holdings Wizard.
- **Update Quotes Only** prompts Quicken to use your Internet connection to download the latest quotes on your holdings and Watch List. Learn more about the Watch List later in this chapter.
- **Edit Account Details** displays the General Information tab of the Account Details dialog, which you can use to enter or edit basic information about the account, including its name, tax-deferred status, account number, and contact information. From this dialog you can also enter information about fees and commission charges for this account. Click Fees to open the Transaction Fees dialog. After you have entered the information, as either a dollar amount or a percentage, click OK to close the Fees dialog and again to close the Account Details dialog.
- **Enter Transaction** opens the investment transaction dialog as described later in this chapter.
- **Reconcile** opens the Reconcile dialog.
- **Update Cash/Share Balance** works as described in "Adjusting the Cash Balance" earlier in this chapter.
- **Reconcile Shares** appears only in investment accounts that are online enabled, it does not appear in manual investment accounts.
- **Security List** opens the Security List. See "Viewing the Security List" later in this chapter.

The menu panel shows:

	Transactions	
⚡	Update Transactions	
⚡	Update Quotes only	
🖉	Edit account details	Ctrl+Shift+E
▭	Enter Transaction	
◎	Reconcile	Ctrl+R
◎	Update cash balance...	
◎	Update share balance...	
◎	Reconcile Shares...	
▤	Security List	
	Reporting	
�量	Account attachments	Ctrl+Shift+A
⊿	Account overview	Ctrl+Shift+O
▣	Investing Activity	
🖶	Print transactions	Ctrl+P
	Global preferences(All registers)	
⚙	Register Row Height Spacing	▸
⚙	Register preferences	
⚙	Customize action bar	

You will see a Checking Account entry here only if the investment account has a linked checking account.

- **Account Attachments** opens the Account Attachment dialog. See Chapter 5 to learn how to work with attachments.
- **Account Overview** opens the Account Overview window.
- **Investing Activity** opens a report about your investing activity for time ranges you can set.
- **Print Transactions** gives you the opportunity to print your Transaction List.
- **Register Row Height Spacing** opens a small menu from which you can set the height of each row in the register as discussed in Chapter 1.
- **Register Preferences** opens the Preferences dialog to the Investment Transactions section. See Appendix B for more information about preferences.
- **Customize Action Bar** opens the Customize Action Bar dialog. From this dialog, you can select additional actions to display on this investment account's action bar, which will display the icons for the items you select in the Customize Action Bar dialog. This customization affects only this investment account.

Exploring the Account Overview Window

When you download transactions from your financial institution, you also receive detailed account balance information. To review this information, select the account in the Account Bar to open the Transaction List. From the Action gear icon's menu, select Account Overview.

The Account Overview window for this account appears as seen in Figure 9-2. Or, you can click the Holdings button next to the Enter Transactions button. You can also add the Account Overview icon to the account's action bar for quick access each time you use the account's Transaction List.

You can review this information in the Account Overview window and compare it to the information in your account statement. You can choose several ways of viewing your holdings. Click the Show menu to see the options shown here.

Some Quicken users prefer using the Portfolio view of the Investing tab to review their holdings. Some prefer the Portfolio view as changes made there are retained, while changes in the Account Overview's Holdings snapshot are not retained. Also, the Portfolio view offers 18 customizable views in the Portfolio, while there are only 4 non-customizable views in the Holdings.

- **Value** displays the following:
  - **Currency** displays if you have enabled multiple currencies.
  - **Quote/Price** shows the quote or price as of the last time you downloaded.

Name	▲	Quote/Price	Shares	Market Value	Cost Basis	Gain/Loss	Gain/L... (%)	Day Gain/Loss	Price Day Change	Price Day Change (%)
⊞ Dycom Industries		81.14	25	2,028.50	1,250.00	778.50	62.28	20.50 ⬆	+ 0.82	+1.02%
⊞ General Motors		35.25	150	5,287.50	3,982.50	1,305.00	32.77	15.00 ⬆	+ 0.10	+0.28%
⊞ Independence Realty Trust		8.77	25	219.25	150.25	69.00	45.92	2.25 ⬆	+ 0.09	+1.04%
⊞ ONE Gas		64.02	50	3,201.00	2,477.50	723.50	29.20	24.00 ⬆	+ 0.48	+0.76%
⊞ USG Corporation		29.52	25	738.00	425.00	313.00	73.65	0.25 ⬆	+ 0.01	+0.03%
Totals:				11,474.25	8,285.25	3,189.00	38.49	62.00		

Online quotes delayed at least 20 minutes. Options quotes are previous day's close. Updated 12/28/2016 at 10:04 am local time.

Figure 9-2 • The Account Overview window contains detailed information about an investment account.

- **Shares** shows the number of shares you currently hold.
- **Market Value** displays today's value of these shares.
- **Cost Basis** shows what you paid for these shares when you bought them, plus or minus any cost-basis–related adjustments, like dividend reinvestments, sales, or corporate actions.
- **Gain/Loss & Gain/Loss %** display your unrealized gain or loss as of the last time you downloaded in both dollars and percentages.
- **Day Gain/Loss** indicates the overall gain or loss based on the latest download prices in dollars.
- **Price Day Change** shows the trend for today for each security and the dollar amount of the change.
- **Price Day Change %** displays the change in price since the previous day's closing price as a percentage.
- **Recent Performance** shows the following:
  - **Market Value** shows the market value as of the last download.
  - **Gain/Loss** and **Gain/Loss %** show the gain or loss in dollars and/or percentage over time.

- **Gain/Loss 1-Month** shows the gain or loss in dollars for the past month.
- **Gain/Loss 1-Month %** shows the percentage of the gain or loss percentage for the past month.
- **Gain/Loss for % 3-Month and 12-Month** shows the gain or loss percentage for these time periods.

• **Historic Performance** indicates the average annual return for each security compared with the average annual return in its industry or category for the past one, three, and five years as a percentage. It also displays the industry and/or category of each holding, expressed as percentages. If you have not held the shares for the entire one-, three-, or five-year period, N/A will display instead of a percent value.

• **Tax Implications** displays tax information about each security. You may need to expand the security lot information by clicking the plus sign in the small square at the left of the security's name to see the tax implications for each lot. However, check with your tax professional for more information.

If you want to adjust your holdings, refer to the section "Adjusting Holdings" elsewhere in this chapter.

Checking Your Account's Status

The current status of your account is displayed in the center of the Account Overview window in the Account Status snapshot. It includes all of the following:

- The **Security Value** of this entire account
- The **Cash Balance** held in this account
- The **Total Market Value**

You will also see the Linked Cash Balance if the account has a linked checking account.

This snapshot also includes the Last Transaction, Last Reconcile, and Last Statement Download dates. You can also see any transactions that need to be compared, as well as any e-mails to the account's financial institution that you need to send or read from the Online Center. Click the blue date shown to the right of Last Statement Download to go to the Online Center for this account.

Seeing the Options

In the Holdings snapshot of the Account Overview, the Options gear menu allows you to do the following:

- **Preferences** opens the Portfolio View Options dialog. These preference settings apply globally to the Account Overview and Portfolio view for all investment accounts.
- **Show Closed Lots** tells Quicken to show transactions that have been closed. This setting also applies to the Account Overview and the Portfolio view for all investment accounts.
- **Get Online Quotes** uses your Internet connection to update your holdings.
- **Go To Full Portfolio** takes you to the Investing tab's Portfolio view.

If you are using Quicken Premier or higher edition and have chosen to update your quotes every 15 minutes, your holdings are automatically updated while Quicken is the active application. To turn on this useful feature, select Edit | Preferences | Investment Transactions, and select the Automatically Update Quotes Every 15 Minutes check box. Click OK or Close to close the Preferences dialog.

The Options menu in the Account Status snapshot offers the following:

- **Reconcile This Account** opens the Account Reconciliation dialog.
- **View All My Accounts** opens the Account List.

Reviewing the Account's Attributes

The bottom snapshot of the Account Overview window displays the account name, its tax-deferment status, and other information about your account. This includes your account number and user name, so be careful if you view this information in a public setting.

From the Option gear's menu in this section, you can do the following:

- **Create a New Account**   Click this to open the Add Account dialog.
- **View/Edit Comments**   This option opens a dialog box in which you can add or edit comments about this account.
- **Set Tax Attributes**   This option opens the Tax Schedule Information dialog.
- **Set Web Pages**   You can enter the Home Page, Activity Page, and one additional webpage address for this account in this dialog.
- **Browse Web Pages**   After you have entered webpage addresses for this account, the option displays a link to those pages.
- **Transaction Fee**   This dialog allows you to enter any fees associated with this account. You may enter both fixed costs and percentages.
- **Create New Loan**   If you are viewing a 401(k) or 403(b) account, you may see an additional option from which you can create a loan that you have taken against this account.

The Edit Account Details button at the bottom of the Account Overview screen opens the Account Details dialog at the General tab. The Change Online Services button opens the Account Details dialog at the Online Services tab.

Click Close to close the Account Overview screen.

Using the Investment Transaction Dialog

You enter transactions into an investment account with the investment transaction dialog. This dialog, which is named for the type of transaction you are entering, is a fill-in form with all of the fields you need to enter transaction details.

To open the investment transaction dialog, click the Enter Transactions button in the Transaction List for the account in which you want to enter the transaction (refer to Figure 9-1). It looks like the dialog shown next. (If the account is a 401(k) account, you may see a Cash Source button in the dialog.)

Investment Actions

To use the investment transaction dialog, you must begin by choosing a transaction type (or action) from the Enter Transaction drop-down list. There are dozens of action types organized into two categories: investment transactions and cash transactions.

Investment Transactions   Investment transactions directly affect your security or investment account balances, unless you have placeholders. See "Working with Placeholder Entries" earlier in this chapter.

- **Buy – Shares Bought** (shown earlier) enables you to add shares to an investment account. The cost of the shares (plus any commissions) is deducted from the account's cash balance (or another account's cash balance).
- **Sell – Shares Sold** enables you to remove shares from an investment account. The proceeds from the sale (net of any commissions) are added to the account's cash balance (or another account's cash balance).
- **Div – Stock Dividend (Non-Cash)** enables you to add shares of a security paid as a dividend.
- **Reinvest – Income Reinvested** enables you to account for investment income (such as dividends) that is reinvested in the security. This is common with dividend reinvestment plans and mutual funds.
- **Inc – Income (Div, Int, Etc.)** enables you to record income from interest, dividends, and capital gain distributions. It also enables you to record miscellaneous income that you can categorize as you wish.
- **Add – Shares Added** enables you to add shares to an investment account without an exchange of cash. You might use this option to add shares received as a gift.
- **Remove – Shares Removed** enables you to remove shares from an investment account without an exchange of cash. You might use this option to remove shares you have given to someone else as a gift.

Each of these options has a keyboard shortcut with which you can access the transaction type, as seen next. Keyboard shortcuts can save some time when entering common transactions. You can also press the first letter of the transaction type; for example, pressing B successively selects Buy – Shares Bought, Bonds Bought, Bonds Sold, and Bought ESPP Shares.

Investment Transactions	
Buy - Shares Bought	Alt+G
Sell - Shares Sold	Alt+R
Div - Stock Dividend (non-cash)	Alt+K
Reinvest - Income Reinvested	Alt+V
Inc - Income (Div, Int, etc.)	Alt+I
Add - Shares Added	Alt+Z
Remove - Shares Removed	Alt+X

- **Adjust Share Balance** enables you to create a placeholder entry transaction to make your share balance agree with your brokerage statement. You can enter cost information later, as discussed earlier in this chapter, in the section "Working with Placeholder Entries."
- **Stock Split** enables you to record additional shares received as a result of a stock split.

- **Return Of Capital** enables you to record the return of part of your investment capital.
- **Miscellaneous Expense** enables you to record investment expenses other than commissions. Unlike most other actions, you can assign a category to miscellaneous expense transactions.
- **Margin Interest Expense** enables you to record the amount of interest paid as a result of purchasing securities on margin.
- **Bonds Bought/Sold** enables you to record the purchase and sale of bonds.
- **Grant Employee Stock Option** enables you to record the receipt of an employee stock option.
- **Exercise Employee Stock Option** enables you to use an employee stock option to buy stock.
- **Reprice Employee Stock Option** enables you to change pricing information for stock options.
- **Bought ESPP Shares** is used to enter transactions for shares you have purchased through an Employee Stock Purchase Plan.
- **Sold ESPP Shares** allows you to enter shares you have sold through an Employee Stock Purchase Plan.
- **Short Sale** enables you to record a short sale of a security.
- **Cover Short Sale** enables you to record the purchase of stock to cover a short sale.
- **Corporate Name Change** enables you to record the change of the name of a company for which you own stock. This preserves the old name information; simply editing the security name in the Edit Security dialog does not.
- **Corporate Securities Spin-Off** enables you to record securities obtained through a spin-off of a smaller company from one of the companies in which you own securities.
- **Corporate Acquisition (Stock For Stock)** enables you to record securities obtained in exchange for other securities you own, normally as a result of a corporate acquisition.
- **Mutual Fund Conversion** lets you record the information for a mutual fund that you currently hold that is being replaced by another fund. Here you record the price per share after the conversion is complete.
- **Cash Transferred Into Account** enables you to record the transfer of cash into the investment account.
- **Cash Transferred Out Of Account** enables you to record the transfer of cash out of the investment account.

 If the investment account has a linked checking account, you will not see the Cash Transferred options.

- **Shares Transferred Between Accounts** enables you to move shares from one Quicken investment account to another.
- **Reminder Transaction** enables you to enter an investment reminder. If the Reminder Transaction has a future date, the reminder will not appear in the alert list until that future date. This reminder will appear as text in your Quicken investment alerts the next time you open Quicken.

Cash Transactions   Cash transactions affect the cash balance in an investment account. These actions make it possible to track an investment account's cash balance without using a linked cash account.

- **Write Check** enables you to record a check written from an investment account.
- **Deposit** enables you to record a cash deposit to an investment account.
- **Withdraw** enables you to record the withdrawal of cash from an investment account.
- **Online Payment** enables you to record an online payment from the investment account's cash balance. To use this feature, the account must be enabled for Online Payment or Online Bill Pay. Chapter 6 discusses Online Payment.
- **Other Cash Transaction** enables you to record any type of transaction that affects the investment account's cash balance.

Completing the Transaction

Investment transaction dialogs and forms are generally self-explanatory and easy to use. Simply fill out the fields in the form, and click one of the Enter buttons. Enter/New enters the current transaction and redisplays the investment transaction dialog so you can enter another transaction. Enter/Done enters the current transaction and dismisses the investment transaction dialog.

Entering Common Transactions

Although page-count limitations make it impossible to review every kind of investment transaction in this book, here's a look at a few common transactions. They should give you a solid understanding of how the investment transaction dialogs work so you can enter your transactions.

Buying Shares

A security purchase normally involves the exchange of cash for security shares. In some cases, you may already own shares of the security or have it listed on your

Watch List. In other cases, the security may not already exist in your Quicken data file, so you'll need to set up the security when you make the purchase.

Start by selecting the investing account with which you want to work. Click Enter Transactions to display the Buy – Shares Bought dialog shown earlier. Enter information about the shares you have purchased:

- **Transaction Date** is the date you purchased the shares.
- **Account** is the name of the account you selected. You cannot change the option chosen from this drop-down list. If the account name is incorrect, click Cancel, open the correct investing account, and start over.
- **Security Name** is the name of the security. If you enter the name of a security that doesn't already exist in Quicken, the Add Security To Quicken dialog, which is discussed later in the section "Adding a New Security," appears so you can add the security to Quicken.
- **Number Of Shares** is the number of shares purchased.
- **Price Paid** is the per-share price.
- **Commission** is the amount of commissions you paid to your brokerage or investment firm.
- **Total Cost** is calculated by Quicken. For Number of Shares, Price Paid, Commission, and Total Cost, you can provide the entry for any three and Quicken will calculate the fourth value.

Enter the total cost and number of shares, and let Quicken calculate the price paid. The total cost and number of shares is what gets reported on IRS Schedule D when you sell the shares. The total cost and number of shares should match exactly what your brokerage reports, and the price per share can be off by a few pennies. It's better to record the information so you can correctly report your transactions at tax time and be confident if you are audited.

- **Memo** lets you enter any comments about this transaction.
- **Use Cash For This Transaction** enables you to specify an account from which the total cost should be deducted. By default, this option is set to use cash from the same investment account. If the brokerage account has a linked checking account, the cash source will default to the linked checking account; this cannot be changed.

When you're finished entering information about the transaction, click one of the Enter buttons. The transaction appears in the Transactions list for the account.

If you want to add security shares to an account without an exchange of cash, use the Add – Shares Added action. Its form asks for most of the same information but does not affect any cash balances. In addition to not affecting the cash balance, Add Shares lets you specify a different acquisition date from the transaction date. This can be helpful if you received the shares as a gift or inheritance so you can track both the date you received the shares and the date the shares were originally acquired.

Selling Shares

A security sale also involves the exchange of cash for security shares. Normally, you dispose of shares you already own, but in some instances, you may sell shares you don't own. This is called selling short, and it is a risky investment technique sometimes used by experienced investors. (To record short sale transactions, use the Short Sale or Cover Short Sale action.)

To sell shares, choose Sell – Shares Sold in the investment transaction dialog to display the Sell – Shares Sold dialog. Enter information about the shares you have sold:

- **Transaction Date** is the date you sold the shares.
- **Account** is the name of the account in which the transaction should be recorded. You cannot change the option chosen from this drop-down list if you are entering a transaction from within the account's Transaction window; if it's wrong, click Cancel, open the correct account register, and start over.
- **Security Name** is the name of the security. You can choose an option from the drop-down list, or if you have many securities, start typing the security name in the field and Quicken will show securities that begin with those letters.
- **Sell All Shares In This Account** tells Quicken to automatically enter the total number of shares you own in the Number Of Shares box.
- **Number Of Shares** is the number of shares sold.
- **Price Received** is the per-share price.
- **Commission** is the amount of commissions you paid to your brokerage or investment firm.
- **Specify Lots** enables you to specify which shares you are selling when you have multiple purchase lots.

You need to be able to instruct your brokerage which lots you are selling. Not all brokerages allow tax lot–specific transactions. The Specify Lots button will be grayed out if you do not have any shares of the selected security in the account where you are entering the sell data. It will also be grayed out if the security uses average cost, like a mutual fund.

EXPERIENCED USERS RECOMMEND

When working in your investing accounts, always ensure you are in the correct investment account and double-check the security name to be sure the security you wish to sell is in that account. Even experienced Quicken users report issues when they try to sell a security that is not in the account or the security name is similar. This is also where entering the correct number of shares, including all necessary decimal places for transactions, becomes critical. If you rounded the numbers or entered any incorrect numbers, you may not be able to record the sale of the number of shares you wish. The Share Balance column in the Investment Transaction list can be useful in troubleshooting this issue, as it shows the exact number of shares you have for each security.

- **Total Sale** is determined by multiplying the per-share price by the number of shares and deducting the commission. These are the proceeds from the sale. You can enter any three of the four fields (shares, price per share, commission, and total) and Quicken will calculate the fourth field.

The technique Quicken uses is determined by the data you enter. However, your broker reports the total sale amount on the 1099B form he or she sends at the end of each year. This is the number you report on Schedule D of your annual income tax report. Therefore, the total sale amount is more critical than the price per share.

- **Memo** lets you enter any comments about this transaction.
- **Record Proceeds?** enables you to specify an account to which the net proceeds should be added. If the investment account has a linked checking account, all proceeds go to the linked checking account. From that linked checking account, you can transfer proceeds to any account in Quicken.

When you click one of the Enter buttons, Quicken records the transaction.

Dividend Payments and Other Income

Many investments pay dividends, interest, or other income in cash. (That's why they're so attractive to an investor!) Recording this activity in the appropriate Transaction List enables Quicken to calculate performance accurately while keeping account balances up to date, as well as helping you at tax time.

Keep in mind that many mutual funds are set up to reinvest income rather than pay it in cash. Do not use the steps in this section to record a reinvestment of income. Instead, use the Reinvest Income action to enter transaction information.

EXPERIENCED USERS RECOMMEND

Use the Specify Lots option when selling your shares for additional control over capital gains. For example, if you want to take advantage of long-term capital gains tax breaks, you could sell shares that have been in your possession for more than 12 months. If you want to record a loss, you could sell shares that cost more than the selling price. Obviously, your options will vary, depending on the lots, their acquisition prices, and your selling price. If you select this option, click the Specify Lots button to display a dialog. (This dialog may include an Enter Missing Transactions button if placeholder entries exist for the security.) Use the dialog to enter shares in each lot you are selling, or select one of the Auto Select options and click OK. If you don't use the Specify Lots button to select lots, Quicken automatically sells the oldest shares (First In, First Out, or FIFO, method). As always, consult your tax professional if you want to select lots other than FIFO to determine what the IRS limitations might be.

To record dividend or interest income, choose Inc – Income (Div, Int, Etc.) from the drop-down list in the investment transaction dialog to display the Income dialog. Enter information about a cash payment on an investment:

- **Transaction Date** is the date of the income event.
- **Account** is the name of the account in which the transaction is to be recorded. You cannot change the option chosen from this drop-down list if you are entering a transaction; if it's wrong, click Cancel, open the correct Transaction List, and start over.
- **Transfer Account** enables you to specify an account into which the income is deposited. Leave this blank if the cash is deposited directly into the investment account. If the investment account has a linked checking account, the linked checking account will be designated as the transfer account and cannot be changed.
- **Memo** enables you to enter a brief note about the transaction.
- **Security Name** is the name of the security. You can choose an option from the drop-down list. If the transaction isn't related to a specific security—for example, interest paid on a cash balance in a brokerage account—you can leave this field blank.
- **Dividend**, **Interest**, **Short-Term Cap Gain Dist**, **Mid-Term Cap Gain Dist**, **Long-Term Cap Gain Dist**, and **Miscellaneous** are fields for entering various types of income. In most cases, you'll use only one or two of these boxes.
- **Total Proceeds** is the total of all income amounts calculated by Quicken.
- **Category For Miscellaneous** is the category you want to use to record miscellaneous income. This field is available only if you enter a value in the Miscellaneous field.

When you click one of the Enter buttons to record the transaction, it appears in the Transaction List.

Other Transactions

Other transactions are just as easy to enter as purchases, sales, and income. Simply choose the appropriate option from the drop-down list in the investment transaction dialog, and enter the transaction information in the form that appears. If you have the transaction confirmation or brokerage statement in front of you when you enter the transaction, you have all the information you need to record it.

You may wonder what the BoughtX and XIn/XOut items in your register's Action column mean. The *X* simply indicates that the action had no impact on the cash balance of the account and the transaction was a transfer between accounts.

If you need additional guidance while entering a transaction, click the Help button (question mark icon) in the Enter Transaction dialog to learn more about the options that must be entered.

To quickly recalculate transactions in an account, use the keyboard shortcut CTRL-Z.

Entering Transactions in the Transaction List

You can also enter investment transactions directly into the Transaction List window. This feature makes entering transactions quicker for experienced Quicken users.

To begin, scroll down to the blank line at the bottom of the register. Click the line to activate it, and enter the transaction date in the Date column. Then choose an action from the pop-up menu in the Action column and press TAB. The two lines for the transactions fill in with italicized reminders of the information you should enter into each field. Fill in the fields with transaction details, and click Enter. Be aware that not all transaction types can be entered directly in the Investment Transaction list. If the form is required, it will pop up automatically.

Editing Transactions

You can quickly edit transactions from your Investment Transaction list. In the register for the account, select the transaction you want to edit. Click in the field you want to modify, and make the desired change. When you're finished, click Enter.

You can also select the transaction and select the Edit action button. The Edit dialog appears. You can also double-click the transaction you wish to edit. Change any of the fields and click Enter/Done.

You can also right-click the transaction to open the context menu. Choose Edit to open the Edit dialog.

NOTE A few transaction types cannot be edited: Exercise Employee Stock Option and Sold ESPP Shares. These transactions must be deleted and re-entered if a change is needed. Additional information on entering uncommon transactions can be found on the Quicken Live Community site. The Quicken Live Community is especially helpful if you have a corporate action, like a merger or a spinoff, that you want to enter in Quicken. Mention the companies involved and you'll get specific detailed instructions on how to enter the merger or spinoff transactions in Quicken.

Working with the Security List

This part of the chapter explains how you can use the Security List to add a new security, choose market indexes, download quotes, edit security details, and more.

Viewing the Security List

The Security List window (see Figure 9-3) simply lists the securities in Quicken's data file. You can use this window to add, edit, delete, or hide securities, including *Watch List securities*—securities you don't own but want to monitor. To open this window, press CTRL-Y. You can also access the list from the Action gear icon menu in an Investment Transaction list or from the Investing tab's Tools menu, select Tools | Security List.

Adding a New Security

To add a new security to your Quicken data file as either a holding or a Watch List item, click the New Security button at the bottom of the Security List window (refer to Figure 9-3). The Add Security To Quicken dialog appears, displaying screens that prompt you for information about a security.

When you click Next, you may be prompted to enter your Intuit ID. Quicken connects to the Internet to obtain information about the security based on its ticker symbol. If it finds the ticker symbol, it displays the information it has downloaded in the Add Security To Quicken dialog. Entering the correct ticker symbol

Figure 9-3 • The Security List window provides many ways with which you can work with your investments.

automates much of the security setup process. Look up the symbol. For example, if you type PG as shown here, you will see a number of other company ticker symbols that start with PG. Click Done to add the security to the Security List.

If Quicken can't find information about the security on the Internet, it displays a dialog enabling you to correct the ticker symbol, or add the security manually. If you made an error when entering the ticker symbol, you can enter the correct symbol in the Ticker Symbol text box and click Next to try looking it up on the Internet again. This security is automatically included in your Quicken Watch List when you add it in this manner.

If you select the Add Manually option, select a security type—Bond, CD, Emp. Stock Option, ESPP, Market Index, Mutual Fund, Other, Stock, or U.S. Savings Bond—and click Next. Another dialog appears, prompting you for additional information about the security, such as its asset class (for a stock), asset class mixture (for a mutual fund), and bond type and maturity and call dates (for a bond). Enter whatever information you have for the security, and click Done to add the security to the Security List.

EXPERIENCED USERS RECOMMEND

Quicken users often ask the Quicken Community how Quicken defines "asset class." Strictly speaking, an asset class is a group of similar securities, such as equity instruments or stocks, income instruments such as bonds, and cash equivalents such as money market accounts. Within each asset class are categories. Quicken uses the shorthand name of "asset classes" to define types or categories of securities. When you enter "asset class" information in Quicken, you are categorizing the asset as one of several different asset "types":

- **Domestic Bonds**   These bonds are issued and traded in the currency of the country in which they are traded. That means they are not subject to fluctuations in currency exchange rates.
- **Global Bonds**   These bonds are traded in any international market, either foreign or domestic. The same bond issue may be offered in several countries at the same time.
- **Large Cap Stocks**   These securities are offered by large, publicly traded companies with a "market capitalization" of at least $10 billion. (Market capitalization is simply a generally accepted value of a company.) In Quicken, the cutoff between small cap and large cap is $4 billion.
- **Small Cap Stocks**   Securities offered by a publicly traded firm with a market capitalization of between $200 to 300 million and $2 to 3 billion.
- **International Stock**   These are securities sold by a company outside of the United States.
- **Cash/Other/Unclassified**   Assets that do not fit one of the other classifications.

If you select Employee Stock Option or ESPP, you start the wizards for those security types.

The security type market index is not the same as an index fund. The term *market index* is only intended for true indexes like the Dow Jones Industrials index. Selecting market index for an index fund will prevent you from using the security as you normally would. For example, if you try to sell a security you have retyped to market index, the security will not show in the security drop-down list in the Sell – Shares Sold form, even if you are in the correct account.

Choosing a Market Index

Within the Security List, you will see a Choose Market Indexes button. This option enables you to add common market indexes, such as the Dow Jones Industrial Average and the S&P 500 Index, as shown here, to the Security List. This lets you download quotes for these indexes at the same time you download security prices.

Add Security to Quicken   ✕

Select Market Indexes to Display in Quicken.

	Name	Symbol
☑	Dow Jones Industrials	DJI
☑	NASDAQ Composite	COMPX
☑	S&P 500 Index	INX
☑	Russell 2000	IUX
☐	AMEX Composite	XAX.X
☑	Dow Jones Composite	COMP
☐	Dow Jones 20 Transportation	TRAN

Note: Except for S&P 500, these indexes do not include dividend income in the rate of return calculations. For most indexes, this will impact returns less than 1%. It will have greater impact for the Dow Jones Industrial Average.

❓   Cancel   Done

- **Show Hidden Securities**   This option will display any securities you've hidden on the Security List.
- **Mark All**   The Mark All button selects Download Quotes for each security and index in the Security List.

To the chagrin of some Quicken users, there is no corresponding Clear All button available.

Working with Individual Securities

When you select a security on the list, three action buttons appear, as seen next. It is with these buttons that you can edit or delete a security as well as run a report. You can also access these actions by right-clicking the security name.

Security		Symbol	Type	Asset Class	Download Quotes	Watch List	Hide	
Abaxis Inc	▲	ABAX	Stock	Small Cap Stocks	☑	☑	☐	
Amazon.com Inc		AMZN	Stock	Large Cap Stocks	☑	☐	☐	Edit Report Delete

Security List

Editing a Security   You can edit a security to correct or clarify information you previously entered for it. Select the security's name in the Security List window (refer to Figure 9-3), and click the Edit button. The Edit Security Details dialog, as seen here, shows what it looks like for a stock. Enter or edit information in the dialog, and click OK to save your changes.

NOTE Quicken gets its asset information from Value Line. As shown in the Asset Allocation Guide, Value Line uses $4.0 billion as the market capitalization value to delineate between large-cap and small-cap domestic stocks. If you download the asset class for a mid-cap stock, it will be assigned Large Cap or Small Cap as its asset class, depending on whether its market cap is above or below $4.0 billion. To access the Asset Allocation Guide, click Investing | Tools | Asset Allocation Guide. To see the information about Value Line, click How Do I Update Asset Classes on the left of the Asset Allocation Guide. Select Common Questions About Downloading Asset Classes | What Asset Classes Are Assigned And Where Does the Information Come From.

Edit Security Details

Name: Amazon.com Inc

Symbol: AMZN   Look Up...

Type: Stock ▼   Edit Types...

Asset class
● Single   Large Cap Stocks ▼
○ Mixture   Define...
☑ Download asset class information
(This will replace your current asset class information.)

☐ Tax free

☐ Matched with online security   Other Info

OK   Cancel

Deleting a Security   Delete removes the currently selected security from your Quicken data file. If this option is grayed out, it has been used in a transaction and therefore cannot be deleted.

Creating a Report   When you select a security and click the Report button at the right of the selected row, you will see a Security Report, which summarizes all activity for the security. From the report window, you can print, export, save, customize, find, or replace information in the report. See more about working with reports in Chapter 15.

Security Type List   Each security in the Security List must be assigned a security type. To see the Security Type List, open your Security List and select any security. Choose the Edit action button to open the Edit Security Details dialog. Click the Edit Types button to open the Security Type List, as shown here, to display a list of security types.

You can use buttons to modify the list:

- **New** enables you to create a new security type. Clicking this button displays the Set Up Security Type dialog, which you can use to enter a name for the security type.
- **Edit** enables you to change the name of the currently selected security type.
- **Delete** enables you to remove the currently selected security type from the list, although you cannot delete predefined security types assigned to an existing security.

Be cautious about editing or deleting security types. You can cause yourself some serious headaches by doing so.

- The **Help** icon displays the Quicken Personal Finances Software Help window with instructions for working with the Security Types. If another help topic appears, type **Security Types** in the search field to open that Help section.
- **Print icon** prints the Security Type List.

Click Done to return to the Edit Security Details dialog, and OK to return to the Security List.

Investing Goal List   Many Quicken users invest for specific goals, such as a college fund or retirement. Quicken provides a list of investment goals you can customize for your own investing needs. You may find investment goals useful for organizing your investments based on what you expect them to do for you. To see the Investing Goal List, open your Security List and select any security.

- Choose the Edit action button to open the Edit Security Details dialog.
- Click the Other Info button in the Edit Security Details dialog.

The Additional Security Information dialog appears. Click Edit Goals to open the Investing Goal List, as seen here.

- **New** enables you to create a new investment goal. Click this button to open the Set Up Investing Goal dialog in which you can enter a name for the goal. Make the goal name short, as you have only 15 characters.
- **Edit** enables you to change the name of the currently selected investment goal.
- **Delete** enables you to remove the currently selected investment goal from the list.

 If the goal is assigned to any securities, you'll see a prompt asking if you're sure. If you answer Yes, your goal is deleted. The securities using that goal will be assigned the first goal in the Investing Goal List.

- The **Help** icon displays the Quicken Personal Finances Software Help window with instructions for working with the Investing Goal List.
- **Print icon** prints the Investing Goal List.

Click Done to close the Investing Goal List, then click OK to close the Additional Security Information dialog, then OK to close the Edit Security Details dialog and return to the Security List.

Downloading Quotes and Investment Information

Quicken enables you to download up-to-date stock quotes, news headlines, and alerts for the securities in your portfolio and on your Watch List. You set up this feature once and then update the information as often as desired. You can even download historical price information so you can review price trends for a security that recently caught your attention.

Because the quote and investment information feature is built into Quicken, it doesn't rely on your brokerage firm for information. That means you can download quotes, headlines, and alerts even if your brokerage firm doesn't offer the downloading of transactions. All you need is an Internet connection and your Intuit ID.

Downloading Online Quotes

Before you can get quotes online, you must tell Quicken which securities you want to include in the downloaded information. To download information, click the One Step Update symbol (the right-curling arrow) on either the Account Bar or the Toolbar to open the One Step Update Settings dialog. Click the Download Quotes And Investment Information check box. Click the Select Quotes link to open the Security List, as seen in Figure 9-3. You can also open the Security List using the keyboard shortcut CTRL-Y.

You can view details about your securities in the Portfolio window, which is covered in greater detail in Chapter 11. This window displays quotes and news headlines for all securities you own or watch. To display this window, choose Investing | Portfolio. Right-click any security and choose Security View, or double-click the security name to open the Security Detail View window, seen in Figure 9-4, to see information about individual securities or market indexes. See "Using the Security Detail View" next in this chapter.

To open the Security Detail View, from the Investing tab, click Portfolio and click the name of the security or index you want to view from the list that displays. If the name does not show, click the right-facing arrow to open the account, Watch List, or Indexes and click the name of the item you want to see. You can also access the Security Detail View window from the Security List,

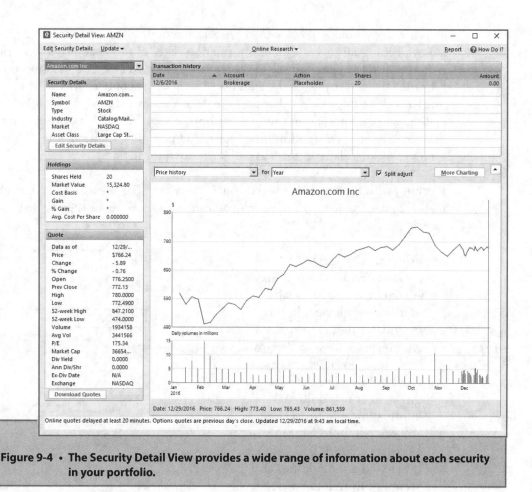

Figure 9-4 • The Security Detail View provides a wide range of information about each security in your portfolio.

which sorts the securities by name. You may also be able to hover your mouse over a security's name to see the small options menu shown here.

You can open the Security Detail View from the Security List by clicking the name of the security or the index.

Using the Security Detail View

The Security Detail View window (see Figure 9-4) offers the most detailed quote information. If you have been faithfully downloading quotes for your securities (or you have downloaded historical quotes, as discussed in the section "Downloading Historical Quote Information" later in this chapter), a chart of the price history appears in the body of the window. You can use the drop-down list in the top-left corner of the window to switch from one security to another. The left side of the window discusses the details about the security, your holdings, and the latest quotes. From this window you can edit the details of your security, download quotes, create additional charts, and do online research. (See "Using Online Research" later in this chapter for more information.)

Working with the Security View Detail Menu Bar   The Security View Detail menu bar has five items from which you can learn more about the selected security:

- **Edit Security Details** opens the Edit Security Details dialog, as seen here. Use this dialog to make any changes in the security, including its ticker symbol, asset class, and security type. See "Downloading Asset Class Information" later in this chapter for additional information about that topic. You can tell Quicken if this is a tax-free security. Click Other Info to open the Additional Security Information dialog in which you can indicate how much income you expect from this security, your goal for this security, your broker's name and phone number, its rating, and any other comments.

Be cautious about editing the security's type or investment goal. These changes can have unintended consequences. For example, changing the investing goal for employee stock options and ESPPs may prevent you from exercising or selling the security.

Click OK to close the Additional Security Information dialog; then click OK to close the Edit Security Details dialog and return to the Security Detail View. There are several options at the top of the Security Detail View screen with which you can find additional information:

- **Update** opens a menu from which you can download quotes, send information to Investing.Quicken.com, download both asset classes and historical prices, and, if necessary, edit the price history of this security.
- **Online Research** offers several tools, as discussed in "Using Online Research" later in this chapter.
- **Report** creates a security report that you can customize to fit your needs.
- **How Do I?** opens the Quicken Help window that discusses securities and security prices.

Click Close to close the Security Detail View.

Viewing Price Information in the Portfolio View   In the Investing tab's Portfolio view, downloaded quotes appear beside the security name or ticker symbol. Stock quotes are delayed 20 minutes or more during the trading day. Quotes for mutual funds are updated once a day by around 6:00 P.M. Eastern Standard Time. Prior to that, you'll see the previous day's prices with a small clock symbol icon beside the price, indicating that the price has not been updated since the previous trading day. Right-click the security in the Portfolio view and select Price History from the context menu. Click Close to exit the Price History and return to the Portfolio view.

Downloading Historical Quote Information

Use Quicken to download up to five years of historical quotes for any security you own or watch. Choose Investing | Update | Historical Prices. Quicken displays the Get Historical Prices dialog, shown here.

If you happen to own a security that is not publicly traded, you won't be able to download historical quote information for it. If you have a source of price data for the security, you can import a price history file.

Choose a time period from the drop-down list at the top of the dialog. Your choices are Five Days, Month, Year, Two Years, and Five Years. Make sure check marks appear beside all securities for which you want to get historical quotes. (Click Mark All to get prices for all securities on the list.)

Some Quicken users have reported trouble when selecting five years of prices for many securities at the same time. Several have suggested that you request data for five years for a single security or one month for several securities.

Then click the Update Now button. Quicken retrieves the information you requested. When it's done, it displays the One Step Update Summary window. Click Close to dismiss the window. Depending on your preference setting, you may not see the One Step Update Summary window unless there is an error.

Downloading Asset Class Information

For each publicly traded security you own or watch, you can include asset class information. This enables you to create accurate asset allocation reports and graphs. Chapter 11 explains how you can use this information to diversify your portfolio to meet your investment goals.

The trouble is that most mutual funds consist of many investments in a variety of asset classes. Manually looking up and entering this information is time consuming and tedious. Fortunately, Quicken automatically downloads this information for you, including your mutual funds.

However, you can change the information at any time. To do so, choose the Investing tab and click Tools | Security List. Click the security you want, and then click the Edit action button. This opens the Security Detail View dialog seen earlier in this chapter. Right-click anywhere on the row for the security you want to change and select Edit. Make sure the Download Asset Class Information check box is selected, close the dialog, and click OK to close the dialog. The next time you update, asset classes are automatically updated.

Making Selections on the Security List

Using check boxes on the Security List, you may select the information you want to download or actions you want to perform for each of your securities. You may choose to:

- Download quotes for each security.
- Include the security on your Watch List.
- Hide the security. However, even if you hide the security, Quicken does not uncheck the Download Quotes or Watch List check boxes.

The Add Security button opens an Add Security To Quicken dialog with which you can enter a new security to the list.

Creating a Watch List

To set up a group of securities you don't own but want to track, create a Watch List. Click the Investing tab and Portfolio. Click Customize, select the Accounts tab, and ensure Watch List is checked in the list of accounts. Click OK to save the change and return to the Portfolio view.

You can designate which securities in your Security List you want to watch by selecting the Watch List check box. From any of the Portfolio views that you chose to display a Watch List, you can click the Add or Edit link to change the securities you are watching. You can also select one or more Portfolio views in which you want to display your Watch List.

Click the right-facing arrow to the left of Watch List, if necessary, to open your current list. All of the securities you have chosen to display on the Watch List will appear. You may change the securities to include in the Watch List in the Security List, as discussed in "Making Selections on the Security List" earlier in this chapter.

You may see a small newspaper icon to the right of a security name or symbol. This is a link. Click it to display a link to the latest information about that security. Click More to open the Investing.Quicken.com page for additional information about the security. (However, you will not see this unless you have set up alerts on Quicken.com.)

Using Investing.Quicken.com for Updates

Using Investing.Quicken.com enables you to track your portfolio's value on the Internet. Although you can do this without Quicken by manually customizing and updating the default portfolio webpage at Investing.Quicken.com, it's a lot easier to have Quicken automatically send updated portfolio information to the page for you.

During the registration process when you installed Quicken and created your Intuit ID and password, the process set up a private Investing.Quicken.com account for you to store your portfolio data.

Exporting Your Portfolio

In Quicken, choose Investing | Update | Update Portfolio On Investing.Quicken .com. The Preferences dialog appears, as shown next.

Click to place green check marks beside each account that you want to track on the Web. If you also want to track Watch List items on the Web, select the Track My Watch List On Investing.Quicken.com check box. Finally, select one of the following upload options:

- **Send My Shares** exports the ticker symbols and the number of shares of each security you own for your portfolio. This enables you to track both prices and portfolio values.
- **Send Only My Symbols** exports just the ticker symbols for your portfolio. This enables you to track prices but not portfolio values.

When you've completed your selections, click OK. The next time you run One Step Update, your account will be updated.

**Figure 9-5 • The Quicken Investing page has a wide variety of ways to work with your
investments.**

To access your Investing.Quicken.com account, go to the Internet from any
location. In the address bar of your browser, type **https://investing.quicken.com**.
You are prompted for your Quicken.com registration member ID and password.
Type the information and click Sign In and your Investing Home page appears,
as seen in Figure 9-5.

Utilizing Quote Lookup

Use the Quote Lookup feature in the Investing Home tab at Investing.Quicken
.com, as shown next, to look up stock ticker symbols. These symbols are required
to use Quicken's Online Research feature for getting quotes and obtaining
information about securities on the Web.

Quotes & Research	Trade Ideas	Alerts	Account Settings ▸ Sign Out
			Help │ Support │ Contact Us

d to Watchlist │ Set Alert │ Quote: ABAX │ Go │ Lookup...

In the Quote field, type the ticker symbol for your security. If you don't know the symbol, just start typing the name in the Quote field. Quicken organizes the results by security type: Stocks, Mutual Funds, ETFs, and Indices. Click the tab of the security type you want, and examine the securities it found that matched the criteria you entered.

Since the Lookup feature opens another browser window, once you are done looking up symbols, close the new browser window to return to the browser window displaying your Investing.Quicken.com information. You can also click the security name that matches the symbol you entered. This will close the second browser window and display the quote information for the security you selected.

Using Online Research

The Investing.Quicken.com site has a number of useful research tools. You can use these tools to find and learn about securities before you invest. This part of the chapter tells you a little about Quicken's online research tools so you can explore them. Many Quicken users find them valuable resources for making wise investment decisions. You can access online research information for a specific security from the Security Detail View window. Press CTRL-Y to open the Security List. Double-click a security, and from the Security Detail View menu bar, select Online Research to open a menu.

- **Get Full Quote and Quotes And Research**   Both of these menu choices take you to the Investing.Quicken.com sign-in site. Sign in to see a wide variety of information about your security.
- **News**   This option opens to the latest news about the security you selected. It can be information ranging from the company's board of directors announcement about a dividend or the latest press release from the company's media department.
- **One-Click Scorecard**   This option displays reports to help you evaluate your security before you invest, using a variety of well-known analysis techniques and strategies.
- **Set Up Alerts**   When you export your portfolio to Investing.Quicken.com you can set online alerts for price changes, volume movement, and any other news that might affect your portfolio.

- **Stock Evaluator**   The Stock Evaluator command opens Investing.Quicken
  .com to the Evaluator section. From this section, both growth trends and the
  financial health of your chosen security are graphed and explained. Another
  useful section of the Evaluator is the Management Performance assessment.
  This section includes price to earnings, price to sales, and price to earnings
  growth ratios.
- **Multiple Security Charting**   Use this option to chart the closing prices of
  up to five securities and include up to three indexes in your chart. To do so:
  - Click Multiple Security Charting to open the Multiple Security Charting
    dialog.
  - Select the period of time you want to cover from the For What Period?
    drop-down list. The default is three months, but you can choose from
    seven more options.
  - Choose the securities you want to chart. To do so, click the name of the
    first security and hold down your CTRL key while choosing up to four more.
  - Select any indexes you want to include. However, you may choose no more
    than a total of five selections, including both securities and indexes.
  - Click Go Online To Chart to complete your chart. Using your Internet
    connection and the Yahoo! Finance page, the chart displays information
    using the first security name (alphabetically) as its base.

You can access these tools as well from the Classic menu. Click View | Classic
Menus to display the extended menu list. Choose Investing | Online Portfolio to
open the Investing.Quicken.com login page. Sign in to open the site.

Assessing Your "Money's Worth"

This part of the book explains how you can use Quicken Personal Finance Software's features to keep track of your property and loans. It starts by showing you how you can use the Property & Debt tab and other Quicken features to monitor expenses related to your assets and debts. It then continues to explain how to use the Investing tab and some useful Quicken tools. This part of the book has two chapters:

Chapter 10:   *Working with Your Assets*

Chapter 11:   *Reviewing Your Financial Position*

Part Four

Working with Your Assets

In This Chapter:

Once you have entered your account transactions into Quicken 2017, as discussed in the previous chapters, Quicken summarizes your entries and calculates their balances. The information displays in a number of places: the Account Bar, the Property & Debt tab, account registers, reports, and graphs. You can consult Quicken's calculated balances and totals at any time to learn about your equity and the expenses associated with your debts.

Assets and debts (or liabilities) make up your net worth. Bank and investment accounts, as discussed in earlier chapters, are examples of assets. Credit card accounts are examples of debts or liabilities. However, you may want to use Quicken Personal Finance Software to track other assets and debts, including your house or family car, as well as any loans related to those assets. By including these items in your Quicken data file, you can quickly and accurately calculate your net worth and financial fitness. It further explains how to set up asset and debt accounts to track your possessions and any outstanding loans you used to purchase them. As you'll learn in these pages, a wealth of information about your net worth is just a mouse click (or two) away.

The Basics

Before you begin, it's a good idea to have a clear understanding of what assets, debts, and loans are and how they work together in your Quicken data file.

Understanding Assets and Debts

An asset is something you own, such as your house, car, computer, smart phone, television set, and furniture. Most assets have value—you can sell them for cash or trade them for another asset.

A debt is something you owe—often to buy one of your assets! For example, if you buy a house, chances are you'll use a mortgage to finance it. The mortgage, which is a loan secured by your home, is a debt. You can use Quicken to track all of your debts so you know exactly how much you owe at any given time.

Reviewing Loans

Debts are often loans, which is simply a promise to pay money. Loans are commonly used to buy assets, although some folks often turn to debt consolidation loans to pay off other debts. You can learn more about paying off current debt in Chapter 13. And while people think of a loan as something you owe (a debt), a loan can also be something you own (an asset). For example, say you borrow money from your brother to buy a car. In your Quicken data file, the loan is related to a debt—money that you owe your brother. In your brother's Quicken data file, the loan is related to an asset—money that is due to him from you.

There are several types of loans, some of which are designed for specific purposes:

- **Mortgage** is a long-term loan secured by real estate. A special type of short-term mortgage is a **balloon mortgage**. Rather than make monthly payments over the full (typical) mortgage term, you pay the balance of the mortgage in one big "balloon" payment. And, if you have substantial equity in your home, you can obtain a **home equity loan** or **second mortgage**. This is a line of credit secured by the equity in your home—the difference between the home's market value and the amount of outstanding debt.
- **Reverse equity loan** (sometimes called a *reverse mortgage*) provides people over age 62 who own their homes with a regular monthly income. The loan is due when the home is sold, usually after the death of the homeowner.
- **Auto loans** are loans secured by a vehicle, such as a car, truck, or motor home.
- **Personal loans** are unsecured loans that require no collateral. Monthly payments are based on the term of the loan and the interest rate applied to the principal.

 "Payable" is an accounting term that means you have an obligation to pay the amount in this account to someone.

When applying for a loan, a number of variables have a direct impact on what the loan costs you, now and in the future. Ask about all of these things before applying for any loan.

Interest Rate

The rate of interest you pay for borrowing someone else's money is the annual percentage applied to the loan principal. Several factors affect the interest rate you may be offered, such as your credit record, the type of loan, the term of the loan, and even your location. Generally speaking, personal loans have the highest interest rates, while mortgage rates are usually the lowest.

Other factors that can affect the interest rate that you pay include the amount of the down payment and even the lender, as rates vary from one lender to another. Two kinds of interest rates can apply to a loan: a fixed rate, which applies the same rate to the principal throughout the loan term, and a variable rate, which applies different interest rates throughout the term of the loan.

A loan's *term* is the period of time between the date of the start of the loan and the date when payment is due in full. Loan terms vary depending on the type of loan:

- Mortgage loan and home equity reserve loan terms are typically 10, 15, 20, or 30 years. Home equity reserve loans are also known as home equity lines of credit (HELOC) or second mortgages.
- Balloon mortgage loan terms are typically 5, 7, or 10 years.
- Vehicle loan terms vary from 3 to 7 years.

Tips for Minimizing Loan Expenses

Borrowing money costs money. It's as simple as that. However, you can do some things to minimize the cost of a loan:

- Shop for the lowest rate.
- Minimize the length of the loan.
- Maximize the down payment.
- Make extra loan payments.
- Ensure your credit history is cleaned up.
- Monitor your credit score with Quicken's Credit Score utility as discussed in Chapter 5.

When evaluating the dollar impact of different loan deals, use Quicken's financial calculators as discussed in Chapter 12. To access these calculators, click the Planning tab and then the Planning Tools button.

Creating Property and Debt Accounts

To track an asset or debt with Quicken, you must set up an appropriate account. All transactions related to the asset or debt are recorded in the account's register. In this section, you'll learn about the types of accounts you can use to track your assets and debts and how to set up each type of account. As you see next, Quicken offers the following Property & Debt account types for tracking assets and debts.

- **House**   A house account is used for recording the value of a house, condominium, or other real estate. When you create a house account, Quicken asks whether there is a mortgage on the property. Quicken can

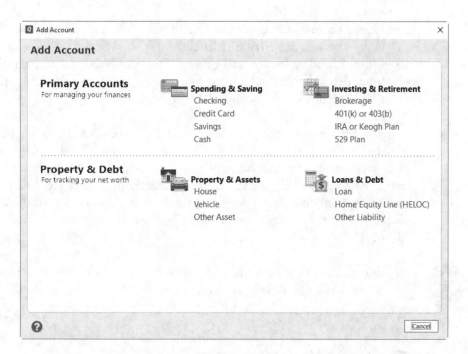

create a related debt account for you or associate the house account with an existing debt account so that both your house asset account and mortgage debt accounts can be established at the same time. And if you are not sure of the value of your home today, use the Zillow connection to get your home's latest value. For more information see "Integrating with Zillow," later in this chapter.

- **Vehicle**   A vehicle account is similar to a house account, but is designed for vehicles, including cars, trucks, and recreational vehicles. You can create a related debt account or link to an existing debt account.

- **Other Asset**   An asset account is for recording the value of other assets, such as personal property. For example, a Quicken data file might include asset accounts for your workshop and its related equipment, your antique china collection, or other personal possessions.

- **Loan**   A loan account is for recording money you owe to others. As mentioned earlier, when you create a house or vehicle account, Quicken can automatically create a corresponding loan account for you. You may also create a loan account for money you lend to others. See "Creating a Lender Loan" later in this chapter.

- **Home Equity Line of Credit (HELOC)**   This type of loan uses the borrower's real property as collateral.
- **Other Liability (not a credit card)**   You can create a debt account to record other debts that are not related to the purchase of a specific asset. Debt accounts show in the Account List as liabilities.

Earlier chapters explained how to use the Quicken Add Account dialog to create new Quicken banking and credit card accounts. To add a new asset or debt account, you need to tell Quicken the type of account you want to create and what name you choose to identify that account. It is always best to give the account a name that clearly identifies the asset or debt. Be descriptive. "Ford Focus" and "Dodge pickup" do a better job identifying the cars than "Car 1" and "Car 2."

When creating a debt account, you may want to include the word "mortgage," "loan," or "payable" in the account name so you don't confuse it with a related asset.

Creating a House Account

You create a house account with the same Add Account dialog you used to set up your banking accounts. Quicken offers a number of ways to open this dialog for an asset or debt account, as well as several types of assets, loans, and debts. In the following example, we are adding a new house asset. The specific steps are as follows:

1. From the Account Bar, click the plus sign or select Tools | Add Account. You can also use the keyboard shortcut of CTRL-A.
2. From the Add Account dialog, choose Property & Assets | House.
3. The Add House (Asset) Account dialog appears with the account name/ nickname field highlighted and ready for you to enter a new name. Type a descriptive name and click Next.
4. Enter the date you acquired the house or use the small calendar to the right of that field.
5. Enter the purchase price of the house, as shown next.

Add House (Asset) Account

Add House (Asset) Account

Tell Quicken about the house you'd like to track.
Don't worry if you don't have all the details- you can make changes to your account later.

When did you acquire this house? 8/19/2005

Purchase price 127,200.00

What's the current value ○ Get an Estimate from Zillow ? Get Zestimate®

⦿ Enter Estimate

It's okay to enter approximate values. You will be able to change them later.

Cancel   Back   Next

You see two options for entering the current value of this house. If you choose to enter an estimate manually, select Enter Estimate to open a field where you can enter this amount. If you choose to connect with Zillow to see how it values this house, see "Integrating with Zillow" later in this chapter.

When you have completed the estimate, click Next to continue. Quicken asks if you have any mortgages on this asset:

- If there is no mortgage associated with this house, click No.
- If you want to track the mortgage for this asset through Quicken, select Yes | I'd Like To Track This Mortgage In Quicken. You are then prompted to add a loan account. See "Creating a Loan Account" later in this chapter
- If you are already tracking this mortgage in Quicken, select Yes | I'm Already Tracking The Mortgage In Quicken and enter the name of the existing account.
- If there is a mortgage but you do not want to track it in Quicken, click Yes and then choose the I Do Not Want To Track The Mortgage In Quicken option.

If you select No or I Do Not Want To Track the Mortgage in Quicken, click Next to continue, and the Account Added dialog appears with the name of your new asset shown with a green check mark. Click Finish.

Loan Details ✕

Loan Details

| House Loan | Name of this loan in Quicken |
| Mortgage ▾ | Loan type |

ⓘ You may need to check your latest loan statement or lender website to complete this form.

Opening date: `7/20/2004` 📅 Date this loan started

Original balance: `125,000.00` 🔢 Amount of this loan on the opening

Current interest rate: `4.250%`

Original length: `15` `Years ▾`

Compounding period: `Daily ▾` ❓

Payment schedule: `Monthly ▾`

Current balance: `28,412.09` 🔢

Monthly payment: `940.81` 🔢 Principal + Interest amount or ❓

❓ Cancel   Back   Next

Figure 10-1 • **For a more complete picture of your financial position, use Quicken to track your assets and debts.**

If you select I'd Like To Track This Mortgage In Quicken and select to track your mortgage manually, you will see a Loan Details window as shown in Figure 10-1.

 You can use Quicken's Attachment feature (covered in Chapter 5) and your scanner to save images of an asset's paperwork, such as the receipt, the warranty, or delivery verification you received, to store as a digital image with your Quicken data file.

Loan Information

If you indicated that Quicken should track a loan for a house or vehicle, it automatically displays the Add Mortgage/Loan Account dialog, which you can use to enter information about the loan. If you set up a debt account, Quicken asks if you want to set up an amortized loan to be associated with the debt. If you selected Yes and I'm Already Tracking The Loan In Quicken, select the debt account from the drop-down list and click Next. You'll then see the Account

INTEGRATING WITH ZILLOW

New in Quicken 2017, Quicken has partnered with the online real estate company, Zillow. Using this service, you can obtain the current value of your main or vacation home whenever you choose, simply by clicking a couple of buttons. To use this service when adding a new house account, select Get An Estimate From Zillow and click the Get Zestimate button to open this window.

Property Valuation	✕

Let us help you find value to your property

Please enter your address

Address
1600 Pennsylvania Avenue

City	State	Zip Code
Washington	DC ⌄	20500

Cancel   Next

Click the Next button to see the results. If there is more than one address showing, select the proper item and click Next. The description of the house at the address you entered appears, as seen here.

Property Valuation	✕

1600 Pennsylvania Ave NW Washington DC 20500   **Zillow**
SingleFamily, 2.0 BA, 3 BR, 55000 sq. ft.   Terms of use

Zestimate® home valuation: $2,131,582.00

☐ Use Zestimate

Property value you would like Quicken
to display: $ 2131582.00

Remind me to update: Quarterly   ⌄

Cancel   Update your property value

(continued)

You can adjust the value you want to display in Quicken. However, at this writing, you may not be able to add commas to separate thousands in the valuation shown in the Zillow screen, but if you choose to update your property value, the amount will appear correctly in the Quicken window.

Note that you have the option to update the valuation of this house. Using the drop-down menu, you will see update options Monthly, Quarterly, Twice A Year, or Yearly. However, should you choose to do so, you can update as often as daily from within Quicken.

Once you have told Quicken what valuation to use, select Update Your Property Value to return to the Add House (Asset) Account window. Your valuation appears in the What's The Current Value box, as shown here.

Add House (Asset) Account

Tell Quicken about the house you'd like to track.
Don't worry if you don't have all the details- you can make changes to your account later.

When did you acquire this house? 8/19/2005

Purchase price 127,200.00

What's the current value ● Zestimate® by Zillow

$2,131,582.00

○ Enter Estimate

Get the current Valuation of your property by looking up Zestimate® provided by Zillow

Zillow

Terms to Use

Cancel   Back   Next

Added screen with the green check mark near the new account's name. Quicken links the asset and debt accounts for you. See how to set up a loan later in this chapter, in the section "Creating a Loan Account."

Be sure to select the appropriate type for your loan so the appropriate interest category is associated with it. Quicken 2017 allows you to change this interest category at any time.

Loan Accounts in Quicken

Quicken makes it easy to track the principal, interest, and payments for a loan. Once you set up a loan and corresponding debt or asset accounts, you can make payments with Quicken using QuickFill, Scheduled Transactions (transaction reminders), or Online Payments (see Chapter 6). The Loan feature keeps track of all the details for you. A loan in Quicken is not the same as an asset or debt account. Quicken uses the loan information to calculate the amount of interest and principal due for each payment of an amortized loan, such as a mortgage or car loan. A loan must be associated with an asset account (if you are a lender) or a debt account (if you are a borrower), as well as an income or expense category to record either interest income or expense.

A mortgage or loan is actually a debt account that has special Quicken features attached to it. Use this option to set up a debt associated with a compounding interest loan, like a mortgage or standard car loan, as explained later in this chapter.

Creating a Loan Account

You can set up a loan in the following ways:

- Create a house, vehicle, or debt account with a related mortgage or loan, Quicken automatically prompts you for loan information. Although you can change the interest category for non–online-enabled loans at any time, you lose flexibility in selecting the loan type if you create the loan after creating the asset.
- From the Account Bar, click the plus sign to add an account. Choose Property & Debt | Loans & Debt | Loan.
- From the menu bar, click Tools | Add Account | Property & Debt | Loans & Debt | Loan.
- From the Property & Debt tab, click Debt | Loan And Debt Options | Add A New Loan.
- Also from the Property & Debt tab, click Property, click Property Options, and select Add A New Loan.

Depending on the location from which you start, Quicken displays either the Add Account or the Add Loan Account dialog. While the information is basically the same, the *type* of loan does matter so that you get the right interest category type. All of the previously mentioned methods except the first bullet point (creating a loan during the asset account creation workflow) enable you to select the loan type. The method described in the first bullet point bypasses the loan type selection and sets the loan with the default type of "loan."

Choose one of the loan providers listed, or if you choose to create a loan account for which you will enter the information manually, click the Manual Loan Account link at the bottom of the dialog. The illustrations that follow are for a manual account.

Be aware! If you choose to download your loan transactions, your loan account register may be read-only and, if so, not be accessible to review and make corrections. Don't do it! Downloading one possibly incorrect transaction per month that cannot be corrected is just not worth it. Set up your loan manually—you will be much happier!

Loan Details

The Loan Details dialog starts by prompting you for the name of the loan, as seen in Figure 10-1. After you have entered a name for this loan, your next choice is the type of loan for which you are creating an account. Click the downward arrow to choose from a list. Choose wisely—you cannot change the loan type or the associated loan interest type category later!

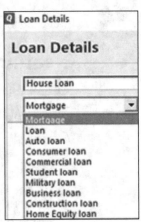

You have the following loan types from which to choose:

- **Mortgage** is a loan for some type of real property such as a house.
- **Loan** is for any type of loan not included in the other options. This loan type may be used for loans from individuals rather than financial institutions, such as borrowing $5,000 from your sister toward some vacation property you will both share.
- **Auto loan** is for vehicle loans, including trucks and travel trailers.
- **Consumer loans** are funds borrowed by a person rather than a business. Lenders for this type of loan are usually financial institutions.
- **Commercial loans** are normally loans to a business from a financial institution. Such loans are often for large purchases, working capital, or real property.
- **Student loans** are used for financing education.
- **Military loans** are designed specifically for those in the service of our country.
- **Business loans** are usually for the day-to-day operating costs of a business, rather than for large real property or equipment purchases.
- **Construction loans** are used when you build a house. These loans are often turned into mortgage loans when construction is completed.

- **Home equity loans** are loans against the equity you hold in your home. Many people use home equity loans to pay for major remodeling, although some home equity loans are taken to pay off other, higher-cost debt.

You are asked for information about the opening date, the original balance, the current interest rate, the original contract length, payment schedule, and so on, as seen in Figure 10-1. It's important to be accurate; get the dates and numbers directly from your loan statement or agreement if possible. Quicken calculates the amount of payment and the interest based on the entries you make, as well as the extra principal, any balloon payment, and the number of remaining payments.

 While Quicken's default compounding period is Monthly, most financial institutions compound interest daily and post it to your account every month. Use the Compounding Period drop-down list to choose Daily if your lender compounds interest daily.

Click Next to continue. The Loan Details dialog continues with the name of the loan at the top. It displays the next payment due date for this loan, based on the opening date you entered in the first screen of the dialog. You may change this date if necessary. Enter any additional information.

- **Other** is used for additional payments on the loan such as escrow funds.
- **Extra Principal Paid Monthly** amounts are those additional principal payments you enter to reduce the total amount of the interest you will pay on the loan, as shown here.

Loan Details	×
Loan Details	

House Loan

Monthly Payment

Next payment due	12/20/2016 🗓 (required)
Principal	$835.72
Interest	$97.17
Other	0.00
Extra principal paid monthly	17.11
	⊙ Extra principal determines tot 🔘
Total Payment:	950.00
	○ Total determines extra princip 🔘

Cancel		Back	Next

- Select **Total Determines Extra Principal** if you want to set the total payment each month and let Quicken determine how much extra principal will be paid, as seen in the following illustration.

Click Next to continue. The Loan Reminder dialog appears as discussed next.

Loan Reminder

When you set up a loan, Quicken creates a reminder. From this dialog, you can tell Quicken to enter the reminder into the register automatically and choose the number of days before the due date that you want the transaction entered. If you do not want Quicken to enter the transaction automatically, leave that check box clear and click Next.

The Loan Payment Reminder dialog appears as shown next. You may edit each field as explained here:

- The **Pay To** field shows the name of the loan if you have indicated that you will enter transactions manually to this loan account. Otherwise, it displays the name of the financial institution from which you borrowed the money. Edit this field by highlighting what appears and typing over the highlighted area.

- The **Due Next On** date can be changed by typing in a new due date.
- The **Amount Due** field originally shows the information you entered in the previous Loan Details dialog. Click Edit to see a split transaction dialog. You can make changes as necessary. Click Cancel or OK to close the Split Transaction dialog. Learn more about split transactions in Chapter 5.
- The **From Account** field indicates the account from which the payment will be paid. Click the downward arrow to change to another account.
- You can change or add three areas in the Details section:
  - Click anywhere in the Details section to open the dialog shown here. From this one dialog, you can change the split categories, create a tag or edit an existing tag, and create a memo for each payment. Note that you have to click the Split symbol in this dialog to make changes to either the Category or the Tag field.
  - When you have made your changes, click OK to return to the Loan Payment Reminder dialog.

- Click **Optional Settings** to set how many days in advance of the payment's due date Quicken should remind you of the payment. The default is 7 days. Click Change to set another time.
- Click **Related Website** to enter a website. This might be the website of your financial institution or any other website that pertains to this loan. This is not required, but can be useful. If you have not yet entered a website, the link will be labeled Add. If you have entered a website, the link will be labeled Change.
- Click the **Sync To Outlook** check box to synchronize your payment date in your Outlook calendar.
- Click **Print Check With Quicken** to let Quicken know you will be paying this payment with a Quicken check.

Click Done to close the Loan Payment Reminder dialog. If you have not entered this loan directly when adding a new house or other asset, a message may appear asking if this loan is to be associated with an asset. Click Add Linked Asset Account if you want to create an asset account for this loan. From the menu that appears, you can choose from Home, Auto, or Other, or click Existing Account to link this loan to an existing asset.

If you choose to add a new asset account, the Add Account dialog appears. If you choose an existing asset, you will see a small icon and the information that this loan is linked to the asset you chose, as shown next. The link icon depends on the type of asset. For example, for a house loan, the icon is a house. Click Done to close the dialog.

Creating a Lender Loan

From time to time, you may be in a position to lend money to someone else. Quicken calls this type of loan a *Lender Loan*. You create this type of account in a slightly different way.

Once you have completed all the necessary paperwork, checked with both legal and tax professionals, and everything is signed and notarized, you are ready to set up the account. Quicken treats this type of loan as an asset, with the value of the asset equal to the amount of money you are lending.

1. Click the plus sign from the Account Bar. Choose Property & Debt | Property & Assets | Other Assets to open the Add Asset Account dialog.
2. Enter a name for the account. Depending on the Quicken edition you use, you may have to choose the purpose for the account, such as Personal or Business. Click Next.
3. Enter the date on which you want Quicken to start tracking this loan, which is usually the opening date of the loan.
4. Enter the asset value, usually the total amount you are lending.
5. If the loan has tax implications, click the Tax button to enter any pertinent information. Otherwise, click Next to continue.
6. The Is There A Loan On This Asset? dialog appears. Select No and click Next, and then in the final dialog, click Finish.
7. Your new loan account appears in the Account Bar. Open the account's register by clicking the account name in the Account Bar.
8. Click the Account Action gear icon and select Convert To A Lending Loan from the drop-down menu. Select that option to convert this asset to a lending loan. A warning appears that this action cannot be undone, as shown here. Select Convert to make this a lending loan.

9. The Loan Details dialog appears as discussed in the "Creating a Loan Account" section, earlier in this chapter. Complete the information, including the current interest rate, original loan length, and payment schedule. Click Next.

10. Make any additions or changes to the monthly payment in the dialog that appears and click Next again.

11. Make your choices in the Reminder dialog and click Next. At the final Reminder dialog, make any necessary changes and click Done. Your new asset account appears with loan information rather than a register. To see the transactions, click Payment Details.

Even if you are lending money to a relative, it is important that paperwork be created and signed by all parties and, in most cases, reviewed by a legal and/or an accounting professional.

Viewing the Asset or Debt Account Register

When you're finished setting up an asset or debt account (and related loans and loan payments, if applicable), Quicken automatically displays the account's register. Figure 10-2 shows what a house account might look like. (Here, the register has a two-line display. To change your display from the default one-line display, press

				Decrease	.	Increase	Amount	Balance
Date ▲	Payee							
▶ ⬠	Memo	Category	Tag					
7/20/2004	Opening Balance					125,000 00	125,000 00	125,000 00
		[House]						
12/20/2016					R	150,000 00	150,000 00	275,000 00
		[House]						
2 Transactions							Ending Balance:	275,000.00

Figure 10-2 • Like other accounts in Quicken, assets and debts have their own account registers.

CTRL-2, which is a toggle between Quicken's default one-line register display and the two-line display shown.) The first transaction, dated 7/20/2004, shows the opening balance, which was the amount paid for the house. The next transaction, dated 12/20/2016, shows an adjustment created when the asset was added into Quicken. If you have entered a house for which you used a manual estimate rather than a Zillow valuation, you will see a link to Zillow, as seen in Figure 10-2. To close the link, click the X in the upper-right corner of the Zillow area.

After you have entered more than one asset account, you'll note that the new accounts are listed alphabetically. In earlier versions of Quicken, the new accounts went to the bottom of the appropriate section in the Account List. Many Quicken users prefer to see their accounts in alphabetical order in the Account List, and this change is in response to those requests. This auto-sorting only works if you have never rearranged your account order. And Quicken, like most computer programs, sorts filenames that have numbers first, then files with text names.

All transactions that affect an asset or debt account's balance appear in the account register. Learn more about using account registers for asset and debt accounts later in this chapter, in the section "Other Asset Transactions."

Optional Tax Information

For asset and debt accounts, click the Tax Schedule button on the Account Details dialog to enter tax schedule information for transfers in and out of the account. While this information is optional, check with your tax professional to see if this information will benefit your tax position. Chapter 14 explains how to set up Quicken accounts and categories to simplify tax preparation.

You can get to the Account Details dialog by pressing CTRL-A and then clicking the Edit button for the account with which you wish to work.

Viewing Loan Information

All loans are associated with asset and/or debt accounts. To view a loan, it must first be set up in Quicken. After you have set it up, you can access the loan information in two ways:

- Click on the loan name in the Account Bar.
- Click Tools | Account List and select the name of the account with which you want to work.

The loan information window appears as seen in Figure 10-3.

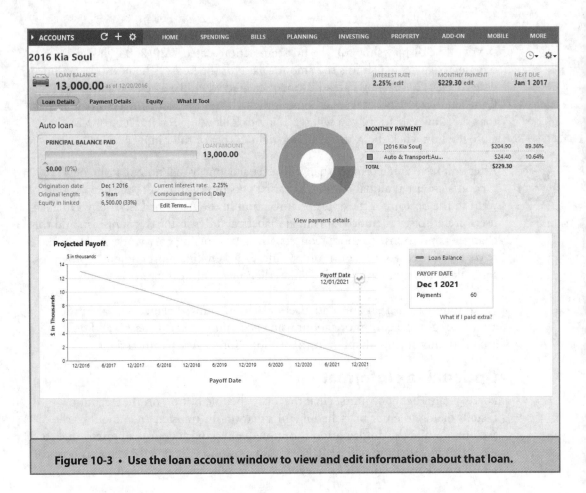

Figure 10-3 • Use the loan account window to view and edit information about that loan.

Making Loan Payments

When you first set up your loan, you told Quicken to create either a loan reminder or a memorized payee, or in some cases, both. Each time you make a payment on a loan, Quicken keeps track of the current loan balance in that loan account. If you have linked an asset to your loan, Quicken tracks your current equity as well. You can make a loan payment in several different ways, each of which is explained here:

- **Use a Loan Reminder** If you instructed Quicken to set up a reminder for your loan payment each month (or other payment schedule), Quicken displays a message reminder. If you have asked Quicken to include the reminder in your register, the payment is already there.

- **Enter the Loan Payment Directly**   You can quickly enter any loan payment into your register by simply typing the payee name, and the information from your special loan payment memorized payee will appear. If you have not memorized the payee, complete the payment entry, and Quicken memorizes both the payee and the transaction so you can use that information each time you make a payment. To create the special memorized payee:

  1. Click the Edit link at the right of the Monthly Payment amount shown at the upper right of the loan account screen. Choose Payment Options and click Memorized Payee.
  2. Click OK to close the dialog.

- **Use the Enter Loan Payment Option**   To enter a payment, click the loan account name in the Account Bar to open the loan. Select the Account Action gear icon, and from the menu choose Enter Loan Payment. The Enter Expense Transaction dialog appears, as shown here. You can also use the Customize Action Bar to add the Enter Loan Payment button to your account action bar.

If you have elected to use the special memorized payee to make your loan payments, you will no longer see the Enter Loan Payment option in the Account Actions menu. Customize the action bar first to add the Enter Loan Payment button; then set up your special memorized payee. The button then remains in the action bar.

Create a Quicken Toolbar Button

Use the special memorized payee to create a customized Quicken Toolbar button to make your payment.

1. Right-click the Quicken Toolbar and choose Customize Toolbar.
2. From the Customize Toolbar dialog, select the Show All Toolbar Choices check box.
3. In the Available Toolbar Buttons list, select Use A Specific Memorized Payee.
4. Click Add to open the Assigned Memorized Payee To Action dialog.
5. Choose the appropriate payee from the Memorized Item drop-down list, as shown here. Enter the account from which this payment will be made and select the Automatically Record Item check box if desired.

Q Assign Memorized Payee to Action		✕
Memorized Item:	2016 Kia Soul ▼	OK
Target Account:	House Checking ▼	Cancel
☐ Automatically Record Item		Help

6. Click OK to close the dialog, and click Done to close the Customize Toolbar dialog. Your new memorized transaction button appears on the Quicken Toolbar.

When it's time to enter the payment, click your new toolbar button. The Confirm Principal And Interest dialog appears. Make any changes necessary and click OK. Your payment is posted into your register. Be sure to save the transaction.

Modifying Loan Information

Once you've created a loan, you can modify it as necessary to record corrections, changes in the interest rate, or changes in payment methods. You can do all these things by clicking the account name in the Account Bar and choosing the Loan Details or Payment Details tab.

NOTE You can also open a loan account window by choosing Tools | Account List and selecting the appropriate account.

At the top of the account window, you see the current balance, interest rate, monthly payment, and the next due date as seen in Figure 10-3. Should you want to make changes to either the interest rate or the monthly payment, click the Edit button to the right of that item. You also have four tabs from which you can view both loan and payment details, the current equity, and a What If tool to help you make decisions about this loan. (See "The What If Tool" later in this chapter.)

Changing Loan Information

Should you need to make changes to other parts of the loan information, use the Loan Details window, as seen in Figure 10-4, to compare the data with the information found on statements or loan agreement papers. You can then make

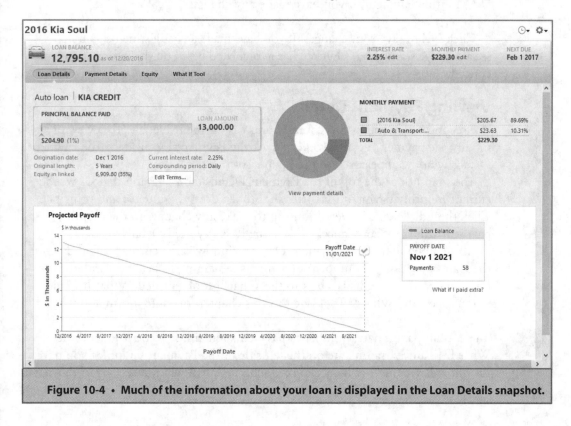

Figure 10-4 · Much of the information about your loan is displayed in the Loan Details snapshot.

any necessary changes to other parts of the loan information, such as the original balance or payment schedule.

- **Origination Date**   Usually, this is the date the loan started.
- **Original Length**   Use your loan statement papers to find this balance if you didn't enter it when you set up the account.
- **Equity In Linked**   This amount calculates the amount of equity you have in the assets to which this loan is linked.
- **Current Interest Rate**   This can vary, depending on your loan.
- **Compounding Period**   While Quicken defaults to Monthly, normally banks and other lending institutions compound interest daily. Change this to Daily if that is true for this loan.
- **Payment Schedule**   This will often be monthly, although some loan terms have quarterly, semi-annual, or even annual payment schedules.
- **Monthly Payment**   This is the total of principal and interest and does not include any other fees.
- **Recalculate**   You may see an additional recalculate button beneath the Monthly Payment, if you have made any changes.

Click OK to save your changes. If you have made any adjustments, you may see a message stating that Quicken has recalculated based on the information you entered.

Viewing Payment Details

The second tab in the loan account window is Payment Details. To review or modify the payment details, you can click the Payment Details tab. The Payment Details window appears as seen in Figure 10-5.

The snapshot at the top of the Payment Details tab is a graph that shows the current monthly payment for this loan, broken down by interest and principal. Click the Edit Payment Details button to make any changes to the monthly payment. Click OK or Cancel to close the Edit Payment Details dialog.

At the upper left of the Payment Details window is the current payoff date for the loan, as well as the number of payments remaining to be paid. Underneath the number of payments is a link to the What If tool, entitled "What If I Paid Extra." See "The What If Tool" later in this chapter for more information.

The current payoff date, number of payments remaining to be paid, and the What If I Paid Extra link are on the left side of the Payment Graph. If you have the Show Payment Graph check box unchecked, you will not see any of this data.

Figure 10-5 • The Payment Details window in a loan account contains both current payment information and a register showing the latest payments on the account.

The Full Payment Schedule   Click the View Payment Schedule button at the top-right of the Payment Details window when the Show Payment Graph box is checked. This information is based on your current Loan Details and Loan Payment fields. You can also add the View Payment Schedule button to the account action bar.

Click the printer icon to print the report to your default printer or to a file. Click Done to close the dialog.

Payment Detail Register

The register at the bottom half of the Payment Details window shows each principal payment that was made on this account since the loan began. The payments that show on this register are only the principal amounts.

EXPERIENCED USERS RECOMMEND

If you are on a laptop or just have your monitor resolution set to the Quicken minimum, you may see only one transaction line at a time. You can see more transaction lines by toggling to a one-line display (CTRL-2), maximizing the register (F11), or setting your preferences to use pop-up registers (Edit | Preferences | Register | Register Appearance | Use Pop-Up Registers).

To see the entire payment, go to the account register from which the payment was made. You can change what shows in this register by choosing the filter drop-down lists at the top of the register.

You can clear the graph to show more payments in the register. Click the check box to the left of Show Payment Graph to toggle the graph on and off.

- The Dates drop-down list allows you to select the date range you want to see in the register.
- The Types and Transactions lists let you tailor the register to your needs.
- The Reset button returns the filters to their default settings.

Retaining the filters for future Quicken sessions is a preference. Click Edit | Preferences | Register | Register Appearance | Remember Register Filters After Quicken Closes.

The Equity Button

Click the Equity button to see information about this loan and its associated asset, as well as the current net value or equity in the asset, as shown next. If there is more than one loan associated with this asset, both will be displayed.

The amount of your equity in this asset is shown as both a percentage and a net value. If you click on the link to the left of Net Value, a small graph appears showing the change in your equity over the last year, as seen next.

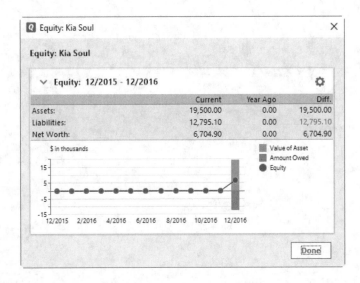

- Click the Options gear icon at the right of the Equity graph to customize the graph. You can also click the Help Reduce My Debt link to be taken to the Debt Reduction dialogs. See Chapter 13 to learn about budgets and debt reduction in Quicken.
- Click Done to close this equity dialog.
- Click the See All Properties button to see the Property view of the Property & Debt tab.

The What If Tool

The What If tool tab at the top of your loan account window opens a worksheet that allows you to see the effects if you made some different financial choices for this account. When the window opens, you see the What If Payoff Schedule at the right side of the window, as seen in Figure 10-6. This schedule, based on the current terms, shows the projected payoff date, total interest paid this year, total interest paid to today's date, and the projected total interest that will be paid using your choices for paying off the loan.

Within the tool itself, you can see projected changes if you make additional payments each month or a one-time payment. In the example shown in Figure 10-6, we have chosen to pay an extra $200.00 per month on the car loan. After we click the See Results button, notice the change in both the graph and the What If Payoff Schedule. By adding this $200.00, we will pay off this loan more than two years early and save about $337.52 in interest.

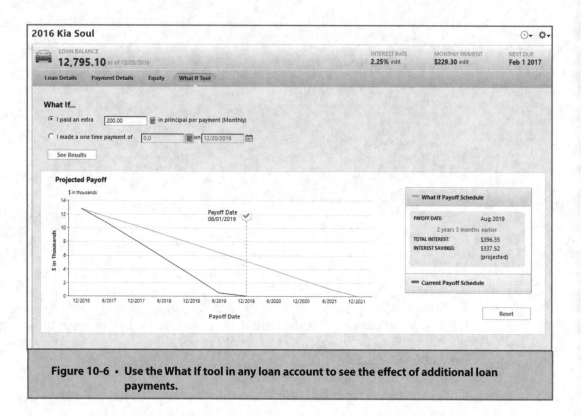

Figure 10-6 • Use the What If tool in any loan account to see the effect of additional loan payments.

You can click Current Payoff Schedule to review that information once more. Then, to see the differences again, click What If Payoff Schedule.

When you have finished working with the What If tool, click the Reset button at the lower right of the What If tool window to return to the current information, or close and reopen Quicken. The changes are not saved.

Action Gear Options

At the upper right of the loan account window is the Action gear icon from which you can choose the following options, most of which are links:

- **Edit Account Details**   Click this link to open the Account Details dialog you saw when setting up the account.
- **Enter Loan Payment**   This link opens the Enter Transaction dialog from which you can enter a payment into the appropriate banking (or credit union) register. However, if you are using a memorized payee instead of the reminder, you will not see this dialog.

- **Update Balance**   This option opens the Update Balance dialog, which allows you to enter a new balance for the loan and the effective date of that change.
- **Transfer Money**   Select this option to open the Quicken Transfer Money dialog, which is discussed in Chapter 6.
- **Full Payment Schedule**   This is the same report shown when you click the View Payment Schedule button.
- **Account Attachments**   See Chapter 5 to learn more about adding attachments to register entries.
- **Account Overview**   This link opens a customizable graph showing information for the total date range of this loan. Click the Action gear icon to change the date range.
- **Print Transactions**   With the dialog that opens when you select this option, you can print transactions in the register for time periods you choose.
- **Export To Excel Compatible File**   This option allows you to send the loan information to Microsoft Excel (or compatible programs).
- **Reminders To Show In Register**   This option is the same as the Reminders icon option shown earlier in this chapter.
- **Two-Line Display**   With this option selected, each transaction in the register shows in two lines. Clear the check box to have each transaction show on only one line.
- **Sorting Options**   This link lets you sort by 11 additional alternatives in addition to the default Date sort.
- **Register Columns**   Use this link to tell Quicken what columns you want to see in your register.
- **Register Preferences**   This option opens the Quicken Preference dialog to the Register Preferences section. See Appendix B for more information about setting Preferences.
- **Customize Action Bar**   From this dialog, you can set the icons you wish to see in the action bar, next to the Action gear icon. These icons are in addition to the Show Reminders icon, which is the Quicken 2017 default.

Other Asset Transactions

Part of tracking assets is keeping track of their current values and modifying account balances when necessary. Like bank or investment accounts, which are discussed in earlier chapters, activity for an asset account appears in its account register.

The best way to open an asset's register is to click the name of the account in the Account Bar. The asset account's register appears. If you do not see your account listed in the Account Bar, you may need to change the account's display. Press CTRL-A to open the Account List and select the Show Hidden Accounts check box to show all of your accounts.

In this section, you'll see how you can record changes in asset values due to acquisitions and disposals, improvements, market values, and depreciation.

Adding and Disposing of Assets

The most obvious change in an asset's value occurs when you add or remove all or part of the asset. For example, you may have a single asset account in which you record the value of all of your sports-related equipment. When you buy a set of golf clubs, it increases the value of the account. Similarly, if you sell your small outboard motor, it decreases the value of the account.

In many instances, when you add or dispose of an asset, money is exchanged. In that case, recording the transaction is easy: simply use the appropriate bank account register to record the purchase or sale, and use the asset account in the Category field. Make sure you use the category enclosed in square brackets [ ].

If the asset was acquired without an exchange of cash, you can enter the transaction directly into the asset account using the Gift Received category (or a similar category of your choice) to categorize the income. Similarly, if the asset was disposed of without an exchange of cash, you can enter the transaction into the asset account register using the Gifts Given or Charity category (or other category) to categorize the write-off.

You can also just record the transaction as an internal transfer in the asset account. If the asset account name is Sports Equipment, an internal transfer in the Sports Equipment account would use the category [Sports Equipment]. You may see a prompt warning you that you are recording a transfer back into the same account. Click Yes to save the transaction.

If you have completely disposed of the asset and no longer need the account, don't delete the account! Doing so will remove all income and expense category transactions and uncategorize all transfer transactions related to the account. Instead, consider hiding the account to get it off account lists. In addition, while

---

EXPERIENCED USERS RECOMMEND

One of the most useful features of Quicken is the Account Attachments feature. This feature allows you to digitally attach copies of property tax statements, home improvement receipts, and other paper items that may add to the basis of your property. You can scan any of these documents and save the scanned copy in the same file with your Quicken data. See Chapter 5 for a full explanation of the process.

you are working with hiding your accounts, be very cautious about using the Close Account feature. Closing an account in Quicken 2017 is permanent.

Updating Asset Values

A variety of situations can change the value of a single asset. The type of situation will determine how the value is adjusted. Here are three common examples.

Recording Improvements

Certain home-related expenditures are sometimes considered improvements that increase the value of your home. It's important that you keep track of improvements, because they raise the property's basis, thus reducing the amount of capital gains you may have to record (and pay tax on) when you sell the house. Your tax advisor can help you determine which expenditures can be capitalized as home improvements.

Since most home improvements involve expenditures, use the appropriate spending account register to record the transaction. Be sure to enter the appropriate asset account (House, Condo, Land, and so on) in the Category field, and enclose the account name in square brackets [ ].

Adjusting for Market Value

Real estate, vehicles, and other large-ticket-item assets are also affected by market values. Generally speaking, real estate values go up, vehicle values go down, and other item values can vary either way depending on what they are.

To adjust for market value, click the Action gear icon | Account Overview and in the Asset Status section, select the Asset Status Options gear icon | Update My Account Balance. The Update Account Balance dialog appears. Use this dialog to enter the market value in the New Balance field and then enter the date of this new value in the Date field. Be careful, as the default date of the change is today's date. Click OK to close the dialog.

You can also click the Action gear icon and choose Update Balance.

When you click OK, the entry is added to the account register as a reconciled transaction. The category for this transaction defaults to Misc. You may change this category by clicking in the Category field and entering the category you want to use.

If you don't want the adjustment to affect any category or account other than the asset, choose the same asset account as a transfer account. When you click OK, a dialog will warn you that you are trying to record a transfer into the same account. Click OK again.

Recording Depreciation

Depreciation is a calculated reduction in the value of an asset. Depreciation expense can be calculated using a variety of acceptable methods, including straight line, sum of the year's digits, and declining balance. Normally, it reduces the asset's value regularly, with monthly, quarterly, or annual adjustments.

Depreciation is commonly applied to property used for business purposes, since depreciation expense on those assets may be tax deductible. If you think depreciation on an asset you own may be tax deductible, use Quicken to track the depreciation expense. Otherwise, depreciation probably isn't worth the extra effort it requires to track. As always, consult with your tax professional to be sure.

To record depreciation, create an entry in the asset account that reduces the value by the amount of the depreciation. Use a Depreciation Expense category to record the expense.

Keep in mind that you can set up monthly, quarterly, or annual depreciation transactions as scheduled reminders in the Bill & Income reminders. This automates the process of recording them when they are due. See more about scheduling payments and being reminded in Chapter 7.

The Property & Debt Tab

Asset and debt account information, as well as an overview of your financial standing (net worth), are part of Quicken's Property & Debt tab. Open the Property & Debt section by clicking its tab. Within the Property & Debt tab are three views with which you can view your financial standing in useful graphic format. You access these views with three buttons: Net Worth, Property, and Debt.

Depending on your monitor's size, some of the tabs may be shortened. For example, instead of the Property & Debt tab, the tab is labeled Property on my laptop screen.

Each of these views displays graphs and report snapshots to help you understand your true financial position. An example is the two graphs you see when you click the Net Worth button, as shown in Figure 10-7. Click either the Net Worth Summary Report or the Account Balances Report button to display additional information about your net worth accounts. Together, these snapshots paint a picture of your overall financial situation. You can see the Account Balances Report button at the lower left of the Net Worth By Account Type snapshot.

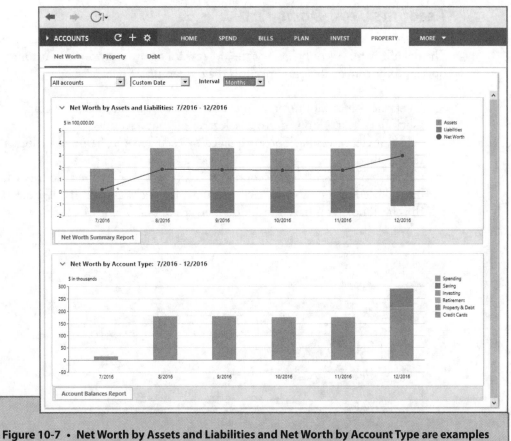

Figure 10-7 • Net Worth by Assets and Liabilities and Net Worth by Account Type are examples of the graphs available in the Net Worth view of the Property & Debt tab.

Exploring the Net Worth View

As you click the button to open the Net Worth view, you'll see both the Net Worth by Assets and Liabilities graph and the Net Worth by Account Type graph, as shown in Figure 10-7. You can customize the information shown in this view, but you cannot customize the information for each graph separately.

There is much more information available within the Net Worth view than first meets the eye. At the top of the section are three drop-down lists with which you can customize information to meet your requirements.

Accounts Drop-Down List

The first drop-down list displays the accounts you want to use for your graphs. The default is All Accounts. Click the downward arrow and choose Custom to open the Customize dialog. From this dialog you may

- Click the Select All button to include all of your accounts in the graph.
- Click the Clear All button to deselect all of your accounts.
- Select or clear the check box displayed by each account name to include it in the graph.
- Click the Show (Hidden Accounts) check box to display the accounts you have chosen to hide so you can opt to include them as well. If you do not see the check box, you have not hidden any accounts.

When you have completed your selections, click OK to close the dialog.

Time Period Drop-Down List

The second drop-down list in the Net Worth button's view allows you to set the time period for your graphs. You can choose from the Last 12 Months, the Last Year, the Last 3 Years, the Last 5 Years, the Last 10 Years, or the default time period, which is the Earliest to Date.

Use the Custom Date option to set the calendar period to display in the graph.

Set the Interval to Display

The three choices on the Interval drop-down list are Months, Quarter, and Year. For example, if you want to see what your financial position has been for the last three years, you might choose to display the information by quarter instead of months to see the general trend.

Net Worth by Assets and Liabilities

The first snapshot in the Net Worth view is Net Worth by Assets and Liabilities, as shown earlier in Figure 10-7. This graph uses a stacked column to indicate your net worth for the period you choose. In our example, we have chosen to display all of the accounts for the last three years. We chose quarterly intervals to get an idea of how our savings and investment plan has worked for that time period. The period covered by the graph shows above the display. We can change the information displayed on the graph by changing the options in any of the drop-down lists.

The green bar represents your assets, the muted red bar represents your debt, and the red circle represents your net worth. Ideally, the green bars should get taller while the muted red bars get shorter. The net effect is a rise in the net worth line, as seen in Figure 10-7. If the net worth line is below the baseline of the graph, you're in some serious financial trouble because your debts exceed your assets.

How you perceive the colors may depend on your monitor's settings.

When you position your mouse over a specific area on the net worth line of this graph, you see your net worth as of that date, as shown here. When you position your mouse on a green area, a similar report appears showing exactly what your assets were worth as of that date. Similarly, put your mouse in the debt area to see how much you owed at that date. Click any bar location to open another chart that displays your assets and liabilities in charts. Click Done to close the chart.

Depending on your selections and accounts you have set up in Quicken, you may see one or two charts. If you have both asset and liability accounts selected, you will see two charts: one for assets and a second chart for liabilities. If you have only asset or only liability accounts selected, you will see only one donut.

The size of the portions in the donut chart may vary depending on the number of accounts you have chosen to display. The charts are sized by the number of account-type legend entries. Therefore, if you have more account types for assets, the assets chart may be smaller than the liabilities chart. This can be a bit disconcerting to see your assets looking smaller than your debts. If you have chosen only one or two asset and liability accounts, the "donuts" in the chart may appear to be the same size.

Keep in mind that, by default, this graph represents all of your accounts in Quicken—including your banking and investment accounts. It's a true view of your net worth trend for the accounts and time period you choose to display.

Net Worth Summary Report

Below the Net Worth by Assets and Liabilities graph, you'll see a button labeled Net Worth Summary Report. The report that appears when you click this button displays your information in both graphic and report format, as seen in Figure 10-8. (This report can also be displayed by selecting Reports | Net Worth & Balances | Net Worth.) As with any report or graph, the information is fully customizable. Click the X to close the report and return to the Net Worth view. See Chapter 15 to review your many options when customizing reports.

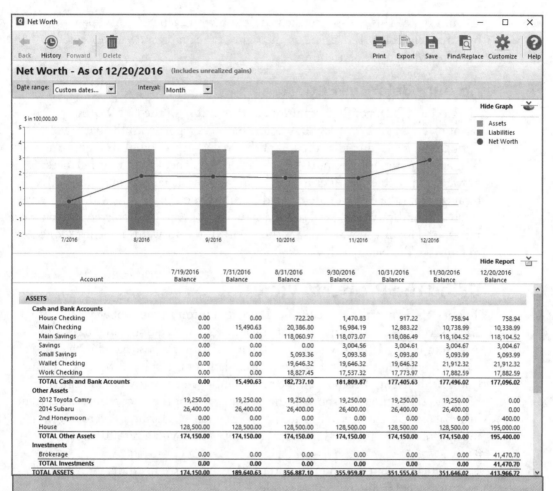

Figure 10-8 • **The Net Worth report and graph show how well your financial plans are working.**

Any accounts you have hidden in Quicken are not included in your Net Worth reports unless you choose to include them by customizing the report.

Net Worth by Account Type

By default, the Net Worth by Account Type graph appears in the lower portion of the screen when you select the Net Worth button in the Property & Debt tab. This graph shows the percentage of your net worth represented by each of your account types. This is also a stacked bar graph with each account type represented by a different color. The legend to the right of the graph shows what color indicates which type of accounts.

Account Balances Report

The Account Balances Report button, at the bottom of the Net Worth by Account Type graph, opens the Account Balances report with the date range settings you have entered at the top of the Net Worth views. This report can also be opened by choosing Reports | Net Worth & Balances | Account Balances. However, the default settings for the report you see using that method show your balances from the earliest date entered in your Quicken account with no interval (such as monthly, weekly, and so on) set. Click the X to close the report. You see a message asking if you want to save the report. If the answer is no, click Don't Save to return to the Net Worth view.

Using the Property View

To open the Property view, click the Property button in the Property & Debt tab. Each of your assets and any associated liability show in a horizontal bar graph, as seen in Figure 10-9. If you have two current liabilities associated with one asset, as shown in the House account, each liability is displayed with a different color. At the right of each asset, the total equity you currently hold in this asset displays. The equity that shows is the current value of the asset minus the current loan balance. If you have refinanced an asset, such as your house, zeroed-out mortgages may be included in the total equity value with a zero balance.

Depending on your screen or monitor, you may not see the different colors because the color differences are subtle.

The drop-down list box at the top of the screen lets you select which of your accounts you want displayed in this graph. While All Accounts is the default choice, you may choose from several options:

- Personal Accounts Only
- One specific account (each shows by the account name)
- Custom (which opens a list of all of your asset accounts so you may choose two or more)

Click the Property Options button at the right side of the screen to open a menu from which you can choose among the following:

Figure 10-9 · **Bar graphs in the Property view display both assets and any associated debt.**

- Add A House Asset Account
- Add A Vehicle Asset Account
- Add Other Asset Account
- Add A New Loan

Each item on the Property Options menu has a small white plus sign in a green circle to its left. You open the appropriate Add Account screen when you click that green circle icon or click the adjacent text.

Creating a new account from the Property Options menu saves a step or two when adding a new account, as the Add Account dialog opens directly to the type of account you are creating.

Within the graph itself are similar icons to the right of each asset name. Use these green circle icons to open a menu with which you can perform the following actions.

Link Existing Loan To This Property   This option opens a list of existing loans from which you can choose the loan to link to this property (asset).

Link Existing Line Of Credit To This Property   Choosing this option opens another list menu that displays all your current credit accounts from which you can choose.

Unlink Existing Liability From This Property   When you choose this option from the list, any current loans that have been associated with this asset are displayed. Click the one you want to unlink from this asset. If no liability (loan or line of credit) is currently linked with the property (asset), you will not see this option.

New Loan   Selecting this option opens the Add Loan Account dialog. If you have not downloaded yet today, when you select New Loan, Quicken will connect to the Internet and download an updated list of financial institutions.

EXPERIENCED USERS RECOMMEND

The ability to link credit accounts with assets can be valuable. However, unless you have set up a line of credit as a "credit" account instead of a loan, Quicken does not make this information available as an "existing line of credit." Since you cannot change the account "type" after you have entered it, be cautious when creating your new accounts.

Opening the Debt View

Clicking the Debt button opens the Debt view, which by default displays two graphs that show your current debt position, as seen in Figure 10-10. Each graph portrays your liability information in a slightly different format. At the top of the graphs are several drop-down lists that let you select the accounts with which you want to work, the time period to cover, and the intervals to be displayed. A legend appears at the right telling you what color the graph uses for each debt listed.

The first drop-down list lets you choose which accounts you want to use in the graphs. You have your choice of the following:

- **All Debt Accounts** sets the graph to display all of your debts. This is the default setting.

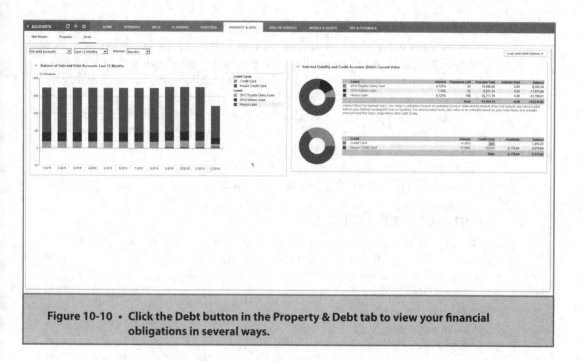

Figure 10-10 • **Click the Debt button in the Property & Debt tab to view your financial obligations in several ways.**

- **Credit Cards Only** displays just the amounts you owe to credit card companies.
- **Loans Only** shows all of your current loans, including any mortgages. If you move your mouse cursor over any section of the stacked bar graph, a small message appears that displays the balance of that loan at that point in time.

If you have designated a liability as "Other Liability" in the Add Account dialog, you may see an option for "Other Liabilities Only," which displays all items of this account type.

- **Custom** opens a Customize dialog that lets you choose which accounts to display. Click Select All to display all of your debts. Click Clear All and choose only the debts you want to display in your graph. Clicking the Show (Hidden Accounts) check box will enable you to include those debts that you have hidden in Quicken for selection in the graphs. Click OK to close the dialog and return to your graph.

Specific debt account names let you create a graph that shows only one of your debt accounts.

The second drop-down list offers a variety of dates for which you can set your graphs. Most of the options are self-explanatory; however, when you click Custom Date, a dialog appears that you can use to set the period for which you want each graph to display. Be aware that in this dialog, unlike most dialog boxes in Quicken, you have to click in the To field to change the date instead of using the TAB key to move to it. In this dialog, pressing the TAB key when you enter a date in the From field moves your cursor to the OK button. Click OK to save your date selection and return to the Debt view.

The third drop-down list lets you choose between three interval options for your graph's display: Months, Quarter, and Year.

Loan and Debt Options

At the top right of the Debt view is a drop-down list, labeled Loan and Debt Options, offering additional options, as discussed next:

- Add A New Loan
- Refinance Calculator
- Loan Calculator
- Add A Credit Card

Both of the "Add" choices open the Add Loan/Credit Card Account dialog with which you can quickly create a new account of the type you selected. Again, if this is the first time you have done any online activity for the day, Quicken will retrieve the list of financial institutions when you click the Add A New Loan or Add A Credit Card drop-down item. The Calculator options open either the Refinance or the Loan Calculator for your use. Learn more about Quicken's useful financial calculators in Chapter 12.

Balance of Selected Debt Accounts Graph

As seen in Figure 10-10, the first graph you see in the Debt view of the Property & Debt tab is a stacked bar graph that shows your total debt by year for a period you designate. This graph includes a legend explaining the color used for each debt item account included in the graph.

Using the drop-down lists at the top of the screen, you can tell Quicken to show a wide variety of accounts, dates, and intervals to make the information meaningful to you.

Current Value Graph

The second graph in the Debt view of the Property & Debt tab displays the current value of the debts you selected in the first drop-down list at the top of the page, as seen in Figure 10-10. Each drop-down list selection you make displays the information in a slightly different way and includes somewhat different information. As you can see, the Selected Liability and Credit Accounts (Debt): Current Value graph displays information both as a chart and with columns of information. How you have chosen to display your debt accounts in the Debt view's first drop-down box will affect what shows on the Current Value graph. Depending on your choices, the information about the (nonhidden) debt accounts is shown in two sections: Loans and Credit. If you have other debt accounts that are not credit or loan, you will see a third debt type: Other Liabilities.

If you only have one debt account with a balance for a particular debt type, a chart may not be displayed for that debt type. No chart is displayed if the balance of the debt account is positive instead of negative. This can happen when you have a credit due you on a credit card account.

Loans   If you have selected All Debt Accounts or Loans Only in the first drop-down list, you will see the following:

- **Interest** displays the rate of interest for each loan.
- **Payments Left** shows you how many more payments you have through the life of the loan or debt.
- **Principal Paid** shows the amount of principal you have paid on this loan since its inception.
- **Interest Paid** totals the interest you have paid to date. Remember, interest is the amount you pay to rent someone else's money.
- **Balance** shows what you still owe on this debt. It shows as a minus because it subtracts from your net worth.

Credit   This section displays the credit cards you have entered into Quicken. If you do not have any credit card accounts set up in Quicken, you will not see this section in the Debt view. The information displays in chart form for the options you chose in the drop-down boxes. You see the following:

- **Interest** displays the interest rate being charged on each card. If it does not show, click the Set button to open the Interest Rate dialog. Enter the interest rate for the card as shown on your monthly statement, and click OK to close the dialog. You may also use this dialog to change the interest rate for the credit card. Click the current rate to open the Interest Rate dialog and enter the new rate.

- **Credit Limit** displays the credit limit of the card. The amount does not show if you have not entered the limit. Click the Set button to open the Credit Limit dialog. Type the amount of this card's credit limit, and click OK to return to the graph.

You can also change the credit limit by clicking the existing value and entering a new amount.

- **Available** displays the amount you can still charge on this card. It is your credit limit minus the current balance.
- **Balance** displays the amount you owe on this card to the credit card company as of the date you set.

If you have not set the interest rate or the credit card limit on any of your credit accounts, Set buttons appear, as seen in Figure 10-10. (The Set buttons are very small and you may miss them. In Figure 10-10, look for Credit Card and on that line, look at Credit Limit to see an example of this button. If you have set the interest rate but not the card limit, only one Set button appears. You may adjust the interest rate and credit limits with the appropriate Set button.

1. Locate the account you wish to adjust and, in the proper column, click the Set button.
2. From the dialog that appears, you may set an interest rate or a credit limit. Type in the information and click OK.

You may also adjust any number that appears in blue in the graph. For example, when our credit card company complies with our request to lower our credit limit, we do the following:

- Click the amount shown in blue in the credit limit column for the appropriate account.
- In the Credit Limit dialog that appears, type the new amount.
- Click OK to close the dialog and return to the Debt snapshots in the Property & Debt tab.

Accessing Property and Debt Account Registers

To learn more about the transactions and balances for a specific account, you can view the account's register:

- Click the name of an account in the Property view in the Property & Debt tab's screen.

- Click the name of the account from the Account Bar.
- Click the account's name from the Current Value graph in the Debt view of the Property & Debt tab.

With any of the three methods, the account's register will open. The register lists all transactions entered into that account, as well as the ending balance. As with all of the Quicken registers, you can enter transactions directly into the register. Quicken automatically calculates and enters other transactions such as principal payments for a mortgage or other loans.

Viewing the transactions and entering or editing the transactions will work in all loan registers, except online loan registers. You cannot edit the transactions in those registers.

Creating Alerts for Property and Debt Accounts

Although Chapter 7 introduced you to Quicken Alerts, there are some special alerts that relate directly to your property.

Setting Up Property and Debt Alerts

To set up an alert, begin by opening the Tools menu and clicking Alerts Center. Click the Setup tab and choose General. Click the name of the alert you want to set from the options on the left side of the window to display its options on the right. Of the several options available, two alerts apply specifically to your property. The Reminders alerts are discussed at length in Chapter 7.

- **Insurance Reappraisal** notifies you before an insurance policy expires so you can either reevaluate coverage or shop for a new policy.
- **Mortgage Reappraisal** notifies you before a mortgage changes from variable to fixed (or fixed to variable) so you can consider refinancing. Even if your mortgage doesn't convert, you can use this alert to remind you periodically to check for better mortgage deals.

Both alerts work in much the same way. For each alert, enter a name and date in the right side of the window. For example, to set insurance policy expiration dates, click in the Policy Name field that contains the name of the policy holder with which you want to work. You can change the name or add a new policy holder (the insurance company). You'll see that your text appears on the right side of the box. Use your TAB key to move to the Exp. (Expiration) Date field. Enter the expiration date.

The Lender Name or Policy Name field (depending on the alert you have chosen to work with) is right-justified when entering the text. That can appear odd if you are expecting the text to appear at the left side of the field.

Select one of the options at the bottom of the window to indicate how you want the alert to appear: as text in the alert list or as a pop-up dialog that appears when you start Quicken. Finally, use the drop-down list to specify the length of time the alert should remain in the list and click OK.

Repeat this process for each alert you want to set. When you're finished, click OK.

Working with Property and Debt Alerts

Once you have established property and debt alerts, you can manage them in several ways:

- Open the Alerts Center's Show All tab by clicking Tools and choosing Alerts Center. Select an alert and click the Delete button to remove an alert.
- In the Alerts Center's Setup tab, you can uncheck an alert category to prevent all the alerts in that category from being displayed in any way.
- If you have made changes in the Alerts Center's Setup tab, click OK to save your changes and close the Alerts Center window.

Reviewing Your Financial Position

In This Chapter:

- *Working with the Portfolio view*

- *Using the Portfolio X-Ray*

- *Studying your performance*

- *Exploring asset allocation views*

- *Updating your investments*

- *Working with reports*

- *Utilizing Investing tab tools*

- *Using the asset allocation guide*

- *Analyzing your portfolio*

- *Previewing your buy/sell decisions*

- *Estimating capital gains*

- *Setting investment alerts*

As you enter your investing transactions into Quicken, whether manually or automatically via Transaction Download, Quicken builds a portrait of your investment portfolio and performance. If you're serious about investing, you can use this information to evaluate your investing position and fine-tune your portfolio to diversify and maximize returns.

Chapter 11

Quicken's Investing tab offers a wide range of tools, including reports, graphs, alerts, analysis tools, and reference materials, that you can use to evaluate and strengthen your investment positions. This chapter takes a closer look at the features that can make you a better investor.

Using the Investing Tab

The Investing tab should be your first stop for evaluating your investment position. Each of its views includes snapshots with calculated information and links to more information within Quicken and on the Quicken.com Investing page. Because the Investing tab always displays the most recent information it has, its windows are most useful immediately after downloading quotes, news, and research information, as discussed in Chapter 9. If you are using Quicken Premier or a higher version, you can tell Quicken to download quotes for you every 15 minutes. To do so, select Edit | Preferences | Investment Transactions | Automatically Update Quotes Every 15 Minutes. And even if you are downloading quotes every 15 minutes, the quotes are still 20 minutes delayed. If you need your quote data that up to date, you are better off using your broker's site, which likely gives you real-time quotes for free.

Quicken must be the active window for this to work. If you are using another program or have minimized Quicken, Quicken will not update quotes until you make it the active window.

Click the Investing tab to open the Investing tab window. By default, the first time you open the Investing tab, the Portfolio view appears, as seen in Figure 11-1. If you have visited the Investing tab before, you may need to select the Portfolio view, as Quicken remembers the last view on the Investment tab you visited. Additional information is available in the views found by clicking the Portfolio X-Ray, Performance, Allocations, or Tax Optimizer button as discussed later in this chapter.

If you don't want to wait for the Portfolio X-Ray to load each time you click the Investing tab, do not leave the Investing tab before clicking another view within it.

This part of the chapter takes you on a guided tour of Quicken's Investing tab so you know exactly how you can use it to monitor your investments.

Name			Quote/Price	Shares	Market Value	Cost Basis	Gain/Loss	Gain/L... (%)	Day Gain/Loss	Price Day Change	Price Day Change (%)	
◢ Brokerage					40,965.70	27.00*	*	*	*	0.00		
⊞ Amazon.com Inc	🔖	⊘	764.72	20	15,294.40		*	*	*	0.00		
⊞ Ancestry.com		⊘		180	0.00		*	*	*	0.00		
⊞ Boeing Co	🔖	⊘	152.24	70	10,656.80		*	*	*	0.00		
⊞ Microsoft	🔖	⊘	59.95	250	14,987.50		*	*	*	0.00		
⊞ Solar Winds		⊘		150	0.00		*	*	*	0.00		
Cash					27.00	27.00						
◢ Small Savings					5,093.99	5,093.99	0.00	0.00	0.00			
Cash					5,093.99	5,093.99						
◢ Watch List (add) (edit)												
◢ Indexes												
Dow Jones Industrials		⊘	18,202.62									
NASDAQ Composite		⊘	5,246.41									
Russell 2000		⊘	1,222.64									
S&P 500 Index		⊘	2,144.29									
Totals:					46,059.69	5,120.99*	40,938.70*	799.43*	0.00			

*Placeholder Entries for missing data are used in these calculations.

Online quotes delayed at least 20 minutes. Options quotes are previous day's close. Updated 12/6/2016 at 2:31 pm local time.

Figure 11-1 • The Portfolio view in your Investing tab shows your current investment holdings.

Working with the Portfolio View

The Portfolio view of the Investing tab displays all of your investments in one place. You can view your information in a wide variety of ways to show exactly what you need to see to understand the performance, value, or components of your portfolio. You can open the Portfolio window by clicking the Portfolio button in the Investing tab or by pressing CTRL-U from any location in Quicken. You can also add the Portfolio button to the Quicken Toolbar.

Using Portfolio View Options

You can quickly customize the Portfolio window's view by using the Show, Group By, and As Of drop-down lists right beneath the Portfolio, Portfolio X-Ray, Performance, and Allocations buttons, seen next. You can further customize the view by clicking the Customize button. There are many view combinations—far too many to illustrate in this book. Here's a brief overview so you can explore these options on your own.

| Portfolio | Portfolio X-Ray | Performance | Allocations | Tax Optimizer | | Update ▼ | Reports ▼ | Tools ▼ |

Show: Value ▼ | Group by: Accounts ▼ | As of: 11/30/2016 📅 | Customize | ⚙ Options ▼

Using Show Options   The Show drop-down list enables you to specify the view by which you want the information displayed. You can customize each of the nine predefined views and have additional nine customized views as shown here. You can use the Customize button, discussed later in this section. You can also create nine "custom" views to see data in ways most useful to you.

Show: Value ▼
- Value
- Recent performance
- Historic performance
- Fundamentals
- Quotes
- Mutual funds
- Asset allocation
- Tax implications
- Employee stock options
- Custom1
- Custom2
- Custom3
- Custom4
- Custom5
- Custom6
- Custom7
- Custom8
- Custom9

Using Group By Options   The Group By options enable you to select the order in which securities appear. The drop-down list offers six options: Accounts, Industry, Security, Security Type, Investing Goal, and Asset Class. These options correspond to information entered as part of a security's definition, either manually when you add the security to Quicken or automatically when you download asset class information. Learn how to add securities and how to download security information in Chapter 9.

Using Portfolio Date   Use the As Of drop-down list to set the date for which you want to view the portfolio. For example, suppose you want to see what your portfolio looked like a month ago before a particularly volatile market period. You can either enter that date in the text box or click the calendar button beside the text box to display a calendar of dates, and then click the date you want to display. The view changes to show your portfolio as of the date you specified.

You can use several date keyboard shortcuts in the date field, or you can use the small calendar at the right of the As Of field. Press M for the beginning of the month and H for the end of the month. Find more keyboard shortcuts in Appendix A or search Help using the phrase "keyboard shortcuts."

Customizing a View

Quicken offers an incredible amount of flexibility when it comes to displaying information in the Portfolio window. In addition to the nine pre-configured views found in the Show drop-down list, you can quickly customize any of the existing 18 views. However, you cannot delete or hide any of these views.

To customize a view, begin by using the Show drop-down list to choose the view you want to customize. Then click the Customize button to the right of the Show, Group By, and As Of drop-down lists. The Customize Current View dialog appears with the Available and Displayed Columns lists displayed, as shown next. Note that the definition for the item chosen in the Available Columns list shows beneath that list. Set options as desired in the dialog, and click OK to change the view.

Selecting Columns to Show   To display a column of information, select it in the Available Columns list and click the Add button beside it. To hide a column of information, select it in the Displayed Columns list and click the Remove button. You're not removing the information—just choosing not to display it. You can change the order in which columns appear by selecting a column name in the Displayed Columns list and using the Move Up or Move Down button to change its order in the list.

A short explanation of the column's data displays with a yellow highlight at the bottom of the Available Columns list for the column you currently have selected. This feature is handy when you are trying to decide which columns will be most useful to you.

Displaying Symbols Rather Than Names   To display a security's ticker symbol rather than its name, select the Show Symbols In Name Column check box found at the lower right of the Customize Current View dialog. Or you can display both the name and symbol by leaving the Show Symbols In Name Column check box blank and adding the Ticker Symbol column to the Displayed Column list.

Return to Default   Click the Reset View button at the lower left of the Customize Current View dialog to return this view to the default settings.

Selecting Accounts to Include   As you are customizing your view, you can specify which accounts you want to appear. Click the Accounts tab, shown next, and toggle the check marks to the left of the account names in the Accounts To Include In This View list. Only those accounts with a check mark will appear. You can specify the order in which accounts appear by selecting an account name in the Accounts To Include In This View list and clicking the Move Up or Move Down button.

Click Select All to include all of your accounts, or click Clear All to clear all of the check marks and start over. To include hidden accounts in the Accounts To Include In This View list, select the Show (Hidden Accounts) check box, as seen in the illustration. To reset the view to the default settings, click the Reset View button.

Selecting Securities to Include　In the Customize Current View dialog box, click the Securities tab to specify which securities should appear. Toggle the check marks to the left of the security names in the Securities To Include In This View list. Only those securities that are selected will appear. To include hidden securities in the Securities To Include In This View list, select the Show (Hidden Securities) check box.

Click Select All to include all of your securities, or click Clear All to clear all of the check marks and start over.

When you have finished creating your new view, click OK to return to the Investing tab's Portfolio view.

 When you create a new investment account, it is automatically added to all Portfolio views. However, when you create a new security, it is not automatically added to any Portfolio views. If you have added a new security, be sure to customize the Portfolio views in which you want the new security to appear.

 In some unusual circumstances, such as when you buy a security, sell all of your holdings and then buy it again, you may have to re-add the security to the Portfolio views.

Setting Portfolio View Options

Click either the Options Action icon (the small gear icon) or the word "Options" at the far right of the Portfolio view to customize the current view, as explained earlier, as well as to perform two additional tasks.

Portfolio Preferences　From the Investing tab Portfolio view, click Options | Portfolio Preferences to open the Portfolio View Options dialog. This option enables you to specify the period for return calculations and the tax rate used in the Portfolio window, as shown here. Setting these options enables you to fine-tune the way Quicken makes Portfolio window calculations, which is also shown here.

The Show Return Calculations From area offers options for determining the period and tax rate for which Quicken calculates the return on investment:

- **Earliest Available Date**, the default, includes all periods for which you have entered transactions into Quicken.
- A blank field allows you to enter a starting date for calculations. All transactions between the starting date you enter and the current date are included in the calculations. Alternatively, you can use the calendar icon to set the date.

 Setting this date allows you to see how an investment that you may have held for many years has been performing for a more recent period—for example, how it has performed for the last year instead of since you purchased it. This can be handy if you are trying to identify investments that performed well in the past but have recently underperformed.

- **Tax Rate Used In Portfolio View** allows you to choose tax rates that should be used in tax calculations for capital gains. If you are utilizing Quicken's Tax Planner, as covered in Chapter 14, keep the default, Use Tax Planner Rate, selected. Otherwise, choose the rates that are appropriate for your financial situation. Check with your tax professional for further information about your specific situation. Click OK to save your changes and return to the Portfolio view.

Show Closed Lots   This option tells Quicken that you want to display lots that have been closed.

Using the Portfolio X-Ray

If you use the Premier edition of Quicken 2017, the Portfolio X-Ray is available to provide investment information through a partnership with Morningstar. Using this tool can help you, the investor, get a clearer view of both the weaknesses and strengths of your portfolio.

To use the Portfolio X-Ray:

1. Choose the Investing tab and select Portfolio X-Ray.
2. Select the Get Started button. Quicken connects to Morningstar to retrieve data for the securities in your Quicken investment accounts.
3. The first time you access Portfolio X-Ray, a license agreement from Morningstar may appear. Click Yes, I Agree, and Continue.
4. The Portfolio X-Ray view appears as seen in Figure 11-2.

Figure 11-2 • The Portfolio X-Ray view displays information about your investments

If you have not yet entered any investment accounts, you will be prompted to add them when you click the Get Started button in the Portfolio X-Ray view.

Reviewing the Portfolio X-Ray Options

As with the several other views in the Investing tab, the Portfolio X-Ray view has several options.

From the Accounts drop-down list, you can choose an "x-ray" of all of your accounts, only the Investing accounts, only the Retirement accounts; you can create a customized list; or you can select specific accounts.

With the Custom option, you may choose to show one or more of your investment accounts. Click to choose an account. Clear the check box if you do not want to view information about an account. If you have hidden accounts, select the Show (Hidden Accounts) check box to include them in the list. Use the Refresh X-Ray button to reload the information.

Use the securities drop-down list to see information on one or more of your securities. Like the accounts drop-down list, you click to choose a security and include hidden securities. You also can clear the check box in this list if you do not want to see information. As with the accounts drop-down list, use the Refresh X-Ray button to reload the information.

The X-Ray's Options

Within the X-Ray itself is a wealth of information. Note the two options, X-Ray Interpreter and Stock Intersection, as seen in Figure 11-2.

The X-Ray Interpreter   The first tab, X-Ray Interpreter, offers the following information:

- **Asset Allocation**   This section reviews your holdings and indicates the risk of your investment mix. It explains what this asset mix indicates for long-term and short-term goals.
- **World Regions**   In this section, the X-Ray analyzes the mix of your holdings worldwide.
- **Stock Sectors**   This section indicates the mix of your holdings in various stock sectors.
- **Change Benchmark**   You may change the benchmark for the Stock Sectors section to the S&P 500 or other portfolios with a similar investment style to your current holdings.
- **Stock & Bond Style**   In these areas, your portfolio's style is discussed.
- **Stock & Bond Stats**   Here, statistical information is displayed comparing your portfolio to benchmark holdings.
- **Stock Type**   This section shows a breakdown of your current holdings compared to the benchmark you select.
- **Fees & Expenses**   The ratios and potential capital gains information displays in this section. Again, you may change the benchmark for this data.
- **Top 10 Underlying Holdings**   In this section, the percentage of your total holdings is displayed by item.

Stock Intersection   This section displays the top 50 items of your portfolio, as seen in Figure 11-3. Each item is shown as a percentage of your total portfolio. It indicates each item's industry sector and when you obtained the item.

Figure 11-3 • Use the Morningstar Stock Intersection information to better understand your investments.

User Guide The User Guide explains in more detail what each section of the X-Ray means.

Studying Your Performance

If you are using Quicken's Premier (or higher) edition, the Performance button's view in the Investing tab displays graphs, such as the one seen next, and tables of information about your investment performance. You can customize many of the snapshots that appear in the Performance view using commands on each snapshot's Options menu. You can further customize the Performance view window by using the drop-down list options at the top of the Performance view window. All of the snapshots on Performance and Allocations views are controlled by the drop-down list selections.

Portfolio Value vs. Cost Basis

The Portfolio Value vs. Cost Basis graph uses a line graph and a bar graph to illustrate your portfolio's cost basis—which may or may not be the amount you've invested—and its market value. Ideally, you want the tops of the bars to appear above the line, indicating that your account is worth more than you spent to buy the securities.

EXPERIENCED USERS RECOMMEND

The Investment Performance report shows the average annual return (AAR) for each investment. One of my clients thought this report presented the return on investment (ROI), which is a different calculation.

- To compute ROI, you subtract the total cost of an investment from the total gain and divide that result by the total cost.
- To calculate the AAR, you add the annual return percentage rates and divide that result by the number of years.

To see ROI information, from the Investing tab, click Portfolio | Customize. From the Customize Current View dialog, choose any of the five ROI calculations from the Available Columns list and add your choice(s) to the Displayed Columns list on the right side of the dialog. Click OK to display the information, which is shown in percentages.

Be aware the investment amount is over the lifetime you have owned the security, so if you have bought, sold, and then bought some more, you may not get the results you expect.

The Options menu (click the gear icon at the right of the graph) offers additional choices for this graph:

- **Go To A Full Screen View Of This Graph** displays a graph with only your portfolio value versus cost basis information as of the custom date you set in the Performance Date Range drop-down list. If you did not set a date, it uses today's date.
- **Show Value/Cost Basis Report** tells Quicken to show the information in a report format. You can hide the report and see only the graph, or you can hide the graph and see only the report with one click on either the Hide Report or Hide Graph icon.
- **Go To Full Portfolio** returns you to the Investing tab's Portfolio view.

Growth Of $10,000

The Growth Of $10,000 chart illustrates how an investment of $10,000 in your portfolio has grown over the period you choose. You can select check boxes beside popular investment indexes to compare your investment performance to one or more indexes, as shown here.

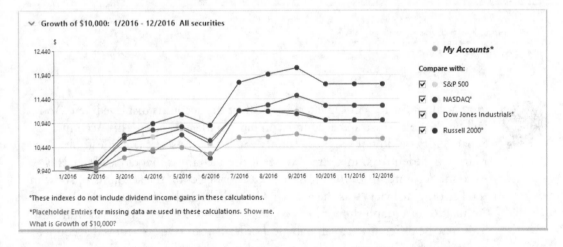

If you have not updated recently and choose an index to compare to the performance of your securities, you may see a message prompting you to do an additional download.

Average Annual Return

The Average Annual Return chart displays the one-year, three-year, and five-year return on each of your investment accounts. If the account has one or more securities in the one-, three-, or five-year period, there will be an average annual return reported for the account. If the account did not exist or no lots of the account's securities existed during the one-, three-, or five-year period, the average annual return will show as N/A, as seen next. If you would like to include additional market indexes on your graph, you can add them using the Security List's Choose Market Indexes button.

Account	1 Year	3 Year	5 Year
MMA Account	6.63%	5.30%	7.23%
Brokerage 1	4.84%*	N/A%*	N/A%*
Current IRA	2.21%*	N/A%*	N/A%*
Inherited Investments	0.0%	0.0%	3.62%
Company Y IRA	N/A	N/A	N/A
XYZ Financial	N/A	N/A	0.0%
My 401(k)	0.0%	0.0%	0.0%
All Listed Accounts	**6.12%***	**5.32%***	**7.05%***
Dow Jones Industrials*	4.83%	4.15%	8.48%
NASDAQ Composite*	5.67%	8.67%	14.74%
Russell 2000*	8.20%	2.43%	10.51%
S&P 500 Index	5.97%	5.71%	11.32%

⌄ Average Annual Return ⚙

*These calculations do not include reinvested dividend income.
*Placeholder Entries for missing data are used in these calculations. Show me.
What is Average Annual Return?

NOTE Your account settings in Quicken 2017 affect the accounts displayed here. You will not be able to see any accounts you have marked as Keep This Account Separate. If you do not see the accounts you expect to see, check the Tools | Manage Hidden Accounts screen to see if the account is marked as Keep This Account Separate. Also, the drop-down list for selecting the accounts to show in the Performance view lists the accounts in alphabetical order, while the Average Annual Return graph shows the accounts in the order listed in the Account List. This may be different from alphabetical order if you have ever moved accounts around in the Account List. This also applies for the Allocations view.

The options for this section let you change the information's display:

- Both **Show Security Performance** and **Show Security Performance Comparison** open a report, similar to the Portfolio view, showing how your securities have done as of a date you choose.

- **Historical Prices** opens the Get Historical Prices dialog, shown next, from which you can tell Quicken to download historical prices for one or more of your securities for the last five days, the last month, year, two years, or five years. Place check marks in front of the name of each security for which you want pricing. The Mark All and Clear All buttons can help you make your selections. Click Update Now to use your Internet connection to download the data. The One Step Update Summary dialog displays when the download is complete. If you have the preference set to only show the One Step Update Summary when there is an error, you may not see it here. Click Close to close the dialog and return to the Investing tab's Performance view.

Depending on whether or not you have elected to store your Intuit ID in the Password Vault, you may see a prompt to enter your Intuit ID user ID and password when you click Update Now to retrieve the historical prices.

Exploring Asset Allocation Views

The Allocations view of the Investing tab displays a number of customizable snapshots of your investment data in both graphical and tabular formats. Each snapshot has links to other features. Each of the graphs that appear in the Allocations view can be customized using commands on the graph's Options menu. Buttons beneath each chart enable you to go to a full-sized graph in a report window or view a related report. You can further customize the Allocations view window by selecting one of the drop-down list options: All Accounts, Investing Only, Retirement Only, or one of your accounts. You can also select Custom to select specific accounts you want to display.

You have the same options using the securities drop-down list. Again, select All Securities or Custom to choose specific securities or show hidden securities. In both drop-down lists, click OK to close the dialogs.

Reviewing Your Asset Allocation

Asset allocation, which is covered in detail later in this chapter, refers to the way in which your investment dollars are distributed among different types of investments. It's a measure of how well your portfolio is diversified.

The Asset Allocation graph displays two donut charts: Actual allocation and Target allocation. Actual allocation indicates your portfolio's current diversification, as shown next. The illustration shows that the majority of the securities in All Accounts are invested in Domestic Bonds. Target allocation is the allocation you set up with Quicken's Portfolio Rebalancer, seen later in this chapter, in the section "Using the Portfolio Rebalancer."

If you have not yet set target allocations, clicking Set Target under the Target graph opens the Asset Allocation Guide, where you can select Set Your Target Allocations in the left pane and then click the linked word "Set" in the right pane. You can also set the target allocations directly by selecting the options gear and then Change Target Allocations.

Allocation By Account

Also in the Allocations view of the Investing tab are two additional charts, shown next. The Allocation By Account chart indicates how your portfolio's market value is distributed among the investing accounts you have entered into Quicken.

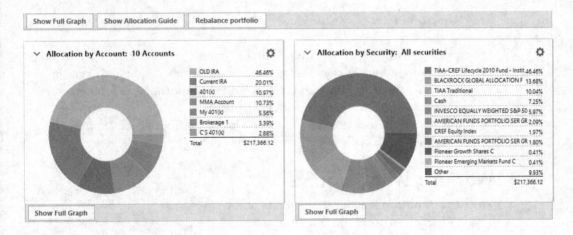

Allocation By Security

The Allocation By Security chart indicates how your portfolio's market value is distributed among the different securities.

Mutual Fund Ratings from Morningstar

If you use Quicken Premier or a higher version, Quicken displays up-to-date ratings from Morningstar, an investment research organization that rates mutual funds based on a variety of criteria. Ratings for mutual funds you track in Quicken are automatically downloaded with asset class and related information. The more stars, the higher the rating.

Updating Your Investments

The Update button at the right of all views in the Investing tab works with your Internet connection to keep your portfolio up to date:

- **Quotes** downloads the current quotations for either your entire portfolio or the securities you have selected.

If it seems your portfolio values are not updating when you run the Quotes download, check your Download Quotes and Watch List selections in the Security List. Press CTRL-Y to open the Security List.

- **Historical Prices** opens the Get Historical Prices dialog discussed earlier in this chapter.
- **Update Portfolio On Investing.Quicken.com** opens the Preferences dialog for Investing.Quicken.com. Learn more about Investing.Quicken.com in Chapter 9, and learn more about Preferences in Appendix B. You may not see this option until you have set up Quicken.com.
- **One Step Update** opens the One Step Update Settings dialog from which you can tell Quicken which accounts you want to update.

Working with Reports

The Reports button's menu, shown here, offers a wide variety of reports you can customize to meet your needs. See Chapter 15 for additional information about creating reports in Quicken 2017.

- **Capital Gains** reports can be for any date range you choose and can be subtotaled by Short- vs. Long-Term, Month, Quarter, Year, Account, Security, Security Type, Investing Goal, and Asset Class.
- **Investing Activity** reports display the activity, income (or loss), and capital gains for your accounts, based on the date range you set. This report is only available in Quicken Premier and higher versions.
- **Investment Asset Allocation** reports can be displayed both as graphs and reports. Use the Date Range drop-down list to tell Quicken the date range you want to display.

- **Investment Income** reports display the income and expenses related to your investments. These can be customized by date range, subtotals, or organization, such as Income & Expense or Cash Flow Basis.
- **Investment Performance** reports show the return and average annual return on your accounts based on the date range and subtotal options you choose.

When you customize the Investment Performance report, you may choose to display the cash flow detail, as well as displaying the cents as in other reports. To do so, ensure the check box by Cash Flow Detail is checked in the Show area of the Customize Investment Performance dialog. This is the only report that allows you to display that information.

- **Investment Transactions** reports show complete data about your transactions for time periods you designate. You can subtotal in several different ways as well as customize the date range of the report to meet your needs.
- **Maturity Dates For Bonds And CDs** creates a detailed report of when your instruments will mature.
- **Portfolio Value** displays the total value of your holdings in both a graph and a report. This report can be customized by date range and subtotal intervals to show your information in the way you want to see it.
- **Portfolio Value & Cost Basis** reports show the cost and value of each of your securities as of the date and subtotal interval you specify.
- **All Reports** opens the same menu you see when clicking Reports on the menu bar.

A plethora of other customization options is available in the Customize Report dialogs. See Chapter 15 for a discussion of many of the options.

Utilizing Investing Tab Tools

The Tools button's menu gives you access to the valuable estimators and guides provided by Quicken. See "Using the Asset Allocation Guide," "Previewing Your Buy/Sell Decisions," and "Estimating Capital Gains" later in this chapter.

Using Investment Analysis Tools

In addition to the Quicken.com-based investment research tools discussed in Chapter 9, Quicken offers a number of built-in tools that can help you learn more about investing and analyze your investment portfolio.

This part of the chapter introduces these analysis tools so you can explore them more fully on your own.

Using the Asset Allocation Guide

Many investment gurus say that an investor's goals should determine his or her asset allocation. If you're not sure what your asset allocation should be, Quicken includes a wealth of information about asset allocation, including sample portfolios with their corresponding allocations. You can use this feature to learn what your target asset allocation should be to meet your investing goals. Then you can monitor your asset allocation and, if necessary, rebalance your portfolio to keep it in line with what it should be.

Using the Asset Allocation Guide

The Asset Allocation Guide, shown in Figure 11-4, explains what asset allocation is, why it's important, and how Quicken can help monitor it in your portfolio.

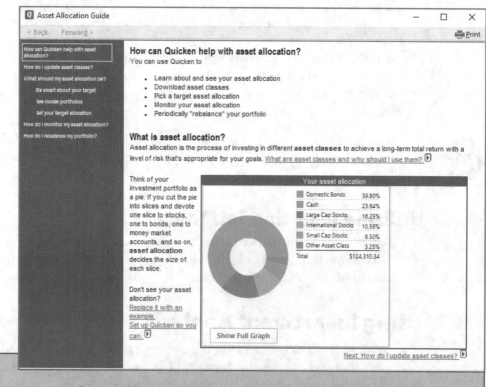

Figure 11-4 • Use the Asset Allocation Guide to learn about investing in different asset classes.

Choose Investing | Tools | Asset Allocation Guide. The Asset Allocation Guide window appears.

To take full advantage of this feature, read the information on the main part of the window. You can click links within the text or in the left column to learn more about specific topics. If you're new to asset allocation, you may find the See Model Portfolios link especially useful. It shows suggested asset allocations based on risk and returns for a number of portfolios. Click Close to return to the Investing tab.

Monitoring Your Asset Allocation

To monitor the asset allocation of your portfolio, you must enter asset class information for each of your investments. You can do this in two ways:

- **Manually enter asset class information**   Although this isn't difficult for stocks, it can be time consuming for investments that have an asset class mixture, such as mutual funds.
- **Download asset class information**   If you have a connection to the Internet, this is the best way to enter this information. With a few clicks, Quicken does all of the work in seconds. The information is complete and accurate. Learn how to download asset class information in Chapter 9.

Viewing Your Asset Allocation

If you have chosen to display all of your accounts and all of your securities in the Asset Allocation graph in the Allocations view's Asset Allocation snapshot, the donut chart that appears in the Asset Allocation Guide window is the same chart you see in your Asset Allocation snapshot in the Allocations view of your Investing tab. To get more information about a "piece of the pie," hover your mouse on a donut slice in either location. A yellow box appears, displaying the asset class and percentage of portfolio value.

Setting Your Target Asset Allocation   If you know what you want your asset allocation to be, you can set up a target asset allocation. Quicken then displays your target in the donut chart beside the current asset allocation chart on the Investing tab's Allocations button's Asset Allocation snapshot so you can monitor how close you are to your target.

Display the Allocations view of the Investing tab window. Then choose Change Target Allocations from the Options gear icon menu at the right of the Asset Allocation snapshot. The Target Allocation dialog appears.

If you have not yet set a target allocation, the link under the target graph will be Set Target. You can click Set Target to open the Asset Allocation Guide or click Options | Change Target Allocations to enter the allocations directly.

Enter the desired percentages for each asset class. When the total of all percentages equals 100, click OK to save your settings. The Target chart in the Asset Allocation snapshot of the Investing tab window reflects your new allocation settings. If your percentages do not add up to 100 percent, the difference appears as Unclassified.

You can also change your allocation percentages by clicking the Change Target link under the Target graph.

Using the Portfolio Rebalancer

If your current asset allocation deviates from your target asset allocation, you may want to rebalance your portfolio. This means buying and selling investments to bring you closer to your target asset allocation.

Keep in mind that brokerage fees and capital gains impacts are often involved when you buy and sell securities. For this reason, you should carefully evaluate your investment situation to determine how you can minimize costs and capital gains while rebalancing your portfolio. If small adjustments are necessary to bring you to your target asset allocation, you may not find it worth the cost to make the changes. Use this information as a guideline only! As always, consult your tax professional for additional information about your specific situation.

Quicken can tell you exactly how you must change your current asset allocation to meet your target asset allocation. In the Asset Allocation snapshot of the Investing tab's Allocations view, click the Options gear icon and select Rebalance Portfolio. The Portfolio Rebalancer window appears as seen in Figure 11-5. It provides instructions and shows you how much you must adjust each asset class to meet your targeted goals.

Click Close to return to the Investing tab.

Analyzing Your Portfolio

Quicken's Portfolio Analyzer enables you to look at your portfolio in a number of ways. To display it, first turn on Classic menus by clicking View | Classic Menus. From the Classic menu, click Investing | Investing Tools | Portfolio Analyzer. You'll find these options on the left sidebar:

Figure 11-5 • Use Quicken's Portfolio Rebalancer to allocate your investments.

- **Performance** shows your portfolio's average annual rate of return.
- **Holdings** lists your investment accounts and then shows a donut chart of your top ten holdings. Because most experts recommend that no single security take up more than 10 percent of your portfolio, you may find the percentage distribution helpful when considering diversification.
- **Asset Allocation** displays your current actual and target asset allocation so you can see how close you are to your target. See "Using the Asset Allocation Guide" earlier in this chapter.
- **Risk Profile** shows how "risky" your portfolio is when compared to the risk associated with specific classes of investments.
- **Tax Implications** summarizes your realized and unrealized year-to-date (YTD) capital gains or losses. Capital gains and losses are broken down into

two categories: short term and long term. For additional information about tax implications, consult your tax professional.

What's great about the Portfolio Analyzer is that it provides tables and charts to show information about your portfolio and then it explains everything in plain English so you know what the tables and charts mean. Using this feature regularly can really help you learn about the world of investing and how your portfolio measures up. To give it a try, choose Investing | Investing Tools | Portfolio Analyzer from the Classic menu. When you have finished reviewing the information, click Close to return to the Investing tab.

You can have your cake and eat it too. If you want to refer to the Portfolio Analyzer often, but don't want to have to switch from Standard to Classic menus to do so, with Classic menus selected, add the Portfolio Analyzer to the Quicken Toolbar. Then you'll have easy access to the Portfolio Analyzer from both Standard and Classic views.

You may want to return to the Standard menus. If so, click View | Standard Menus. Or, you may decide you like having menu access to every Quicken feature. If so, keep the Classic Menu selection.

Previewing Your Buy/Sell Decisions

In the Quicken Premier (and higher) editions, you will find a feature called Buy/Sell Preview, which offers a quick and easy way to see the impact of a securities purchase or sale on your finances—including your taxes.

From the Investing tab when using both Standard and Classic menus, choose Tools | Buy/Sell Preview. In the top half of the Buy/Sell Preview window that appears, enter information about the proposed purchase or sale. Quicken automatically enters the most recent price information for a security you own or watch, but you can override that amount if necessary.

If you choose to model a sell, ensure you select an account with an open position for that security first; otherwise, you will see an error message when you click Calculate.

When you're finished setting options, click Calculate. Quicken displays its results in the bottom half of the window, as seen here.

The Buy/Sell Preview feature works with Quicken's Tax Planner, as discussed in Chapter 14, to calculate the net effect of a sale on your expected tax bill or refund. Check with your tax professional for additional information. Click Done to close the Buy/Sell Preview window and return to the Investing tab.

Estimating Capital Gains

Quicken's Capital Gains Estimator enables you to estimate capital gains or losses and their related tax implications before you sell a security. The information it provides can help you make an informed decision about which security to sell.

Getting Started

Choose the Investing tab and click Tools | Capital Gains Estimator. The Capital Gains Estimator's welcome window appears. If you have used the tool before, you may see a message about previous proposed sales holdings changes.

Start by reading the information in the main part of the window. It explains what the Capital Gains Estimator does and offers links for learning more about specific terms and topics. Then click each of the links in the left side of the window, in turn, to step through the process of setting up the Capital Gains Estimator for your situation. You'll be prompted to name and choose a scenario, select taxable investment accounts to include, set your tax rate, and enter capital loss carryover information. When you enter complete and accurate information, Quicken can provide a more accurate indication of tax impacts.

Deciding What to Sell

Both Quicken Deluxe and Quicken Premier users (and users of the higher editions of Quicken as well) have the What If Scenarios. However, those who use Quicken Premier (or higher editions) have the What Should I Sell feature along with the What If Scenarios. With the What Should I Sell link, you can tell Quicken both the money you want to make and identify your goals for a sale. After you enter this information, click the Search button at the bottom of the window.

A dialog appears while Quicken makes complex calculations to meet your goals. When it's finished, you can click the View Results button in the dialog to display a scenario with the results as well as Quicken's recommendation.

Manually Adding Proposed Sales

If you prefer, you can manually indicate proposed sales in the What If Scenario window. Step 1 shows all the securities you hold in the accounts you selected during the setup process. You can add a proposed sale in two ways:

- **In the Current Holdings (Step 1) section**, click the name of the security you want to sell. Then enter the number of shares and sales price in Step 2. If you have multiple purchase lots for the security, this automatically sells the oldest lots first.
- **In the Current Holdings (Step 1) section**, if necessary, click the plus sign (+) to the left of the security that you want to sell to display the purchase lots. Then click the lot you want to sell. This enables you to specify exactly which lots are to be sold in the Proposed Sales area.

No matter which method you use, the sale is added to the Step 2 area of the window, which lists all of the proposed sales.

To adjust the number of shares to be sold, click in the Shares To Sell field for the proposed sale (in the Step 2 area), and enter a new value. The value you enter must be less than or equal to the number of shares purchased in that lot.

You can set up proposed sales for up to three scenarios—just click the Scenario link on the left side of the window to see and set that scenario's options. You can mix and match any sales you like to reach your goal.

Reading the Results

When all the information has been entered, you can see the true power of the Capital Gains Estimator. It tells you about the proceeds from the sales, as well as the gain or loss. If you scroll down in the What If Scenarios screen, you'll find more information about the proposed sale and its tax implications in the Step 3 area, including the gross profit and net proceeds from proposed sales. You can click links to view the results of additional calculations, such as the tax situation before and after executing the proposed sales and gain or loss on the proposed sales. Do the same for each scenario to see how they compare—then make your selling decision. Click Close to return to the Investing tab.

Setting Investment Alerts

Investment alerts are downloaded automatically with quotes and news headlines, as discussed in Chapter 9. To open the Alerts Center from the Quicken menu bar, click Tools | Alerts Center. When you select a specific alert, or a group of alerts, the Show All tab shows the alerts you have selected to track. To see the available alert selections, click the Setup tab of the Alerts Center. Ten investment alerts are available for your use:

- **Price And Volume** consists of two alerts. Price and Volume alerts notify you when a security's price rises above or falls below values you specify, as well as when the sales volume of a security exceeds a value you specify. News alerts give you the latest information about your securities, such as earnings announcements or analyst actions. The options for these are at Investing.Quicken.com. Once on the Quicken site, you will see that you can also add Portfolio alerts with which you can set alerts for your current portfolio or set up a watch list.
- **Reminders** has two options:
  - **Download Quotes**, which reminds you to download information so that your portfolio is up to date.
  - **Maturity Date**, which reminds you when a CD or bond reaches its maturity date.
- **Ratings And Analysis** lets you set two notifications:
  - When information becomes available for stocks you track
  - When information becomes available for mutual funds you track
- **Capital Gains/Losses** lets you set alerts for the following:
  - **Tax Implications On Sale** notifies you of your tax implications when you sell a security.
  - **Cap. Gains For The Year** notifies you if you exceed your capital gains limit for the year.
- **Tax Efficient Investments** provides you with information about investments that are more tax efficient than those you already have.
- **Mutual Fund Distributions** provides you with information about mutual fund distributions.

- **Securities Holding Period** provides you with information about holding periods for securities you own.

Many Quicken users report the most useful alerts are Price And Volume, Maturity Date Reminder, Stocks Ratings And Analysis, and Cap. Gains For The Year. These alerts give timely information without information overload.

Setting Up Alerts   To set up investment alerts, click Tools | Alerts Center | Setup. Quicken displays the Setup tab of the Alerts Center window. (See Chapter 7 for more detail on setting alerts.) On the left side of the window, click the name of an alert you want to set, and then set options for the alert in the right side of the window. (You must set some alerts, such as the Price And Volume alert, on Quicken.com.) You can disable an alert by removing the check mark beside its name. When you are finished making changes, click OK to save them.

Deleting Alerts   To remove an alert, select Tools | Alerts Center, and click the Show All tab. Then check the alerts you wish to delete and click Delete. A warning message appears telling you the alert will be deleted. Click OK to confirm your deletion. If you want the alert to continue, click Cancel. Either choice returns you to the Show All tab of the Alerts Center.

Looking Toward Tomorrow

This part of the book tells you about Quicken Personal Finance Software's planning and reporting features, which you can use to plan for your retirement, major purchases, and other life events. It covers Quicken's built-in financial calculators, as well as features that can help you save money to make your dreams come true. You are introduced to the many tax tools that are available in Quicken to help you prepare for tax time and, finally, you'll learn how to use Quicken's powerful reporting capabilities. The four chapters are

Part Five

Planning for Your Future

Chapter 12

In This Chapter:

- *Planning your steps*

- *Setting plan assumptions*

- *Viewing plan results*

- *Setting "What If" options*

- *Using "What If" results*

- *Finding more planning tools*

- *Learning about financial calculators*

- *Accessing the financial calculators*

- *Working with the Retirement Calculator*

- *Running the College Calculator*

- *Evaluating the Refinance Calculator*

- *Planning with the Savings Calculator*

- *Using the Loan Calculator*

Quicken can help you with all of your financial decisions and give you direction regarding how much you may need to save for the future. To most of us, the future is an unknown, a mystery. After all, who can say what will happen tomorrow, next year, or ten years from now? However, when you think about your future, you can usually come up with a few events for which you can plan: marriage, the purchase of a home, the birth of children (and their future education), and a comfortable retirement. (These are just examples—everyone's life runs a different course.) These events, as well as many unforeseen events, all have one thing in common: they affect your finances. In this chapter, you'll learn how Quicken's tools can help you plan for many of life's milestones.

Planning for Retirement

It may seem strange to start planning for what may happen 20 or more years from now. Throughout your life, you work and earn money to pay your bills, buy the things you and your family need or want, and help your kids get started with their own lives. However, there comes a day you may choose to retire from going to work every day. Regular paychecks stop coming, and you find yourself relying on the money you've been saving for those many years.

Retirement planning may be one of the most important financial planning jobs facing individuals and couples. Since this "job" requires long-term planning and, in many cases, sacrificing something today to create a secure tomorrow, we start with some planning steps and suggestions.

Most retired people live on fixed incomes. That's not a problem, as long as the income is fixed high enough to support a comfortable lifestyle. You can help ensure that there is enough money to finance your retirement years by planning and saving now. As longevity increases, planning is even more important today. In our country, people are living longer than ever. Your retirement dollars may need to support you for 25 years or more, at a time when the cost of living will likely be even higher than it is today.

With proper planning, it's possible to finance your retirement years without putting a strain on your working years. Tracking your current expenses and finding ways to reduce current spending so you can save more are important as well. By closely monitoring the status of your retirement funds, periodically adjusting your plan, and acting accordingly, your retirement years can be the golden years.

Planning Your Steps

Retirement planning is much more than deciding to put $5,500 in an IRA every year. It requires careful consideration of what you have, what you'll need, and how you can make those two numbers the same.

Assess What You Have

Take a good look at your current financial situation. What tax-deferred retirement savings do you already have? A 401(k)? An IRA? Something else? What regular savings do you have? What taxable investments do you have? The numbers you come up with form the basis of your final retirement funds.

Be sure to consider property that you can sell to contribute to retirement savings. For example, if you currently live in a large home to accommodate your family, you may eventually want to live in a smaller home. The proceeds from the sale of your current home may exceed the cost of your retirement home. Consider any income-generating property that may continue to generate income in your retirement years or could be sold to contribute to retirement savings.

Determine What You'll Need

What you'll need depends on many things. One calculation suggests you'll need 80 percent of your current gross income to maintain your current lifestyle in your retirement years.

Time is an important factor in calculating the total amount you should have saved by retirement day. Ask yourself two questions:

- **How long do I have to save?** Take your current age and subtract it from the age at which you hope to retire. That's the number of years you have left to save.
- **How long will I be in retirement?** Take the age at which you plan to retire and subtract it from the current life expectancy for someone of your age and gender. That's the number of years you have to save for. No need to pull out your calculator—Quicken will do the math for you as you enter your information in the Lifetime Planner.

Develop an Action Plan and Stay with It

Once you know how much you need, it's time to think seriously about how you can save it. This requires putting money away in one or more savings or investment accounts. Use the Lifetime Planner in Quicken to get you started. See "Getting Started with the Quicken Lifetime Planner" next in this chapter. After you have created the plan, stick to the plan!

The most important part of any long-term plan is consistency. For example, if you plan to save $5,000 a year, don't think you can just save $2,000 this year and make up the $3,000 next year. There are two reasons: first, you can't "make up" the interest lost on the $3,000 you didn't save this year, and second, you're kidding yourself if you think you'll manage to put away $8,000 next year. If you consider deviating from your plan, just think about the alternative: making ends meet with a job bagging groceries or waiting tables when you're 73 years old.

Getting Started with the Quicken Lifetime Planner

To help you prepare for many of life's financial goals, Quicken 2017 includes several comprehensive planning tools. From the Planning tab, you have access to all of Quicken's built-in planning features, including the Quicken Lifetime Planner's main plan assumptions and the various plan assumption dialogs (refer to Figure 12-1). Once you have set up your plan, simply view the Lifetime Planner to see an up-to-date view of how well your plan is working.

Here's how it works. You start by entering plan assumptions, which include information about you, your current finances, and your tax rate. Quicken makes

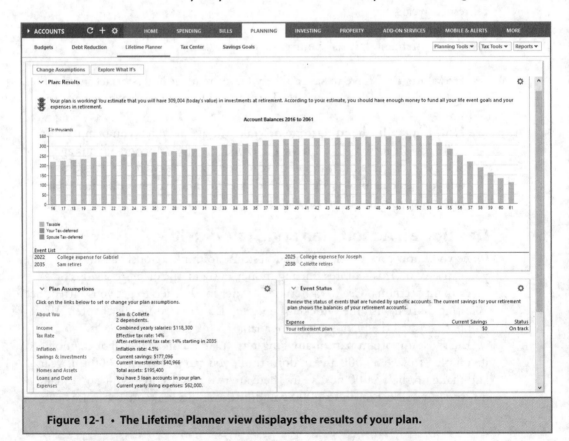

Figure 12-1 · The Lifetime Planner view displays the results of your plan.

calculations based on what you entered to display plan results. As you continue working with Quicken, entering transactions that affect your finances, Quicken updates the result of the plan.

Setting up Quicken Lifetime Planner assumptions does take a bit of time. However, the benefits of using this feature far outweigh the time it takes to enter the information. If you don't have the time to set up the Quicken Lifetime Planner today, schedule time in the near future. This can even be a family project on a rainy Saturday afternoon. If you are raising a family, helping them see how to plan and save can be a very valuable lesson.

NOTE You can enter information into the Lifetime Planner all at once or over time. Once you have entered information into the planner, Quicken retains the information for you and you can continue where you last were working.

This section explains how to set assumptions for the various topics within the Quicken Lifetime Planner and how to view the results of your plan in the Planning tab.

Setting Plan Assumptions

The easiest way to see what plan assumptions you will need to make is to view the Plan Assumptions area of the Lifetime Planner. Click Planning | Lifetime Planner. When you first see the planner, the Plan: Results area is blank, waiting for your input, as seen here. Select About You to begin your plan.

To begin, start by entering information in the Plan Assumptions. To set details for an assumption category, click its link. Each link opens a dialog you can use to enter information. Here's a look at each category.

About You

Clicking the About You link displays the About You dialog, shown next. Its fields are pretty self-explanatory: your name and date of birth. When you're finished entering information in the dialog, click Done to save it.

Here are some other items to consider when entering data into the About You dialog.

Include Spouse (or Partner)   If you select the Include Spouse check box, you can enter information about your spouse or partner into the Spouse column of the dialog. If you don't wish to include anyone else in your plan, leave those boxes blank.

If you choose not to include your spouse, all the other plan assumption dialogs will show the spouse options grayed out and inactive. If, in working through the other plan assumption dialogs, you change your mind and want to include your spouse, you will need to return to the About You assumption dialog and enter the information about your spouse.

Life Expectancy   You can either enter what you think might be your life expectancy or enter your birthdate and click the Calculate button to display the Calculate Life Expectancy dialog. Set options in the dialog, and Quicken tells you how long you may live. Of course, this is an estimate based on current research into life expectancy; you may or may not live to reach the age Quicken suggests, or you may live even longer. Click OK to dismiss the Calculate Life Expectancy dialog.

Many Quicken users set a life expectancy as 95 or longer to ensure their savings will last throughout their lives.

Children and Dependents   To enter information about children or other dependents, click the New button at the bottom of the dialog. This displays the Add Child/Dependent dialog, in which you can enter the name and date of birth for a dependent. Once you click OK, the person's name and age are added to the list. Repeat this process for each child or dependent you need to add. Once a child or dependent has been added, you can select his or her name and click the Edit button to change information about him or her, or click the Delete button to remove him or her permanently from the plan, or turn on the Exclude From Plan check box so Quicken doesn't use him or her in its calculations. When you have finished making entries, you will see a window as shown. Click Done to close the About You dialog.

Q Quicken Planner: About You   ✕

Quicken Planner: About You

Choose whether you want to include your spouse or partner in the plan. If you and your partner are not legally married, click the Help icon for more information.

☑ Include spouse   Yourself   Spouse

First name | Sam | Collette
Date of birth | 12/11/1968 📅 | 11/23/1971 📅
Retirement age| 67 | 67
Life expectancy| 85   Calculate...| 90   Calculate...
Current age: | 47 | 45
Years until retirement: | 19 | 22

Children and dependents
───

Enter any children
or dependents that | Gabriel   12 years old
you currently | Joseph   9 years old
support as well as
any you plan to
add in the future.

☐ Exclude from plan   New...   Edit...   Delete

❓   Done

The focus, or location, of your cursor may not automatically go to the first name field, so you may have to click in the field to begin entering information.

Income

Clicking the Income link displays the Income dialog. This section has three separate tabs of information. Select the appropriate tab to enter salary, retirement benefits, and other income information for you (and your spouse or partner, if you choose).

Salary The Salary tab enables you to record information about current and future salary and self-employment income.

To add an income item into your Plan Assumptions section, click Income to open the Quicken Planner: Income dialog. In the Salary tab, click the New button to display the Add Salary dialog. Then set options to enter information about the income item. The Add Salary dialog is extremely flexible, enabling you to enter start and end dates for a salary—which is useful for income from seasonal employment, as seen next. If you don't need to enter specific dates, choose Already Started from the When Does This Salary Start? drop-down list and one of the retirement options from the When Does This Salary End? drop-down list. When you click OK, the salary item is added to your income.

For each item you add, Quicken automatically includes adjustments that specify when the item begins and ends. You can add other adjustments if you know about changes that will occur in the future. Select the item in the top half of the dialog, and then click the New button in the Adjustments to [*item name*] in the bottom half of the dialog. Enter information in the Add Salary Adjustment dialog. Click OK to close the dialog. The information is added to the bottom half of the Salary tab of the Income dialog.

After you have completed the entries in the Salary tab, you can select any of the salary or adjustment items and click the Edit or Delete button to change or remove them, respectively. You can also select an item and select the Exclude From Plan check box to exclude its information from the Quicken Planner.

Retirement Benefits   The Retirement Benefits tab enables you to enter information about Social Security or pension benefits you are currently receiving or to estimate future benefits.

To estimate future Social Security benefits, enter the age at which you expect to begin collecting benefits and click the Estimate button. The Estimate Social Security Benefits dialog appears, as seen next. You have two options:

- **Use Rough Estimate** enables you to select a salary range option to estimate benefits.
- **Use Mail-In Estimate From SS Administration** enables you to enter the amount provided by the Social Security Administration on your annual Social Security statement.

When you click OK, the amount appears in the Retirement Benefits tab.

Currently, the Social Security retirement age for those born between 1943 and 1959 is 66, while those born in 1960 or later may receive full Social Security benefits at age 67. There has been some talk about raising the retirement age for those born after 1978 to 70, although as of the date of this manuscript, that has not been enacted.

To add a pension, click the New button at the bottom of the Retirement Benefits tab of the Income dialog. This displays the Add Pension dialog. Enter information about the pension, and click OK to add it to the Retirement Benefits tab. In that tab, you can select the pension and click Edit or Delete to change or remove it, or select the Exclude From Plan check box to exclude it from the Quicken Planner's calculations.

Other Income   The Other Income tab of the Quicken Planner: Income dialog enables you to enter income from other sources, such as gifts, child support, and inheritances. Don't use this tab to enter income from investments or rental properties; the Quicken Lifetime Planner provides specific locations for that data.

Click the New button in the Other Income tab to enter an income item. An interesting option in this dialog is the ability to specify how you plan to use the funds: either for savings and investing or to pay expenses. The option you select determines how this income is used in the plan. If you're not sure what to select, leave it set to the default Use It To Pay Expenses option. When you click OK, the

---

EXPERIENCED USERS RECOMMEND

If you have misplaced or don't want to wait for the Social Security Administration's annual mailing, you can create a personal account at the Social Security Administration's website and view your benefit estimates at any time. Go online to www.ssa.gov. From there, select Online Services and choose the Get Your Social Security Statement link. Once you sign up on the website, you get an annual reminder e-mail rather than an annual postal mailing.

item is added to the Other Income tab's list. You can edit, delete, or exclude the item from the plan as desired.

When you have entered all the income items, click Done to close the Quicken Planner: Income dialog.

Tax Rate

Clicking the Tax Rate link in the Plan Assumptions snapshot displays the Average Tax Rate dialog, as seen here. You have two options:

- **Demographic Average** enables you to estimate your tax rate based on where you live and what your income is.
- **Tax Returns** enables you to estimate your tax rate based on the total income, total federal taxes, and total state taxes from your most recent tax returns.

You can also enter an estimate of your post-retirement tax rate, which may be lower. Click Done to close the Quicken Planner: Average Tax Rate dialog.

Inflation

Clicking the Inflation link displays the Estimated Inflation dialog, which includes a field you can use to enter the inflation rate you want to use for your plan. Quicken suggests an inflation rate of 3 percent, which is the average inflation rate since 1927, but you can enter any rate you think is correct in the text box. Click OK to save your estimate.

Quicken users who want to plan more conservatively may want to enter a higher inflation rate.

Savings & Investments

Clicking the Savings & Investments link in the Plan Assumptions snapshot displays the Savings And Investments dialog, which is organized into three tabs, as seen next. Use these dialogs to enter information about current bank and investment accounts, as well as contributions you make to bank or investment accounts. To enter a contribution that you or your spouse make to a bank account, select an account from the list above and click New below to add a contribution. Use the Return tab to enter the return you expect to earn on your investments.

Quicken Planner: Savings and Investments

| Savings | Investments | Return |

1. Select the bank accounts that you want to be part of your plan.
   To indicate how the account will be used in the plan (to pay for college, for example), click "Details".

Account Name	Intended Use	Balance
House Checking	General expenses	$759
Main Checking	General expenses	$10,339
Main Savings	General expenses	$118,105
Savings	General expenses	$3,005

New... □ Exclude from plan   Details...
    ☑ Show excluded account

Contributions to House Checking

2. To enter the contributions that you or your spouse make to a bank account, select an account from the list above and click "New" below to add a

Start	End	Yearly Amount
Already started	12/2035 (Sam retires)	12.0% of salary
Already started	11/2038 (Collette retires)	3.5% of salary

New...   Edit...   Delete   □ Exclude from plan

Done

Savings

Click the Savings tab to list all of the bank accounts you have set up in Quicken, along with their ending balances.

If you have omitted any accounts from Quicken, now is a good time to add them if you want them to be part of your plan. Click the New button at the upper half of the dialog to display the Add Account dialog, as you learned in earlier chapters.

Quicken automatically assumes that each bank account will be used for general expenses. You can change this assumption by selecting an account and clicking the Details button. Choose a new purpose from the drop-down list in the Account Details dialog that appears and click OK. Until you use Quicken's calculators and planners, general expenses is the only offered option. However, if you have entered information into one of the Quicken plan assumption topics, such as college expenses in the Expenses topic, an option for that expense appears in the drop-down list.

If you or your partner makes regular contributions to one of your bank accounts, you can enter information about that contribution in the Savings dialog. In the top half of the dialog, select the account that receives the contribution. Then click the New button at the bottom of the dialog. Use the Add Contribution dialog that appears to indicate how much you contribute. The dialog walks you through the process of entering information based on whether the contribution is a percentage of a salary or a base amount that increases each year. Click Done to close the Add Contribution dialog.

Investments

The Investments tab lists all of the investment accounts you have set up in Quicken, along with their current market values. Remember, since market value is determined by security prices, the market value is only as up to date as the security price information in Quicken that you have most recently entered or downloaded.

This tab works just like the Savings tab. You can click the New button in the top half of the dialog to open the Add Account dialog to enter a new investment account. Choose an existing account, and click the New button in the bottom half of the dialog to enter regular contribution information for any selected investment account. You can also specify the intended use for any account by selecting the account name and clicking the Details button.

As of the date of this writing, there is a bug with the contribution limits in the Lifetime Planner. The limit is much lower than it should be. To get the actual maximum contribution allowable for 2017, you need to use multiple contributions when using A Percentage Of Your Salary option, or use the An Amount That Increases Each Year By option to specify the dollar amount.

Return

The Return tab enables you to specify your expected rates of return for pre-retirement and post-retirement investments. If you select the separate rate of return check box near the top of the dialog, additional text boxes appear, enabling you to enter different rates of return for taxable and tax-deferred investments. At the bottom of the dialog, you can enter the percentage of the taxable return that is subject to taxes. This is normally 100 percent, but for your situation, the percentage may be different. Click Done to close the Quicken Planner: Savings And Investments dialog.

Homes And Assets

Clicking the Homes And Assets link displays the Homes And Assets dialog, which is organized into two tabs. This is where you can enter information about currently owned assets and assets you plan to purchase in the future.

EXPERIENCED USERS RECOMMEND
Check with your tax professional for the current limits of contributions to any retirement plan such as a 401(k) or an IRA, whether traditional or Roth. Current limits for the calendar year 2017 are • 401(k) = $18,000 • 401(k) Catch-up for those 50 and older = $6,000 • IRA = $5,500 • IRA = Catch-up for those 50 and older = Add $1,000 for a total of $6,500

Homes and Asset Accounts   The Asset Accounts tab, seen next, lists all of the asset accounts you have created in Quicken, including accounts for your home, vehicle, and other assets. If you have additional assets that have not yet been entered in Quicken and you want to include them in your plan, click the New button and use the Add Account dialog that appears to create the new account. Review how to add a new asset account in Chapter 10.

Notice that the value on the two cars in the illustration shows a current value of zero. There is a reported bug in Quicken 2017 that the estimated value field is missing from the Add Vehicle dialog, so new vehicle accounts may show the current value to be zero.

If you plan to sell an asset, you can enter information for that sale. Select the asset in the top half of the dialog, and then click the Sale Info button. A series of dialogs prompts you for information about the asset's purchase and sale date and price, as well as other information that affects how much money you can expect to receive and pay taxes on. Quicken adds this information to your plan. Click Done to close the Sale Information dialog. If you change your mind about selling the asset, click Sale Info again and select I Do Not Plan To Sell This Asset in the second screen of the dialog.

Three buttons at the bottom of the Homes And Assets dialog enable you to associate loans, expenses, and income with a selected asset. This is especially important when working with assets you plan to sell, since the sale of the asset should also end associated debt, expenses, and income.

- **Loans** enables you to link existing loans to the asset or add new loans, including home equity loans. It also enables you to enter information about planned loans—for example, if you plan to use a home equity loan to build an addition on your house sometime next year. You can also enter information about planned payoffs—perhaps you're settling an estate and will be getting an inheritance and plan to use it to pay down your house mortgage. Review entering loan information in Chapter 10.

When you click New to add a loan, the dialog is titled Add Loan Account instead of just Add Account.

- **Expenses** enables you to enter property tax information as well as other expenses related to the asset. For a home, this might include association fees, homeowner's insurance, and estimated maintenance and utility costs. For a car, this might include registration, fuel, service, and insurance. For each expense you add, Quicken prompts you for information about the expense, including how you expect to pay for it—with money in a specific bank account or with a loan. It even enables you to set up a monthly savings target to pay for the item. Remember not to enter these same expenses in the Expenses dialog.
- **Income** enables you to enter information about income you expect to earn from the asset. This is especially useful if you own rental property. The dialog that appears when you add an income item is almost the same as the Add Other Income dialog. It even allows you to specify how you plan to use the income: for investment or to pay expenses. Click Done to close the Loans, Asset Expenses, or Other Income dialogs.

Planned Assets   The Planned Assets tab lets you enter information about any assets you plan to purchase in the future. For example, suppose you indicated in the Asset Accounts tab that you plan to sell your home or car on a specific date. If you plan to replace it with another home or car, this is where you will enter information about the replacement. Quicken uses dialogs that walk you through the process of entering details about the future purchase. Once you've entered planned asset information, you can select the asset in the list and add loans, expenses, and income for it, as well as choose the accounts you plan to use to pay for it. Click Done to close the Quicken Planner: Homes And Assets dialog.

Loans And Debt

Clicking the Loans And Debt link in the Plan Assumptions snapshot displays the Loans And Debt dialog, which is organized into three tabs: Loan Accounts, Planned Loans, and after you have set up your debt reduction plan, Existing Debt Plan. Use these dialogs to enter information about current and planned loans, as well as information from your debt reduction plan.

The Existing Debt Plan tab does not appear until you have set up a debt reduction plan.

Loan Accounts   The Loan Accounts tab, shown next, displays information about current loans. This information comes from loans you have set up within Quicken. To add another loan that isn't already recorded in Quicken, click the New button to display the Add Loan Account dialog, which is covered in Chapter 10. If you plan to pay off a loan before its last payment date, you can click the Payoff button to enter future payoff information. And our example is another good reason to use Quicken: seven years to pay off a car loan at 4.7 percent! By using Quicken you can improve your credit rating so you can get a better rate or help reduce your spending so you can save more to have cash available for large purchases like a new vehicle.

Q Quicken Planner: Loans and Debt		✕

Quicken Planner: Loans and Debt

Loan Accounts	Planned Loans

Enter any loans you currently have. For more information on tracking loans in Quicken, click "Help".

If you want to enter a loan associated with an asset, such as a home loan, go to the Homes and Assets section. If you plan to pay off a loan early, click "Payoff".

Description	Start Date	Length	Current Balance
2012 Toyota Camry ...	9/2012	7 Years	$8,563
2014 Subaru Loan	4/2014	7 Years	$17,879
House Loan	11/2001	30 Years	$91,789

New...   ☐ Exclude from plan   Payoff...

2012 Toyota Camry Loan

Original Loan Amount:	$19,250
Payment:	$270
Interest Rate:	4.7%
Remaining Payments:	34
Date of Last Payment:	9/2019

❓   Done

Planned Loans   The Planned Loans tab enables you to enter information about loans you plan to make in the future. This does not include any loans you may have already entered in the Homes And Assets dialog discussed earlier in this chapter. Instead, this is for loans that are not associated with any particular asset, such as a personal loan you plan to use for a 30th anniversary cruise.

Existing Debt Plan   The Existing Debt Plan tab includes information from the Debt Reduction Planner, which is covered in Chapter 13. If you have credit card and other debt, it's a good idea to create a debt reduction plan as part of your overall planning strategy. Click Done to close the Quicken Planner: Loans And Debt dialog.

> **NOTE**   If you include your debt reduction plan here, you should exclude the included loan and credit accounts/expenses in the Loan Accounts tab/Expenses tab, as applicable, so as to not double-count the expenses.

Expenses

Open the Expenses dialog, shown here, by clicking the Expenses link. This section is organized into four tabs. Use these tabs to enter information about your living expenses, as well as any adjustments to expenses and the expenses for college or other special events.

Living Expenses   The Living Expenses tab uses two techniques to help you enter your estimated living expenses:

- **Rough Estimate** enables you to enter an estimate of your annual living expenses. Using this technique is quicker, but it may not be as accurate as using the Category Detail option.
- **Category Detail** enables you to have Quicken calculate an estimate of your annual living expenses based on transactions already entered in your Quicken data file. This technique is more accurate than Rough Estimate, especially if you have been using Quicken for some time and have a good history of transactions. If you select this method, you can click the Details button that appears in the middle of the dialog to display the Living Expenses Category Detail dialog. Toggle check marks in the list of categories to include or exclude specific categories and enter monthly amounts as desired. When you click OK, Quicken annualizes the amounts and enters them in the Living Expenses tab. A trick to be able to keep seeing the estimated amount for the category but not have it counted against the plan's expenses is to set the Monthly Amount to $0 and leave the category checked.

One thing to keep in mind here: don't include expenses that you may have already included for an asset. For example, if you included car insurance expenses in the Homes And Assets dialog as an expense associated with an automobile, don't include them again here. Doing so would duplicate the expense and overstate your annual expenses. In addition, don't include expenses that are otherwise accounted for in other topics of the Lifetime Planner, such as taxes or retirement contributions.

At the bottom of the dialog, you can enter a percentage of surplus cash—any cash left over after paying living expenses—that you want to put into savings. Don't skip this last box—it can make a big difference on your plan outcome. If you don't elect to sweep some percentage of your surplus cash to savings, it's assumed the surplus is spent, which can reduce your plan balances drastically.

Adjustments   The Adjustments tab enables you to enter any adjustments to your expenses that are related to intended changes in your life. For example, perhaps you plan to hire a nanny to take care of your child while you go back to work. You can add this planned expense as an adjustment for a predefined period. When you click the New button in the Adjustments tab, the Add Living Expense Adjustment dialog appears. When you are done adding information, click OK to close the Add Living Expense Adjustment dialog.

College Expenses   The College Expenses tab enables you to plan for the education of your children—or yourself! Clicking the New button in this tab displays the Add College Expenses dialog, which walks you through the process of entering expected college expenses for a plan member. You'll have to do a little homework to come up with realistic estimates of college costs, including tuition, room, board, books, and supplies. Remember, if you underestimate expenses, your plan won't be accurate. The dialog also prompts you for information about expected financial aid, student loans, and student contributions to cover all sources of financing. If you have a college fund—such as an educational IRA—already set up for the college expense, you can associate it with the expense to indicate how it will be paid for. Click Next to advance through the dialogs, and click Done to close the Add College Expenses dialog. Accounts marked "Separate" will not be available for inclusion in the Lifetime Planner. So if you have set your children's 529 accounts to be "Separate," you will not be able to include them in the Lifetime Planner.

Be aware that some of the dialogs in the Add College Expenses dialog may use a very small font.

Special Expenses   The Special Expenses tab includes any expenses you may have already added in the Homes And Assets dialog and enables you to enter other one-time or annual expenses you expect to incur. Use this for items like a vacation, special anniversary, or large purchase. When you click the New button, Quicken prompts you for information about the expense, including the amount and how you expect to finance it. Click Next to advance through the Add Special Expense dialogs. Close the Add Special Expense dialog, and click Done to close the Quicken Planner: Expenses dialog.

EXPERIENCED USERS RECOMMEND

Quicken even gives you help in finding outside funding for college expenses. Once you have created a plan that includes college expenses, follow these steps for some Internet links to help you or your student find college funding.

1. From the Planning tab, click the Lifetime Planner button.
2. In the Plan: Results | Event List, choose the appropriate college event.
3. The College Event summary dialog appears for that event. Click Internet Resources in the left-hand column of the College Expense Plan that appears. With your Internet connection, open one of the resource links listed for additional discussions of funding college costs.
4. Click the X to close the plan.

Reviewing and Changing Assumptions

You can review and modify your plan assumptions at any time. Quicken offers a number of ways to do this.

The Plan Assumptions Snapshot

Once you enter assumptions into the Quicken Planners, a brief summary of your entries appears in the Plan Assumptions snapshot in the Planning tab (refer to Figure 12-1), shown next. To open this window, choose Planning | Lifetime Planner.

∨ **Plan Assumptions**	⚙

Click on the links below to set or change your plan assumptions.

About You	Sam & Collette 2 dependents.
Income	Combined yearly salaries: $185,300
Tax Rate	Effective tax rate: 14% After-retirement tax rate: 14% starting in 2035
Inflation	Inflation rate: 4.5%
Savings & Investments	Current savings: $177,096 Current investments: $40,966
Homes and Assets	Total assets: $195,400
Loans and Debt	You have 3 loan accounts in your plan.
Expenses	Current yearly living expenses: $9,913.

You can click links in the Plan Assumptions snapshot to open the same dialogs discussed earlier in this chapter. Review and change plan assumptions as desired, and click Done or OK, depending on the dialog, to save your changes.

The Planning Assumptions Window

Another way to review plan assumptions is in the Planning Assumptions window, as seen in Figure 12-2. This method shows more detail than the Plan Assumptions snapshot. To open this window, choose Planning | Lifetime Planner. (You can access the Planning Assumptions window from the gear icon in any of the four sections of the Lifetime Planner. From the menu shown when you click the gear icon, select Review Or Change Plan Assumptions.)

Use links on the left side of the Planning Assumptions window to navigate quickly from one category to another. The details appear in the main part of the window. Each assumption category offers two links:

- **How Is This Used?** explains how the information in that category of assumption is used in the plan.
- **Edit** enables you to edit the assumptions for that category, using the same dialogs discussed earlier in this chapter.

Planning Assumptions			×
			🖶 Print

Assumptions

About you
Income
  Salary
  Retirement benefits
  Other income
Taxes & Inflation
  Taxes
  Inflation
Savings & Investments
  Savings
  Investments
  Rate of Return
Homes & Assets
  Current homes & assets
  Future homes & assets
Loans & Debt
  Current loans
  Debt reduction
  Future loans
Expenses
  Living expenses
  Adjustments
  College expenses
  Special expenses

About you　　　　　　　　　　How is this used? | Edit

	Sam	Collette
Age	47 years old	45 years old
Life Expectancy	85	90
Retirement Age	67	67
Retirement Date	12/2035	11/2038
Years Until Retirement	20	22
Years In Retirement	18	23
Children and dependents		Age
Joseph		9 years old
Gabriel		12 years old

Salary　　　　　　　　　　How is this used? | Edit

Your Salary	Amount	Annual Increase	Self Emp.	Pay SS Tax
My Income (Already sta...	$67,000	Inflation	No	Yes
Annal Salary (Already st...	$67,500	Inflation	No	Yes
Your spouse's Salary	Amount	Annual Increase	Self Emp.	Pay SS Tax
Annual Salary (Already ...	$50,800	Inflation	No	Yes

Retirement benefits　　　　　　　How is this used? | Edit

Your Social Security Benefits	
Age you elected to start collecting	67
Date you elected to start collecting	12/2035
Worker Benefits	$30,000 *

Figure 12-2 • Use the Planning Assumptions dialog to change information in your Lifetime Planner.

Viewing Plan Results

When you have entered all of your information, the results of your saved plan, the plan assumptions, the status of any planned events, and your monthly savings targets can be viewed as shown in Figure 12-1, earlier in this chapter. You can use this screen to review your savings plans and change them if you need or want to. Click a link to open the associated planner and change data as desired.

As with the information displayed in the other Quicken tabs, you can print the Plan Results, Assumptions, Event Status, and Monthly Savings Targets by clicking File | Print Lifetime Planner. Sadly, the Plan Results graph may not print.

If you see a message that there is not enough space to draw the graphics in the Lifetime Planner, it is not a problem with your computer; it is a bug within Quicken. Also, you are not able to adjust the size of the Planning Assumptions snapshot as the size is determined automatically by the program.

The top of the Plan: Results area tells you whether your plan is working and how much you should have in investments at retirement. Amounts are in today's dollar values; to view them in future dollar values, choose Show Amounts In Future Value from the gear icon pop-up menu at the top-right corner of the Plan: Results snapshot. You can toggle the graph back to today's dollar values by selecting the gear icon and selecting Show Amounts In Today's Values.

The graph beneath this summary shows your taxable and any tax-deferred savings. The shape of this graph often shows a steady increase until the year you retire and then a gradual decrease. Many of us would prefer to see a continuing increase or, at least, no change after retirement. Clicking any column opens a Plan Summary dialog for that year showing income and expenses, as shown next. You can use the <<Prev Year>> and <<Next Year>> buttons in the dialog to scroll through the years in the graph. This enables you to see the detailed numbers that make up the graph columns—very helpful! Plan results change automatically based on a variety of changes within your Quicken data file:

- When the account balances referred to in the plan change, the plan changes accordingly.
- When you change plan assumptions, the plan changes accordingly.
- When you use Quicken's planners to plan for major purchases, college, retirement, and other events that affect your finances, the plan changes to include these events.
- When you play "what if" with assumptions and save the changes as your plan, the plan changes accordingly. You'll see how to enter "what ifs" a little later in this chapter, in the section "The 'What If' Alternatives."

Viewing Event Status Items

Quicken also keeps track of your progress toward certain events and savings targets. It displays this information in the Planning tab of the Lifetime Planner. (Refer to Figure 12-1.)

Income and Expenses Summary (2025)   ✕

<< P_rev Year   Next Year >>   Print...   C_lose

Plan Summary (2025)
(All amounts are reported in today's value.)

Income Summary

Income	
Salaries	
My Income	$67,000
Annal Salary	$67,500
Annual Salary	$50,800
Total Salaries	$185,300
Pension Benefits	
My pension	$0
My pension: Survivor's Benefit	$0
Total Pension Benefits	$0
Social Security Benefits	
Self	$0
Spouse	$0
Total Social Security Benefits	$0
College Incomes	
Financial Aid for Gabriel	$19,000
Student Contribution for Gabriel	$20,000
Gifts Contribution for Gabriel	$2,000
Financial Aid for Joseph	$17,000
Student Contribution for Joseph	$19,000
Gifts Contribution for Joseph	$1,000
Total College Incomes	$78,000
Total Income	$263,300

The Event Status snapshot displays information about events in your plan that are funded with specific accounts. From this section, click Your Retirement Plan to open the My Retirement Plan window, shown next, which looks a lot like the Plan Assumptions window. Click the X in the upper-right corner to close and return to the Lifetime Planner.

Viewing Monthly Savings Targets

The Monthly Savings Targets snapshot of your Lifetime Planner displays information about your savings toward events in your plan.

Clicking any link for an expense displays the summary area for that expense in the Plan Assumptions window. You can review and modify event information in that window. When you are done reviewing the event, click Done or OK to return to the Lifetime Planner.

The "What If" Alternatives

Once you've entered assumptions, created plans for specific events, and viewed your plan results, you might wonder how a change in one or more assumptions would affect the plan. You can use the "What If" Event Scenarios feature to see how the changes would affect the plan without changing the plan itself.

EXPERIENCED USERS RECOMMEND

When working with the Plan Comparison chart you may notice a slow response when applying the What If changes. Also, if you make a change that is too subtle, it may be hard to distinguish the lines.

As an example: You've been offered a job in another state. The job pays about the same salary that you make now, but you can move to a town where your living expenses would be greatly reduced. You can see how the job change would affect your financial plans for the future by playing "what if" to modify existing assumptions, and then see the old and new plan results side by side.

Setting "What If" Options

Each of the snapshots of the Lifetime Planner in the Planning tab has a gear icon from which you can play What If. From the gear icon menu, select What If I Did Something Different? to open the What If window. The first time you use it, the window displays the account balances shown in your plan results.

Choose a goal option from the drop-down list at the top-left corner of the window. Then click appropriate links on the left side of the window to open dialogs to change assumptions.

Each time you make a change, the Plan Comparison chart changes. The original plan shows as a turquoise line and the change as a lavender line. (Depending on your monitor's settings, the colors may look slightly different.)

Using "What If" Results

When you've finished changing assumptions and viewing results, you can click one of the three buttons at the top of the What If window as seen earlier:

- **Reset What If** clears all of the assumptions you changed while playing "what if." This enables you to start over.
- **Save What If As Plan** saves the assumptions you changed while playing "what if" as your actual financial plan. When the window closes, you'll see the results in the Planning tab change accordingly.
- **Close Without Saving** simply closes the window so you can continue working with Quicken. Your settings are not saved.

Finding More Planning Tools

Quicken offers additional tools found in the Planning tab: Budgets, which are covered extensively in Chapter 13, and financial calculation tools, which are found in the Planning Tools drop-down list. These tools are discussed at length next in this chapter.

A Look at Quicken's Financial Calculators

Quicken includes five financial calculators you can use to make quick financial calculations: the Retirement Calculator, the College Calculator, the Refinance Calculator, the Savings Calculator, and the Loan Calculator. These calculators make complex calculations simple. Each calculator can help you enter more complete information into the Lifetime Planner and greatly assist you when looking at your financial options.

Learning About Financial Calculators

All five of the financial calculators share the same basic interface. Although they are similar in appearance, each has a specific purpose. It's important that you use the correct calculator to get the job done.

In most instances, you begin by telling the calculator what part of the formula you want to calculate. For example, when calculating a loan, you can calculate the loan amount or the periodic payment. Then you enter values and set other options in the calculator's dialog to give Quicken the information it needs to make its calculations. Clicking a Calculate button completes the process. Quicken is fast; the results appear as soon as you click Calculate—if not sooner.

Accessing the Financial Calculators

To view the financial calculators, click the Planning tab and choose the Planning Tools button. The five calculators appear at the bottom of the menu, as shown here. If you don't see the Planning tab, click View | Tabs To Show | Planning to display it.

Projected Balances, the first item on the Planning Tools menu, is covered in Chapter 7.

Using the Financial Calculators

When you are ready to try Quicken's financial calculators, the rest of this chapter provides some detailed instructions for using each of them. All of the calculators open with one or more fields showing the text "CALCULATED" or "calculated." (Some financial calculators use uppercase and others lowercase.) Click the Calculate button to change that text to the calculated number.

Working with the Retirement Calculator

The Retirement Calculator can help you calculate some of the numbers you need to plan for your retirement. To open it, choose Planning | Planning Tools | Retirement Calculator. The Retirement Calculator appears as seen in Figure 12-3.

As you will note at the top of the calculator, you may calculate for three different values:

- **Annual Retirement Income** calculates the annual amount of retirement income you'll have based on the values you enter.
- **Annual Contribution** calculates the minimum amount you should contribute to a retirement account to achieve the values you enter.
- **Current Savings** calculates the amount of money you should currently have saved to achieve the values you want when you retire.

Select an option, and then enter or select values and options throughout the dialog. Most options are pretty straightforward and easy to understand. When you're finished, click the Calculate button to see the results. Click Done when you're finished.

Figure 12-3 • Use the Retirement Calculator to estimate your retirement income.

Here's a closer look at the options in the Retirement Calculator.

Retirement Information

Retirement Information options enable you to enter the values Quicken should use in its calculations. The values you must enter vary depending on the Calculate option you select. For example, if you are 47 years old, plan on retiring at age 67, and want to know how much to save each year to achieve an annual income at retirement of about $26,000 in today's dollars, calculate for the annual retirement income, as seen in Figure 12-3.

Current, Retirement, and Withdrawal Until Age   Use these fields to enter your age today, the age at which you plan to retire, and your estimation of how long you will need to withdraw from this retirement fund.

Current Savings and Annual Yield   These fields are used to calculate how much you should have saved to meet the goals you set up. Enter the interest rate you are receiving to calculate the annual yield from those savings.

Inflation Rate   Inflation options make complex calculations to account for the effect of inflation on your savings dollars. Use this field to enter your best guess as to the future inflation rate, or use Quicken's default of 4 percent.

What you put in this field influences two other options in the Retirement Calculator:

- **Increase Based On Inflation Rate** makes calculations assuming that the annual contributions will rise with the inflation rate.
- **Show In Today's $** makes calculations assuming that the Annual Retirement Income After Taxes entry is in today's dollars and not inflated.

Tax Assumptions   Tax Assumptions options enable you to indicate whether your retirement savings are in a tax-sheltered investment or a non-sheltered investment. If you select the Non-Sheltered Investment option, you can enter your current tax rate, and Quicken will automatically calculate the effect of taxes on your retirement income. By experimenting with this feature, you will see why it's a good idea to use tax-sheltered or tax-deferred investments whenever possible.

Calculate

Depending on the option you choose at the top of the Retirement Calculator, clicking the Calculate button does the computation for you. If you change any amounts, click Calculate a second time to see the results of your change.

View Schedule

Clicking the View Schedule button displays a printable list of deposits made and income withdrawn, with a running balance total. Use the vertical scroll bar to view the theoretical balance in the retirement account as our subject reaches each age.

- Use the question mark to open Quicken's Help screen to answer questions about financial calculators.
- Select the printer icon to print a complete schedule by year.
- Click Done to close the Deposit Schedule window.
- Click Done to close the Retirement Calculator.

Running the College Calculator

The College Calculator enables you to calculate savings for the cost of a college education. Choose Planning | Planning Tools | College Calculator. The assumption in this calculator is that you will continue to save the entire time the student is in school.

Select a Calculate option from these choices at the top of the Calculator:

- **Annual College Costs** calculates the annual tuition you'll be able to afford based on the values you enter.
- **Current College Savings** calculates the amount of money you should currently have saved based on the values you enter.
- **Annual Contribution** calculates the minimum amount you should contribute to college savings based on the values you enter.

Then enter values and options throughout the dialog. As with the other calculators, the available options are straightforward. When you click Calculate, Quicken calculates the results. When you are finished, click Done.

Annual College Costs   Use this field to enter your best guess at the cost of college per year when the person for whom you are saving enrolls in school.

Years   Both the Years Until Enrollment and Number Of Years Enrolled fields will influence the outcome of the calculations. If you have a 12-year-old who, you assume, will be attending college in six years and plans on attending for only four years, enter that information.

Current College Savings   This field shows either what you have already saved for this person's education or, when used as the calculate field, what you should have saved to date to meet the other college goal requirements. Entering the yield you currently receive and your best guess at the inflation rate helps Quicken show you more realistic numbers.

Although the calculator is named the "College Calculator," many Quicken users find that their students want to attend vocational training rather than a four-year school. Consider the current costs for specialized technical training, and use the College Calculator to determine how much you will need to save for that specialized training.

Calculate

The Calculate button computes the requested value.

Schedule

Clicking the Schedule button displays the College Savings Plan, a printable list of deposits made and money withdrawn for tuition, with a running balance total. The schedule will show the withdrawals for the period you defined in number of years enrolled, which may or may not be four years. The last X years of the schedule will show the withdrawals, where X is the number of years enrolled. Click Done to close the College Savings Plan dialog, and click Done once again to close the Calculator.

Evaluating the Refinance Calculator

With housing values increasing, many of us think about refinancing our home. Quicken 2017 provides a handy tool to help determine whether refinancing will really save money and, if so, how much. Choose Planning | Planning Tools | Refinance Calculator. The Refinance Calculator appears, as shown next.

Enter values for your current mortgage and proposed mortgage in the various fields to calculate your monthly savings with the new mortgage. When you are finished, click Done.

Existing Mortgage

Existing Mortgage options enable you to enter your current total monthly mortgage payment and the amount of that payment that is applied to property taxes and other escrow items. Quicken automatically calculates the amount of principal and interest for each payment. If you already know the principal and interest amount, you can enter that in the Monthly Payment box and leave the Impound/Escrow Amount box empty. The result is the same.

Proposed Mortgage

Proposed Mortgage options enable you to enter information about the mortgage that you are considering to replace your current mortgage. The Principal Amount may be the balance on your current mortgage, but it could be more or less, depending on whether you want to refinance for more or less money. (Refinancing often offers a good opportunity to exchange equity for cash or to use cash to build equity.)

If you would have to pay closing costs or points to complete the refinancing, enter them in the appropriate fields. This will help Quicken compute a more accurate break-even point.

Break Even Analysis   Break Even Analysis options are optional. If you enter the closing costs and points for the proposed mortgage, Quicken will automatically calculate how long it will take to cover those costs based on your monthly savings. If there are no savings, the calculations show as a negative number. Click Done to close the Calculator.

Planning with the Savings Calculator

The Savings Calculator lets you calculate savings annuities, that is, periodic payments to a savings account or an investment. Choose Planning | Planning Tools | Savings Calculator to open the Savings Calculator.

As with the other calculators, this calculator offers three options:

- **Ending Savings Balance** calculates the total amount saved at the end of the savings period based on the values you enter.
- **Regular Contribution** calculates the minimum amount you should regularly contribute to savings based on the values you enter.

- **Starting Savings Balance** calculates the amount of money you should currently have saved based on the values you enter.

Save For

The Save For drop-down box offers several options in which to enter values for Quicken to use in its calculations. Enter what you have today, the interest rate you are receiving, and the period of time you want to save. The drop-down list offers four options from which Quicken will calculate:

- Years
- Quarters
- Months
- Weeks

Inflation

Inflation options make complex calculations to account for the effect of inflation on your savings dollars. Enter your best estimate at the future inflation rate. Quicken will use this entry to determine the result of the option you chose at the top of the Savings Calculator screen.

When you have entered all of the information, click Calculate to show the outcome. As with other calculators, use the View Schedule button to see the result of the calculations.

Like the Retirement Calculator Schedule, this schedule can be printed. To print this schedule, click the printer icon at the lower-left corner of the schedule.

After you have completed your calculations, click Done to close the Deposit Schedule dialog, and click Done again to close the Savings Calculator.

Using the Loan Calculator

Perhaps the most used calculator is the Quicken Loan Calculator. With this tool you can quickly calculate the principal or periodic payment for a loan. Choose Planning | Planning Tools | Loan Calculator to open the Loan Calculator.

This handy tool will calculate the total loan amount if you enter the payments, interest, and other requested information. Its most common use is to calculate the total payment per period—usually a monthly payment, as shown next.

Select one of the options, enter information in the remainder of the dialog, and click Calculate. Getting the answer is a lot quicker and easier with Quicken's Loan Calculator than using one of those loan books or creating formulas in an Excel spreadsheet to do the job. When you're finished, click Done.

You may calculate for two different options:

- **Loan Amount** calculates the amount of the total loan, given the interest rate, number of years, how many payments per year, and the interest rate on the loan.
- **Payment Per Period** calculates how much your payment would be each month (or other period) to pay off the loan amount you enter, given the interest rate, number of years you would have to pay back the loan, and how many times a year you would make payments.

Loan Information

Loan Information options enable you to enter values for Quicken to use in its calculations. The information you must enter varies depending on the Calculate option you select.

Annual Interest Rate   Enter the interest rate for this loan in the Annual Interest Rate field.

Number Of Years, Periods Per Year, and Compounding Period   This tells Quicken how many years the loan is for and the number of times per year you will be paying on this loan. While 12 payments per year is the norm, you may choose any number. The number you choose influences the calculator's computations, so choose wisely.

EXPERIENCED USERS RECOMMEND

If you have young people in your life, use the calculators as a teaching tool. Perhaps your teen wants to buy a car. He (or she) has saved nearly $5,000 from yard work and other neighborhood jobs. Grandpa and Grandma have an older, well-maintained car worth about $7,800 and are willing to sell it and finance the balance for your teen. However, the teen must pay interest. Show him or her the cost per month for just the balance on the car, which does not include insurance, gas, oil, or other maintenance. This might convince him (or her) to find a regular yard maintenance job or jobs in the neighborhood.

Although the default entry in the Compounding Period is Monthly, most financial institutions compound daily and enter the total to your account at the end of each month.

View Schedule

Clicking the View Schedule button displays a printable amortization table that lists the payment number, the amount of the principal and interest paid at each payment, and the ending balance for the loan. Click the Print button at the top of the schedule to open the Print dialog and choose a printer. Click Print from the Print dialog to create your paper copy. Click Close to close the dialog.

Calculate

The Calculate button at the bottom of the calculator performs the calculation based on your choices and the information you have entered.

Saving Money by Reducing Debt

Chapter 13

In This Chapter:

- *Taking control*

- *Using the Debt Reduction Planner*

- *Understanding Quicken's automatic budget*

- *Working with your automatic budget*

- *Forecasting for your future*

- *Understanding why we save*

- *Saving strategically*

- *Using Savings Goals*

Economic ups and downs have emphasized the importance of saving money and reducing debt. Budgeting and saving to prepare for life events is an important part of financial management. Savings enable you to make major purchases or take family vacations without increasing debt. Long-term planning and saving can allow you to help your kids through college, handle emergencies, and have a comfortable retirement.

This chapter tells you about tools within Quicken Personal Finance Software that can help. If you're in debt and can't even think about saving until you dig your way out, this chapter offers some help as well. It starts by covering Quicken tools for reducing your debt.

Reducing Your Debt

Consumer credit is a huge industry in our society. Many of us find that paying for something with a piece of plastic is much easier than paying with cold, hard cash. The "buy now, pay later" attitude has become an acceptable way of life. It's no wonder that many Americans are deeply in debt.

Those credit card bills can add up quickly and wreak devastation on a budget. And making just the minimum payment on each one only helps the credit card company keep you in debt—and paying interest—as long as possible. If you're in debt, don't skip this part of the chapter. It'll help you dig yourself out so you can build a solid financial future.

Taking Control

It's difficult to save money if most of your income is spent paying credit card bills and loan payments. If you're heavily in debt, you might even be having trouble keeping up with all your payments. But don't despair. There is hope! Here are a few simple things you can do to dig yourself out of debt:

- **Break the Debt Pattern** Your first step to reducing debt must be to break the pattern of spending that got you where you are. Eliminate all but one or two major credit cards for emergencies, such as car trouble or unexpected visits to the doctor. The cards that should go are the store and gas credit cards. They can increase your debt, but they can be used in only a few places.
- **Reduce Your Credit Limits** High credit limits are a trap. The credit card company or bank flatters you by offering to lend you more money. What they're really doing is setting you up so you'll owe them more—and pay them more in monthly finance and interest fees.
- **Shop for Cards with Better Interest Rates** If you do not pay off the balance of a credit card at the end of each billing period, you pay the interest on that balance. The balance and interest rate determine how much it costs you to have that special picture or name on a plastic card in your wallet. Low-interest credit cards are still widely available; try a web search. But before you apply for a new card, read the terms carefully. Many offer the low rates for a short, introductory period—often no longer than 6 or 12 months. Some offer the low rate only on new purchases, while others offer the low rate only on balance transfers or cash advances. Be sure to find out what the rate is after the introductory period.

NOTE Be sure that any fees involved in a balance transfer are not more than the savings you will receive with the new, lower interest rate!

- **Consolidate Your Debt**   Consolidating your debt may be one way to dig yourself out. By combining balances into one debt, whether through balance transfers to a single credit card or a debt consolidation loan, you're better able to pay off the balances without causing financial hardship. This is sometimes the only option when things have gotten completely out of control and you can't meet your debt obligations. However, make sure you have cut up the old cards so you don't add new debt to the older, consolidated amount.

 If you do choose to use a debt consolidation company, investigate them thoroughly before you give them any money.

- **Use Charge Cards, Not Credit Cards**   Understand the difference between a credit card and a charge card:
  - **Credit cards** enable you to buy things on credit. If each month you pay less than what you owe, you are charged interest on your account balance. Most major "credit cards," such as Visa and Discover, are true credit cards. Most store "charge cards" are also credit cards.
  - **Charge cards** enable you to buy things on credit, too. However, when the bill comes, you're expected to pay the entire balance. You don't have to pay any interest, but if you don't pay the entire balance on time, you may have to pay late fees and finance charges.

The benefit of charge cards is that they make it impossible to get into serious debt. Using these cards can prevent you from overspending.

- **If You Can't Stop Spending, Get Help**   Some people who are deeply in debt may have a spending problem. They can't resist buying that fifth pair of running shoes or that trendy new outdoor furniture. They don't need the things they buy, but they buy them anyway. There's nothing wrong with that if your income can support your spending habits, but if your net worth is less than $0, it's a real problem—one that might require counseling to resolve. The next time you make a purchase, stop for a moment and think about what you're buying. Is it something you need? Something you can use? Something you can justify spending the money on? If you can't answer yes to any of these questions, don't buy it. If you feel you have to buy it anyway, it's time to seek professional help.
- **Live Debt Free**   It is possible to live debt free—and you don't have to be rich to do it. Just stop relying on credit to make your purchases and spend only what you can afford. Imagine how great it would feel to be completely debt free. It's worth a try, isn't it?

Using the Debt Reduction Planner

Quicken's Debt Reduction Planner is a great tool to help you reduce your debt. After you enter information about your financial situation, Quicken develops a debt reduction plan for you. The Debt Reduction Planner is thorough, easy to use, and an excellent tool for teaching people how they can get out of debt as quickly as possible, saving hundreds (if not thousands) of dollars in interest charges.

If you're in serious debt—actually having trouble making ends meet because you can't seem to get any of your debts paid down—a pair of scissors (for cutting up charge cards), a telephone (to call your credit card companies to get your interest rates reduced), and the Debt Reduction Planner (to come up with a solid plan for reducing your debt) are probably your three best tools for getting things under control.

Here's what the Debt Reduction Planner can help you do that you might not be able to do on your own. The Planner will

- Objectively look at your debts and organize them by interest rate. Use the Planner to see the debts with the highest interest rate (these cost you the most) and ensure they are the first to be paid, thus saving you money.
- Show you the benefit of using some of your savings to reduce the balances on your most costly debt.
- Create an itemized plan based on real numbers that you can follow to reduce your debt.
- Show you, with a nice graph, in dollars and cents, how much money you can save and how quickly you can become debt free by following the plan.
- Help you to stop dreading the daily mail and its package of bills or the phone calls from bill collectors. Use the Debt Reduction Planner to get things under control.

While you can track and include all of your debt in the plan, Quicken suggests you begin with the debt that costs you the most (the debt with the highest interest rate). These debts are often one (or more) credit card accounts. That means setting up accounts for your credit cards rather than simply tracking monthly payments as bills paid. Chapters 4 and 5 discuss the two different ways to track credit cards in Quicken.

The wording on the first debt reduction plan screen you see is a little different depending on which accounts you have already set up. If you have not created any accounts, there is a line just above the Get Started button that says "Add your Accounts to get started." If you have created accounts other than credit cards and loans, the line will say "Add your Credit Card and Loans Accounts to get started."

Using the Debt Reduction Planner with Your Currently Entered Debt Accounts

To get started with the Debt Reduction Planner, from the Planning tab, choose the Debt Reduction button. The Debt Reduction Planner appears with its Get Started button, as seen next. What you see next depends on whether you have entered information about your debt into Quicken.

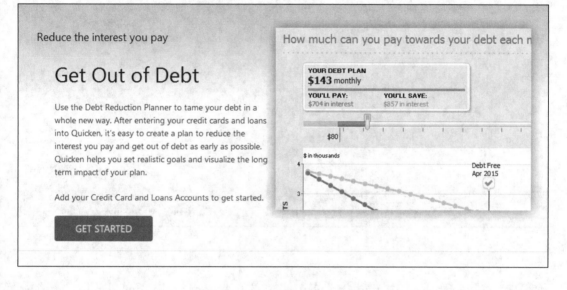

If you have not yet entered any credit card or other debt into Quicken, you are prompted to do so after you click the Get Started button. The Add Account dialog appears so that you can enter any credit cards or other personal loans. (See Chapters 1 and 4 if you need to review how to enter a new account in Quicken.) See the section "Starting the Debt Reduction Planner from Scratch" later in this chapter to work with new accounts in the Debt Reduction Planner. Click the Get Started button to start. This takes you to the Identify Your Debt screen.

- If you have entered credit cards and other debt accounts but have not yet created a debt reduction plan, you will see the Get Started button without a tagline suggesting you add accounts. You can click the Get Started button to start, which will take you to the Identify Your Debts screen.
- If you have already entered debt information, you will see a dialog that reflects the balances you have currently entered, as seen in Figure 13-1. The balance of this example assumes at least some of the information about what you owe is already entered into Quicken.

Budgets   Debt Reduction   Lifetime Planner   Tax Center   Savings Goals   Planning Tools ▾ Tax Tools ▾ Reports ▾

① IDENTIFY YOUR DEBTS   ② GET THE DETAILS   ③ MAKE A PLAN

Identify the debts you want to reduce

Listed below are the debts you currently track in Quicken. Click Include or Remove to choose which debts to include in your plan.
Being complete is important. If a debt is missing, click Add an account to add it to the list.

ACCOUNTS TO INCLUDE IN THIS PLAN	BALANCE		OTHER DEBT ACCOUNTS	❓ Why not include these? BALANCE
Credit Card	$1,895.00		2012 Toyota Camry Loan	$8,563.34
House Credit Card	$3,679.64		2014 Subaru Loan	$17,878.66
Total in Plan:	**$5,574.64**		House Loan	$91,788.81

Tip: Be sure to include all credit card and other high-interest debt in your plan.

❓   NEXT

Figure 13-1 • Identifying your current financial obligations is often the first step in controlling debt.

NOTE If you have an existing debt plan, click Plan Actions | Edit Your Plan to get to the Identify Your Debts screen.

What Do You Owe?   The first step in creating a plan is to recognize what you owe. By default, Quicken has designed the Debt Reduction Planner to help you decrease high-interest debt before long-term debt, which Quicken assumes to have lower interest. However, you may add any debt account to the plan. Figure 13-2 shows the third and final step of a debt reduction plan that saves the planner more than $2,200 in interest.

1. To include an account in your debt reduction plan, click the Plan Actions button at the right side of the Debt Reduction Plan window, as seen in Figure 13-3. If you have not yet set up a plan, click the Get Started button to begin.
2. Click Edit Your Plan to open the Debt Reduction Planner dialog seen in Figure 13-1. Note that your current credit cards appear on the left side of

Figure 13-2 • The Debt Reduction Planner in Quicken helps you create a plan to reduce your current debt.

the Planner in the Accounts To Include In This Plan section. Other debt accounts, such as your mortgage, appear on the right side of the screen in the Other Debt Accounts section. If you have an existing plan and choose Edit Your Plan, your account selections will reflect your previous plan selection, which may or may not be with credit cards first. If you delete your existing plan or are setting up a brand-new one by clicking the Get Started button, Quicken selects the credit card accounts first.

A non-zero ending balance is the criteria for displaying debt accounts in the Identify Your Debts screen. If you have future-dated payments that pay your account balance down to zero, you will not see these debt accounts in the Identify Your Debts screen. Also, debt accounts with a positive balance (one on which you have paid more than you owe) will not be included.

3.   Position your mouse cursor to the left of the account you want to add to the Planner. Click the Include link that appears. The account now appears as part

Figure 13-3 • The final window of the Debt Reduction Planner shows your projected payoff dates and schedule.

of your plan in the column on the left side and is no longer included with the Other Debt Accounts column on the right side of the Planner.

When you hover your mouse over any of the account names in the panel on the left, the Remove link appears. Conversely, when you hover your mouse over any of the text in the panel on the right, the Include link becomes available.

4. To remove an account from the plan, position your mouse cursor to the right of the account, and click Remove. The account is not included in the plan and appears in the Other Debt Accounts section of the Planner dialog.

5. After you have selected all of the debts you want to include in your plan, click Next.

Get The Details   The Get The Details section of the Debt Reduction Planner appears. Here is where you enter the current interest rates and the minimum

EXPERIENCED USERS RECOMMEND

One of the hardest parts of starting a new plan is facing how much you owe, both the grand total and the monthly payments. It is often so overwhelming that people stop right there. The thought of paying off thousands of dollars of debt, in addition to feeling like the task is impossible, often causes family arguments and, sometimes, avoidance techniques such as compulsive shopping or other non-productive activities.

Quicken makes the first task—identifying your total debt load—easier with the Debt Reduction Planner. Most users suggest you start working with the Planner. One of the beauties of the Planner is that you do not have to include all of your debt. Try using just the credit cards (or even just the credit card with the highest balance or interest rate) at first. Then, when those balances are zero, consider applying the Planner to your car and mortgage payments. Using the Planner in "small bites" can greatly relieve the shock and stress of seeing how much debt you actually owe.

payments for each of the accounts you've included in your plan. If you have not yet entered this information into Quicken, you can find this information on your latest credit card statement or from the financial institution's website. If the current interest rate or minimum payment amounts are different from what is shown, do the following:

1. Enter the actual interest rate in the Interest Rate field for each account. When you click in that field, the current information is highlighted. If the information is not correct, type in the correct rate.
2. Click in the minimum payment field for each account. If there is an existing amount, it will be highlighted and you can type in the proper amount. If you enter a minimum payment that does not meet the minimum based on the interest rate you entered, you'll see a warning message, shown next. The minimum payment is calculated based on the ending balance of the account, not on the current balance. Adjusting your ending balance to match the current balance may allow you to enter the minimum payment specified by your credit card company.

	INTEREST RATE (APR)	MINIMUM MONTH	
Credit Card	14.99 %	$3	Based on this Interest Rate your minimum payment must be at least $43
House Credit Card	17.99 %	$92	

Tip: Review your statements or visit your financial institutions' web sites to get the correct numbers. For credit cards, look for a "Purchases" or "Standard APR" to find the interest rate.

Some Quicken users have reported their financial institutions' minimum payments are less than the minimum calculated by Quicken. The only workaround is to accept the Quicken-calculated minimum payment. However, this can be a good thing, as your debt will be gone sooner.

You will not be able to continue until you make any necessary corrections. When the corrections are made, the Next button becomes available. Click Next to continue.

Make A Plan   The Make A Plan dialog is the workhorse section of the Debt Reduction Planner. You'll see that Quicken first calculates the plan based on your current payment amounts, as seen in Figure 13-4. This dialog has several information areas with which you can work to create a plan that gets you out of debt sooner.

1. Your Debt Plan is shown above the chart of the Make A Plan dialog. As you start your planning, the amount displayed shows how much interest you will

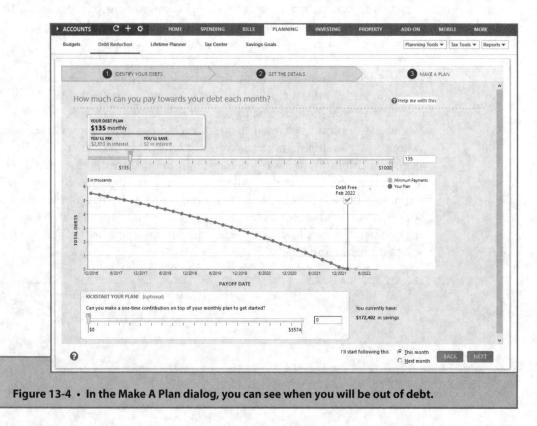

Figure 13-4 • In the Make A Plan dialog, you can see when you will be out of debt.

be paying if you continue paying the same monthly payments. Below the minimum payment information is a chart showing when you will be debt free making just the minimum payment on each outstanding account. It's the total of the minimum amounts, so as you pay off each debt, you begin paying more than the minimum on the remaining debts. For example, if you have two debts with minimum payments of $100 and $50, the minimum payment plan has you continue to pay $150 each month after you have paid off the first debt, so you will be paying more than the minimum of the second debt. The Your Debt Plan summary may appear anywhere along the slider above the chart, depending on the accounts and minimums in your plan.

2. Move the slider or enter a new amount into the field to the right of the chart to see how much you will save by paying more than the minimum payment each month. The yellow line in the chart is the plan based on your minimum payment amounts. The green line shows the impact of paying more than the minimum each month, or making an extra one-time payment, or both.

At the bottom of the Make A Plan dialog, Quicken displays another slider that lets you tell Quicken how much you could pay on the debt if you choose to make a one-time payment from your savings and nonretirement investments, as seen in Figure 13-4. Shown at the right of the Kickstart Your Plan slider are the balances of accounts you have that might be used to pay down your debt.

The Help Me With This link at the upper-right side of the Make A Plan dialog offers several suggestions to help with your plan.

Once you have entered your plan amounts, finish your Debt Reduction Planner session by telling Quicken when you plan on starting the new payment schedule, using the option at the bottom right of the plan next to the word "Back."

- Click This Month if you intend to pay more than minimum payments starting with this month's payments.
- Click Next Month if you've already paid the minimum for this month and want to start paying more than the minimum next month.
- If you are satisfied with your plan, click Next to see your completed plan, as seen in Figure 13-3.

In your Debt Reduction Plan dialog, use the Plan Actions button to explore other plan options or delete the current plan and start over. You can click the legends at the right of the graph to see summary information on either your plan or minimum payments. See "Modifying Your Plan" later in this chapter for more information. If you have had your plan for a few months, you may also see the original plan in gray in the legends.

You can opt to display the plan graph or include the minimum payment graph along with the graph for your plan. Click the Show Minimum Payment Graph check box to toggle between the two displays.

Use the What If button to experiment with other plan options, change the pay-off order, and update your plan.

- Click the downward arrow in the Payment Schedule section to hide the schedule of upcoming payments. You can also click the See Full Schedule link at the bottom right of the Payment Schedule section to see the scheduled payments, as seen next. This schedule also shows the projected balance for each account after the plan's payment schedule is met. Scroll to see the result when the balances are all zero. You can also print a 6 Month or a 12 Month Plan from the My Payment Schedule dialog.

- Click Print 6 Month Plan or Print 12 Month Plan in the My Payment Schedule dialog to open the Print dialog from which you can preview or print the payment schedule for the next 6 or 12 months. This schedule also shows the projected balance for each account after you meet the plan's payment schedule.

Click Done to close the schedule and return to your plan.

Modifying Your Plan

Once you have created a plan to reduce your debt, you can adjust it at any time. To review the plan, go to the Planning tab and choose the Debt Reduction button. Your current plan appears. Click the Plan Actions button and choose from one of the menu options:

- Click Explore Other Plan Options to open the Experiment With Other Plan Options dialog as described in "Use the What If Option" later in this chapter.
- Click Delete This Plan to delete your current plan and start over.
- Choose Edit Your Plan from the drop-down menu to work with your current plan.

You can open the Experiment With Other Plan Options dialog by either clicking the What If button or clicking the Plan Actions button and then selecting Explore Other Plan Options from the drop-down list.

Editing Your Plan   When you choose Edit Your Plan you are returned to the Identify Your Debts dialog, where you can remove or include any of your accounts. Once you have made changes, click Next to continue.

1. In the Get The Details dialog, make any necessary changes to interest rate and/or minimum payments. Click Next to open the Make A Plan dialog. Make any changes in the Make A Plan dialog. Perhaps you've decided to pay an additional $50 per month to reduce debt faster.
2. If you've decided to take more money from savings, indicate how much. Whatever the choices, indicate as appropriate and click Next to complete your modifications.
3. Position your mouse cursor and click any "tick" on the Projected Payoff Date and Savings graph lines to see how much you will owe at a specific date. The yellow line shows your Minimum Payments plan, and the green line shows Your Plan lines in the Projected Payoff Date and Savings graph.

Your plan displays the monthly payment, total interest you will pay, the interest savings, the payoff date, and how much time you will save over paying just minimum payments.

The yellow bar represents how long it will take to pay off your debt by making minimum payments, and the green bar shows the results of your new debt reduction plan. As seen at the right of the projected payoff date and savings chart in Figure 13-3, the green bar to the left of Your Plan tells you your interest savings, and the yellow bar to the left of Minimum Payments displays the total interest you will pay when making those minimum payments. If you have created a second plan, you may see a gray bar by the words "Original Plan," indicating the results of your first plan.

Use the What If Option

You may be pleased with your debt reduction plan as it stands but curious about what would happen if you applied your income tax refund to your debt, or increased or decreased the monthly payment amounts. The What If option allows you to see these changes without really changing the plan. To see your options, select the What If button to open the Experiment With Other Plan Options dialog, as seen in Figure 13-5.

Figure 13-5 • You can experiment with different payment options without changing your plan in the Experiment With Other Plan Options dialog.

Change Your Monthly Payment   Either use the sliders or type a new amount directly in the payment field in the Experiment With Other Plan Options dialog. Position your mouse key on a tick on each graph line to see the total due at that point in time. Note that the second graph line in this dialog is blue, indicating your possible alternative plan.

Try a One-Time Payment   Considering selling that gas-guzzling second car? Did you win the sports pool at work? If you come into some extra cash, think about applying those funds directly to your debt load. Enter the amount in the payment field, or use the slider to see how those extra funds would lessen your debt load.

Change Payoff Order   By default, Quicken maximizes your interest savings by selecting the order in which you pay off your credit card debt. You can use another method if you choose. Click the Change Order button to open the Change Payoff Order dialog as seen next. From this dialog you can

- See the default order, which maximizes your interest savings
- Use the debt snowball method
- Choose the order yourself

EXPERIENCED USERS RECOMMEND

One of the suggested methods of paying off debt is the snowball method. Using this method, people start by paying as much as possible on the debt with the lowest balance while paying minimum payments on the rest of their debt. Then, when they have paid off the first debt, they apply the same method to the debt with the next lowest balance and so on. The main advantage to this system is a feeling of accomplishment; one debt is gone forever.

While this method may not save the debtor as much interest as when paying off the item with the highest interest rate first, people use this plan when they face a very high debt load and feel overwhelmed.

You can decide what method, or combination of methods, works the best for your financial situation. The main goal is to get out of debt and then stay away from the debt merry-go-round.

Select the Custom Order option to tell Quicken the order in which you plan to pay off your debts. When you select that option, small blue up and down arrows appear to the left of each debt. Click the upward-pointing arrow to move a debt up in the list and the downward-pointing arrow to move it down.

Click OK to save any changes to the Change Payoff Order dialog, or click Cancel to return to the Experiment With Other Plan Options dialog.

At the Experiment With Other Plan Options dialog, click Update My Plan if you have made changes you want to keep. If you are satisfied with your current plan, click Cancel to return to your Debt Reduction Plan screen.

Starting the Debt Reduction Planner from Scratch

If you have not entered any of your credit cards or other debt into Quicken, the Debt Reduction Planner will prompt you to do so. To get started, from the Planning tab, choose the Debt Reduction button. The Debt Reduction Planner appears with its Get Started button. Click the Get Started button. The Add Account dialog appears.

1. From the Add Account dialog, select Credit Card to advance to the next screen.
2. Enter your financial institution's name or select it from one of the lists. You can also use Advanced Setup, choosing I Want To Enter My Transactions Manually, to enter your information without downloading. If you need more help adding your accounts, review Chapters 1 and 4.
3. Enter the date of your latest credit card statement, and enter the balance as of that date.

4. Click Next to complete the setup of your debts. At this point, you'll see the Account Added screen. If you are going to add more accounts, click the Add Another Account button rather than the Finish button. Clicking the Finish button starts the debt reduction plan's Identify Your Debts screen. If you aren't paying attention, you'll be "stuck" in the debt reduction plan without all of the accounts you wanted to include in the plan. You can click the menu path Tools | Add An Account to add any accounts you might have missed. When you have finished adding accounts, click the Planning tab to return to the debt reduction plan's Identify Your Debts screen, and the newly added accounts will be shown in the Other Debt Accounts section of the screen.

5. Repeat Steps 1 through 4 for each debt with a balance. Once all of your debts are entered, they will be reflected on the Identify Your Debts dialog in the Debt Planner. When your information is complete, click Next to continue.

6. In the Get The Details dialog, enter the interest rate shown on your credit card statements for each item. You can move between the fields with your TAB key. Quicken will automatically enter the correct minimum payment based on the interest rate you enter.

7. Click Next to open the Make A Plan dialog. Follow the directions described in the "Make A Plan" section shown earlier.

Budgeting with Quicken

When money is tight and you're interested in meeting financial goals, it's time to create a budget and monitor your spending. However, if you're serious about managing your money, consider creating a budget *before* you need one. Although Quicken's categories give you a clear understanding of where money comes from and where it goes, budgets enable you to set up predefined amounts for each category, thus helping you to watch and control spending.

Budgets also make it easier to create forecasts of your future financial position, for example, to see how much cash will be available next summer for a vacation.

The idea behind a budget is to determine expected income amounts and specify maximum amounts for expenditures. This helps prevent you from spending more than you earn. It also enables you to control your spending in certain categories. For example, say you realize that you go out for dinner a lot more often than you can really afford. You can set a budget for the Dining category and track your spending to make sure you don't exceed the budget. You'll eat at home more often and save money.

If you don't like the word "budget," consider it a "spending plan" or even a "making better use of our money" plan.

This section explains how Quicken works with budgets and how you can use the budgeting tools to set up a budget and use it to keep track of your spending. Hopefully, you'll see that budgeting is a great way to keep spending under control.

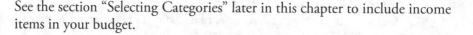

Quicken's Automatic Budget

Quicken automatically generates a budget for you based on past transactions. You can edit the budget it creates to meet your needs, or you can create a budget from scratch.

The quickest and easiest way to create a budget is to let Quicken do it for you based on your income and expenditures. For Quicken to create an accurate budget, however, you must have several months' worth of transactions in your Quicken data file. Otherwise, the budget may not reflect all regular expenses. By default, the budget does not include any income items.

See the section "Selecting Categories" later in this chapter to include income items in your budget.

To get started, choose the Planning tab and click the Budgets button. Click the Get Started button to open the Create A New Budget dialog. Quicken assigns the default name of Budget 1. If you wish to change the name, highlight it and type in your own. Click Advanced Budget Settings to set a Budget Year. The default is the calendar year (January through December), but you can use a different calendar for your budget. For example, if you earn most of your income during the school year, you might want to start your budget year in September.

Once you have named your budget and set any additional options, such as the calendar year, click OK to create the new budget, as seen in Figure 13-6.

If you do not see the Get Started button, click the Budget Actions button and select Create New Budget.

Your automatic budget appears for the period you selected, as seen in Figure 13-6. As you can see, the automatic budget graphs the top expenses and puts all of the other expenses into the Everything Else category.

When creating a budget, Quicken can use as few as three months' worth of expenses, but it is better to have more transactions.

← → C⌄				
▸ ACCOUNTS C + ⚙	HOME SPENDING BILLS **PLANNING** INVESTING PROPERTY ADD-ON MOBILE MORE			
Budgets Debt Reduction Lifetime Planner Tax Center Savings Goals			Planning Tools ▾ Tax Tools ▾ Reports ▾	

Graph view ▾ Yearly ▾ ◂ 2016 ▸	Budget Actions ▾

SPENDING **$5,590** Jan 2016 - Dec 2016		Budget: $7,165 ✓ $1,575 LEFT

			Budget
− HOME EXPENSES	852	213 left	1,065
Bills & Utilities: Home Phone	852	213 left	1,065 ▮▮
+ Everything Else		424	
− Personal Expenses	4,738	1,362 left	6,100
Auto & Transport: Gas & Fuel	531	133 left	664
Other Bills & Utilities	1,773	443 left	2,216
Bills & Utilities: Television	454	114 left	568
Education: Student Loan	732	183 left	915
Fees & Charges: Bank Fee	24	6 left	30
Home: Rent	600	200 left	800
Other Shopping	624	284 left	908
+ Everything Else		5,643	

⊕ Select categories to budget

Figure 13-6 • Quicken can create an automatic budget based on the transactions you have entered.

Understanding Quicken's Automatic Budget

Quicken creates its budget based on the amount you spent on each category and the total number of months in which you spent money in that category.

The average is for the full month of each of the prior months. Therefore, if you are creating the budget on June 24, 2017, and you have 12 months or more of transactions, the first full month included in the average is June 2017. For a phone bill or other regular monthly bill, this may not make much difference. For an irregular expense like gas or groceries, knowing the first month in the average is a full month might make a big difference on the calculation.

NOTE Quicken rounds all amounts to the nearest dollar in Budget dialogs.

Working with Your Automatic Budget

As seen in Figure 13-6, Quicken's automatic budget has a wealth of information. Since we are looking at our budget in the Yearly view, the total annual spending summary is displayed. Each bar shows the total budgeted for the time period selected, the amount you have spent, and the amount you have left over or have overspent.

Bars with the lighter color indicate a planned expense, such as from a transaction reminder that is due during the month. Darker color indicates expenses that have already occurred for the month. So early in the month, the bars may be light colored because no actual expenses have yet occurred.

The Graph View

In the Graph View, seen in Figure 13-7, each category has a green, gray, or red bar:

- A green bar means you have spent what you budgeted or less.
- A red bar means you have spent more than you budgeted. In both cases, the actual amount you spent shows as a number on the bar.
- A gray bar means there are no transactions for the current period in that category.
- A light green or red portion within a bar means you have scheduled reminders for the future in that category. The sum of any reminder transactions shows as a number within the bar as well.

Figure 13-7 • The Quicken automatic budget shows your spending.

Graph View Filters   The graph view has several filters from which you can choose. If you have more than one budget, the first filter toggles between them. The next filter toggles between the graph view and the annual view. (See "The Annual View" later in this chapter.) If you have only one budget, the first filter options are Graph and Annual Views.

Use the date filter in the graph view to set the time period with which you want to work. Your choices are

- **Monthly**   Use the arrows to the right and left of the current month to look at previous and future months.
- **Quarterly**   This option shows your budget by quarters. The previous and future filters to the left and right of the selected quarter's name allow you to see all four quarters of the year.
- **Yearly**   This filter option shows the current year's budget information, as seen in Figure 13-7. If you click the left or right arrows in the year shown at the right of the time period option, a dialog appears from which you can add a budget for that year, as seen here. In our example, we clicked the right arrow twice. We then saw the dialog prompting us to enter a budget for 2018.

- **Quarter/Year To Date**   This option reflects the transactions and budgets for the current quarter (or year) through today's date.
- **Last Three/Six Months**   Choosing this filter displays transactions and budgeted amounts for the last three or the last six months, no matter when in a quarter you are viewing the information.

You can select Yearly and use the back button on the date to get last year's budget. This will display an annual graph for all of the transactions you entered for the last year. If you have not yet created a budget for the previous year, you will see the prompt for the prior year.

Click the small plus sign to the left of Everything Else at the bottom of your expenses to see the items included in that figure. That plus sign changes to a minus sign when the "Everything Else" categories display. Click the minus sign to close the list. If you use custom category groups, you may see more than one instance of Everything Else.

You can learn more detail about any category's spending by hovering your mouse over or clicking the red, gray, or green bar for that category.

Selecting Categories   To add a category to the budget, click Select Categories To Budget at the bottom left of the Budget window. This displays the Select Categories To Budget dialog.

Select the categories you want to budget by clicking the check box to the left of each category name. To ensure all categories are listed, including any hidden categories, click the Show Hidden Categories check box at the lower left of the dialog. If you have created custom category groups, the custom category group name will appear on the left side of the dialog, along with the standard category groups such as Personal Income and Personal Expenses. To learn more about creating custom category groups, see Chapter 4.

The Paychecks and Detailed Loan Payments category groups enable you to choose how you want to budget your paycheck and loan payments. For example, the Paychecks group allows you to budget based on your net salary or your gross salary with all associated categories. If you do not see these special category groups, you need to set up a paycheck reminder to see the Paycheck group, and for Detailed Loan Payments, you must have a loan with a loan payment reminder.

After you have marked all the categories you want to budget, click OK to close the dialog and return to your budget.

 To use a specific category group in your budget, you must choose at least one of the categories within that group in the Select Categories To Budget dialog.

Budget Actions   The Budget Actions button at the upper right of your budget screen opens a menu, as seen here. From this menu, you can

- **Select Categories To Budget**   This option opens the Select Categories To Budget dialog described earlier.
- **Switch To Annual View**   See "The Annual View" section later in this chapter to learn about the annual view of a Quicken budget.
- **Budget Reports**   This option allows you to create both a current and a historical budget report.
- **View Options**   Use the choices on this menu item to tell Quicken how to display your budget items:
  - **Show Cents** includes the cents in each amount.
  - **Include Reminders** includes scheduled payments in your budget amounts.
  - **Show Parent Category Rollup** shows the parent category as a sum of all the budgeted subcategories. With this option selected, you cannot edit the budget amount for the parent category. If you want to simplify your budget by tracking only parent categories, select this option and uncheck the subcategories for the parent categories you wish to use.
  - **Edit Budget Name** displays a dialog with which you can type a new name. Click OK to close the dialog.

- **Duplicate This Budget**   Click this option to open the Duplicate Budget dialog.
- **Delete This Budget**   This option opens the Delete Budget dialog.
- **Create New Budget**   This option opens the Create A New Budget dialog.
- **Budget Preferences**   Choose this option to tell Quicken which specific transfers to exclude or include in your budget.

Columns in the Graph View   The column labeled Budget in the graph view indicates the budgeted amount for each category for the date range you selected in the date filter.

The amount in the (unlabeled) balance column is the difference between the amount you have budgeted for a specific time period and the amount you spent during that same time period.

Everything Else   The Everything Else amount is the sum of all categories you have chosen not to include in your budget. You can

- Budget the "Everything Else" amount by assigning an amount to create a collective budget for all of the categories contained in this total. To do so, click the white cross within the green circle at the right of the "Everything Else" line. A new line appears in your graph showing the total spent in that collective "category" for the time period selected. The green circle with the white cross is available only when you choose the Monthly filter in the graph view of your budget.
- Eliminate or reduce the Everything Else amount by adding those categories to your budget.

Other Budget Choices   As you are working in the default Monthly filter of the graph view of your budget and select a specific category, you'll see several additional tools, as shown here:

Groceries	165	85 left	⚙	250

- The Rollover Options tool (crossed arrows) allows you to create or change rollover categories and amounts. See "Using Rollovers in Quicken Budgets" later in this chapter.

- Click the Budget Amount Options tool (small gear icon) to open a menu from which you can choose to:
  - Apply the current (month) budget amount to each of the remaining months' budgets for the current year.
  - Apply the current (month) amount to every month of the next year.
  - Edit the yearly budget. This is handy for seeing the budgeted amounts for each of the 12 months of the current year so you can easily see how the average was determined.
  - Calculate the average budget.
  - Set the current month's budget amounts based on the average spending for this category.
  - Get help setting a budget amount. This choice opens the Quicken Help screen to the Budget Amount information.
- Set a different amount in the Budget column.
- Click the Category History icon (small bar chart) to see the category's transaction history for the current year, as shown next. The History tab shows all of the transactions in columnar form, while the Transactions tab shows only the transactions for the time period you have selected to display in the graph view's date filter. Click the X at the upper right of the report to close the history. You can also press ESC on your keyboard to close the Category History.

You can also open a category's history by clicking anywhere on that category's red or green bar in the graph view of your budget.

The Annual View

The annual view of your Quicken budget displays information in a columnar format, as shown in Figure 13-8. This view gives you the opportunity to assign budget amounts and scrutinize your spending. To switch to annual view, select the drop-down list arrow in graph view.

Filters in Annual View   When you work in the annual view of your budget, you can choose from among several filters. If you have created more than one budget, you can choose the other budget. You can choose to see your budget at any time in graph view.

The Year filter gives you the opportunity to apply your budget to both the last and next calendar years. Use the left arrow to open the Add A Budget for 20*xx* (*xx* being whatever the previous year is) to work with the previous year's information. Click the right arrow to work with the next calendar year or to set up next year's budget, if you have not yet done so.

The Details filter, seen in Figure 13-8, allows you to see the current year's budget information displayed in four ways:

- **Details** shows both the budgeted amount and the actual amount spent in each category for each month. In this view, click in any category to see some additional information about that category, as shown next. Select any of the three icons to see additional information about that category.

	August			September			October			November			December			2016 Summary
	BUDGET	ACTUAL	BALANCE	BUDGET	ACTUAL	BALANCE	BUDGET	ACTUAL	BALANCE	BUDGET	ACTUAL	BALANCE	BUDGET	ACTUAL	BALANCE	BALANCE
Auto & Transport: Gas & Fuel	100	136	-36	100	193	-93	181	181	0	150	308	-158	155	0	155	-132
Other Bills & Utilities	334	334	0	609	609	0	829	829	0	0	0	0	443	0	443	443
Bills & Utilities: Television	91	91	0	91	91	0	91	91	0	182	182	0	114	0	114	114
Education: Student Loan	183	183	0	183	183	0	183	183	0	183	183	0	183	0	183	183
Fees & Charges: Bank Fee	6	6	0	6	6	0	6	6	0	6	6	0	6	0	6	6
Home: Rent	0	0	0	200	200	0	200	200	0	200	200	0	200	0	200	200
Other Shopping	58	58	0	0	0	0	374	374	0	193	193	0	283	0	283	283
Totals	1,105	1,141	-36	1,353	1,446	-93	2,055	2,055	0	1,078	1,236	-159	1,599	0	1,599	1,312

Figure 13-8 · The annual view shows details about your budget.

- **The Bar icon** creates a category history report.
- **The Gear icon** opens a budget actions menu.
- **The Rollover icon** presents a menu you can use to work with rollovers, as discussed in "Using Rollovers in Quicken Budgets" next in this chapter.

You also have access to the Budget column where you can enter a new budget amount. Use the Action gear icon to open a menu that allows you to apply the budgeted amount forward or to all of the current year. (You do not see the gear icon until a category is selected.) You can also set the budget for the chosen month based on the average spending in this category for this current year or see help on setting the budget amount. You can see information for future months by clicking the Show Detail For Future Months check box at the lower right of the dialog.

	October ▼			November ▼			December ▼		
	BUDGET	ACTUAL	BALANCE	BUDGET	ACTUAL	BALANCE	BUDGET	ACTUAL	BALANCE
− **Personal Expenses**	1,864	1,864	0	913	913	0	1,384	0	1,384
Auto & Transport: **Gas & Fuel** ▮▮ ⚙ 🗐	181	181	0	150	150	0	155	0	155

- **Balance Only** shows the amount over or under budget for each category for each month. Click the Show Balance In Future Months check box to show the current budget balance in each of the months following the current month.
- **Budget Only** displays only the budgeted amount for each category for each month. Click in any month to make the budget amount field active, where you can change the budget amount or access the Budget Amount Options icon (small gear).
- **Actuals Only** shows the actual amount spent during each month for each category. You cannot make any changes to this filter's display.

Using Rollovers in Quicken Budgets

A budget rollover is an element of a budget category. As stated in Quicken Help, "Budget categories that have rollovers carry their cumulative balances from one month to the next." The idea is that there are many categories for which you don't have a set amount each month, such as groceries or household repairs. By using rollovers, you can account for these monthly spending variations over the year. A good example might be an annual budget of $1,800 for household repairs. This amount would show as $150 per month. If in one month you spent $70, if you choose to make Household Repairs a rollover category, you could "roll over" $80 to the next month to add to that month's total ($150 – $70 = $80). Quicken gives you the option to roll over both negative (you've spent more than you budgeted for that month) and positive (you did not spend as much as you budgeted) amounts.

EXPERIENCED USERS RECOMMEND

When working with Quicken budgets, occasionally there may be one-time items you do not want to include, such as a large down payment on a new car. Normally, Quicken would categorize this expense as an Auto & Transport expense, but the amount would certainly skew your budget if it were included. You might consider creating a subcategory under Auto & Transport entitled Down Payment and then excluding that item from your budget. See "Creating Your Own Budget" later in this chapter to understand how to exclude a category or subcategory from a budget.

Budget categories do not automatically "roll over." You have to add this attribute to each budget category to which it applies. To do so:

1. Click the Planning tab. If the Planning tab does not show, from the Quicken menu choose View | Tabs To Show | Planning.
2. From the Planning tab, click the Budgets button.
3. In either graph or annual view, select a category in your budget and click the small criss-cross icon to open a list of options, as seen here:
   - **Turn Rollover Off** turns off any rollover characteristic you've set before.

⊠	Turn rollover off
⊠	Rollover balances at the end of each month
⇒	Rollover only positive balances at the end of each month
?	Rollover help

   - **Rollover Balances At The End Of Each Month** tells Quicken to include the amount you have left, whether positive or negative, in the next month's totals.
   - **Rollover Only Positive Balances At The End Of Each Month** tells Quicken to include only positive amounts in the next month's totals.
   - **Rollover Help** is a shortcut to the What Is A Budget Rollover? section of Quicken Help.

Creating Your Own Budget   Although Quicken's automatic budget is great, you might want to create an alternative budget to see "what if" scenarios and then compare your original budget with the alternative one.

To create another budget, from the currently displayed budget (either view), click Budget Actions | Create New Budget, or click the Get Started button. This opens the Create A New Budget dialog from which you can make changes. Enter a name for your customized budget and click OK.

A new Quicken budget appears, based on the average spending for each category. If the time between your first budget and creating this budget is minimal, you probably don't have enough change in your spending, so the new budget appears the same as the original budget.

Working with More than One Budget   If you have created more than one budget, you can choose the budget with which to work. From the Planning tab, click Budgets. Click the Budget Name drop-down list to see your choices. Click the budget you want to use.

To edit a budget's name, select the budget name and click the Budget Actions button at the upper-right corner of the budget window. Select View Options | Edit Budget Name from the drop-down list. Enter a name in the Edit Budget Name dialog that appears, and click OK. The Edit Budget Name dialog in the View Options menu is the only place to edit the budget name.

Deleting a Budget   If you have created more than one budget, you can delete one or more of the existing budgets. To delete a budget, select the budget name. From the Budget Actions menu, choose Delete This Budget. The Delete Budget dialog appears. Click Delete to eliminate this budget or Cancel to close the dialog. If you delete all of your budgets, you will see the Get Started screen in the Budgets view of the Planning tab.

Showing a Budget in Your Home Tab   You can display your budget graph in either the Main View or a customized view of the Quicken Home tab's window. With this feature, you can keep an eye on the budget that interests you most. To choose which budget to display, in the Budget section of the Main View tab, click Options | Show Budget from the menu that appears. A list of the budgets you have created appears. Choose the budget you want to show in this view. It replaces the original budget.

You can add a budget to other views that you may have customized. Choose the view with which you want to work and click Customize. Use the Customize View dialog to choose Budget in the Available Items list, and click Add to move it to the Chosen Items list. Click Save to close the dialog.

Open the view, and in the budget snapshot, click the gear icon and select Show Budget from the menu. Note you will see the Show Budget option only if you have more than one budget. A list of the budgets you have created appears. Choose the budget you want to show in this view. See more information about creating customized Home tab views in Appendix B.

Where Does Your Money Go?

Now that you have been working with the various planners and reports available in Quicken, you are probably getting more comfortable understanding just where your hard-earned dollars are going. If you've used the Debt Reduction Planner and created a budget, you may also be thinking about the future and how your financial situation will be improving. Quicken offers several tools that help you understand where you will be spending your funds. Using either Quicken's reminders feature, which shows transaction reminders in your register, or the Projected Balances tool will help you to understand what expenditures are coming up in the near future. Then, in the second part of this section, we'll discuss saving your money.

Remember when you got your first piggy bank? It may not have looked like a pig, but it had a slot for slipping in coins and, if you were lucky, a removable rubber plug on the bottom that made it easy to get the coins out when you needed them. Whoever gave you the bank was trying to teach you your first financial management lesson: save money.

As an adult, things are a little more complex. See the later section "Understanding Why We Save," which explains why you should save, provides some saving strategies, and tells you about the types of savings accounts that make your old piggy bank obsolete.

Forecasting for Your Future

Forecasting uses known and estimated transactions to provide a general overview of your future financial situation. This "crystal ball" can help you spot potential cash flow problems (or surpluses) so you can prepare for them. Quicken helps you see your projected balances and can also help you create savings goals.

Projected Balances

Quicken helps you keep up with what your account balances will be in the future with the Projected Balances report. This report can be found in the Bills tab, or by choosing the Planning tab and then Planning Tools | Projected Balances. However, the graph is more useful when you have set up reminders, as discussed in Chapter 7.

You can set the range for the Projected Balances report for the next 7 days, next 14 days, next 30 or 90 days, or the next 12 months, or even customize a range that suits your requirements. See the following illustration for an example of the Projected Balances report for the next 12 months. Some Quicken users find this report not particularly useful, as it is small and sometimes difficult to discern the balances from the lines when there is a large variation in the account balances.

Reminders

Quicken 2017 allows you to display a reminder about future bills in your register. The reminder appears with a small "bill due" icon at the left of the register entry. You can set the range for these bill reminders for the same periods as the Projected Balances report. See more information about reminders in Chapter 7.

Understanding Why We Save

Most people save money so they have funds available when they are needed. Others save for a particular purpose. Still others save because they have so much they can't spend it all. Here's a closer look at why saving makes sense.

- **Saving for "rainy days"**   When people say they are "saving for a rainy day," they probably aren't talking about the weather. They're talking about bad times or emergencies—situations when they'll need extra cash. If your paychecks stop coming, do you have enough savings to support yourself or your family until you can get another source of income? On the "rainy day" scale, this could be a torrential downpour. Your savings can be a good umbrella.
- **Saving for a goal**   Planning for your future often includes planning for events that affect your life—and your wallet. Saving money for specific events can help make these events memorable for what they are, rather than what they cost.
- **Saving for peace of mind**   Some people save money because events in their lives showed them the importance of having savings. Children who lived through the Depression or bad financial times for their families grew up to be adults who understand the value of money and try hard to keep some available. They don't want to repeat the hard times they went through. Having healthy savings accounts gives them peace of mind.

Saving Strategically

There are two main ways to save: when you can or regularly.

- **Saving when you can**   When money is tight, saving can be difficult. People who are serious about saving, however, will force themselves to save as much as possible when they can. Saving when you can is better than not saving at all. One suggestion given by financial specialists is to "pay yourself first." This means that you consistently take a portion of any income and put it into a savings account. The amount really doesn't matter; it is the consistency that creates the habit.
- **Saving regularly**   A better way to save money is to save a set amount periodically. For example, consider putting away $25 every week or $200 every month. Timing this with your paycheck makes sense; you can make a split deposit for the check. A savings like this is called an annuity, and you'd be surprised at how quickly the money can accumulate.

There are different types of savings accounts, each with its own benefits and drawbacks. Check with your financial institution (or do an Internet search) to see what products might best meet your needs. A short list of possibilities are

- Standard savings accounts
- Payroll savings

- Certificates of deposit
- Money market accounts
- Interest-bearing checking accounts

Because current interest rates are still low, none of these options is a very good choice for building savings. Try doing an Internet search for reputable financial institutions that offer better interest rates.

Using Savings Goals

Quicken's Savings Goals feature helps you save money by "hiding" funds in an account. You set up a savings goal and make contributions to it using the Savings Goals window. Although the money never leaves the source bank account, it is deducted in the account register, thus reducing the account balance in Quicken. If you can't see the money in your account, you're less likely to spend it.

EXPERIENCED USERS RECOMMEND

Kind of sounds silly, doesn't it? Using Quicken to transfer money from your checking account to another account that doesn't even exist?

But don't laugh—the Savings Goals feature really works. One Quicken family used a similar technique when they had their second child. They simply deducted $50 or $75 from their personal checking account balance, thus giving the illusion that there was less money in the account than was really there. They were saving money by thinking twice about writing a check for something they really didn't need. The same method prevented any bounced checks. When they had the opportunity to buy some nearly new play equipment from a neighboring family whose children started college, there was enough money in this "secret" account to pay for the swing set and other equipment for their growing family.

Give it a try and see for yourself!

Getting Started

Open the Savings Goals window by choosing Planning | Savings Goals. The Savings Goals startup screen appears. Click Get Started to open the Create New Savings Goal dialog as seen here. If you do not see the Get Started button, click Goal Actions and select New Savings Goal from the drop-down list.

Enter your goal's name, the amount you want to save, and the date by which you want to have saved the money. The finish date should be shortly before you leave for your second honeymoon or before the date when you are taking the entire family to the family reunion in New York City. Click OK to close the dialog. Your Savings Goals dialog appears as shown in the following illustration.

The name of the savings goal cannot be the same as any Quicken category or account.

Contributing Funds to a Savings Goal

To contribute funds to a savings goal, select the Contribute icon (the white cross in a small green circle) or the Contribute text to open the Contribute To Goal *<goal name>* dialog.

In the From Account drop-down list, select the account from which you want to transfer the money. The balance and name of that account appear in the bottom of the dialog. Then enter the amount of the transfer in the Amount box. By default, Quicken suggests the projected monthly contribution amount, but you can enter any amount you like. When you've finished, click OK.

If you make a contribution, Quicken will create an entry in the account register of the account from which the money was contributed. It also updates the progress bar and information in the Your Savings Goals dialog. To show this entry:

- Click the Goal Actions button in the Your Savings Goals dialog.

- Click Show Savings Goal Transactions In Register And Reports. Your entry appears in the register of the selected account. This menu item is a toggle. Click once to select—a green check mark indicates it is selected. Click once again to deselect—a grayed-out check mark indicates it is not selected.

When you create a savings goal, Quicken creates a Savings Goals account to record the goal's transactions and balance. This account is shown, with the total of your contributions, at the bottom of your Account Bar.

To automate contributions to the goal, you can create a scheduled transaction to transfer money periodically from one of your bank accounts to the savings goal asset account. Scheduled transactions are covered in Chapter 7.

Meeting Your Goal

Once you have met your savings goal, you can either withdraw the funds from the savings goal so they appear in a Quicken account or delete the savings goal to put the money back where it came from.

Withdrawing Money   You can withdraw funds from your savings goals should you need to do so. Click the Planning tab and choose Savings Goals. All of your savings goals will appear. If you have more than one goal, select the one from which you want to withdraw money. Click the Withdraw icon (a small white minus sign in a red circle) or just the word Withdraw. The Withdrawal From *<goal name>* dialog, which works much like the Contribute To Goal dialog, appears. Use it to remove funds from the savings goal and put them back into the account from which they were contributed. Unlike the Contribute To Goal dialog, your only choice is to put the funds back into the account from which they were deducted. Enter the amount and the date of withdrawal. Click OK to close the Withdraw From *<goal name>* dialog.

You can make contributions to a goal from more than one account. Any withdrawal would then be limited to the maximum contributed from the specific account. For example, if you contributed $500 from Checking and $1,000 from Savings to your goal, the maximum you could withdraw from the goal to be added to Checking is $500.

If you funded your goal from multiple accounts, if you try to withdraw more money than you funded from an account, you will see a warning: "You have not saved enough money to complete this transfer." The maximum amount you can transfer back to the funding account will be listed on the left side of the Withdrawal From *<goal name>* dialog.

Editing a Savings Goal   To edit an existing savings goal, from the Planning tab, click Savings Goals. Select the Edit Goal gear icon in the goal you want to change. The Edit Savings Goal dialog appears. Enter the new goal amount and/or finish date. Click OK or Cancel to close the dialog.

Deleting a Savings Goal   To delete a savings goal, right-click its name in the Account Bar and, from the context menu, select Edit/Delete Account. From the Account Details dialog that appears, select the Delete Account button at the bottom left of the window. A message appears that the account will be permanently removed and all transfers put back into the account from which the transfers were made. You must type Yes to confirm the deletion and then click OK to close the dialog. If you decide not to delete the account, click the Cancel button. You can also delete a goal directly from the Savings Goals view.

1. Click the Planning tab and select Savings Goals.
2. Click the Action gear icon to the right of the goal's name. From the list that appears, choose Delete Goal. The Delete Savings Goal dialog appears. The dialog states that all funds will be returned to their source accounts and allows you to determine what to do with the Savings Goal account.
3. Choose Remove It From Quicken Completely to remove all record of this goal.

   –Or–

   Choose Keep It As A Zero Balance Asset Account For My Records.
4. Click Cancel to stop the action or OK to close the dialog.

Planning for Tax Time

Chapter 14

In This Chapter:

- *Including tax information in accounts*

- *Connecting tax information with categories*

- *Using TurboTax*

- *Working with the Tax Planner*

- *Creating scenarios*

- *Minimizing taxes by maximizing deductions*

- *Utilizing the Itemized Deduction Estimator*

- *Exploring the Tax Withholding Estimator*

- *Understanding the Tax Center*

Tax time is no fun. You have to spend hours sifting through financial records and filling out complex forms. When you're done with the hard part, you may be rewarded with the knowledge that you can expect a refund. However, it is more likely that your reward will be the privilege of writing a check to the federal, state, or local government—or worse yet, all three.

Fortunately, Quicken Personal Finance Software can help. You can save time with its reporting features. By using the tax planning and monitoring tools that are available through Quicken's Tax Center, the next tax season may be a little less stressful. This chapter will show you how.

Tax Information in Accounts and Categories

As mentioned briefly in earlier chapters, Quicken accounts and categories can include information to help you at tax time. This section explains how you include tax information in accounts and categories. Although the tax line items for transfers are set up automatically when the account is created, you can change them if needed. Before you make any changes to the Quicken defaults, however, consult with your tax professional.

Including Tax Information in Accounts

You can include tax information in each account you establish in Quicken. Use the Tax Schedule dialog included with each account to enter the information.

1. Choose Tools | Account List or press CTRL-A to display the Account List window.
2. Click the Edit button that appears to the right of the account name or right-click the account name in the Account Bar and select Edit/Delete Account. (Hidden accounts appear in the More Accounts link in the Account Bar.)
3. In either case, the Account Details dialog appears. At the bottom of the Account Details dialog, click the Tax Schedule button to display the Tax Schedule Information dialog, shown here.

Tax Schedule Information	✕
Tax Schedule Information	

(Optional)
Choose the tax schedules to associate with transfers in this account.

Transfers in: | Form 1040:Other income, misc. ▼
Transfers out: | Form 1040:IRA contribution, self ▼

[?]   OK   Cancel

You will not see the Tax Schedule button if you have turned off the display of the Planning tab. You can turn on the Planning tab using View | Tabs To Show | Planning.

4. Use the Transfers In and Transfers Out drop-down lists to map account activity to specific lines on tax return forms and schedules. In our example, all transfers into the account are miscellaneous income items and track to Form 1040 of the individual tax return, while all transfers out go into an IRA and

will appear on that line of the tax return. You may have to scroll either up or down the drop-down list within the Transfer In or Transfer Out field to find the appropriate tax line item.

 There are a few tax line items set as default for various types of accounts, such as IRAs. Changing the default could cause a problem on your tax return. Be sure to check with your tax professional before changing any default item.

5. When you're finished, click OK twice: once to close the Tax Schedule Information dialog box and again to close the Account Details dialog box. You will return to either the Account List or the main screen, depending on your location when you started the process. Repeat the process for all accounts for which you want to enter tax information.

Keep in mind that if you use the Paycheck Setup feature to account for all payroll deductions, including any retirement plan contributions, you may not have to change the settings for many of your accounts. (That's another good reason to set up your regular paychecks in Quicken. Chapter 7 explains how to do this.) However, as with all things tax related, check with your tax professional.

 Remember, when working with accounts and categories, and especially subcategories, you cannot use names that contain the characters : } / { | ^.

Connecting Tax Information with Categories

Quicken automatically sets tax information for many of the categories it creates. You can see which categories are tax related and which have tax form lines assigned to them in the Category List window, as seen in Figure 14-1. To open the Category List, click Tools | Category List or press CTRL-SHIFT-C.

If this information does not appear, click the Action gear icon at the far right of the Category List (under the New Category button), and ensure Tax Line Item is checked, as seen here. Concentrate on the categories without tax assignments; some of these may require tax information, depending on your situation.

Use the Set Up Category dialog to enter or modify tax information for a category.

1. Open the Category List window by choosing Tools | Category List.

Category	Usage	Type	Description	Group	Tax Line Item	Hide	Action
Shopping	7	Expense	Shopping	Personal ...		☐	
Books	0	Expense	Books	Personal ...		☐	
Clothing	0	Expense	Clothing	Personal ...		☐	
Electronics & Sof...	2	Expense	Electronics & Software	Personal ...		☐	
Hobbies	0	Expense	Hobbies	Personal ...		☐	
Sporting Goods	1	Expense	Sporting Goods	Personal ...		☐	
[Small Business XX...	1	Transfer				☑	
[Small Savings]	1	Transfer				☑	
Tax	0	Expense	Taxes	Personal ...	☑	☐	
Fed	0	Expense	Federal Tax	Personal ...	☑ W-2:Federal tax withheld, self	☐	
Property Tax	0	Expense	Property Tax	Personal ...	☑ Schedule A:Real estate taxes	☐	
State	0	Expense	State Tax	Personal ...	☑ W-2:State tax withheld, self	☐	
Travel	0	Expense	Travel	Personal ...		☐	
Air Travel	0	Expense	Air Travel	Personal ...		☐	
Hotel	0	Expense	Hotel	Personal ...		☐	
Rental Car & Taxi	0	Expense	Rental Car & Taxi	Personal ...		☐	

Figure 14-1 • You can set tax-related items in the Category List.

2. Select the category for which you want to enter or edit tax information to highlight the category.
3. Right-click the category and choose Edit from the context menu.

You can also click the small arrow that appears in the Action column of any category to display the Edit menu.

4. Click Edit to open the New Category dialog and choose the Tax Reporting tab. (If the category is a transfer category, Edit does not appear on the context menu.)
5. If the category's transactions should be included on your tax return as either income or a deductible expense, select the Tax Related Category check box.
6. Then use the Tax Line Item For This Category drop-down list to choose the form or schedule and line for the item. (You can expand this list by selecting the Extended Line Item List option.) A description of the tax line item you chose appears at the bottom of the dialog, as shown next. Keep scrolling to see all of the options.

7. Click Save to return to the Category List. The tax line item you chose appears on the same line as your category, as seen here.

8. Repeat this process for all categories that should be included on your tax return. Keep in mind that you can also enter tax information when you first create a category, as explained in Chapter 4.

Tax Reports

You can make tax time easier with several tax reports included in Quicken. Quicken creates all of these reports from the tax information settings for the accounts and categories in your Quicken data file. You can learn more about Quicken's reporting feature in Chapter 15.

To create a specific report, select Reports | Tax from the menu bar. Choose the name of the report from the menu:

- **Capital Gains** summarizes gains and losses on the sales of investments, organized by the term of the investment (short or long) and the investment account.

- **Tax Schedule** summarizes tax-related transactions, organized by tax form or schedule and line item.
- **Tax Summary** summarizes tax-related transactions, organized by category and date.

Remember, you can start with a standard report, with the default settings and organization, and then customize it to meet your own requirements.

And, if you are using the Quicken Premier (or higher) edition, there are three additional options. All allow you to print reports from which you can enter information directly into the appropriate federal income tax schedules.

- Schedule A–Itemized Deductions
- Schedule B–Interest and Dividends
- Schedule D–Capital Gains and Losses

You can specify any date range for Capital Gains, Tax Schedule, and Tax Summary reports, but for Schedule A, Schedule B, and Schedule D reports, you can only select tax years 2016, 2017, or 2018.

Online Tax Tools

From both within Quicken and online, you have access to a number of tools for tax planning and preparation. Click the Planning tab, and then click the Tax Tools button on the right to open a menu, as seen next. Select Online Tax Tools as shown. The Tax Tools menu shown includes the Itemized Deduction Estimator, the Capital Gains Estimator, and the Tax Withholding Estimator, which are available only in Quicken Premier and higher editions. The Online Tax Tools submenu offers two tax-related features and information sources from the TurboTax.com website to help you with your taxes. All you need to take advantage of these features is your Internet connection.

Tax Center	Savings Goals		Planning Tools ▼	Tax Tools ▼	Reports ▼
			Tax Planner		
			Deduction Finder		
			Itemized Deduction Estimator		
			Capital Gains Estimator		
			Tax Withholding Estimator		
Tax Calculators and common tax questions			Online tax tools	>	
Tax forms and publications			TurboTax	>	

EXPERIENCED USERS RECOMMEND

By taking the time to enter tax information into Quicken, you can save hours of time and maybe even some money. You see, by including tax information in Quicken accounts and categories, you make it possible for Quicken to do several things for you:

- Prepare tax reports that summarize information by tax category or schedule. Take these tax reports to your tax preparer and make it a lot easier for him or her to do your taxes. This might even save you money in tax preparation fees!
- Display tax information in the Tax Center window, which shows an up-to-date summary of your tax situation. Knowing how you stand now helps to prevent surprises at tax time.
- Save time using the Tax Planner, a Quicken feature that uses information from your Quicken data file based on tax information you enter. If you do a little work here, you can save a lot of work later. See "Working with the Tax Planner" later in this chapter.
- Distinguish between taxable and nontaxable investments, so you can create accurate reports on capital gains, interest, and dividends. That way, tax-exempt income and taxable income are separated for preparing your tax returns!
- Use TurboTax to prepare your tax return based on information imported right from your Quicken data file.

So, by spending a few minutes setting up tax information for your accounts and categories, you can save time and money at tax time and know your tax situation all year long.

Here's a quick look at the online tax tools. The next time you're thinking about taxes, be sure to check these out.

Tax Calculators and Common Tax Questions

Using your Internet connection, the Tax Calculators option displays the Intuit TurboTax page, with links to various online tools for making tax and other financial calculations, as shown in Figure 14-2. You will see both video links and links that offer tax guides for specific categories. There are even links to apps for smart phones and social media sites.

Tax Forms and Publications

Using your Internet connection, choosing Tax Forms And Publications opens another TurboTax page from which you can link to both federal and state returns as well as other official IRS forms.

When you click the IRS Forms And Publications link, the Internal Revenue Service site appears from which you can download many federal forms. The forms

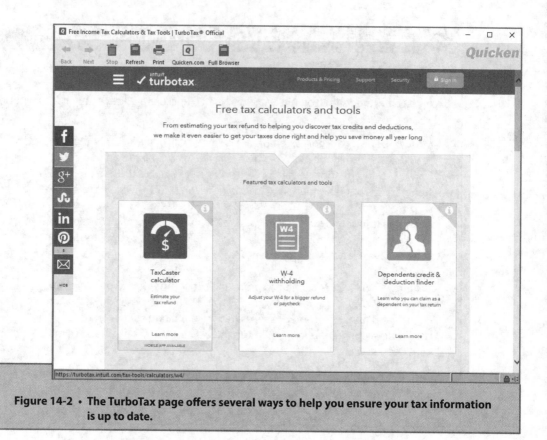

Figure 14-2 • The TurboTax page offers several ways to help you ensure your tax information is up to date.

are Acrobat PDF files that appear in either a web browser window or an Adobe Acrobat Reader window. (You must have the freely distributed Adobe Acrobat Reader software to open and print these forms.) You may fill out some of the forms online and print them from the website, or save them on your computer. Others must be downloaded or printed and then filled out by hand.

Click any state link to go to that state's website, from which you can download your forms. Most states offer additional information and publications on their sites as well as the tax forms. As with the federal forms that you download from the IRS page, most state forms download as Acrobat PDF files.

Adobe Reader is often included with computers you purchase "off the shelf." In Windows 8.1 and Windows 10, press the Start button to view the Start screen and look for the Adobe Reader tile or app. Click Start | All Programs to see if it is already on your computer in Windows 7 or earlier.

About TurboTax

If you're tired of paying a tax preparer to fill out your tax return for you, but you're not quite confident enough about your tax knowledge to prepare your own return by hand, it's time to check out TurboTax online tax-preparation software. It's a great way to simplify tax preparation.

TurboTax works almost seamlessly with Quicken to complete your tax return. Just follow the instructions in this chapter to set up your accounts and categories with tax information. Purchase the TurboTax program either online to be downloaded or the boxed program from your local store. Then, from within TurboTax, import your Quicken data. TurboTax takes you through an easy interview process to make sure you haven't left anything out—much like the interview you might go through with a paid tax professional. TurboTax then calculates the bottom line and makes it possible for you to file the return electronically or print it on your printer.

Using TurboTax

Intuit offers several versions of TurboTax, each of which you can access online. You can learn more about them by opening the Planning tab in Quicken and selecting Tax Tools | TurboTax | File Your Taxes With TurboTax. Using your Internet connection, the link takes you directly to the TurboTax Products and Pricing page.

You can choose from several options. With each option, you can start "for free" from this page. With so many options available, depending on your personal situation, TurboTax programs meet the tax filing requirements of nearly all of us.

All online editions featured on this page require no payment until you file the return. Of course, you can also purchase either a downloadable or a CD version of each program directly from this site.

- **TurboTax Free Basic Edition** is for taxpayers with basic tax preparation needs. It includes just the 1040EZ form.
- **TurboTax Deluxe** can perform tax calculations for taxpayers who own a home, make donations, or have childcare or medical expenses. In other words, most of us. You can also use TurboTax Deluxe for tax calculations for investments.
- **TurboTax Premier** offers all of the functionality of TurboTax Deluxe and includes tax calculations for taxpayers who own stocks, bonds, mutual funds, or rental properties.

- **TurboTax Home & Business** offers all of the functionality of TurboTax Premier and includes tax calculations for small businesses, such as sole proprietorships or single-owner LLCs.
- **TurboTax Business** (click the View CD/Download Products link at the right of the page) provides tax preparation for corporations, partnerships, and multimember LLCs while maximizing business tax deductions. It does not include the means to prepare your personal taxes.

Import TurboTax File

From the Planning tab's Tax Tools menu, select TurboTax | Import TurboTax File to import last year's TurboTax information. Many Quicken and TurboTax users store a copy on an external device, such as an external hard drive or flash drive. This backup copy ensures the safety of the tax information. When it is time to prepare your current year's tax return, you can import the information from either a location on your computer or an external device.

For more information about backups and Quicken, see Appendix A.

Export TurboTax Reports

Use the last two links in the TurboTax submenu to quickly create and send both the Tax Schedule and Capital Gains reports into the TurboTax program. When you choose either of the menu items, a file is created with the .txf extension (i.e., transfer files) and that file can be quickly imported into the TurboTax program.

Planning to Avoid Surprises

One of the best reasons to think about taxes before tax time is to avoid surprises on April 15. Knowing what you will owe before you owe it can help ensure that you pay just the right amount of taxes up front—through proper deductions or estimated tax payments—so you don't get hit with a big tax bill or tax refund.

You may think of a big tax refund as a gift from Uncle Sam. Well, it isn't. The money that Uncle Sam has been using, interest free, for months is actually *your* money. When you overpay your taxes, you're giving up money that you could be using to reduce interest-bearing debt or earn interest or investment income. Making sure you don't overpay taxes throughout the year helps you keep your money where it'll do *you* the most good.

Quicken Personal Finance Software's tax planning features, like the Tax Planner and Tax Withholding Estimator, can help you avoid nasty surprises.

Other built-in tax tools, like the Deduction Finder and Itemized Deduction Estimator, can save you money and help you make smarter financial decisions. From the Planning tab's Tax Tools menu, you will find all of these features. Each tool offers options to help you plan and monitor your tax situation.

Quicken offers built-in tax planning tools that you can use to keep track of your tax situation throughout the year. The Tax Planner helps you estimate your federal income tax bill for the 2016 and 2017 tax years. You can add up to three additional scenarios to your planner to help plan for possible changes in your life. In addition, Quicken provides several estimating tools to help you with your taxes. For example, the Tax Withholding Estimator helps you determine whether your withholding taxes are correctly calculated. Finally, the Tax Center in the Planning tab summarizes your tax situation with a number of useful snapshots. Here's a closer look at each of these features.

Working with the Tax Planner

Quicken's Tax Planner includes features from Intuit's TurboTax tax preparation software to help you estimate your federal income tax bill for the 2017 and 2018 tax years. Although this can help you avoid surprises, it can also help you see how various changes to income and expenses can affect your estimated tax bill.

Opening the Quicken Tax Planner Window

To open the Tax Planner, open the Planning tab and choose Tax Center | Show Tax Planner. You can also click Tax Tools | Tax Planner. (If you don't see Tax Tools, expand your screen.) Read the introductory information to get a clear understanding of what the Tax Planner can do for you and how it works.

If you find yourself using the Tax Planner regularly, consider adding a button for it to your Quicken Toolbar. See Appendix B for more information about customizing your Quicken Toolbar.

Viewing the Tax Planner Summary

To see what data is already entered in the Tax Planner, click the Tax Planner Summary link in the navigation bar on the left side of the Tax Planner window. A summary of income tax–related data, as well as the calculated tax implications, appears as shown in Figure 14-3.

Figure 14-3 · The Tax Planner Summary screen shows the tax-related information you have entered.

The Tax Planner window:

Tax Planner

Reset ▾   Copy   Rates   Compare   Print   How Do I?

Year: 2016
Status: Single
Scenario: Projected

How can Quicken help with Tax planning?
Tax Planner Summary
  Wages
  Interest/Dividend Inc
  Business Income
  Capital Gains
  Other Income
    Schedule E
    Schedule F
  Adjustments
  Deductions
    State/Local Tax
  Exemptions
  Other Tax, Credits
  Withholding
  Tax Payments
Details

Tax Planner Summary

Income

Wages and Salaries	40,500
Interest/Dividend Income	1,088
▶Business Income	0
▶Capital Gains and Losses	0
▶Other Income	12,183
Total Income	53,771

Adjustments

▶Adjustments to Income	5,732
Adjusted Gross Income	48,039

Tax Computation

▶Deductions	11,050
Exemptions	12,150
Taxable Income	24,839
Income Tax	3,262
▶Other Taxes & Credits	0
Total Tax	3,262
Marginal Rate	15.0%
Average Rate	6.7%

Tax Due

Withholding, W-4	4,755
▶Est. Tax Pmts	0
Refund Due	**1,493**

◀ Previous   Next ▶

Entering Tax Planner Data

Data can be entered into the Tax Planner from three different sources:

- TurboTax data can be imported into Quicken. In the main Quicken application window, from the Planning tab, choose Tax Tools | TurboTax | Import TurboTax File. Then use the dialog that appears to locate and import your TurboTax data. You can use this information to project current-year amounts in the Tax Planner.

You can also open the TurboTax import dialog by clicking File | File Import | TurboTax File.

- User-Entered data can override any automatic entries. Use this to enter data that isn't entered any other way or that has not yet been entered into Quicken—such as the $100.00 cash you donated to your local food bank.

(As your tax professional will mention, it is always best to get a receipt for cash donations.)

- Quicken Data is automatically entered into the Tax Planner if you have properly set up your tax-related Quicken categories with appropriate tax return line items, as discussed in "Tax Information in Accounts and Categories" earlier in this chapter.

Here's how it works. Click a link in the navigation bar on the left side of the Tax Planner window or in the Tax Planner Summary screen (refer to Figure 14-3) to view a specific type of income or expense. Then click a link within the window for a specific item. Details for the item appear in the bottom of the window. If the detail information doesn't show, click Show Details to expand the window and show the details. If desired, change the source option and, if necessary, enter an amount.

The options you can choose from vary depending on whether TurboTax data is available or the item has transactions recorded in Quicken. For example, if TurboTax data is not available but transactions have been entered in Quicken, you can either select the User Entered option and enter a value in the Annual Total column or select the Quicken Data option and enter an adjusting value in the Adjustment column. This makes it easy to manually override any automatic entries created by the data you have entered into Quicken.

Repeat this process for any Tax Planner items you want to check or change. The Tax Planner automatically recalculates the impact of your changes.

To reset values quickly to amounts automatically entered by Quicken, choose Reset on the Tax Planner's button bar and click Reset To Quicken Default Values.

Creating Scenarios

The Scenarios feature of the Tax Planner enables you to enter data for multiple scenarios—a "what if" capability that you can use to see tax impacts based on various changes in entry data. For example, suppose you're planning to get married and want to see the impact of the additional income and deductions related to your new spouse. You can use a scenario to see the tax impact without changing your Projected Value scenario.

To use this feature, click the Scenario link in the upper section of the navigation bar on the left side of the Tax Planner window (refer to Figure 14-3). The Tax Planner Options screen appears, as seen next. Click the Scenarios down arrow to choose a different scenario from the drop-down list.

![Tax Planner window screenshot]

If Quicken asks whether you want to copy the current scenario to the scenario you chose, click Yes if that new scenario hasn't yet been created. Choose options from the Tax Year and Filing Status drop-down lists to set the scenario options. Then click the Next link at the bottom of the window to save your scenario settings. If necessary, change the values in the new scenario.

When creating or editing a scenario, you must choose the scenario first before you change the tax year or filing status.

To compare one scenario to another, click the Compare button in the Tax Planner window's button bar. A Tax Scenario Comparisons dialog appears, showing the results of each scenario's calculations. When you're finished viewing the comparative information, click OK to dismiss the dialog.

Finishing Up

When you're finished using the Tax Planner, click the Close button on the title bar. This saves the information you entered and updates the Projected Tax calculations in the Tax Center. (Learn about the Tax Center later in this chapter, in the section "Understanding the Tax Center.")

Meeting the Estimators

You can find some of the most useful tips to aid your tax planning under the Tax Tools button in the Planning tab. From helping you find and itemize your tax deductions to helping you determine your tax refund (or payment), each tool can help you make your tax situation clearer. The more you know about taxes that you must pay, the better you will be able to manage your money to ensure there are funds to pay them.

Minimizing Taxes by Maximizing Deductions

One way to minimize taxes is to maximize your deductions. While Quicken can't help you spend money on tax-deductible items—that's up to you—it can help you identify expenses that may be tax deductible so you don't forget to include them on your tax returns.

Quicken offers two features to help maximize your deductions. The Deduction Finder asks you questions about expenditures to determine if they are tax deductible. The Itemized Deduction Estimator helps make sure you don't forget about commonly overlooked itemized deductions.

Deduction Finder

The Deduction Finder uses another TurboTax feature to help you learn which expenses are deductible. Its question-and-answer interface gathers information from you and then provides information about the deductibility of items based on your answers.

Working with the Deduction Finder Window

To open the Deduction Finder, open the Planning tab and choose Tax Tools | Deduction Finder. An Introduction dialog may appear, as shown next. Read its contents to learn more about Deduction Finder and then click OK.

Introduction to Deduction Finder dialog:

Introduction to Deduction Finder

1) Deduction Finder lets you select from over 100 deductions and find out whether or not you are likely to qualify to take the deduction.

2) Answer some simple yes/no questions for each deduction you are interested in.

3) Based on your answers, Quicken will tell you if you are likely to be eligible for that deduction.

4) Learn more about the deductions or have Quicken automatically set up a category to track expenses related to each deduction.

5) Click the Action Plan tab to print a summary of those deductions you are eligible for and recommend next steps.

☑ Show next time Deduction Finder is started   OK

If you do not want to see the introduction the next time you open the Deduction Finder, clear the Show Next Time Deduction Finder Is Started check box.

Figure 14-4 shows what the Deductions tab of the Deduction Finder window says about the tax implications of paying mortgage interest on a first or second home.

Use the buttons to work with the Deduction Finder window:

- **See Introduction** displays the Introduction window so you can learn more about how Deduction Finder works.
- **Clear Checkmarks** removes the check marks from items for which you have already answered questions.
- **Print** prints a summary of deduction information about all the deductions for which you have answered questions.
- **How Do I?** opens the Quicken Personal Finances Help window, where you can find additional information about using the Deduction Finder.

Finding Deductions

As you have seen, the Deductions tab of the Deduction Finder window uses clearly numbered steps to walk you through the process of selecting deduction types and deductions and then answering questions. It's easy to use. You

---

Figure 14-4 • The Deduction Finder can help determine what items you can deduct on your federal tax return.

need only choose the type of deduction from the drop-down list. As you see, Employee is the first option. Click the downward arrow to see the options in that section. You don't have to answer questions about all the deductions—only the deductions you think may apply to you. When you've finished answering questions about a deduction, the result appears near the bottom of the window. You can then move on to another deduction.

The Summary tab of the window, seen next, summarizes the number of deductions available in each category, the number for which you answered questions, and the number for which you may be eligible to take deductions based on your answers to the questions.

When you've finished answering questions, you can click the Action Plan tab to get more information about the deductions and the things you may need to do to claim them. Although you can read the Action Plan information on-screen, if you answered many questions, you may want to use the Print button on the button bar to print the Action Plan information for reference.

When you have completed your entries and printed your Action Plan, click the Close button to close the Deduction Finder.

Utilizing the Itemized Deduction Estimator

The Itemized Deduction Estimator feature, which is available in the Quicken Premier and higher editions, helps make sure you don't overlook any itemized deductions, specifically the deductions on Schedule A of your tax return, for which you might qualify. It does this by guiding you through a review of deduction ideas and providing the information you need to know to determine whether you may qualify. To get started, open the Planning tab and choose Tax Tools | Itemized Deduction Estimator. The How Can I Maximize My Deductions? window appears. As shown in Figure 14-5, you can select a deduction idea from the navigation bar at the left of the window and an additional dialog appears.

Follow the instructions in the middle column of the Welcome window. You'll be prompted to enter information related to itemized deductions, taxes paid (as seen in Figure 14-5), interest paid, charitable contributions, and other items. The instructions are clear and easy to follow. Each time you enter information that can change your taxes, the Projected Refund Due or Projected Tax Due amount in the lower-right corner of the window changes. Your goal is to get a projected refund due amount as high as possible or a projected tax due amount as low as possible.

None of the entries you make in the Itemized Deduction Estimator feature will affect your Quicken data or any other tax-planning feature within Quicken. Make changes and experiment as much as you like. When you are done, click Close.

Figure 14-5 • In Quicken Premier (and higher editions) find additional Schedule A deductions using the Itemized Deduction Estimator.

Capital Gains Estimator

If you are tracking your investments in Quicken Premier or a higher edition, the Capital Gains Estimator can help you calculate the taxable consequences of selling an investment. See Chapter 11 for a detailed explanation of this tool.

Exploring the Tax Withholding Estimator

Quicken's Tax Withholding Estimator feature, also available in Quicken Premier and higher editions, helps you determine whether your W-4 form has been correctly completed. It does this by comparing your estimated tax bill from the Tax Planner to the amount of withholding tax deducted from your paychecks.

Using the Tax Withholding Estimator Feature

To get started, in the Planning tab, choose Tax Tools | Tax Withholding Estimator. The Am I Under Or Over Withholding? window appears.

Read the information and follow the instructions in the middle column of the window. You'll be prompted to enter information related to withholding taxes. Since the instructions are clear and easy to follow, they're not repeated here. Each time you enter data, the Projected Refund Due or Projected Tax Due amount in the lower-right corner of the window changes. If a refund is due, you will see a message telling you that you may be overwithholding. Consider increasing the deductions you claim on your W-4 at work if the refund number is sizeable.

None of the entries you make in the Tax Withholding Estimator feature affect your Quicken data or any other tax planning feature within Quicken, so don't be afraid to experiment.

Acting on the Results of Tax Withholding Estimator Calculations

What do you do with this information once you have it? Well, suppose your work with the Tax Withholding Estimator feature tells you that you should change your W-4 allowances from 1 to 2 to avoid overpaying federal withholding taxes. You can act on this information by completing a new W-4 form at work. This will decrease the amount of withholding tax in each paycheck. The result is that you reduce your tax overpayment and potential refund.

In some states, changing your federal withholding allowances on your W-4 changes your state withholding as well. Be careful you do not end up under withholding your state taxes if you change your federal withholding rate.

Periodically Checking Withholding Calculations

If you are entering all of your information into Quicken, including your paycheck information, consider using the Tax Withholding Estimator feature every three months or so to make sure actual amounts are in line with projections throughout the year. Whenever possible, use actual values rather than estimates in your calculations. And be sure to act on the results of the calculations by filing a new W-4 form, especially if the amount of your projected refund due or projected tax due is greater than you anticipated. Click Close to close the Tax Withholding Estimator.

Understanding the Tax Center

Quicken summarizes all information about your tax situation in the Tax Center, as seen in Figure 14-6. Here's a quick look at what you can find in the Tax Center window.

Projected Tax

The Projected Tax snapshot provides a summary of your upcoming projected tax return, including the amount that you'll have to pay or get back as a refund. If any items in the Projected Tax section need to be completed, a small flag will appear to the left of the item.

Show Tax Planner		
∨ Projected Tax	⚙	**∨ Tax Calendar** ⚙
Filing Status	Married-Joint	10/15/2016 Tax returns are due for the first extension
Tax Year	2017	12/31/2016 Last day to establish a Keogh plan
Wages/Salary (self)	40,500	1/14/2017 Quarterly estimated taxes are due
Wages/Salary (spouse)	0	1/29/2017 You should have received W-2 forms
Interest/Dividend Income	0	1/29/2017 You should have received 1099 forms
Business Income	0	1/29/2017 Early filing deadline
Capital Gains/Losses	0	2/13/2017 Last day to continue tax exemption status
Other Income	0	2/26/2017 Forms W-2 and W-3 for household employees are due
Total Income	0	4/15/2017 Income tax returns are due
Adjustments to Income	0	4/15/2017 Last day to make qualified IRA contributions
Adjusted Gross Income	0	4/15/2017 Last day to get an extension on your taxes
Deductions (Itemized Deduct...	12,600	4/15/2017 Quarterly estimated taxes are due
Exemptions	8,100	Set Up Alerts
Taxable Income	0	
Other Taxes and Credits	0	**∨ Tax-Related Expenses YTD** ⚙
Total Tax	0	Education:Student Loan 732.00
Marginal Tax Rate	10.0%	
Average Tax Rate	0.0%	
Withholding/W-4	0	Assign Tax Categories Show Tax Schedule Report
Estimated Tax Payments	0	

Figure 14-6 · The Tax Center displays information about your current tax situation.

The information in this snapshot is based on the Tax Planner's Projected scenario, discussed earlier in this chapter. From the Options menu in the Projected Tax section of the Tax Center you can

- Open the Tax Planner.
- Create a Tax Summary Report. This report can also be created by clicking the Show Tax Summary Report button at the bottom of the Projected Tax section of the Tax Center.

Watch for small red flags that appear to the left of any item in the Projected Tax snapshot. Quicken is warning you that this item may not be complete.

Tax Calendar

The Tax Calendar snapshot warns you of upcoming IRS tax deadlines. From here you can create Tax Alerts from either the Options menu or the Set Up Alerts button at the bottom of the section.

While quarterly estimated taxes are due on January 15, April 15, June 15, and September 15, if those dates fall on a holiday or a weekend, the actual payment is due the next working day.

Tax-Related Expenses YTD

The Tax-Related Expenses YTD snapshot summarizes all of your year-to-date tax-related expenses. Quicken automatically calculates this information based on the transactions you enter throughout the year. All expense categories that are marked "tax-related" and have transactions appear in this list. The Options available from this section are as follows:

- **Find Other Deductions** opens the Deduction Finder, explained in the section "Deduction Finder" earlier in this chapter.
- **How Will These Deductions Affect My Taxes?** opens the Tax Planner.
- **Create A Tax Schedule Report** opens a report for the current tax year showing information and schedules for the Form 1040, as well as Schedules A and B. In Quicken Premier and higher editions, Schedules A and B reports for tax-related categories are included.
- **Link Categories To Tax Forms** opens the Category List so that you can associate categories with specific tax-line items as explained in "Including Tax Information in Accounts" earlier in this chapter.
- **Go To Category List** opens the Category List.

The Assign Tax Categories button at the bottom of this section opens the Category List. The Show Tax Schedule Report button opens the report described earlier.

Taxable Income YTD

The Taxable Income YTD snapshot summarizes all of your year-to-date tax-related income. Quicken calculates these totals based on the transactions you enter throughout the year. All income categories that are marked "tax-related" and have transactions appear in this snapshot. If you have chosen to enter your net paycheck and have not told Quicken that this amount is tax related, nothing will appear in this list except a link to set up your paycheck.

If you have any non–paycheck-related taxable income, such as dividend income from investments, the Taxable Income YTD snapshot will not be blank.

The Options menu of this section of the Tax Center offers the following options:

- **Report My Net Worth** creates a net worth report as of the current date. See Chapter 15 for more information about net worth reports.
- **How Does This Income Affect My Taxes?** opens the Tax Planner.
- **Go To Category List** opens the Category List.

The Add Paycheck button at the bottom of the section opens the Paycheck Setup dialog. The process is explained in detail in Chapter 7.

Tax Alerts

Tax alerts are only visible in the Alerts Center, which is where you go to set alerts related to your tax situation. You can access the Tax Alerts feature through the Options menu in the Tax Calendar or from the menu bar by choosing Tools | Alerts Center | Setup. In the Setup dialog, you have three options related to taxes.

If necessary, click the plus sign to the left of the Taxes item in the Alerts Center's Setup tab to expand the tax-related alerts.

- **Withholding Threshold** enables you to set a value of dollars withheld from your paycheck to alert you if your payroll withholding is too much or not enough. However, this alert only works when you set up your paycheck in Quicken.
- **Schedule A – Personal Deductions (Schedule-A Reminder)** displays information about the types of personal deductions you can claim on Schedule A of your tax return.

- **Important Tax Dates** notifies you in advance of tax calendar events, such as estimated tax due dates and extension deadlines.

Learn more about setting alerts in Chapter 7.

You can also see tax alerts in the Alerts snapshot that you can add to your Main View on the Home tab or into another view you create on the Home tab.

Creating Quicken Reports

Chapter 15

In This Chapter:

- *Reviewing report and graph types*

- *Creating reports and graphs*

- *Working with a report window*

- *Customizing reports and graphs*

- *Working with subreports*

- *Saving reports and graphs*

- *Exporting your reports*

- *Printing reports and graphs*

After you have downloaded or entered your financial data, you may need to see an explanation of your current position. Quicken offers a variety of reports and graphs, each of which can be customized to meet your needs. After data is entered into Quicken, Quicken crunches the numbers for you, provides reports and graphs to analyze your spending habits, helps you find ways to save money, helps when you prepare your taxes, and formats your data to submit information to financial institutions when you apply for loans or credit cards.

Quicken Reports Overview

Although the Reports button in the Spending tab offers nine reports that you can create dealing with spending and income, many other reports are available throughout Quicken. You can access reports from the Reports button in both the Planning and Investing tabs as well as the Reports & Graphs Center. In this chapter, you'll learn about the various types of reports and graphs Quicken offers. Then you'll learn how you can use a variety of techniques to quickly create reports and graphs based on the information in your Quicken data file, regardless of where it appears.

Reviewing Report and Graph Types

Within Quicken are two kinds of reports and graphs: the Quicken standard reports and those you can customize to meet your needs. By starting with any of Quicken's standard reports you can design reports and graphs to reflect the information you want to see. Here's an overview of each type of report.

Standard Quicken Reports

When you click Reports on the menu bar, Quicken displays a number of standard reports and graphs, organized by topic: Banking, Comparison, Investing, Net Worth & Balances, Spending, Tax, EasyAnswer, and Graphs, as well as links to the Reports & Graphs Center and Credit Score.

This section discusses standard reports found in the Deluxe and Premier editions of Quicken 2017. If you are using the Home & Business or Rental Property Manager edition of Quicken, there are even more reports available for your use.

EXPERIENCED USERS RECOMMEND

Many Quicken users have found that reports and graphs are their reward for taking the time to download, enter, and reconcile their accounts. You can quickly create a report of everything you've spent on cell phone bills since the first of the year, for example, or summarize the total income from your second job.

Your tax preparer may appreciate you even more when you next walk in the office with a complete list of all of your income and every expense—including your itemized charitable contributions, and property tax amounts. Those reports may even save you some money when that tax person sends your bill!

For example, the Banking report options include Banking Summary, Cash Flow, Cash Flow By Tag, Missing Checks, Reconciliation, and Transaction reports that clearly contain your banking-related information. EasyAnswer reports and graphs, as seen next, answer specific, predefined questions, such as, "Where did

I spend my money during the period…?" and "How much did I spend on…?" You select a question and then provide optional information, such as a date range, payee, or account. Quicken gathers the information and generates the report or graph.

Customized and Saved Reports

You create custom reports and graphs based on standard reports and graphs. This multiplies your reporting capabilities, enabling you to create reports or graphs that show exactly what you need to show. When you save your custom reports and graphs, they can be recalled with just a few mouse clicks to display current information.

EXPERIENCED USERS RECOMMEND

Recently a new user asked how to find the beginning and ending balances on his transaction report from last month. When he looked at the report again, he saw that the beginning balance for the account (or accounts when including more than one bank account) is shown at the top of the report and the ending balance shows on the bottom line entitled "Balance." You may find as well that most of the Quicken reports do have the information you need—you just have to look a bit at the report you've created.

Another person asked why one of her checks showed up in the Income category of her report. When she double-clicked that transaction, she found she had entered that check into the register with an income category rather than an expense category. Once she found the error, it was easily corrected—she just had to change the category.

Creating Reports and Graphs

With Quicken, creating a report or graph is as simple as clicking a few buttons. You can use several techniques: choosing a report or graph from the Reports menu, setting options in the Reports And Graphs window, using the Reports button, and choosing commands from contextual menus. In this section, you'll learn to use all of these techniques.

Reports & Graphs Center

The Reports And Graphs window (see Figure 15-1) offers one way to create reports and graphs. Open the Spending, Planning, or Investing tab, and from the Reports button, choose All Reports | Reports & Graphs Center to display it. You can also access the Reports & Graphs Center from the Quicken menu bar by clicking Reports | Reports & Graphs Center.

Consider adding the Reports & Graphs Center icon to your Quicken Toolbar to open the center without using menus.

Reports and Graphs	— □ ✕
	Preferences ? How Do I?

Quicken Standard Reports

- Itemized Categories
- Itemized Payees
- Itemized Tags
- Spending by Category
- Spending by Payee
- Current Spending vs. Average Spending by Category
- Current Spending vs. Average Spending by Payee
- Income and Expense by Category
- Income and Expense by Payee
- Current Budget
- Historical Budget

▶ Comparison
▼ Investing

- Capital Gains
- Investing Activity
- Investment Asset Allocation
- Investment Income
- Investment Performance
- Investment Transactions
- Maturity Dates for Bonds and CDs
- Portfolio Value
- Portfolio Value and Cost Basis

▶ Tax
▶ Net Worth & Balances
▶ EasyAnswer

My Saved Reports

- Cash Flow

[Manage Toolbar Reports]   [Manage Saved Reports]

Figure 15-1 • Use the Reports & Graphs Center to create both written and graphic reports.

Click one of the sections in any of the Quicken Standard Reports sections to display a list of the available reports and graphs seen in Figure 15-1. The icon that appears to the left of the report name indicates what you are choosing. Those items that have both the graph and the report symbols to their left let you choose between the two when you create the report.

To create a standard report or graph, click its name. Set the Date Range option in the settings field. Click the Customize button to further customize the report or graph, as explained in the section "Customizing Reports and Graphs." Then click Show Report or Show Graph to display the report or graph. Figure 15-2 shows an example of the report we created.

Figure 15-2 • Quicken's standard reports display your financial picture with only a mouse click.

The All Reports Menu

In the Spending, Planning, and Investing tabs, you see a Reports button from which you can open the All Reports menu. This menu is the same as the menu you see in the Reports option on the Quicken menu bar.

To create a report or graph from the All Reports menu, click a topic submenu, and then click a report name. Quicken creates the report with default date settings, usually the current year to date, as seen earlier in Figure 15-2. Click Reports & Graphs Center from the All Reports submenu to go directly to the Reports & Graphs Center. Sort within reports with the drop-down lists.

 You can set the default date range in Preferences. Click Edit | Preferences | Reports And Graphs and then set the dates you want in the Default Date Range and Default Comparison Date Range.

If you start creating reports and find that you often want to change settings or adapt the report in some way, you can tell Quicken to open the customization dialog at the time you select a report to create. To set this preference, click Edit | Preferences | Reports And Graphs; then, from the Customizing Reports And Graphs section, click Customize Report/Graph Before Creating, as shown next. Click OK to close the Preferences dialog. Then, the next time you want to

---

Preferences   ✕

Select preference type: Select preferences:

Startup   **Reports and Graphs preferences**
Navigation
Setup   ┌─Default date range──────────────────────┐
Calendar and currency   │ Last 12 months ▼ from: 1/10/2016 to: 1/9/2017 │
Backup   └──┘
Web Connect
Alerts   ┌─Default comparison date range───────────┐
Investment transactions   │ Prior year perioc ▼ from: 1/10/2015 to: 1/9/2016 │
Investing.Quicken.com portfolio   └──┘
Register
Data entry and QuickFill   ┌─Report toolbar──────────────────────────┐
Notify   │ ⦿ Show icons and text   ◯ Show icons only │
Write checks   └──┘
Downloaded transactions
Transfer detection   ┌─Customizing reports and graphs──────────┐
Reports and Graphs   │ ⦿ Customizing creates new report or graph │
Reports only   │ ◯ Customizing modifies current report or graph │
Intuit ID, Mobile & Alerts   │ ☑ Customize report/graph before creating │
                                     └──┘

                                     ☑ Cash-basis reporting if applicable

 ?   OK   Cancel create a report, the Customize dialog will appear before the report displays. Learn more about customization in the "Customizing Reports and Graphs" section later in this chapter.

Reports from Other Menus

You can also create a report by using the menus in certain windows. This normally creates a report based on information selected within the window. For example, you could create a Register report for a specific account. From the register for that account, click the Action gear icon and choose More Reports | Register Report, as seen next.

A mini-report button also appears in an account register window when you activate the Payee or Category field. Clicking this button displays a pop-up mini-report of recent activity for the payee or category. Clicking the Show Report button in the mini-report opens a report window with the information. And if you hover your mouse over the word "Split" in a transaction, the mini-report icon is available from each separate category.

Contextual Menus

The contextual menu that appears when you right-click while pointing to an item sometimes includes a command that will create a report for the item. For example, right-clicking the name of a payee in the account register window displays a context menu that includes the Payments Made To and Launch Mini-Report For Payee *nnnnn* options at the bottom of that context menu. If you right-click a deposit's payee, the report will be Payments Received From.

You can also create a report from almost all Quicken screens by using the shortcut CTRL-P or File | Print *nnnnn,* where *nnnnn* is the Quicken screen. As with the other report types, you can print a hard copy, print to a PDF file, or "print" to a tab-delimited file that you can use in Excel.

Working with Reports and Graphs

Although Quicken's standard reports and graphs often provide just the information you need, you may want to do more with them. In this section, you will see how you can customize reports and graphs, save the reports and graphs you create so they're easy to recall, and print reports and graphs so you have hard copies when you need them.

Working with a Report Window

When you create a report or graph, it appears in a report window, as seen in Figure 15-2. Each report or graph has a number of features and options, discussed next, with which you can customize the report to meet your specific needs.

Toolbar Icons

The report window includes a number of toolbar icons, shown here, that work with report contents:

Spending by Category								— □ ✕
Back	History	Forward	Delete		Print	Export	Save	Find/Replace Customize Help

- The **Back** arrow returns you to the Reports & Graphs Center when you have created your report from that center. The arrow does not appear if you have created your report from a Reports button within the Spending, Planning, or Investment tab. If you have created a subreport, you may see both forward and back arrows.
- The **History** icon displays a list of the parent report and all subreports you have created. Click the History icon and select the name of a subreport to display it. Choose the Show Report List option to display the Report History navigation bar. This is a list of all of the subreports related to the current report. Click the Hide Report List to close the navigation bar.
- The **Forward** arrow is available only if you have clicked the Back button, and it allows you to move through subreports.
- The **Delete** icon deletes the report from the current Report History List. This button is gray if the report has not been added to the report list. See more about the report list in the section "Saving Reports and Graphs," later in this chapter.
- Click the **Print** icon to send the report or graph to the printer or a file.
- Click the **Export** icon to display a menu. From this menu, you can export the contents of the current report in several ways. See "Exporting Your Reports" later in this chapter.
- Select the **Save** icon to save the current report. See "Saving Reports and Graphs" later in this chapter for more information.
- The **Find/Replace** icon opens the Find And Replace dialog. See Chapter 5 for more information about using Find And Replace.
- Use the **Customize** icon, which looks like a small gear, to use the Customize dialog to tailor the currently displayed report.
- The last item on this toolbar is the familiar question mark **Help** icon.

Hiding or Displaying Report Detail

You can show or hide the details for some reports by clicking a plus (+) or minus (–) button beside a report line. Some reports include additional items that allow you to change what appears on the current report without using the Customize dialog. These items appear under the report title and include

- The **Expand All** and **Collapse All** buttons do the same thing as the plus and minus signs by individual categories, but for all groups in that report.
- The **Edit** drop-down list, which displays in transactions reports, allows you to:
  - Resolve a placeholder in an investment transaction report (if any exist).
  - Delete a selected transaction (or a group of transactions). Note that this process deletes the transaction from both the report and the account register.

- Recategorize the selected transaction (or group).
- Retag the selected transaction or group of transactions.
- Rename selected payees.
- Edit transaction memos.

 When you double-click a transaction shown on a report, Quicken opens that transaction in the appropriate account register. You can return to the report by clicking the report's name at the bottom of the register.

- **Date Range**, **Column**, **Sort By**, and **Subtotal By** fields allow you to change the focus of the current report. What you see in a report varies according to type.
- **Show/Hide Graph** and **Show/Hide Report** toggles allow you to show and hide either the graph or the report.
- **Update To Show** offers additional options for the report you've run.

EXPERIENCED USERS RECOMMEND

When you see Uncategorized as a category or payee on any report, double-click the amount to drill down to each transaction so that you can add a category or payee. Because many financial institutions download checks without your category, you may have quite a number of uncategorized transactions in one report. As explained in Chapter 6, ensure that you review each downloaded transaction and categorize it if necessary.

Not only do you have to categorize the checks you download, it's very likely your checks will download without a payee name. It's far easier to recall the payee and category as you write the checks than it is to do it days or even weeks later. Instead of waiting for the check transactions to download, enter your checks in your account register as you write them. You'll capture the payee and category, and your account balance will be more accurate. Then when the check clears, the downloaded transaction will match the transaction you entered.

Spending Trends

A useful tool you will see in some Quicken reports is the Spending Trend report. You see the symbol (shown here) in both the Spending by Payee and Spending by Category reports. Click the Spending Trend symbol to the left of a category or payee to see a small graph, also shown next, that shows the trend for this category or payee over the last year. Click Done to close the graph and return to your report.

To choose only one bank for a report, use the Accounts tab in the Customize dialog and clear the check marks from all the other accounts.

Customizing Reports and Graphs

You can customize just about any report or graph you create so it displays only the information you choose. Customization options vary from one type of report or graph to another, so it is impossible to cover all variables in this chapter. Here are the most common options so you know what to expect. When you can customize it, however, depends on how you create it.

When you create a report or graph using the Reports And Graphs window (refer to Figure 15-1), you can customize it before or after you create it.

When you create a report using other commands, you may be able to customize it only after you have created it, unless you have set your preferences to always display the Customize dialog.

 EasyAnswer reports do not display a Customize button when you use the Reports & Graphs Center to create them; however, once the report is displayed on your screen, the Customize icon is available from the toolbar.

 You can adjust the columns on many reports by placing your mouse cursor on the line between headings. A small horizontal arrow appears. Hold down your left mouse button and drag the line to the left or right as you require.

Using the Customize Dialog

To customize a report or graph, click the Customize button in the options area for the report or graph in the Reports And Graphs window or the Customize button at the top of the report window (refer to Figure 15-2). The Customize dialog, as shown next, appears. The dialog's full name includes the name of the report or graph.

The Customize dialog includes up to seven tabs of options that you can set to customize the report:

- **Display** enables you to set display options for the report, such as the title, row and column headings, organization, number formatting, and columns.
- **Accounts** lets you select the accounts that should be included in the report. Quicken will include transactions or balances in this report for only the accounts you specify.
- From **Categories**, you can select the categories to include in the report. If you choose, you can use this tab to include only transactions for which the payee, category, or memo contains certain text.
- The **Payees** tab shows options from which you can select the payees to include in the report. If desired, you can use this tab to include only transactions for which the category, payee, or memo contains certain text.
- The **Tags** tab lets you select the tags you want to show in your report.

To include hidden tags, categories, and other items, you will have to unhide them in their respective sections.

 When working with split transactions where some items have tags and others do not, ensure you have cleared the Not Tagged check box in the Tags tab in the Customize dialog so that the nontagged items are not included in your report.

- If you have created any category groups, you may also see a Category Groups tab in Summary, Comparison, or Budget reports. See Chapter 4 for more information about creating this type of group.
- The **Advanced** tab offers different options, depending on the standard report with which you are working. For example, you can set additional criteria for transactions to be included in the report, such as amount, status, and transaction type. It is also from this Advanced tab that you can tell Quicken to exclude all transfers you make between your accounts, as seen next.

Q Customize Spending by Category	×

Date range: Year to date ▾   From: 1/1/2016   To: 11/30/2016

Display	Accounts	Categories	Payees	Tags	Category Groups	**Advanced**

Transactions

Amounts: All ▾

Status
☑ Not cleared
☑ Newly cleared
☑ Reconciled

☑ Tax-related transactions only
Transaction types: All transactions ▾

Transfers: Exclude all ▾
Subcategories: Show all ▾

☑ Show me change alerts for this rep

[Show Report] [Show Graph] [Cancel]

- The **Securities** tab, available on some reports, allows you to choose the securities you want included in the report. From this tab, you can also instruct Quicken to include hidden securities.
- The **Actions** tab, seen in the Investment Income and Investment Transactions reports, lets you opt to display only certain investment actions you have taken, such as purchases or sales.

- The **Security Types** tab, again only available in some investment reports, lets you determine which security type is displayed on the report.
- The **Investing Goals** tab allows you to create a report that displays the current status of your various investing goals.

Once you have set options as desired, click the Show Report or Show Graph button as necessary.

Some of the investing and tax schedule reports are available only in the Premier or higher editions of Quicken.

If the custom report or graph isn't exactly what you want, that's okay. Just click the Customize button in the report or graph window and change settings in the Customize dialog to fine-tune the report or graph. When you click OK, Quicken creates a new report. You can repeat this process until the report or graph is exactly the way you want it.

Using QuickZoom

Quicken's QuickZoom feature helps you create a report or graph on the fly. Simply double-click a report line item, graph bar, or legend item. Quicken generates and displays a subreport for the item you double-clicked. Click the Back arrow to return to your original report.

Working with Subreports

Each time you make changes to an existing report or graph or create a QuickZoom report, Quicken creates a subreport. As you can imagine, it's easy to accumulate quite a few of these subreports when experimenting with Quicken's reporting features. This can be reduced somewhat by changing your preference settings. Select Edit | Preferences | Reports And Graphs | Customizing Reports And Graphs, and select Customizing Modifies Current Report Or Graph. Click OK to close the Preferences dialog.

To view a specific subreport, choose its name from the History menu in the report window's toolbar. The view changes to the report. You can also choose Show Report List from the History menu in the toolbar to display the Report History List. Click the name of the report you want to view to display it.

You can click the Back or Forward button at the top of the navigation bar to move among subreports you have already viewed.

To delete a subreport, display it and then click the Delete icon in the toolbar. You can also delete any subreport (other than the first one in the report list) by

right-clicking the subreport name in the Report History List and selecting Delete
This Report from the context menu.

Saving Reports and Graphs

You may customize a predefined report to create a report you want to be able to
see again and again. Rather than creating and customizing the report from scratch
each time you want to see it, you can save the report's settings. Then, when you
want to view the report again, just select it from a list and it appears. You can do
the same for graphs.

Saving a Report or Graph

To save a report or graph, start by creating, customizing, and displaying it. When
it looks just the way you want, click the Save icon in the report window's toolbar.
The Save Report dialog appears as seen here.

Enter a name and description for the report or graph in the appropriate boxes.
To save the report or graph in a specific folder, choose the folder name from the
Save In drop-down list. You can create a new folder by clicking the Create New
Report Folder option, which appears on the Save In drop-down list. Enter a name
for the folder in the dialog that appears, and click OK. To save all versions of the
report that you create, select the Save Report History check box. When you're
finished setting options, click OK to save the report.

Viewing a Saved Report or Graph

When you save a report or graph, it appears in a number of places throughout Quicken, organized by folder if you have saved them into specific folders. Your saved reports and graphs appear in the My Saved Reports area of the Reports And Graphs window, as seen in Figure 15-3. Click the name of the report or graph, change the date range if you choose, and click Show Report or Show Graph to display it.

Saved reports and graphs also appear on the Reports menu as My Saved Reports & Graphs. (This submenu appears only if at least one report has been saved.) Choose a report name to display it. If you have a lot of saved reports, you will see an item, More Saved Reports & Graphs, which you can click to open the Reports And Graphs window.

Working with Saved Reports

Quicken offers two tools for managing saved reports: the Manage Saved Reports and Manage Toolbar Reports dialogs. When you choose the Reports & Graphs Center from the menu and look at the My Saved Reports pane, you will see one or two buttons at the bottom of the pane: Manage Toolbar Reports and Manage Saved Reports, as referenced in Figure 15-3.

Manage Toolbar Reports   When you click the Manage Toolbar Reports button, its dialog appears. This dialog allows you to add saved reports to the Quicken

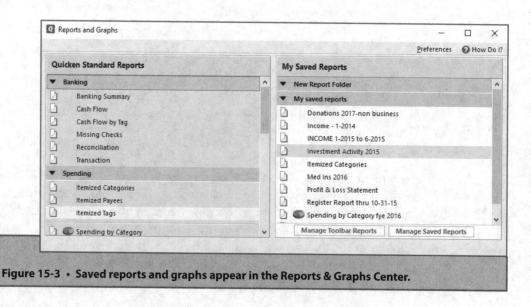

Figure 15-3 · Saved reports and graphs appear in the Reports & Graphs Center.

Toolbar for easy access, as seen next. (This option appears only when you have chosen to show the Quicken Toolbar. Click View | Show Toolbar if you do not see this button on the My Saved Reports pane of the Reports And Graphs dialog.)

In the dialog, click the check box of each report you want to show as an icon in the Quicken Toolbar. Then, click OK to save your settings. You will see the icon on your toolbar. If the name is long, the entire name may not appear. (If you do not see the text for your report's icon, right-click in the toolbar and choose Customize Toolbar | Show Icons And Text. Click Done to close the Customize Toolbar dialog.)

If you have created your own folders for your saved reports, as described next in "Manage Saved Reports," you can choose to have one or more of those folders display on the Quicken Toolbar as well. When you click a saved report folder icon on the toolbar, it will appear as a pop-up menu button that lists the reports within it. Learn more about customizing the Quicken Toolbar in Appendix B.

Manage Saved Reports   The Manage Saved Reports dialog, shown next, enables you to organize saved reports by folder, edit report settings, or delete reports. Select the item you want to work with in the report list, and click the appropriate button.

- **Create Folder** displays the Create New Report Folder dialog. Enter a name for the folder in the Name box, and click OK. The folder appears in the list.
- **Move To Folder** displays the Move To Report Folder dialog. When you select a report from the list, this button becomes available. Click the Move To Folder button to open the dialog, and select a different folder from the Name drop-down list. Click OK when you've made your choice, and the report is moved to that folder.
- Select a current folder, and the **Rename Folder** button becomes available. From the dialog that appears when you click this button, enter a new name for the folder in the Name box and click OK. The folder's name changes.
- When you have selected one of the saved reports, the **Edit** button is available for use. This button allows you to enter a new name and description for the report. Click OK to save your changes.
- **Delete** removes any selected item. When you click this button, a confirmation dialog appears. You must click OK to delete the item permanently. Remember, when you delete a folder you are deleting all the items in that folder. Should you want to save any of the items, move them before deleting the folder.
- **Done** closes the Manage Saved Reports dialog and returns you to the Reports And Graphs window.

Exporting Your Reports

Another method of working with your reports is to export them into other formats or programs. From your report's toolbar, choose the Export icon to view this menu. As you can see, there are three choices, each of which is explained in the sections that follow.

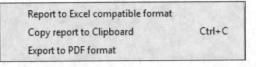

Report To Excel Compatible Format

Use this option to save your report into a .txt file that can be used with the Microsoft Office Excel program. The file is saved as a tab-delimited file with the file extension .txt. To save your file in this format:

1. From the Export menu, choose Report To Excel Compatible Format to open the Create Excel Compatible File dialog.
2. Browse to find the folder into which you want to save this file, and click that folder.

Enter a name for your file, and click Save. The file will have a .txt extension. The new file is saved into the folder you designated, and you are returned to your report window. A small message appears telling you the export was successful and notes the location of the Excel file. See "Work with Your Saved Excel File" next to see how to open the file in Excel.

Work with Your Saved Excel File

Once you have saved the file, you can work with it in Microsoft Excel. To do so:

1. Open Microsoft Excel. (The illustrations in this section refer to Microsoft Excel 2016, but the application works in similar ways with earlier versions.)
2. Click File | Open. Choose Text Files instead of All Excel Files as the type of file for which you want Excel to look. Locate the folder into which you saved your file. When the folder opens, select the file you saved and click Open. The Text Import Wizard appears.

Text Import Wizard - Step 1 of 3   ?   ✕

The Text Wizard has determined that your data is Delimited.

If this is correct, choose Next, or choose the data type that best describes your data.

Original data type

  Choose the file type that best describes your data:
    ⦿ Delimited   - Characters such as commas or tabs separate each field.
    ◯ Fixed width - Fields are aligned in columns with spaces between each field.

Start import at row: 1 ⬍   File origin: 437 : CEM United States   ⌄

☐ My data has headers.

Preview of file \\BOBBI-PC\Users\Public\123.TXT.

```
1 Cash Flow - Last quarter
2
3 7/1/2016 through 9/30/2016
4
5 Category7/1/2016- 9/30/2016
```

Cancel   < Back   Next >   Finish

3. Ensure that Delimited is selected. Normally, this is the default option. Click Next.
4. Make sure that Tab is selected from the Delimiters column. Click Next to continue.
5. At the last step, choose General and then click Finish to complete the import.

Your Excel worksheet appears, as seen next. You may have to make the columns wider to see the information on the report. If so, place your cursor on the line between the column letters and drag to the right.

You may also have to format the numbers to display as dollars and cents. To do this, highlight the cells with numbers in them and click the $ tool on the ribbon. Save the file in an Excel format. To do so:

1. Click File.
2. Click Save As. From the Save As dialog, choose an Excel Workbook format and click Save.

Copy Report to Clipboard

Use this option to copy the report into another Windows program. Quicken sets your keyboard shortcuts to the Windows Standard, so you can also use the keyboard shortcut CTRL-C as shown on the menu. To "paste" this report into another program, use the keyboard shortcut CTRL-V. You can even use this method to copy the report into Excel, a much easier process than the one Quicken recommends.

To verify the Windows Standard keyboard shortcuts are set as your preference, click Edit | Preferences | Setup | Keyboard Mappings to see that Windows Standard is selected.

Export to PDF Format

PDF stands for Portable Document Format. This format, patented by Adobe Systems, allows the reader to view and/or print a document from nearly any computer or word processor. This option is particularly useful if you are saving the report to e-mail it or sharing the file with someone who does not have either Quicken or Microsoft Office. To save as a .pdf file:

1. From the Export menu, click Export To PDF Format.
2. The Print dialog appears. In the Printer field you will see "Quicken PDF Printer on *nnnn*" rather than your regular printer.
3. Click Print. The Save To PDF File dialog appears. Locate the folder into which you want to save your file, type a name, and click Save. Your file is now saved with a .pdf extension.

Printing Reports and Graphs

One of the best things about reports and graphs is the ability to print and share them with others. You can create hard copies for your paper files, you can print a copy to take to your tax professional (and make that person very happy), or you can include professional reports with a loan application.

To print a report, subreport, or graph, begin by displaying it in the report window. Then click the Print icon on the window's toolbar. The Print dialog appears, as seen in Figure 15-4. Set options as desired and click Print.

Here's a look at the available options:

- **Print To** options determine the destination of the printed report or graph. You have two choices:
  - **Printer** prints to the printer you choose from the drop-down list, which includes all printers, faxes, and related devices you have set up in Windows.
  - **Export To** makes it possible to export the report information in one of three formats you choose from the drop-down list: Text File, Tab-Delimited (Excel-Compatible) Disk File, or PRN (123-Compatible) Disk File. This option is only available if you are printing a report.
- **Print Range** determines which pages will print. You can use this if the printed report is more than one page. The default setting is All, which prints

Figure 15-4 • Printing reports means you can share your financial information with other authorized entities.

all pages of the report. To print a range of pages, select Pages and then enter the page numbers for the page range you want to print.

- **Copies** determines how many copies of the report will print. If you enter a value greater than 1, you can select the Collate check box to collate the copies as they are printed.

- **Page Scaling** options enable you to resize a report or graph to a specific percentage or to fit on a certain number of pages. These options are only available for certain printers.

- **Print What** lets you toggle between two check boxes to determine whether to print a graph or report or both. The available options depend on what's in the report window.

- **Orientation** determines how the printed report will be viewed. The options are Portrait or Landscape. These are standard options offered by all programs. The icon beside each orientation option illustrates it.

- **Ink Color** allows you to choose between three options to determine the ink color and quality of the printout: Color (available only if a color printer is selected from the Printer drop-down list), Grayscale, or Draft.
- **Fonts** lets you use the two Change Font buttons to change the header and body typefaces of the report or graph. Clicking the button displays the Font dialog, which you can use to set standard font options, such as font, size, and style.
- **Preview** shows a thumbnail preview of the document. You can click the buttons in the Viewing Page area to scroll through all pages of the report. To change the margins for the document, click the Adjust Margins button. The Preview area changes to offer boxes for entering margin values. To view a full-size preview, click the thumbnail in this area or click the Preview button at the bottom of the dialog.
- **Viewing Page** dialog allows you to scroll through the pages of your report to see how each page will look when printed.

Appendixes

This part of the book provides some additional information you may find helpful when using Quicken Personal Finance Software. These appendixes explain how to work with Quicken data files and how to customize Quicken.

Part Six

Managing Quicken Files

In This Appendix:

- Creating a new data file

- Opening, saving, and copying Quicken data files

- Protecting a data file

- Protecting existing transactions

- Working with passwords

- Setting backup preferences

- Backing up your data

- Restoring data files

- Importing files into Quicken

- Exporting Quicken files

- Working with additional file operations

- Setting up printers

- Setting up for check printing

- Using keyboard shortcuts

Appendix A

Quicken 2017 stores all the information you enter in a Quicken data file. This file includes all account and category setup information, transactions, and other records you enter into Quicken. Technically speaking, your Quicken data file consists of a single file with the QDF extension.

Commands under Quicken's File menu, shown next, enable you to perform a number of file management tasks, such as creating, opening, backing up, restoring, password protecting, importing and exporting, and copying portions and years of data files, as well as validating and repairing your data files. This appendix discusses all of these tasks.

Working with Multiple Data Files

Chances are you won't need more than the Quicken data file you created as part of the Quicken Setup process, covered in Chapter 1. However, if you need to keep financial records for someone else, such as a community group or an aging relative, you can easily create a new Quicken file. If a separate tax filing is needed for a group or a person, you will need to create a separate Quicken file.

Creating a Data File

Start by choosing File | New Quicken File. A dialog appears, asking whether you want to create a new Quicken file or a new Quicken account. (Some users confuse the two and try to use the File menu's New command to create a new financial account.) An account is a part of a Quicken file, and a Quicken file can contain any number of accounts. (You learned how to create an account in Chapter 1.) Select New Quicken File, as shown here, and click OK.

> **New Quicken File** ✕
>
> ## New Quicken File
>
> ⦿ **New Quicken File**
>   A new collection of accounts, categories etc. separate from the file you are using now.
>
> ○ **New Quicken Account**
>   Add a new account such as a single bank account or credit card, to the Quicken file you are currently using.
>
> ❓   [OK]   [Cancel]

A Create Quicken File dialog appears. Use it to enter a name for the data file. Although you can also change the default directory location, it's easier to find the data file if it's in the Quicken subdirectory of your Documents folder with other Quicken data files. It is also easier to find the Quicken file if it is renamed with no spaces or other special characters. Click OK.

Consider making your filename eight characters or less. While most modern programs can use longer filenames, there can be occasional issues if the filename is longer than eight characters.

The Intuit ID page appears. (Note that you cannot even create a test file without creating—or entering—an Intuit Quicken ID.) After you enter your Intuit ID, Quicken asks if you want to sync to mobile. Select Don't Use Mobile and click Next. The Registration Successful page appears. Select Add Account to create the first account for this new entity and continue as you did your first Quicken file. Refer to Chapter 1 for step-by-step instructions or just to refresh your memory.

Opening, Saving, and Copying Quicken Data Files

The first four options on the File menu help you work with your Quicken files. Use these commands to create a new file (as discussed earlier), open an already existing Quicken file, save a copy of your current file, and determine the location of the file on your computer.

Opening a Different Data File

If you have more than one Quicken data file, it's important that you enter transactions into the right one. You can see which data file is currently open by looking at the filename in the application window's title bar, shown next. Note that the title bar shows the version of Quicken that you are using, the file in which you are working, and the tab with which you are currently working.

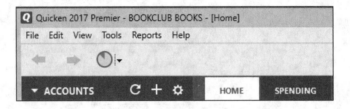

To open a different data file, choose File | Open Quicken File, or press CTRL-O, and use the Open Quicken File dialog that appears to select and open a different file. Only one Quicken data file can be open at a time. To open the new file, click on the name of the file and click OK. Alternatively, simply double-click on the filename.

You can also create shortcuts to each of your Quicken data files and name the shortcuts so it's easy to tell you are opening the correct file.

You may note a folder named "BACKUP." See "Backing Up Your Quicken Data File" later in this appendix to learn more about Quicken backup files and folders.

Save A Copy As

Use this menu command to open a dialog with which you can save an exact copy of your current file to another location. This other location can be a flash (sometimes called a "thumb") drive, another location on your network, or an external hard disk. If you have a CD or DVD burner on your computer, you can use your computer's CD or DVD writing software to copy the file to a CD or DVD.

NOTE You can use the Save A Copy As dialog to rename your file as well.

Quicken makes it easy for you to copy your currently open file.

1. Click File | Save A Copy As. The Copy Quicken File dialog appears, as shown here.

2. If you want to save the file in a folder other than the default Documents | Quicken folder, select the folder into which you want to save this Quicken file by choosing the folder from the drop-down list.
3. Select the location for your copied file, give it a new name such as "myfilecopy" to distinguish it from your original file, and click OK. Your file is now copied to the other location.
4. A message appears stating that your file has been copied successfully and showing the name you gave it. You are asked if you want to open the copied file. If you click Yes, you see an additional prompt asking if you want to close the current file. To return to your currently open Quicken file, click No.

Show This File On My Computer

You can immediately find where your current file is located by choosing File | Show This File On My Computer. When you click this command, Quicken opens a Windows Explorer window showing where the currently open file is located on your computer.

Password-Protecting Quicken Data

Besides the ability to use one password for all your Quicken data, Quicken offers two more types of password protection for your data: file passwords and transaction passwords. This section shows how these options work.

Protecting a Data File

When you password-protect a data file, the file cannot be opened without the password. This is the ultimate in protection—it prevents unauthorized users from even seeing the data in your Quicken file.

Setting Up the Password

Choose File | Set Password For This Data File to display the Manage Data File Password dialog. If you choose to set a custom password for your data file, click Use My Custom Password to open the text boxes. Enter the same password in each text box, and click OK. Remember, passwords are always case-sensitive, meaning if you've used capital letters when setting your password, you must enter your password with capital letters. For example, if your password is *cHe4sRt8e*, entering *che4srt8e* will not open the file.

EXPERIENCED USERS RECOMMEND

Setting custom passwords for both your data and individual transactions is a way to ensure that your records are protected. While no method can protect you completely, having several levels of passwords can certainly help ensure your files are secured.

Secure passwords contain at least 12 to 14 characters and include uppercase and lowercase letters, numbers, and symbols. Using your name or the name of someone in your family or any number combination that can be discovered easily, such as birth dates or street addresses, is highly discouraged.

Opening a Password-Protected Data File

When you open a data file that is password protected, the Enter Quicken Password dialog appears. You must enter your password correctly and then click OK to open the file. As mentioned earlier, passwords are "case-sensitive." That means if you've used capital letters when setting your password, you must enter your password with capital letters.

If you are updating to Quicken 2017 from Quicken 2011 or earlier, the allowable password length changed in Quicken 2012. If the password you used in earlier versions was 15 or 16 characters, you may have a problem getting Quicken 2017 to accept your password. Try re-entering your password and leaving off the last one or two characters. You could also change the password in the older Quicken version before you update to Quicken 2017.

Changing or Removing a Password

1. To change the password, choose File | Set Password For This Data File to display the Manage Data File Password dialog. Click the Change link to continue.
2. Enter the existing password in the Existing Password text box and then the new password in both the Create New Password and Confirm Password text boxes.
3. Click OK to save your new password and close the dialog box.

To remove the password, choose File | Set Password For This Data File to display the Manage Data File Password dialog. Select the I Do Not Want To Use A Data File Password button. Enter the existing password in the Existing Password text box to approve the change and click OK to close the dialog.

Protecting Existing Transactions

When your existing transactions are password protected, the transactions cannot be modified unless the password is properly entered. This prevents unauthorized or accidental alterations to data.

Setting Up the Password

Choose File | Set Password To Modify Transactions to display the Password To Modify Existing Transactions dialog. Enter the same password in the top two text boxes, as seen next. Then enter a date through which the transactions are to be protected, and click OK. This is an especially useful tool when you have completed entering all of your transactions for the year and are ready to run your reports for your income tax return. Protecting your transactions through the end of the year will ensure that you don't inadvertently change a number that might affect your return.

Manage Data File Password

Manage Data File Password

What password would you like to use?

( ) Set a custom password

Create New Password [   ] Show

Confirm Password [   ] Show

( ) Use this data file without a password

OK   Cancel

Transaction passwords may be up to 16 characters in length.

Modifying a Password-Protected Transaction

When you attempt to modify a transaction that is protected with a password, the Transaction Password Required dialog appears. You must enter your password correctly and then click OK to modify the transaction.

Changing or Removing a Password

Choose File | Set Password To Modify Transactions to display the Change Transaction Password dialog. Enter the current password in the Old Password box, and then enter the same new password in the two boxes beneath it. (To remove a password, leave the two bottom boxes empty.) Click OK.

Working with Passwords

Here are a few things to keep in mind when working with passwords:

- File passwords can be up to 15 characters, while transaction passwords can contain up to 16 characters. Both passwords can contain any character, including a space.
- Passwords are case-sensitive. That means, for example, that "PassWord" is not the same as "password." (By the way, do *not* use "password" as your password!)

- If you forget your password, you will need to use the Password Recovery process as described in Chapter 1. Write your password down and keep it in a safe place.
- Your data file is only as secure as you make it. Quicken's password protection can help prevent unauthorized access to your Quicken files, but only if your password is effective.
- Consider including numbers; capital and lowercase letters; or symbols such as !, ?, or * in your password.
- Do not use personal birthdays, addresses, or other such information as your password.
- Do not use the password you use for your financial institutions as a Quicken file or transaction password.

Password Error Messages

After you have established your passwords, you may see error messages when trying to open a file or change a transaction. Before you contact Quicken Support, consider these possibilities:

- Is your CAPS LOCK key on? If you have inadvertently pressed the CAPS LOCK key on the left side of your keyboard, you may be typing in all caps. Remember, your passwords are case-sensitive.
- Is your NUM LOCK key off? When your password contains numbers and you enter those numbers from the ten-key pad at the right side of your desktop keyboard, you may be entering symbols instead of numbers if you have turned off the NUM LOCK key.
- Are you in the right data file? If you have more than one data file on your computer, you may have opened the wrong one by mistake.

Try another password. Many of us have several passwords that we use, and you may be entering the wrong password.

If you have recently changed your password and have just restored from a backup copy, you may have restored a file with an old password. Try that old password.

You can also use the converse—if you have recently changed your password and you can't remember the new password, try using your old password on a recent backup file.

 The sudden onset of a long-established password suddenly not working can be a sign of data file corruption. Should this happen to you, the best solution is to restore a backup taken prior to the start of the password issue.

Backing Up Your Quicken Data File

Imagine this: you set up Quicken to track all of your finances, and you record or download transactions regularly so the Quicken data file is always up to date. Then one evening, when you start your computer to check your e-mail or enter a cash transaction into Quicken, you find that your hard drive has died. Not only have your plans for the evening been ruined, but your Quicken data file is also a casualty of your hard drive's untimely death.

Throughout this book, you've been encouraged to back up your data files. If you back up your Quicken data as regularly as you update its information, the loss of your Quicken data file will be a minor inconvenience, rather than a catastrophe. In this section, you'll learn how to back up your Quicken data file and how to restore it if (or when) the original data file is lost or damaged.

As part of your backup plan, consider restoring your backed-up data on a regular trial basis to ensure the backup device is working properly.

Setting Backup Preferences

By default, Quicken reminds you to run a manual backup every third time you leave your Quicken program. However, you can change this prompt in Quicken Preferences. The Backup Preferences dialog also allows you to tell Quicken how often to automatically save a copy of your files. Open the Backup Preferences dialog by clicking Edit | Preferences | Setup | Backup. The dialog appears as seen in Figure A-1.

About Automatic Backups

Quicken creates a Backup folder in the same location where your data files are stored. Every fifth time you open your Quicken file, Quicken creates a backup file of your information and stores that record in the Backup folder. While this is useful if your data file becomes corrupted or there is a software or hardware error, storing the file on your hard drive does not protect you against hard drive failures.

Each automatically backed up file is saved as *QData*-YYYY-MM-DD.ap.hh.mm .QDF-backup. (Data filename - four-digit year - two-digit month - two-digit day - AM or PM - two-digit hour - two-digit minute.QDF-backup.) Manual backups are formatted as *QData*.QDF-backup or *QData*-YYYY-MM-DD .QDF-backup, depending on whether or not you opted to include the date.

Figure A-1 • Use Quicken Backup Preferences to tell Quicken how you want to back up your Quicken files.

As seen in Figure A-1, you can read about backups in Quicken Help and even open your current backup directory (folder). You can change both the number of times Quicken saves your file to this folder and the number of copies maintained in that folder. Enter any number between 1 and 99 to change from the default of 5. Each file is saved with the word "backup." The date and time of the backup are recorded in the Backup folder for automatic backups. The time does not appear in manual backups.

If you use the Quicken Attachments feature discussed in Chapter 5, be aware that there must be enough room on the media to which you are backing up for any of your attached files, or any attachments will not be backed up with the file.

EXPERIENCED USERS RECOMMEND

One of the points all users stress is that eventually all hard drives and other devices will fail. The *only way* to protect yourself in the event of such a failure is by having a current backup of your data. By far, the most secure backup file is the one that resides somewhere *other* than near your computer. Otherwise, if your computer is stolen or damaged in a tornado, fire, or other disaster, your backup disks might also be lost.

For a small fee, Quicken Online Backup can help protect your data by making it easy to back up your data to a secure server far from your computer and other backup files. After you have signed up for Quicken's Online Backup, you simply follow the same steps as a manual backup, but choose to save your data online rather than to a physical device at your location.

If your Quicken data is important to you, check out this feature. Open the Quicken Backup window by clicking File | Backup And Restore | Back Up Quicken File. Click the Learn More link under Quicken Online Backup in the Quicken Backup window to get the details on this useful service. You can test it free for the first 30 days, and the service's interface is easy to use.

For more information about backing up, see "Backing Up Your Data" later in this appendix.

Setting Manual Backup Reminders

This Preferences setting tells Quicken how often you want to be reminded to back up. A manual backup allows you to change the location for your backed-up file.

Consider alternating your manual backup locations. For example, back up to a flash drive on Monday and Wednesday, to an external hard drive on Tuesday and Thursday, and to a CD or DVD on Friday and the weekend.

Backing Up Your Data

While you are using Quicken, you begin the backup process by choosing File | Backup And Restore | Backup Quicken File or by pressing CTRL-B at any time. This displays the Quicken Backup dialog for the currently open Quicken data file. As you see in Figure A-2, we are saving our file to a Backups folder on a USB drive named "I."

Select one of the following backup location options.

Figure A-2 • The Quicken Backup dialog lets you tell Quicken how, when, and where to back up your data files.

Back Up On My Computer Or Hard Drive (CD/DVD, Hard Drive, Thumb Drive)

This option enables you to back up to another disk, either on your computer or on one that's accessible via a network. If you select this option, you can use the Change button to locate and select a backup disk and directory. It's a good idea to alternate between two disks for backup purposes. This means you'll always have two versions backed up in case one version is corrupt. Choosing a backup location other than your hard disk, such as a thumb (flash) drive (for small files) or an external hard disk, protects your data by placing it away from your regular hard drive. (Backing up to your computer's internal hard disk defeats the purpose of backing up!) If you want to automatically append the current date to the backup filename, select the Add Date To Backup File Name check box. (These instructions assume you have selected Back Up On My Computer.) Keep in mind that your computer may not be able to write directly to a CD-R or DVD-R. Even though the option says only CD, you can back up to either a CD or DVD. If you choose to back up to an optical disk such as a CD or DVD, you might have to back up to your hard disk and then burn the resulting file to disk.

1. Select Back Up On My Computer Or Hard Drive (CD, Hard Drive, Thumb Drive).
2. The folder into which your backed up file will be saved is displayed. To back up to another folder or location, click Change.
   a. Select the drive, folder, and location into which you want to save your backed-up files.
   b. Click OK.
3. Click Back Up Now. Your Quicken data file briefly disappears and a small message appears telling you that Quicken is backing up your data.
4. When the backup is complete, the data file's windows reappear and a dialog informs you that the file was backed up successfully. Click OK to dismiss the dialog.

Many Quicken users keep more than two backups. Subtle data corruption can go unnoticed for some time. Having a wide date range of backups to choose from should you need to restore may save you a lot of data re-entry time. Quicken, Inc., does not recommend storing your Quicken file on a network drive and working with your file across your network. While backing up to a network drive can work effectively for many, it's a good idea to store your actual Quicken data file in the Quicken subfolder in your Documents folder on your computer.

Use Quicken Online Backup

Choose this option to back up to a server on the Internet, using Quicken's Online Backup service, which is available for a nominal fee. You can learn more about this service by selecting Learn More in the Use Quicken Online Backup section to connect to the Quicken Online Backup website.

If you have an online backup account, click the I Am Already An Online Backup Customer link to enter your account ID and password.

- When working with online backup through Quicken, there have been issues with some firewall hardware and software. Refer to the product's documentation to forestall any problems.
- Make sure you keep a record of your Quicken Online Backup account ID and password. If you forget it, you'll have to contact Quicken Support to complete your backup.

- Antivirus and non-Quicken backup programs may interfere with Quicken Online Backup.
- Quicken Online Backup cannot access files stored on CDs, DVDs, or flash drives.

The Quicken Community sees many questions about renewing your online backup when the subscription runs out. However, Quicken states that it will renew the subscription using the same credit card that was used originally.

EXPERIENCED USERS RECOMMEND

Many Quicken users have shared a common backup issue, whether it be to CDs, DVDs, or flash drives. The issue is "my Quicken data did not back up properly." In addition, there seem to be as many error messages as there are different CD/DVD burning programs available. Many of these errors are due to formatting issues. In most cases, one way to solve the question is as follows:

1. To back up to a CD or DVD, create a folder on your desktop.
2. Right-click a blank area on your desktop.
   a. Click New | Folder. Name your folder and press ENTER.
   b. Use Quicken to back up your file to that folder.
3. Use the backup file on the desktop to burn to your CD or DVD following the manufacturer's directions.
4. After you have verified that the backed-up file is on your external device and can be accessed by Quicken, delete the icon for the temporary folder on your desktop.
5. Remember that some CD/DVD programs will not accept filenames longer than 31 characters. This is another good reason to keep your filenames short!

Try following the same procedure if Quicken does not back up to your flash drive. Occasionally, flash drives are formatted by the manufacturer and can cause some of the same issues as CDs or DVDs.

Do check the size of your Quicken data file and the amount of space available on your CD or DVD. If, for some reason, your Quicken data file is too large to fit on the available space, the file will not back up. Since many CD and DVD programs determine the backed-up file size, if there is a question in your mind, you're better off burning to a new, blank disk.

Remember that files burned to a CD or DVD may be "read-only," meaning you cannot work with files on that optical device directly. For this reason, it is a good idea to use external hard drives or similar devices for backup and store your active Quicken data file on your computer's hard drive.

Restoring Data Files

In the event of loss or damage to your data file, you can restore from a recent backup. You can restore from an external file or one on your hard drive. Each process works in a similar way.

If you just want to check something in a backup file, be sure you are not restoring the backup over your working file, or you may lose your more recent data. The Save A Copy As option on the Quicken File menu is helpful in creating a copy of your working file (just in case) before restoring a backup.

Start the restoration process by opening Quicken and clicking File | Backup And Restore | Restore From Backup File. You may restore from one of Quicken's automatic backups, a backup file that you created, or an online backup.

To restore from one of Quicken's automatic backups:

1. Click Restore From Automatic Backups, as shown next.

Restore from Backup File   ✕

Restore from Backup File

◉ Restore from automatic backups
Periodic backups created automatically by   Open Backup Directory

Select file to restore
BOOKCLUB BOOKS-2016-10-24.PM05.10.QDF-backup

○ Restore from your backup

[   ]   Browse ...

○ Restore from online backup
Requires Quicken Online Backup   Learn more...

❓   Restore Backup   Cancel

---

2. If no backup files appear, click Open Backup Directory to locate the Quicken Backup folder. This process opens the folder in Windows Explorer, and you

will have exited the backup dialog. Once you find the backup file you want, you have to restart the restore process.

3. Select the file you want to restore and click Restore Backup. If the file you want to restore is the currently opened file, you are prompted to write over the current file or to create a copy of the file. Many Quicken users create a copy for safety's sake. You can always delete that copy in the future should you not need it.

4. To restore a backup file that you have created, ensure the device on which the file is stored is connected to your computer.

5. Click Restore From Your Backup | Browse to locate and select the appropriate backup file.

6. Click Restore Backup. If a file by the name of the file you are trying to restore exists, you'll see a message asking what you want to do. If you are restoring your backed-up file over the current file, choose Overwrite The Open File With Restored File (This Cannot Be Undone). Overwriting a file means replacing all the information that is in the current file. This cannot be reversed, so make very sure that is what you want to do!

7. If you choose to create a copy of the backed-up file, click Create A Copy. You see a message that the file was restored and are asked if you want to open the restored file.

8. To restore a file from your online backup, choose Restore From Online Backup to log into Quicken Online Backup. You see a list of the last 90 days of backups.

9. Select the file you want to restore. After Quicken has restored your files, click OK to close the confirmation message.

10. To open your restored file, click File | Open.

Moving a Quicken Data File Between Two Computers

Quicken, Inc.'s technical support staff is often asked how to move a Quicken data file from one computer to another. In fact, this question is so common that we are including it here.

The best way to move a data file from one computer to another is with the Backup and Restore Backup File commands. Begin by opening the file in Quicken on the computer on which it resides. Then follow the instructions in this appendix to back up the file to removable media, such as a thumb (or flash) drive, CD, DVD, external hard drive, or a network drive (preferably one that is connected to the other computer). Then start Quicken on the other computer and follow the instructions in this appendix to restore the backup copy. When you're finished, the Quicken data file is ready to use on the new computer.

EXPERIENCED USERS RECOMMEND

Many computer users are confused about the difference between backing up their files and copying their files. When should you back up and when should you copy? In today's computing world, that's a great question. When personal computers first came into general use, the storage devices, such as floppy disks, held much less information than today's spacious devices. The 3½-inch floppy disks that were used most often held only 1.44MB of information. Today's flash (or thumb) drives (those small storage devices about 3 inches×0.75 inches) measure their capacity in gigabytes. (When you remember that 1,024MB is 1GB, you get an idea of the storage capacity of a flash drive.) In order to save data efficiently and safely, earlier backup programs compressed the information to fit on the small media. One had to use the same program to restore the information back to the hard disk.

Today, all Quicken files, including the backups, are encrypted for security. When you run the Quicken Backup utility, Quicken appends the word "backup" to each file during the process. This tells Quicken that the file is not the current working file.

With today's large external hard disks, saving space may not be as important as easy retrieval of your data. If that is the case, consider using either of the two Copy commands offered by Quicken. These commands copy the information rather than save it as a backed-up file. While Quicken recommends the Backup and Restore utility when moving data files from one place to another, the Copy options are available, and with them, you can easily retrieve your data and get back to work.

However, the two Copy commands are different. File | Save A Copy As will create a byte-for-byte copy. The byte-for-byte copy will be the same size as the original file. File | File Operations | Copy, seen next, will create a record-by-record copy, which may clear space taken up by records you have deleted from your data file. The record-for-record copy may be smaller than the original file.

File	Edit	View	Tools	Reports	Help		
New Quicken File...						
Open Quicken File...					Ctrl+O	
Save a Copy As...						
Show This File on My Computer						
Set Password for This Data File...						
Set Password to Modify Transactions...						
Backup and Restore					▶	
File Import					▶	
File Export					▶	
File Operations					▶	Copy...
Printer Setup					▶	Year-End Copy...
Print Checks...						Validate and Repair...
Print Home...					Ctrl+P	Find Quicken Files...
✓ 1 C:\Users\Bobbi\Documents\Quicken\BOOKCLUB BOOKS						
2 C:\Users\Bobbi\Documents\Quicken\Bobbi's Quicken Data						
Exit						

It's important to remember that once you begin making changes to the file on the new computer, the file on the old computer will no longer be up to date. This means that if you want to use the file on the old computer again, you need to complete the backup and restore process to move the file back to that computer. As you can imagine, if you often move the file from one computer to another and back, it can be difficult to keep track of which version of the file is the most up to date.

Although you can make your Quicken data file "portable" by keeping it on removable media so you can access it from any computer, this is not the recommended method. Flash drives, CDs, and DVDs are even more susceptible to data loss and damage than an internal or external hard disk. Quicken users have reported numerous problems using this technique; don't add your own problems to the list. A networked drive may not be a good place to store your file either, at least if you are going to keep it networked while you work on it.

Additional File Procedures

The File menu contains links to several other tasks.

Importing Files into Quicken

Importing information into Quicken can make your financial life much easier. As discussed in earlier chapters, importing data such as downloading information from your financial institution saves you time.

From within Quicken, click File | File Import to open the submenu that shows your options. As you can see, several types of files can be imported:

- **Web Connect Files** are those files created by financial institutions that do not have Direct Connect availability. You download these files onto your hard drive and then import them into your Quicken data file. See Chapter 6 for detailed information about Web Connect files.

Web Connect files have the file extension .qfx. This can be easily confused with Quicken transfer files, which use the file extension .qxf. Be sure you select Web Connect Files when trying to import files downloaded from your financial institution.

- **QIF Files** are Quicken Interchange Format files that have been created in a third-party program for importing into Quicken. While not all programs support this format, many financial programs do.

- **Quicken Transfer Format (.qxf) Files** are files that permit the exchange of banking data with other Quicken data files, such as Quicken Essentials for Mac. As of this writing, .qxf files may not transfer investment transactions between Quicken files.
- **Import Security Prices From CSV File** allows you to utilize security price reports in this format. CSV stands for comma-separated value. This import type can be handy for repairing security price history corruption or importing security price history for non–publicly traded securities.
- **TurboTax Files** can be imported into Quicken for tax planning.
- **Microsoft Money Files** can, in many cases, be quickly converted into Quicken data files if Microsoft Money 2007 or 2008 is installed on your computer. The last version of Microsoft Money was released in 2008 and was supported only through January 2011. Microsoft Money versions prior to 2007 cannot be easily converted.

Exporting Quicken Files

Several types of files appear on the File Export menu. These file types are used to transfer information between Quicken products, such as Quicken for Mac, as well as the Windows versions of Quicken:

- **QIF Files** are used to export Quicken data from one Quicken account to another Quicken account or to another Quicken file.
- **Quicken Transfer Format (.qxf) Files**, as explained earlier, are Quicken financial data files used to transfer data files from Quicken for Windows to Quicken for Mac. Click File | File Export | Quicken Transfer Format to open the Export To Quicken Transfer Format dialog. By default, the file with which you are working is the filename you will export. Click Save. You will see a message box when the export file is created successfully. You will then need to import this .qxf file into your Quicken Essentials file.

See this article for more information about transferring files to Quicken for Mac: https://www.quicken.com/support/converting-quicken-windows-quicken-mac-2016.

- **Export TurboTax Tax Schedule Report** and **Export TurboTax Capital Gains Report** allow you to transfer TurboTax files (.txf) into other programs.

Working with Additional File Operations

There are four options listed in the File Operations menu. As shown earlier, you see Copy, Year-End Copy, Validate And Repair, and Find Quicken Files. Each option is discussed next.

Copy

This copy command enables you to copy all or portions of the current data file to a different disk or save a copy with a different name. While similar to the Save A Copy As command discussed earlier in this appendix, this command gives you choices regarding what time period to include in the copied file, as well as a choice to include uncleared and investment transactions. It also may clear unused space in the Quicken file.

When you choose File | File Operations | Copy, the Copy File dialog appears. Click Browse to choose a location for your file if you want the copied file stored in a location other than the current folder. The new filename will be the same as the current file, but will have "Cpy" at the end of the filename, as shown here. You can change the name if you choose. Select the date range that is to be included in the copy, and clear the check box if you do not want to include earlier, uncleared transactions. While you may choose to clear the Include All Prior Investment Transactions, consider keeping them for a more complete record of your investment transactions. Click OK to make the copy.

> **NOTE** The Quicken Copy command may cause issues if you are using mobile sync or Express Web Connect.

If there is already a Quicken file with the same name in your Quicken folder, you will receive a prompt to give a new name to the file copy. Type a new name for this second file copy, and click OK.

When the copy is finished, a dialog asks if you want to continue working with the original data file or the new copy. Select the appropriate option, and click OK to continue working with Quicken.

The process does not change the original file in any way. Perhaps you want to copy categories, scheduled transactions, and memorized payees to a new file without the transactions. Or, perhaps there is a date range in which you had some major changes in your financial life and want to review those transactions.

Making a Year-End Copy of a Data File

Many Quicken users create a special copy of their data at the end of each year. This "Year-End Copy" is NOT a requirement. However, this option allows you to copy all reconciled transactions prior to this year (or the date you set) and remove those transactions to save room on your hard drive or to have only current year information in your file. The Year-End Copy command creates two special copies of your data file. Choose File | File Operations | Year-End Copy to display the Create A Year End Copy dialog, shown next, and set options for the two files.

Current Data File   The Current Data File section allows you to set options for the file you will continue working with in Quicken.

Do Nothing. My Current Data File Will Remain Unchanged   This option simply saves a copy of the current data file as-is.

I Only Want Transactions In My Current Data File Starting With This Date   This option enables you to enter a starting date for the files in the data file you will continue to use. For example, if you enter 1/1/2016, all reconciled transactions *prior* to that date will be removed from the data file.

Archive Data File   The Archive Data File section allows you to set options for creating an archive copy of the file. An archive is a copy of older transactions saved in a separate file. You can set two options:

- Enter a complete path (or use the Browse button to enter a path) for the archive file.
- Enter the date for the last transaction to be included in the file. For example, if you enter 12/31/2015, the archive file will include all transactions in the current file, up to and including those transactions dated 12/31/2015.

Creating the Files   When you click OK in the Create A Year End Copy dialog, Quicken creates the two files. It then displays a dialog that enables you to select the file you want to work with: the current file or the archive file. Select the appropriate option (normally Current File), and click OK to continue working with Quicken.

> **EXPERIENCED USERS RECOMMEND**
>
> Many Quicken users do not use the Create A Year End Copy utility. With today's large hard disks and fast machines, large Quicken data files are not an issue as they may have been when hard disks were small and computers didn't run at warp speed.

Checking the Integrity of a Data File

The Validate And Repair command facilitates checking the integrity of a Quicken data file. This command is particularly useful if you believe that a file has been damaged. It is a good idea to copy your file to an external device, such as a CD or external hard drive, before you perform the Validate And Repair function—in other words, perform a backup before working with this utility!

The Validate And Repair utility is one that many experienced Quicken users recommend as the first step when there are problems with your Quicken file. Of course, this is after you perform a backup!

When you choose File | File Operations | Validate And Repair, the Validate And Repair Your Quicken File dialog appears, as shown next. By default, the current file is selected, but you may click Browse to select another file to check if you choose.

Validate and Repair Your Quicken File ☒

Validate and Repair Your Quicken File

If you suspect data damage in your Quicken file, use this utility to validate the data, report on any issues found, and then repair the damaged file.

File to validate and repair: **BOOKCLUB BOOKS.QDF**   Browse...

☑ Validate file | ⚠ **Important:** Validate your Quicken data file if you suspect data damage.

☑ Rebuild investing lots | ⚠ **Important:** This takes a few minutes to complete. If errors are found, your cost basis valuations could change.

☑ Delete investing price history | ⚠ **Important:** Delete your investing price history only if you suspect data damage. Your price history will be rebuilt after deletion, but prices older than five years will be lost.

☐ Reset all Quicken printer settings (this will not affect your financial data)

❓   OK   Cancel

There are four specific operations that affect your data in different ways:

- **Validate File** should be run when you feel your data might be corrupted. Ensure you have performed a backup on your file before you run this process.
- **Rebuild Investing Lots** reviews your investing information. Current valuation amounts could change if this file has errors. Ensure you have performed a backup on your file before you run this process.
- **Delete Investing Price History** attempts to repair any data damage in your investing files. Ensure you have performed a backup on your file before you run this process. You will still need to re-enter any prices you've entered manually. You may have to perform a separate step to replace the price history.

If you have securities that are no longer traded publicly, such as with an acquisition or merger, that price history is not rebuilt. However, you can still recover price histories from online resources and enter them manually. Learn more about entering investment prices in Chapter 9.

- **Reset All Quicken Printer Settings** simply fixes any issues with your printer setup. You may have to reset the check and report print settings after this procedure is complete, but none of your financial information is affected.

Click OK to start each selected process. After each process completes, Quicken displays a text file that tells you whether the file has any problems.

Some Quicken users use this process and add one more step. If you hold down the CTRL and the SHIFT keys when clicking OK, you perform an additional validation step called a Super Validate. This additional step may find more errors in a damaged file. As always, before you perform any function that may affect your financial transactions, back up your file!

> **EXPERIENCED USERS RECOMMEND**
>
> One additional thought when working with files you suspect are damaged: try uninstalling and then reinstalling your Quicken program. Often, it is something that has been scrambled within the data and its interface with the program that can cause your files to appear damaged. Just remember to back up *before* you uninstall the program.

Setting Up Printers

The last section of your File menu discusses how to set up your printer for various Quicken tasks. From the File menu, click Printer Setup to set the printer for reports and graphs as well as checks. Since many Quicken users have one printer devoted to printing checks, Quicken offers a separate setup procedure for checks.

Set Up for Report and Graph Printing

Select For Reports/Graphs to open the Printer Setup For Reports And Graphs dialog box, shown here. Each section has options:

Printer Setup for Reports and Graphs   ×

Printer Setup for Reports and Graphs

Printer: Brother PC-FAX v.2.1 on USB002   ▼   Properties

Margins
Top: 0.50   Bottom: 0.50

Left: 0.50   Right: 0.50

Fonts
Heading Font

Body Font

OK   Cancel

- The Printer text box displays your default (standard) printer. Click Properties to open a dialog box specific to that printer.
- The Margins section lets you set top, bottom, right, and left margins.
- In the Fonts section, you can select the size of report and graph headings as well as the font size for your reports.

Click OK to close the dialog box after you have made your selections.

Setting Up for Check Printing

Quicken's ability to print checks enables you to create accurate, legible, professional-looking checks without picking up a pen (or a typewriter). In this section, you'll learn how to print the checks you enter in the Write Checks window.

Before you can print checks from Quicken, you must obtain compatible check stock. Quicken supports checks in a number of different styles.

First choose the type of printer you use, either Page Oriented (as most printers are today) or Continuous, sometimes used with multipart checks that are packaged together.

Then, indicate the type of check stock you use:

- Standard checks print just checks. There's no voucher or stub.
- Voucher checks pair each check with a similarly sized voucher form. When you print a voucher check, the transaction category information, including splits and tags, can be printed on the voucher portion.
- Wallet checks pair each check with a stub. When you print a wallet check, the transaction information is printed on the stub.

 Wallet checks are being phased out and have been replaced by Check 21 Compatible Wallet checks.

- Wallet checks (Check 21 Image Compatible).

Use the drop-down lists and option buttons to specify settings for your printer and check stock. The following are a few things to keep in mind when making settings in this dialog.

Partial Page Printing Options

If you select the Page-Oriented option and either Standard or Wallet checks in the Check Printer Setup dialog, you can also set options for Partial Page Printing

Style. This enables you to set up the printer for situations when you're not printing an entire page of checks.

- **Edge** is for inserting the page against one side of the feeder. The left or right edge of the checks enters the feeder first.
- **Centered** is for centering the page in the feeder. The left or right edge of the checks enters the feeder first.
- **Portrait** is also for centering the page in the feeder, but in this case, the top edge of each check enters the feeder first.

If your printer supports multiple feed trays, you can also set the source tray for partial and full pages by choosing options from the Partial Page Printing and Full Page Printing drop-down lists.

Continuous Printing Options

If you select the Continuous option and either Standard or Wallet checks in the Check Printer Setup dialog, the dialog changes to offer two Continuous options:

- **Bypass The Driver**   Select this check box for a continuous printer that skips checks or prints nothing.
- **Use Low Starting Position**   This should be turned on for a continuous printer that cuts the date or logo off your checks.

Checking the Settings for Page-Oriented Checks

If you're using page-oriented checks, you can check your settings by printing a sample page on plain paper. Here's how:

1. Click the Alignment button in the Check Printer Setup dialog.
2. In the Align Checks dialog, choose the Full Page, Two Checks, or One Check button. The Fine Alignment dialog appears.
3. Click Print Sample.
4. When the sample emerges from your printer, hold it up to the light with a sheet of check stock behind it. The sample should line up with the check.
5. If the sample does not line up properly with the check stock, set Vertical and/ or Horizontal adjustment values in the Fine Alignment dialog. Then repeat Steps 2 through 4 until the alignment is correct.
6. Click OK in each dialog to accept your settings and close it.

A catalog and order form for checks may have been included with your copy of Quicken. If so, you can use it to order checks. With your Internet connection, you can order checks online from within Quicken by clicking the Order [check type] Checks button in the Write Checks window or by clicking the Order [check type] checks link below the check style field in the Select Checks To Print dialog.

Quicken must also be set up to print the kind of checks you purchased. You do this once, and Quicken remembers the settings.

Print (Current Location)

The final option in the printer section allows you to print from your current location. For example, if you are using Portfolio in the Investing tab, the option will read "Print Portfolio." Note the CTRL-P keyboard shortcut to the right of this option. Use that shortcut from nearly every location within Quicken to print from that location.

Although CTRL-P works from many locations, the Planning tab's Budgets view is one where it does not work.

Using Keyboard Shortcuts

If you have been working with computers for a long time and are comfortable with your keyboard, Quicken has a number of keyboard shortcuts that can save time. When you see a keyboard combination to the side of a menu command, it means that you can press that combination of keys and achieve the same result as when you click that command on the menu. For example, by choosing Open Quicken File on the File menu, you see the keyboard shortcut CTRL-O. Hold down the CTRL key on your keyboard, press the O key, and release both keys to open an existing Quicken file.

For more information about the keyboard shortcuts available in Quicken 2017, press the F1 key (or from the Quicken menu bar, click Help | Quicken Help). Select Search Quicken Help and, in the search box, type **keyboard shortcuts**.

Mapping Your Keyboard

By default, Quicken's shortcuts are the traditional Windows shortcuts, such as CTRL-C for copy and CTRL-V for paste. However, Quicken has its own set of shortcuts, which you can choose in Preferences. To change your preferences, click Edit | Preferences | Setup | Keyboard Mappings. Choose Quicken Standard and click OK.

Customizing Quicken

In This Appendix:

- *Creating custom Home tab views*

- *Re-creating the Summary view*

- *Crafting an Analysis & Reports view*

- *Customizing the Toolbar*

- *Telling Quicken your preferences*

- *Converting your older Quicken files to a new computer*

- *Changing multiple transactions*

- *Using the Emergency Records Organizer*

Once you have become familiar with Quicken Personal Finance Software, you may want to fine-tune parts of the program to meet your specific needs. While there are options for changing the look of Quicken throughout this book, other customization options, such as customizing the Toolbar, may be useful to you. This appendix explains many ways you can customize Quicken.

Customizing Quicken's Interface

Quicken offers many customization possibilities. Since the Home tab is often the opening point for many Quicken users, this part of the appendix explains how to customize both the Home tab and the Quicken Toolbar.

Creating Custom Home Tab Views

We mentioned earlier that you could customize views in the Home tab to see specifics about your Quicken data. You can create multiple Home tab views, each of which shows the "snapshots" of summarized financial information that you want to display.

If you've upgraded to Quicken 2017 from an earlier version, you may already have custom views set up in your Quicken data file. You have access to these views on the Home tab, where you can switch from one to another, modify them, and delete them, as discussed in this section.

Displaying the Home Tab Views

To get started, click the Home tab near the top of the Quicken window. Quicken displays the Main View. Before you customize this view, it displays three other snapshots: See Where Your Money Goes, Stay On Top Of Monthly Bills, and Budget Your Spending. Once you've customized the Home tab, it displays the views you added to it. Each view can contain one or more snapshots.

Modifying the Current View

Click the Customize button shown beneath the Main View title to change the current view. The button opens the Customize View dialog, as seen next. Scroll

---

Q Customize View   ✕

Customize View

View Name: | Main View |

Available items:

- – Overview
  - Alerts
  - All accounts
  - Calendar
  - My Web Links
  - Online Updates
- Banking
  - Banking Account Activity
  - Banking Account Details
  - Bill and Income Reminders
  - Credit Card Accounts
  - Expenses
  - Income Year-to-Date

Alerts, Reminders, and Scheduled Bills and Deposits

[Add »]
[« Remove]

[Move Up]
[Move Down]

Chosen items:

- See Where Your Money Goes
- Stay On Top of Monthly Bills
- Budget

? | Delete This View | | Save | | Cancel |

through the Available Items list to choose what to include in your customized view. Move items from the Available Items list on the left to the Chosen Items list on the right with the Add button. To rearrange the order of items in the Chosen Items list, select an item and click Move Up or Move Down. Repeat this process until the items appear in the view in the order you prefer.

Make changes as desired, and click Save to save them.

Removing an Item   To remove an item from the view, select the Customize button and select the item you want to remove in the Chosen Items list and click Remove. This action simply moves the item back to the Available Items list.

Creating a New View

By creating multiple views, you can make several versions of the Home tab window, each with a specific set of information. You can then quickly switch from one view to another to see the information you want.

In the Home tab window, click the Add View button that appears parallel to the Main View button, but at the right side of your screen. The Customize View dialog appears.

Enter a name for the view in the View Name box. The default name will be "View 2" or the next available number. Follow the instructions in the previous section to add items to the view, and click Save. Your new view appears on your screen.

Switching from One View to Another

If you have created more than one view for the Quicken Home window, each view has its own menu button at the top of the Home tab window. The view currently in use is underlined, as seen next. To switch from one view to another, simply click the button for your chosen view.

▶ ACCOUNTS	C + ⚙	HOME	SPEND	BILLS	PLAN	INVEST	PROPERTY	BUSINESS	MORE ▼
Main View	Summary View	Analysis & Reports View						⊕ View Guidance	Add View
Customize									

Deleting a View

To delete a view, select the button for the view you want to delete. Click Customize to open the Customize View dialog. Then choose the Delete This View button. Click Yes in the confirmation dialog that appears. The view is deleted. You must have at least one view in the Home tab, meaning you cannot delete the "last" view.

Re-creating the Summary View

In earlier versions of Quicken, a Summary view displayed a number of snapshots with useful information about your banking accounts. If you liked this view, as many did, you can easily create it, as described next.

1. Open the Home tab, and click Add View. The Customize View dialog appears. First, type **Summary View** or any name you prefer in the View Name field. If any information appears in the Chosen Items list, click the first item, hold down your SHIFT key, and click the bottom item to select the entire list. Then, select Remove to remove the highlighted items. They are still available in the Available Items list on the left, as you are only removing them from the Chosen Items list in the current view.
2. Start by selecting Alerts in the Available Items list, and click Add. (You learn about setting alerts in Chapter 7.) You will note that all of the items are in this order within the six sections: Overview, Banking, Investing, Property & Debt, Planning, and Tax. However, if you have not yet added an investment account, you will not see the Investing section.
3. Add the following from the Banking section of the Available Items list: Spending And Savings Accounts, Credit Card Accounts, and Bill And Income Reminders, in that order. When you click Save, you'll see a Summary View, similar to the one that was in previous Quicken versions, as seen in Figure B-1.

The layout depends on your screen width and the order in which you have placed the snapshots. To get the layout you want, change the width of your Quicken window and/or the order in which the snapshots display.

In your new Summary View, all snapshots include an Options menu that displays as a small gear icon and buttons that you can use to work with that snapshot. For example, the Alerts snapshot at the top of the view has both buttons and Options menu commands for showing and setting up alerts. You can click links to view the account register, set up balance alerts, and set interest rates in any of the snapshots. You have seen many of these options throughout the book. Try exploring some of the others!

New in Quicken 2017 is the ability to expand or collapse snapshots. To make the adjustment, click the downward arrow at the upper left of each snapshot.

Figure B-1 • Design the Summary View to show your financial position in one location.

Here's a brief summary of each snapshot in your new Summary View:

- **Alerts** The Alerts snapshot lists alerts you have set up. You can click blue links to go to the account or to other applicable alert items that you learn about in Chapter 7.
- **Spending And Savings Accounts** The Spending And Savings Accounts snapshot lists all of your checking, savings, and cash accounts, along with their current or ending balances. Remember, the current balance shows the net of all of the deposits and checks through today's date. The ending balance includes any checks or deposits you have entered that will occur on future

dates. Whether the Spending And Savings Accounts snapshot shows both the current balance and the ending balance or just shows the ending balance depends on whether any of the listed accounts have future-dated transactions. If you have no future-dated transactions in any of the listed accounts, only the ending balance will display in the snapshot. Review Chapter 4 to understand how account balances are displayed.

- **Credit Card Accounts**   The Credit Card Accounts snapshot lists all of your credit card accounts along with their current balances.
- **Bill And Income Reminders**   The Bill And Income Reminders snapshot lists all of your bills, deposits, and other scheduled transactions. It may also display a list of transactions that Quicken thinks you may want to schedule. Buttons beside each selected item enable you to enter, edit, or skip a scheduled transaction or to schedule or ignore a suggested transaction. You may also link each item as described in Chapter 6.

Crafting an Analysis & Reports View

Another useful view is the Analysis & Reports View, which includes both graphs and reports that explain your current financial position. Most of these snapshots give you a glimpse of Quicken's extensive and highly customizable reporting features, as discussed in Chapter 15.

- From the Home tab, click Add View to open the Customize View dialog. Type **Analysis & Reports** in the View Name field. Remove any items in the Chosen Items list.
- Add the following from the Available Items list: Expenses and Income vs. Expenses from the Banking section and Budget from the Planning section, in that order. Click Save to see an Analysis & Reports View, as seen in Figure B-2.
- Select either the Expenses or Income vs. Expenses snapshot to open a detailed snapshot about that section of your view. In the Budget snapshot, click any of the bars to open a mini-report.

 If you have not yet set up a budget, you will see Budget Your Spending with the Get Started button. Clicking the Get Started button takes you to the Budgets view on the Planning tab so you can set up your budget. Learn about setting up your budget in Chapter 13.

Customizing the Toolbar

The Quicken Toolbar is an optional row of buttons along the top of the screen, just beneath the menu bar, as seen here. These buttons offer quick access to

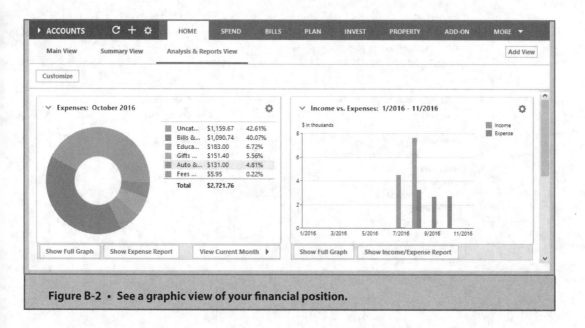

Figure B-2 • See a graphic view of your financial position.

Quicken features. If you do not see the Quicken Toolbar, display it by clicking View | Show Toolbar.

By default, the Quicken Toolbar shows both a left- and right-pointing arrow and the One Step Update button. You can customize the Toolbar by adding, removing, or rearranging buttons or by changing how the buttons display. To do this, you use the Customize Toolbar dialog, as seen in Figure B-3. To open the Customize Toolbar dialog, open the View menu and click Show Toolbar. With the Toolbar displayed, select Customize Toolbar.

Quicken calls the Toolbar items "buttons," but other Quicken users call them *icons*. Either way, they are simply links to other Quicken items.

To customize the Toolbar, make changes in this dialog as discussed next, and click Done.

Adding Buttons

To add a button, select it in the Available Toolbar Buttons list and click Add. Its name appears in the Your Toolbar Buttons list. If you want more items to choose from, click the Show All Toolbar Choices check box to display all the possibilities.

Customize Toolbar

Q Customize Toolbar   ✕

Customize Toolbar

Available toolbar buttons:

Account List
Category List
Go to Investing » Portfolio
Go to Property & Debt » Debt
Online Center
Print
Projected Balances
Recategorize
Reports & Graphs Center
Security list
Tax Planner
Write and Print Checks

[Add ->]
[<- Remove]
[Move Up]
[Move Down]

Your toolbar buttons:

One Step Update
Calculator
Reconcile an Account

☐ Show all toolbar choice

[Add or Remove Saved Reports...]

[Edit Shortcut or Label...]

○ Show icons and text   ● Show icons only

❓ [Reset to Default]   [Done]

Figure B-3 · You can customize your toolbar with shortcuts to your most used features.

 You also have more Toolbar button choices if you are using View | Classic Menus.

The Toolbar can display as many buttons as your monitor's display resolution and width allow. If you choose to show both icons and text, you may also see fewer buttons. If you resize your Quicken window to make it smaller, a More button, with two right-pointing arrows, appears on the Toolbar. Click this button to display a menu of buttons and select the button you want.

If you have chosen to display only buttons rather than both buttons and text, you may also see a >>> symbol showing more buttons are available.

Adding Saved Reports to the Toolbar

To add a saved report to the Toolbar, click the Add Or Remove Saved Reports button in the Customize Toolbar dialog. Then select the In Toolbar check box beside each saved report you want to add to the Toolbar. Click Done to save your changes.

Removing or Rearranging Buttons

To remove a button, select it in the Your Toolbar Buttons list and click Remove. Its name is removed from the Your Toolbar Buttons list, but is still available on the Available Toolbar Buttons list should you want to include it at another time.

You can rearrange the order of buttons on the Toolbar by changing their order in the Your Toolbar Buttons list. Simply select a button that you want to move, and click Move Up or Move Down to change its position in the list.

Moving More than One Button

Many Quicken users want to put several buttons on the toolbar at the same time. This is easy to do.

To choose items that are listed in the Available Toolbar Buttons list in a row (one after the other):

1. Select the first button you want to use in the Available Toolbar Buttons list.
2. Hold down the SHIFT key on your keyboard.
3. Click the last item you want to use. Release the SHIFT key. You'll note that the items you chose are "bolded."
4. Click the Add button (or the Remove button if you are taking them off the Quicken Toolbar). As before, the only change is made to the toolbar itself.

To move items that are not in a row, use the CTRL key rather than the SHIFT key. Select each item that you want to move while you are still holding down the CTRL key. Release the CTRL key after selecting the items.

Changing the Appearance of Buttons

At the bottom of the Customize Toolbar dialog are two options that determine how Toolbar buttons are displayed:

- **Show Icons And Text** displays both the Toolbar button and its label.
- **Show Icons Only** displays just the Toolbar button. When you hover over a button, its label appears.

In earlier versions of Quicken, you had the option to display a Global Search field in the Quicken Toolbar. The Global Search has been moved from the Toolbar to the Quicken title bar. It shows with text in a light gray font reading "Search A Payment Or A Deposit."

Restoring the Default Toolbar

To restore the Toolbar back to its "factory settings," click the Reset To Default button in the Customize Toolbar dialog. Then click OK in the confirmation dialog that appears. Click Done to close the dialog and return to the main Quicken window. The Toolbar buttons return to the way they display when you first installed Quicken.

EXPERIENCED USERS RECOMMEND

Many users like the ability to create custom keyboard shortcuts for the buttons on your Toolbar. From the Customize Toolbar dialog:

1. Select the item you want to edit from the Your Toolbar Buttons list on the right of the dialog.
2. Click Edit Shortcut Or Label to open the Edit Shortcut Or Label dialog.
3. Change the label name, create a shortcut key combination, or both, and then click OK.

You can now open that item from your keyboard using the keystrokes shown in the Edit Shortcut Or Label dialog. However, if you remove the button from the Toolbar, the keystroke combination no longer works for that item. In addition, the label change does not appear in the Your Toolbar Buttons list, but it does appear on the Toolbar when you save your customized settings.

Changing a label name is effective only in the Toolbar display when you've chosen to show both buttons and text. It does not change the label that appears when you hover over the button with your mouse.

You can also access the Customize Toolbar dialog by right-clicking anywhere within the Toolbar.

Setting Preferences

Many Quicken users find the Preferences settings give them better control when using the program. While we discuss many of the settings throughout other chapters in this book, this section reviews all of the options you can change and tells you where you can learn more about the features they control.

Telling Quicken Your Preferences

As the name suggests, Preferences allow you to control Quicken's appearance and operations. To access these options, open the Edit menu and choose Preferences to open the Preferences dialog. It lists a variety of categories as follows.

Startup

Startup preferences, shown next, enable you to specify what should appear when you start Quicken. Use the drop-down list to select Home (the default setting), one of the tabs (Home, Bills, Planning, and so on), a specific account register, an investing item, or one of the views within the tabs.

Preferences ☒

Select preference type:

- Startup
- Navigation
- Setup
- Calendar and currency
- Backup
- Web Connect
- Alerts
- Investment transactions
- Investing.Quicken.com portfolio
- Register
- Data entry and QuickFill
- Notify
- Write checks
- Downloaded transactions
- Transfer detection
- Reports and Graphs
- Reports only
- Intuit ID, Mobile & Alerts

Select preferences:

Startup preferences

Startup location

On startup open to: Home ▼

This can also be changed at any time by right-clicking the tab you would like to use and selecting "Start Quicken On..."

Startup actions

☐ Download transactions when Quicken starts

🔒 Password required when Quicken starts: **No** (change)

Quicken colors

Color scheme: Blue (default) ▼

☑ Dim disabled windows

❓   OK   Cancel

If you choose to use pop-up registers in the Register Preferences | Register Appearance dialog, you will not be able to select a specific register to start on.

You can choose what you want Quicken to do when it starts, such as download transactions or require a password, and choose one of the predefined color schemes for the Quicken program: blue (the default), green, purple, teal, or tan. You can also choose to have nonactive (disabled) windows dimmed. Use the slider to determine how much or how little "dimming" should occur.

EXPERIENCED USERS RECOMMEND

Depending on your monitor settings, sometimes changing the color scheme can make Quicken easier for you to read. Also, you can make the font easier to read by selecting View | Use Large Fonts. However, you may find that not all of your information appears in your Quicken window when you use large fonts.

However, some users report issues with using the large font option. Because the monitors on many devices today can be "scaled" to make text and other items larger or smaller, you may have to experiment a bit with your device to achieve the best result.

Navigation   Startup Navigation allows you to choose how you want to get around Quicken:

- **Main Navigation** lets you choose to use the Classic menus (those used prior to 2010). If you choose Classic menus, you also have an option to turn off the tab display.
- **Account Bar** lets you select where to place the Account Bar and whether to display cents in the Account Bar balances. You can also choose to not show the Account Bar with this preference. Clearing the Show Account Bar check box minimizes the Account Bar, enabling you to see more of the Quicken screen with which you are working.
- **Other Options** lets you choose whether to show the Quicken Toolbar. If you have a widescreen monitor, from here you may choose to dock the side bar permanently on the right side of your monitor.

If you choose to display the Account Bar on the right side of your widescreen monitor, as well as choose to display the side bar, the side bar will then dock on the left side of your screen.

Setup

Setup options control basic Quicken operations:

- **Keyboard Mappings** enables you to change what certain standard Windows keyboard shortcuts do. In most Windows programs, the CTRL-Z, CTRL-X, CTRL-C, and CTRL-V shortcut keys perform commands on the Edit menu. In Quicken 2017, these keyboard shortcuts are set to the Windows standard. See Quicken Help for more information about keyboard shortcuts.

 If you are upgrading from a previous Quicken version, the preferences you set in that version may not be the same in Quicken 2017. To ensure the settings are what you want, choose Edit | Preferences | Setup | Keyboard Mappings to verify the settings on your machine.

- **Turn On Quicken Sounds** turns on Quicken sound effects. You may want to leave this check box off if you use Quicken in an environment where sounds might annoy the people around you.
- **Turn On Animation**, which is turned on by default, activates the Quicken animation effects that appear when you complete certain actions.
- **Automatically Minimize Pop-up Windows** automatically minimizes a Quicken window, such as a report window or the Category List window, to the Quicken task bar when you click outside that window. (This is the window behavior in some older versions of Quicken.) With this option turned off, you can have multiple Quicken windows open at once and can manually minimize each one. Note that not all Quicken windows open independently. For example, when the Preferences dialog is open, you cannot open other Quicken pop-up windows.

Calendar and Currency   The folks at Quicken, Inc., realize that not everyone manages their finances on a calendar-year basis or only in U.S. dollars. The Calendar and Currency options enable you to customize these settings for the way you use Quicken:

- **Working Calendar** enables you to choose between two options: Calendar Year is a 12-month year beginning with January, and Fiscal Year is a 12-month year beginning with the month you choose from the drop-down list.
- **Multicurrency Support** assigns a "home" currency to all of your current data, placing a currency symbol beside every amount. You can then enter amounts in other currencies by entering the appropriate currency symbol.

It is not necessary to set this option unless you plan to work with multiple currencies in one of your Quicken data files.

Backup   The Backup options enable you to customize the way Quicken's Backup feature works. You can choose to have Quicken automatically do backups on your computer's hard drive, as well as choose to be reminded to do manual backups on any drive you want. See Appendix A for a complete discussion of how and when (*do it often!*) to back up your data.

Web Connect   The Web Connect options enable you to customize the way Quicken's Web Connect feature works. Web Connect, as discussed in Chapter 6, is a method for downloading transaction information from your financial institution into your Quicken data file.

- **Give Me The Option Of Saving To A File Whenever I Download Web Connect Data** displays a dialog after a Web Connect session that enables you to save the downloaded Web Connect information to a file.
- **Keep Quicken Open After Web Connect Completes** tells Quicken to keep running after Web Connect completes a download from the Web.

Alerts

Alerts preferences enable you to set the lead time for calendar notes to appear in Alerts snapshots as well as the Alerts Center. Learn about alerts in Chapter 7. Chapter 7 also discusses the Billminder feature that displays your scheduled bills and deposits. You can select a lead-time period to display from the drop-down list; timing options range from Last Month to Next Month. The items you display in the Billminder have no effect on the lead time you've set for alerts.

Warnings allow you to change all Quicken warnings back to their default. Click Reset Quicken Warnings, and a message appears that all warnings are reset. This can be helpful if you turned off a warning by selecting the Don't Show Me This Again check box and now realize you really did want to see the warning.

Investment Transactions

The Investment Transactions options let you customize the way the Investment Transaction lists look and work. Learn about the Investment Transaction lists in Chapter 9.

This option does not appear if you have turned off the Investing tab display.

- **List Display** determines whether transactions should appear with one or two lines in the list.
- **Sort Choice** determines whether transactions are sorted in ascending or descending order by date.
- **Show Hidden Transactions** displays hidden transactions in the list.
- **Show Attach Button** displays the Attach button beside the Edit and Delete buttons for the current transaction. You may want to turn off this check box if you do not use the Image Attachment feature. Chapter 5 explains how to attach images to transactions.
- **Automatically Update Quotes Every 15 Minutes** updates your stock portfolio with your Internet connection every 15 minutes. This feature comes with Quicken Premier and higher editions. As discussed in earlier chapters, Quicken will only update when it is the active application. If Quicken is open but you are working with another application, quotes will not update until you make Quicken the active program again.

Investing.Quicken.com Portfolio   As explained in Chapter 9, http://investing .quicken.com is an online site where you register and can then track your investment information from any location with Internet access. Your Preferences options are as follows:

- **Select Accounts To View Online** tells Quicken what accounts to view online at Quicken.com and how to send information. You can choose which accounts to use, or use the Select All button to select all of your accounts, or click Clear All to clear your choices and start over.
- **Send My Shares/Send Only My Symbols** tells Quicken what information about your holdings to track.
- **Track My Watch List On Investing.Quicken.com**, if cleared, stops Quicken.com from keeping track of the items you've included in your security Watch List.
- **Change My Investing.Quicken.com Credentials At Next One Step Update**. If you have previously uploaded your portfolio to Investing.Quicken.com, you will see this option. Otherwise, it does not appear.

Register

Register preferences enable you to fine-tune the way the account register works. Five groups of settings appear in addition to the Register preferences themselves. You'll see account register windows discussed throughout this book.

Register Preferences   Register options affect the way the transactions you enter appear in the account register window:

- **Show Date Before Check Number** is the default setting for your registers. Clear this check box to have the check number appear after the Flag or Flag And Status column.
- **Show Memo Before Category** puts the Memo field before the Category field in your account register.

Transaction Entry

- **Automatically Enter Split Data** turns the OK button in the Split Transaction window into an Enter button for entering the transaction. See Chapter 5 for a complete explanation of split transactions.
- **Automatically Place Decimal Point** automatically enters a two-place decimal point when entering dollar figures in Quicken or using Quicken's built-in calculator. For example, if you enter 1543 in the calculator, Quicken enters 15.43.

EXPERIENCED USERS RECOMMEND

Although Quicken tries to assign a category to every transaction, you may see one or more uncategorized downloaded transactions. This happens because Quicken does not recognize the vendor. In addition to blank categories, you may see incorrect category assignments or simply categories that you want to change. Updating or adding the Memorized Payee List as described next should correct both issues.

Quicken assigns categories to downloaded transactions in this order:

1. A transaction in your Memorized Payee List with a matching payee name with the category shown for that payee.
2. Your financial institution has associated a standard industrial classification (SIC) code with this transaction.

You also have the option to edit the category from the Memorized Payee List. Click Tools | Memorized Payee List, edit the memorized payee, and choose the correct category. This will then memorize the payee name to the correct category for future downloads.

Register Row Spacing   This option, new in Quicken 2017, allows you to change the height on each row on your register. You may choose from Compact, Standard, and Comfortable. Take the time to try each option before you make your decision. This feature is especially useful when working on a mobile device or laptop with a smaller screen.

To test which option works best for you, select an option. Then, click OK and open a register. Then, select Edit | Preferences | Register | Register Row Spacing and select another setting to see how that changes your view. When you have selected the option that works best for you, click OK to close Preferences

Register Appearance

- **Gray Reconciled Transactions** displays all reconciled transactions with gray characters rather than black characters.
- **Remember Register Filters After Quicken Closes** remembers any register filter settings you may have made when you close Quicken so those settings are in place the next time you start the program.
- **Use Pop-Up Registers** opens registers in separate windows, allowing you to have several different windows with a variety of information open at the same time.

The Use Pop-Up Registers option is unavailable if you have chosen a bank, credit card, or an investing account as your Startup Location. See "Startup" earlier in this appendix.

- **Fonts/Colors** displays dialogs with which you can select the font and font size as well as the colors for your register windows.

Data Entry and QuickFill   Data Entry and QuickFill options allow you to fine-tune the way Quicken's QuickFill feature works.

Data Entry

- **Use Enter Key To Move Between Fields** enables you to use either the ENTER or TAB key to move from field to field when entering data.
- **Complete Fields Using Previous Entries** enters transaction information using the information from previous entries.
- **Recall Memorized Payees** uses memorized payees to fill in QuickFill entries. This option is not available if the Complete Fields Using Previous Entries option is disabled.
- **Automatically Open Drop-Down Lists In QuickFill Fields** automatically displays the drop-down list when you advance to a field with a list.
- **Capitalize Payees And Categories** automatically makes the first letter of each word in a payee name or category uppercase.
- **Show Buttons On QuickFill Fields** displays drop-down list buttons on fields for which you can use QuickFill.

QuickFill and Memorized Payees

- **Automatically Memorize New Payees** tells Quicken to enter automatically all transactions for a new payee to the Memorized Payee List.
- **Automatically Include On Calendar Payee List** tells Quicken to add automatically memorized payees to the Calendar window. This option is grayed out if you have not checked the Automatically Memorize New Payees check box.
- **Add Address Book QuickFill Items To Memorized Payee List** tells Quicken to add entries from the Address Book to the Memorized Payee List so the address fields are filled in automatically when writing checks.
- **Remove Memorized Payees Not Used In Last *NN* Months** tells Quicken to remove memorized payees that have not been used within the number of months you specify. By default, this feature is turned on, with the number of months set at 14. By entering a value of 6 (for example), Quicken retains only the memorized payees for transactions you entered during the past six months, thus keeping the Memorized Payee List manageable. In this way, you can weed one-time transactions out of the Memorized Payee List. Changing this option does not affect already entered transactions.

A large list of Memorized Payees can affect performance and slow down your Quicken file. Setting this preference not only keeps the list manageable, it helps to keep Quicken speedy.

Notify   Notify options affect the way Quicken notifies you about problems when you enter transactions in the register:

- **When Entering Out-Of-Date Transactions** warns you when you try to record a transaction for a date more than a year from the current date.
- **Before Changing Reconciled Transactions** warns you when you try to modify a previously entered and reconciled transaction.
- **When Entering Uncategorized Transactions** warns you when you try to record a transaction without assigning a category to it.
- **To Run A Reconcile Report After Reconcile** asks if you want to display a Reconcile Report when you complete an account reconciliation.
- **Warn If A Check Number Is Re-used** warns you if you assign a check number that was already assigned in another transaction.
- **When Changing The Account Of An Existing Transaction** notifies you when you change the account of a transaction you have already entered.
- **To Save A Transaction After Changing It** asks you if you want to save the changes you made to the last transaction you changed.

Write Checks   Write Checks preferences affect the way the checks you create appear when printed using the Write Checks window:

- **Printed Date Style** enables you to select a four-digit or two-digit date style.
- **Spell Currency Units** tells Quicken to spell out the currency amount in the second Amount field.
- **Allow Entry Of Extra Message On Check** displays an additional text box for a message in the Write Checks window. The message you enter is printed on the check in a place where it cannot be seen if the check is mailed in a window envelope.
- **Print Categories On Voucher Checks** prints category information, including splits and tags, on the voucher part of voucher checks. This option affects only voucher-style checks.
- **Change Date Of Checks To Date When Printed** automatically prints the print date, rather than the transaction date, on each check.

Downloaded Transactions   Downloaded Transactions preferences control the way Quicken handles transactions downloaded into it from your financial institution. You learn more about downloading transactions into Quicken in Chapter 6.

- **Automatically Add To Banking Registers** saves manually reviewing and accepting each banking transaction, and possibly leaving an unaccepted transaction out of Quicken reports and graphs. Many Quicken users prefer not to use this option. If downloaded transactions occasionally seem to be disappearing, try turning off this preference, at least temporarily. That will help you determine if the missing transactions are due to incorrect downloaded transaction matching.
- **Automatically Add To Investment Transaction Lists** saves you time by entering your downloaded transactions to your investment account "registers" rather than having to manually review and accept each transaction. Even with this preference selected, you will still be prompted to specify lot assignments for Sell transactions.

During Transaction Download
- **Automatically Categorize Transactions** sets the transaction's category based on what you have used before for that payee.
- **Automatically Apply Quicken's Suggested Name To Payee** uses Quicken's "best guess" name for the downloaded transaction. Selecting this option can,

depending on your financial institution, cause some unexpected or strange payee names to appear in your downloaded payees.

- **Capitalize First Letter Only In Downloaded Payee Names** is self-explanatory.

Your Renaming Rules The Renaming Rules options allow you control over how Quicken deals with the differences between the payee names in your records and those of the bank's. See Chapter 6 for a complete discussion of renaming rules.

- **Use My Existing Renaming Rules** tells Quicken to use the rules you have created to name the downloaded payee name.
- Click the **Renaming Rules** button to open the Renaming Rules dialog, which you can use to create, modify, and remove renaming rules.
- **Automatically Create Rules When I Rename Payees** establishes a rule for the payee you have renamed.
- **Let Me Review/Confirm The Automatically Created Rules** tells Quicken you want to see the renaming rule that Quicken has created.

Transfer Detection This option tells Quicken to review each downloaded transaction to see if it is matched with a transaction in another account. If you select this option, when Quicken finds matched transactions, you have two options:

- **Automatically Create Transfers When Detected** makes the transfer from the one account to the other automatically and enters the transaction in both registers. Choosing this setting can have unexpected and undesired results. You may appear to be losing downloaded transactions because they are incorrectly identified as a transfer. If you choose to use the transfer detection feature, consider using the Confirm Possible Transfers Before Entering In Register setting instead.
- **Confirm Possible Transfers Before Entering In Register** directs Quicken to ask you whether the transaction is, indeed, a transfer.

Reports and Graphs

Reports And Graphs preferences include two categories of options for creating reports and graphs. Chapter 15 discusses creating reports and graphs in detail.

Reports And Graphs Preferences Reports And Graphs options enable you to set your own default options for creating reports and graphs:

- **Default Date Range** and **Default Comparison Date Range** enable you to specify a default range for regular and comparison reports. Choose an option from each drop-down list. When you actually run the report, you can then specify any date.

- **Report Toolbar** allows you to tell Quicken how you want your reports selected for the Toolbar to be shown, either showing only icons or both icons and text on your reports.
- **Customizing Reports And Graphs** options determine how reports and graphs are customized and what happens when they are:
  - **Customizing Creates New Report Or Graph**, which is the default setting, creates a subreport based on the report you customize.
  - **Customizing Modifies Current Report Or Graph** changes the report you customize without creating a subreport.
  - **Customize Report/Graph Before Creating** tells Quicken to offer to customize a report or graph when you choose one.

Reports Only   This group of options applies only to reports:

- **Account Display** and **Category Display** enable you to set what you want to display for each account or category listed in the report: Description, Name, or Both.
- **Use Color In Report** tells Quicken to use color when displaying negative numbers.
- **QuickZoom To Investment Forms** tells Quicken to display the investment form for a specific investment when you double-click it in an investment report. With this check box turned off, Quicken displays the investment register transaction entry instead.
- **Remind Me To Save Reports** tells Quicken to ask whether you want to save a customized report when you close the report window.
- **Decimal Places For Prices And Shares** enables you to specify the number of decimal places to display for per-share security prices and number of shares in investment reports.

Intuit ID, Mobile & Alerts

After you have set up your Intuit ID, you can set several preferences for your online (or Cloud) services.

Intuit Profile shows your current Intuit ID, which you use to sign in to all Intuit services. This includes your Intuit ID, your e-mail, and your contact information. When you select Update Your Intuit Profile Information, a Quicken sign-in dialog appears in which you will need to enter your Intuit ID and password. If you select Sign In As A Different User, the following message appears. Your current Intuit ID will no longer be linked with this data file, and you will no longer be able to sync this file with the Quicken Cloud account that uses this Intuit ID. If you have made changes to your Intuit information, you must type **Yes** to confirm the changes and click the Sign Out button. If you simply want to cancel the change, click Cancel.

 When you select Sign In As A Different User, your Password Vault passwords will be cleared for security purposes. You may want to save your Password Vault passwords before signing in as a different user.

Sign in as a different user   ✕

Sign in as a different user

ⓘ **Why do this?**
Do this if you want to use a different Intuit ID with this data file.

When you sign out:
- The Intuit ID below will no longer be linked with this file.
- No accounts in this file will sync with the Quicken Cloud account using this Intuit ID.
- You will need to sign in again with an Intuit ID to use connected services.
- No other files that use this Intuit ID will be affected.
- Your Data File password will remain the same as your existing password.
- Your Password Vault password will be reset to the new Intuit ID password. However, since the Password Vault is linked with the Intuit ID, this would reset and delete all the existing encrypted FI data and passwords. You will need to re-add them later.

⚠ Mobile attachments synced to **this** data file that you **have not yet viewed on your desktop will be lost.** Attachments synced to other data files are not affected.

You are currently signed in with the Intuit ID:

quickenuser@happy.com

Type "yes" to confirm sign out [   ]

❓   [Sign Out]   [Cancel]

If you have not yet done so, you can set up your mobile accounts with Quicken 2017 from this dialog. This process is explained in detail in Chapter 3.

Useful Tips

While most Quicken users find the program exactly to their liking after they use some of the customization features mentioned earlier, others have questions about some specific how-tos.

Converting Your Older Quicken Files to a New Computer

After using the Quicken program for a number of years on a desktop computer, you may decide to get a new laptop and want to upgrade to Quicken 2017. Depending on the version you are running, the best way to do this follows next.

Convert from Quicken 2004 and Newer

These steps apply to converting Quicken 2004 and newer files. If you are converting from Quicken 2003 or older, see "Use Intermediate Versions of Quicken to Convert Your Old Data Files."

1. Back up your old files before you start anything else.
2. On the "old" computer, choose File | File Operations | Validate And Repair or File | File Operations | Validate to ensure your old files are in the best shape possible. (See Appendix A for more information on Validate and Repair.)
3. Install Quicken 2017 on your new computer. The Quicken license agreement allows you to install up to three copies of your Quicken program onto computers within your own household.
4. Copy the files from your "old" computer to your "new" computer, and you're ready to go.

 A handy way to move files from the old computer to the new computer is to back up on the old computer, copy the backup file (or files) to a thumb drive, insert the thumb drive on the new computer, and copy the backup file (or files) from the thumb drive to the new computer.

 When you are installing Quicken, you may see an option asking if you are a new Quicken user. If you inadvertently choose that option, you can still access your data files. Click File | Open Quicken File, and choose the data file you want to use. Your data will be converted to use with Quicken 2017.

Use Intermediate Versions of Quicken to Convert Your Old Data Files

For those users who are using Quicken 2003 or older versions, you may need to use an intermediate version of the program to convert your files to use with Quicken 2017.

Quicken 1 (through Quicken 5) for Windows users must install Quicken 6 and update their files to Quicken 6 for Windows. From there they can convert to Quicken 2004, the intermediate program for Quicken 2005 and later.

You can read more information about converting from older versions of Quicken from a website. Type **http://www.quicken.com/support/how-and-when-use-intermediate-version-convert-older-versions-quicken** into the address bar of your browser. From there you can even download the intermediate programs required to complete your conversion.

If you are unsure which version of Quicken you are using, click Help on the Quicken menu bar and select About Quicken.

Changing Multiple Transactions

As companies merge and life changes, you may have a recurring transaction that needs to be changed. While you can edit the payee, category, tag, or memo for current month and future transactions in the Bills tab, as explained in Chapter 6, you may want to change all of the previous transactions as well. It is not a difficult task to do so; however, as always when making any changes to your data, perform a backup before making those changes.

The process shown here assumes that the transactions are all from the same account.

1. Create a backup of your data file. This is the *most* important step!
2. Open the account in which you posted the transactions.
3. Sort by the name of the item you want to change—in this example, it is the Payee.
4. Click the first item on the list and, holding your SHIFT key down, click the last item on the list. Each of the items is highlighted.

Depending on your monitor and the color preferences you have set for your register, the highlighting may be hard to distinguish.

5. Right-click one of the highlighted selections to open a context menu.
6. From the context menu choose Edit Transactions.
7. The Find And Replace dialog appears.
8. In the With field, enter the new name. Keep in mind that if you are changing something other than the payee, you will need to select the appropriate field in the Replace drop-down list.
9. Click Replace All to replace the payee name.

If you do not want to create a renaming rule, click Cancel. You will find that you may have to choose Cancel for as many transactions as you have selected.

10. You are returned to the Find And Replace dialog. Click Done.

11. You are returned to the register where your new payee name is now showing. (Remember, you've sorted in alphabetical order, so if your new name starts with a different letter, you will have to scroll down the register to see it.) After completing your transaction cleanup, remember to sort your account by date or your preferred register sort order.

You can perform this same process using any register field, including Amount, Category, Memo, and Tag, as well as Check Number, Cleared Status, and Date. You can also perform this same process from the All Transactions register, which enables you to change the info for transactions from multiple accounts at once. You can find the link for the All Transactions register at the top of the Account Bar. However, be sure to run a backup before starting the process just to ensure your data's safety.

Quicken Emergency Records Organizer

Earlier versions of Quicken included an organizational tool in which users could maintain important information about emergency contacts, personal and legal documents, mortgage and investment information, and so on. While the Attachment utility has taken over much of the necessity of using this tool, many Quicken users still rely on this useful tool because of the variety of data it contains, as seen later.

You can still install the Emergency Records Organizer in Quicken 2017. To do so, first run a backup of your data file. Then, from the Quicken menu bar, click View | Classic Menus. In the Property & Debt menu, choose Emergency Records Organizer, as seen next.

Depending on your computer's operating system, a message may appear asking if you want to allow the Quicken, Inc., program to make changes to your computer. Click Yes, and Quicken asks if you want to add the Emergency

Records Organizer to Quicken. If you click Yes, the program is installed and you see a message telling you that the installation was successful.

Using the Emergency Records Organizer

After you have installed the Emergency Records Organizer, you must be using Classic menus to access it.

You can use Classic menus, add the Emergency Records Organizer button to your Quicken Toolbar, then switch back to Standard menus and access the Emergency Records Organizer using the Toolbar button.

1. Click View | Classic Menus.
2. Click Property & Debt.
3. Select the Emergency Records Organizer at the bottom of the menu. The Emergency Records Organizer window opens.
4. Click the Create/Update Records tab.
5. Click the Select An Area down arrow, and click one of the 11 areas in which to enter information.
6. Click an option under Select An Area. The records pane on the right will display text boxes to enter information pertaining to that topic.
7. Enter the relevant information in each field. Press TAB to move between fields.
8. Click Save to save the record when finished.
9. Click New Record to add another record in this topic.

Creating Reports in the Emergency Records Organizer

One of the best uses of the Emergency Records Organizer is to create reports for various professionals in case of an emergency.

- With the Emergency Records Organizer displayed, click the Report tab, click the Report Type down arrow, and choose which report you want.
- Click Sort By Family Members to include all information about each family member separately. Otherwise, it displays by topic area.
- Click Print Topics With No Data Entered to show that data has not been entered about this topic as yet.
- Click Print to print the report. The report goes directly to the printer. If you need more than one copy, you must click Print for each copy. If your default printer is the Quicken PDF printer (or other PDF printer), the report can be saved as a PDF file.
- Click Close to exit the Emergency Records Organizer.

Index